HOST NATIONAL ATTITUDES TOWARD MULTINATIONAL CORPORATIONS

HOST NATIONAL ATTITUDES TOWARD MULTINATIONAL CORPORATIONS

Edited by
John Fayerweather
New York University

Sponsored and Administered by the FMME
Fund for Multinational Management Education

PRAEGER SPECIAL STUDIES • PRAEGER SCIENTIFIC

Library of Congress Cataloging in Publication Data

Main entry under title:

Host national attitudes toward multinational corporations.

Bibliography: p.
1. Corporations, Foreign. 2. Elite (Social sciences)—
Attitudes. 3. Nationalism. I. Fayerweather, John.
II. Fund for Multinational Management Education.
HD2755.5.H67   338.8'8   81-13875
ISBN 0-03-059776-5   AACR2

Published in 1982 by Praeger Publishers
CBS Educational and Professional Publishing
a Division of CBS Inc.
521 Fifth Avenue, New York, New York 10175 U.S.A.

© 1982 by the Fund For Multinational Management Education

23456789   145   987654321

Printed in the United States of America

CONTENTS

v

LIST OF TABLES

LIST OF FIGURES

LIST OF APPENDIXES

INTRODUCTION

As the multinational corporation (MNC) has risen to a central role in international economic relations, a major area of concern has been host nation receptivity to MNC activities. The tremendous contributions of MNCs to economic development in their capabilities for transmission of capital, goods, and skills are broadly recognized. At the same time the cost to host nations both in economic terms and especially in the cultural, social, and political impact of MNC operations is critically questioned.

These conflicting currents in host nations have been widely discussed in the literature of the field. In his penetrating study of tensions created by MNCs, *National Interests and the Multinational Enterprise*, Jack N. Behrman crystallized the issues around the concept of the "love-hate" syndrome (p. 7). Raymond Vernon, in his *Sovereignty at Bay*, analyzed the economic conflicts in MNC-host nation relations but observed that they were not sufficient to explain the existing level of tensions (p. 230). He concluded that "clashing elites, clashing ideologies, and clashing cultures" were important dimensions to include in understanding host nation reactions to MNCs. In *International Business Strategy and Administration*, I have set forth a conceptual model of the interactions of the MNC with the nation-state and nationalism that defines the multiple facets involved in host nation reactions.

These and many other writings have set forth a considerable body of ideas and popular wisdom as to the nature and sources of attitudes toward MNCs. From a scientific point of view, however, this body of literature presents essentially an intriguing mass of hypotheses, many of them apparently logical, many of them conflicting, but all of them untested.

Efforts to systematically determine attitudes toward MNCs and the bases of them have developed rather slowly considering the prominence of the subject. Simple questions such as, "Do you favor more foreign investment in our country?" have appeared for some time in surveys by various organizations. These have provided a rough gauge of opinions, useful in guiding overall government and business decision making, but they give little information as to the full nature of attitudes and may even, as the contents of this book will reveal, be misleading in understanding host national reactions.

What has been needed are quantitative attitude studies to explore at depth the feelings and the factors influencing attitudes in host nations. Over the past decade a handful of researchers have responded to this challenge. As is common in the outcome of pioneer explorations of new territory, their studies have been highly productive in staking out the broad dimensions of the subject while at the same time identifying a multiplicity of problems for further exploration.

The present book is a state-of-the-art report designed to serve two purposes: first, to convey the main findings of studies undertaken thus far, and second, to provide stimulus and guidance for those who will undertake further studies to explore the many facets of the subject opened up by the work reported here. The book contains reports on all of the completed in-depth quantitative studies of host national attitudes toward MNCs of which we are aware. The final chapter presents a synthesis of these reports and also draws on the discussions in a two-day workshop conducted by the Fund for Multinational Management Education in January 1978 in which at least one of the authors of each chapter participated. The workshop was a unique opportunity for those who had varied experiences with quantitative surveys to exchange views on hypotheses, methodologies, and analytical approaches. The combination of our ideas permitted our thinking to advance appreciably beyond our previous individual efforts. The main lines of this synergistic effort appear in the final chapter.

The research studies described here are quite varied, so there is no overall sequential pattern. Those covered in the first five chapters are, however, related in that the questionnaires used for them all had a common core of questions. The first chapter presents the results of surveys I made of elites in Britain, Canada, and France and of business students and management program groups in several countries. It is followed by a factor analysis of the elite data by Peter Sugges and an analysis of evidence of nationalistic bias in the elite data made in collaboration with Katherin Marton. Next come studies by Katherin Marton and John Smetanka in which the core of questions from the elite study were used in Canada on blue collar workers and managers respectively. Marton's research added questions dealing with nationalism, big business, and job satisfaction while Smetanka focused on various structural factors affecting the manager.

The studies described in the other chapters are substantively distinct from each other, though two were undertaken under the sponsorship of the Fund for Multinational Management Education. One by Truitt and Blake deals with attitudes of elites toward MNCs and national firms in Chile and Venezuela while the other is a study by Blake and Driscoll of attitudes of Brazilians about two U.S.-owned pulp and paper companies. Then comes a study by Hilton of attitudes among a cross-section of the Nigerian population toward MNCs, Nigerian firms, and those owned by indigenous Lebanese businessmen. The chapters by Murray and LeDuc and by Graham are similar in that both analyze the change of national attitudes over time, the former in Canada and the latter in Britain and France.

The final contribution by Sauvant and Mennis does not explicitly deal with attitudes toward MNCs but it has been included because the TNE (transnational business enterprise) effect that it explores is potentially a major influence on views of MNCs among businessmen, closely related to the structural factors considered by Smetanka.

1

ELITE ATTITUDES TOWARD MULTINATIONAL FIRMS

John Fayerweather

The future evolution of multinational firms will depend to a large degree on the policy decisions of host nations, made essentially by leadership groups. Thus, knowledge of how elites feel about foreign business firms is a key element in analysis of the outlook for international business.

Assorted expressions of elite attitudes on multinational firms have included official national policies, speeches, and popular writing, but prior to 1970 there were no studies to identify systematically the views of the significant elite groups. To fill this gap, I undertook surveys in Britain and France in late 1970 and in Canada in late 1971. In addition, I administered variations of the questionnaire to business student and management program groups on three continents. The results of these varied surveys are summarized in this chapter.

Major portions of this chapter are extracted from John Fayerweather, "Elite Attitudes toward Multinational Firms," *International Studies Quarterly*, December 1972, pp. 472-90, and "Attitudes toward Foreign Firms among Business Students, Managers and Heads of Firms," *Management International Review*, no. 6, 1975, p. 19. Other reports on this research have appeared in "Attitudes of British and French Elite Groups toward Foreign Companies," *MSU Business Topics*, Winter 1972, pp. 14-24, and "Canadian Attitudes and Policy on Foreign Investment," *MSU Business Topics*, Winter 1973, pp. 7-20.

I am indebted to my colleague, Professor Jean Boddewyn, for help in formulating the questionnaire and preparing the French translation and to my research assistants, Katherin Marton, Richard Sorrenson, and Peter Sugges, for computer analysis of the data. Experts in Britain, Canada, and France, too numerous to list, provided invaluable advice and helped in the survey.

THE SURVEYS

The elite surveys covered four groups—national legislators, permanent government officials, heads of business firms, and labor union leaders. A mail questionnaire was employed for reasons of breadth, economy, objectivity, and anonymity, the latter point applying especially to the government officials. For each group in each country, about 200 questionnaires were mailed.

Mail surveys of foreign cities, especially government and labor groups, are not common, and they present assorted problems. This study provided a variety of useful insights on methodology for such surveys, but space permits noting only a few highlights here. It was assumed that a major handicap to be overcome was the image of a meddling American question asker with little interest in the welfare of the host country. The author has devoted substantial time to seeing problems from the host country viewpoint by means of frequent communication with host nationals. A strong effort was made to convey an image along these lines in the cover letter. With appropriate permission, the author noted in the letter that he had sought advice from specific organizations in each country (for example, the Canadian Institute of International Affairs and the Private Planning Association of Canada). Also, French and Canadian return addresses were used.

While it is difficult to judge the effect of these and other efforts to encourage response, they apparently had a positive result. Some competent advisers were quite doubtful about the prospects of adequate response, especially with some groups like the French *fonctionnaires* who are notably suspicious of *investigateurs*. But the methodology, supported undoubtedly by the strong interest in the subject matter, proved satisfactory. A response of about 25 percent had been expected, giving a statistically satisfactory group of 50 replies per group. In fact the response rates were generally well in excess of this minimum:

	Legislators	Government Officials	Business Heads	Labor Leaders
Britain	30%	29%	25%	41%
Canada	23%	40%	30%	30%
France	26%	39%	25%	47%

The student and management program groups were covered at various stages, first as part of the pretesting of the questionnaire and later as adjuncts to the elite surveys. The first batch of data was collected in early 1970 from business student classes in Japan (Keio University), Korea (Seoul National University), and the Philippines (Asian Institute of Management) and from middle managers in the Japanese Institute of International Studies and Training. Later that year, a somewhat revised questionnaire was administered to students in the French Institute Superieur d'Administration and the London Graduate School of Business. The final version of the questionnaire used in the elite surveys was administered to resident classes of middle managers at the French Centre de Recherches et d'Etudes des Chefs d'Entreprises (CRC) and the London business school in 1970 and to MBAs at McGill University and the University of Western Ontario in 1971. A McGill middle management group was surveyed by mail at the same time and another such group from the University of Western Ontario was included in 1973.

The topics and wording of questions were based on the content of press commentaries on multinational firms, under the assumption that these are representative of the images of MNCs and their impact among literate persons. An initial pretest of the questions was made among U.S. and foreign students at New York University. The number of questions used on the student and management program groups in the pretest stage varied from 40 to 70, and some were reworded. In the three elite surveys a question on labor union recognition had to be varied because of legal differences among the countries; a question on effects of joint ventures was rephrased for Canada because of unsatisfactory results in the European surveys; and three questions were dropped and one was added for Canada. The questions used will appear in the analytical tables. They will be identified by letters sequentially in the analysis, for example, A, B, and so on. In the first mention, the number indicating the sequence in the British questionnaire will be given in parentheses, for example, Q. F(1). There were only slight differences in the sequences in the other questionnaires. The questionnaire was administered in English in all cases except for France and French-Canadians. For the French version, the standard translation and retranslation process was applied.

ANALYSIS OF RESULTS

The main focus of this analysis is on the elite studies, which were designed for systematic comparison. The diversity among the business student and management program groups and the variations in the questionnaire during the pretest stage do not permit a useful analysis of those data. However, as a by-product of the elite studies, they provide an interesting sampling of attitudes in a variety of countries. The respondents are not, of course, representative of the populations of their countries as a whole. Still, the differences among such groups in several countries probably are somewhat indicative of differences among broader groups in the countries. And the groups are in themselves interesting as the raw material from which an important segment of the future decision-making elites will develop. Because of the difference in the character of the data, the analyses of each of the two broad sets of data are presented separately, the elite study first and then the business students and management program groups.

The questionnaire provided for responses on a seven-point scale. The right-left location of response options was varied in an erratic manner to avoid repetitive answers. In the data in this chapter, the responses have been reversed where appropriate, so that 1 always indicates the most favorable attitude toward foreign firms and 7, the least favorable. Except as noted, the data are mean scores for groups. The tables for the elite studies also show averages of mean scores for the four groups for each country. These averages of averages are questionable in statistical methodology but are a convenience for readers in putting the data in perspective.

Significance values are not given for mean scores because they differ from question to question due to differences in numbers of answers and standard deviations. In addition, bimodal response distributions for some questions required use of contingency table testing of significance rather than t values. Providing precise significance values for each relationship in the tables would therefore unduly burden them. In the discussion significance is indicated where appropriate. Beyond that the reader may assume that differences of 0.7 are always significant at the .05 level. Those from 0.4 to 0.6 are sometimes significant, and those below 0.4 are rarely so.

THE ELITE SURVEYS

The analysis of the elite survey data will follow two main approaches: first, consideration of the response patterns on various groups of questions, and, second, exploration of variables that may have a bearing on the response patterns.

Analysis of Response Patterns

The questions on the impact of foreign firms fell into four major subject areas, each of which will be discussed below: overall impact; criteria for appraising impact; effect of performance in four respects (economics, control, culture, and labor); and joint ventures.

Overall Impact

To place the opinions of the leaders in overall perspective, two broad questions were asked at the outset of the questionnaire: (A) how great an effect the operations of foreign companies had on their country, and (B) whether the overall effect was good or bad. The mean responses are shown in Table 1.1. Table 1.2 gives the frequency distribution of responses to question B.

The responses to question A indicate that most of the leaders regard the impact of foreign investment in their country as a matter of substantial magnitude with scores ranging from 4.4 to 6.3 along a scale of 1 = small to 7 = large. As might be expected, the Canadian scores are distinctly higher. With 60 percent of Canadian manufacturing foreign-controlled versus around 10 percent for the British and the French, there is a major difference. If the data hold any surprise, it is that the European and Canadian scores do not differ more.

Question B reveals a moderately favorable overall appraisal by most groups, with scores around 3 (4 would be neutral). Thus, despite a number of negative reactions on specific points which will be noted later, the majority of the leaders

TABLE 1.1. Overall Opinions

Q.A   How great an effect do you believe the operations of foreign companies in X have on X? Small = 1 ; Large = 7

Q.B   In your opinion what is the overall effect on X of the activities of foreign companies in X? Good = 1; Bad = 7

For "X" in all questions read "Great Britain" (British); "France" (French); or "Canada" (Canadian)

		Leg	PG	Lab	Bus	Ave
Q.A	Br.	5.0	5.0	5.2	4.4	4.9
	Fr.	4.5	4.9	4.9	3.9	4.6
	Can.	5.6	6.1	6.3	5.9	6.0
Q.B	Br.	3.2	2.8	4.0	2.9	3.2
	Fr.	3.1	3.1	4.3	2.8	3.3
	Can.	3.5	3.2	4.2	2.6	3.4

Note: Leg = national legislators; PG = permanent government officials; Lab = labor union leaders; Bus = heads of business firms; and Ave = average.

seem solidly favorable in their judgment of the net effect of the role of multinational firms in their countries. The other significant feature is the substantial similarity across countries among the groups: the businessmen, except in Britain, are the most favorable; the two government groups are close to them; and the labor leaders are clearly set apart, with a slightly adverse judgment.*

Criteria for Evaluating Foreign Firms

Table 1.3 gives a picture of the criteria by which the merits of foreign firms are judged. The respondents were asked in question C to rate the impor-

*An obvious question in this whole survey is the possible bias of those who responded as compared with nonrespondents. A full check on this point was not feasible, but a check was made of one group. A random sample of 20 percent of the Canadian Members of Parliament was covered directly by a researcher. (The interviewing was done by Bruce Thordarson with guidance from Julian Payne of the Canadian Parliamentary Centre in Ottawa.) They were asked whether they had returned the questionnaire, and they each answered question B on Table 1.1. Some 30 percent had responded, compared to the 24 percent rate for all M.P.s surveyed. The average of the scores of the nonrespondents on question B was 2.3 and for the respondents it was 3.0 compared to 3.5 for M.P.s responding to the mail questionnaire. These latter figures indicate that the group was either not comparable to the mail respondents or that the direct checking process elicited different responses. However, the main point is the apparent favorable bias among nonrespondents. One cannot with assurance assume a bias of similar magnitude or direction among other groups, but it is at least a fair possibility. Thus, the indications of favorable overall attitudes from the mail survey are reinforced.

TABLE 1.2. Appraisals of Overall Effect of Foreign Firms

	Distribution of Responses (percent)							
	Good 1	2	3	4	5	6	Bad 7	Total Number
Britain								
Leg	18	16	25	20	15	5	2	61
PG	14	30	37	7	5	7	0	59
Lab	4	10	27	22	21	11	5	81
Bus	20	27	22	12	12	6	0	49
France								
Leg	7	36	25	9	15	7	0	55
PG	6	27	33	18	13	3	0	78
Lab	11	15	17	13	10	7	27	92
Bus	19	23	29	17	8	4	0	52
Canada								
Leg	13	24	20	5	24	9	5	45
PG	6	32	26	16	14	5	1	81
Lab	10	18	7	11	22	25	7	72
Bus	23	37	18	8	8	6	0	62

See note for Table 1.1.

tance of eight criteria on a scale from major (1) to minor (7). The table is designed to show the most significant facts—the rank and relative weight of each criterion. The criterion rated as most important by each group is given a rank of 1.0. The rank numbers of the other criteria indicate the difference between their actual scores and those of the top-ranked criteria.

A variety of features appears in Table 1.3. Most obvious is the consistent prominence of the top three criteria. With a few exceptions, economic and control considerations rank close to the top of all lists. There is little statistically significant distinction among the scores of these three in most cases. However, the pattern of differences among countries is interesting. The effects of foreign investment on control of national affairs seem to loom somewhat larger to Canadians than to Europeans. A notable feature is the generally much lower ranking of effects on the national way of life by all elites. It appears that, at least among leadership groups, the highly publicized reaction against the "Americanization" of Canada and Europe is of distinctly less importance than the economic and political effects of foreign investment.

TABLE 1.3. Criteria for Evaluating Foreign Firms (Computed rank order scores: 1 = most important)

	Britain					France					Canada				
	Leg	PG	Lab	Bus	Ave	Leg	PG	Lab	Bus	Ave	Leg	PG	Lab	Bus	Ave
Effect on X national income	1.0	1.0	1.0	1.0	1.0	1.0	1.0	1.1	1.0	1.0	1.5	1.4	1.0	1.2	1.3
	(2.2)	(2.3)	(2.1)	(2.8)		(2.5)	(2.5)	(2.1)	(2.4)		(2.9)	(2.4)	(2.0)	(2.6)	
Effect on balance of payments	1.0	1.0	1.1	1.1	1.1	1.3	1.3	1.1	1.4	1.3	1.1	1.6	1.8	1.1	1.4
Control over national affairs	1.4	1.7	1.6	1.3	1.5	1.2	1.0	1.1	1.5	1.2	1.0	1.0	1.1	1.2	1.1
Benefits for X workers	1.1	2.0	1.0	1.1	1.3	1.3	1.6	1.0	1.9	1.4	1.8	1.6	1.0	1.3	1.4
Opportunities for X managers	1.8	2.4	2.0	1.6	2.0	2.1	3.0	2.7	2.1	2.2	1.5	1.9	1.9	1.0	1.6
Role of X in the world	1.8	2.8	2.1	1.3	2.0	1.1	1.5	1.6	1.7	1.5	1.5	1.4	1.0	1.2	1.3
Changes in X way of life	2.4	3.0	2.6	2.4	2.6	1.8	2.0	2.0	2.1	2.0	2.1	2.3	2.2	2.4	2.2
Opportunities for X investors	3.1	3.4	2.9	2.0	2.8	2.7	3.6	3.2	1.8	2.8	2.1	2.1	1.9	1.2	1.8

Note: X = British, French, or Canadian.

Basis: Question C, "How important should the following considerations be in judging the value of foreign companies operating in X?" Major Importance = 1; Minor = 7.

In the above table the consideration with the lowest average score for each group was given the rank of 1.0. The ranks of the other criteria are the sum of 1.0 plus the difference between their scores and those of the top ranked criteria for the group, for example, for British MPs. Effects on National Income had an actual score of 2.2 and Opportunities for Investors, 4.3. The actual average scores of first item are given in parentheses. See note for Table 1.1.

Among the effects on specific national groups, the labor element stands out as definitely most significant. The highest rating for it naturally comes from the union leaders, but there is substantial reinforcing support from other groups. The chief deviation from this pattern is the high ranking of opportunities for both managers and investors in Canada by businessmen. It seems likely that this is a product of the relatively large scale of foreign investment in Canada. If only 10 percent of manufacturing firms are foreign owned, local investors and managers presumably feel little effect on their opportunities, but at 60 percent or so the impact of foreign ownership is of real concern.

The rankings for the role of the nation in the world may reflect this same sort of reaction. The Canadians generally place this criterion appreciably higher than do the Europeans. One may surmise that the massive impact of U.S. investment makes the Canadians more concerned about its effect on the whole character of their nation. The other score that strikes one in this criterion is the 1.1 for French legislators. One gathers that, among deputies, Charles de Gaulle's preoccupation with the glory of France struck a sympathetic chord.

Another interesting way to look at Table 1.3 is to compare the spread of scores. For British and French business leaders and all Canadian groups, the spreads are 1.4 or less, while for other British and French groups, they tend to be appreciably higher, 1.7 up to 2.6. Doubtless, a number of factors are at work here, but two suggest themselves as possible explanations. First, among the Europeans it is likely that rather specialized interests and responsibilities of government and labor people lead to discrimination as to the importance of criteria, whereas the businessmen have a more diffused picture which results in less discrimination among the effects of foreign investment. The Canadian story, on the other hand, may be one more manifestation of the difference between foreign investment on a major versus a minor scale. The massive impact of foreign firms in Canada elevates all sorts of effects to prominence in the eyes of varied groups.

Effects on the Host Nation

Most of the questions in the survey were designed to elicit attitudes on effects of foreign firms on four aspects of host-nation affairs: economics, control, culture, and labor. The results of these questions will be considered separately and in relation to each other.

Economic Impact. The three questions in Table 1.4 are different ways of looking at the economic impact of foreign firms. Question D suggests a rather broad appraisal of economic contribution. Among British and French elites, with the exceptions of the union leaders, the appraisals here are moderately but clearly favorable. In Canada the weight of opinion is on the other side: all except the business leaders take a negative view. This is an interesting judgment, somewhat at variance with the view commonly heard in Canada that foreign investment has been a good thing for the country economically. This view and the responses to question D are not inconsistent, for one can interpret the latter to mean, "While

TABLE 1.4. Economic Measures

Q.D What do you believe is the net economic result of the operations of foreign companies in X? They give more than they take = 1; They take
more than they give = 7

Q.E In relation to their economic contributions, the dividends, royalties,
and other payments which foreign companies received from their operations in X are: Too small = 1; Too large = 7

Q.F Do you feel that the magnitude of the receipts (dividends, royalties,
etc.) from X overseas operations in relation to their contributions is:
Too small = 1; Too large = 7

		Leg	PG	Lab	Bus	Ave
Q.D	Br.	3.8	3.2	4.8	3.4	3.8
	Fr.	4.1	3.8	5.2	3.3	4.1
	Can.	4.6	4.2	5.2	3.8	4.4
Q.E	Br.	4.5	4.4	4.9	4.3	4.5
	Fr.	4.5	4.5	5.3	4.2	4.6
	Can.	4.7	4.8	5.6	4.5	4.9
Q.F	Br.	3.4	3.7	4.2	3.3	3.7
	Fr.	3.5	4.0	4.4	3.6	3.9
	Can.	3.8	4.0	4.0	3.7	3.9

See note for Table 1.1.

we may benefit economically from foreign investment, the foreign firms gain
even more." But the implication nonetheless is that, compared with the Europeans, Canadian leaders are skeptical about the balance of economic gains.

Question E is essentially an appraisal of the items which enter into the
balance of payments. Here the elites take a distinctly more negative view. In
effect, the data say that the balance of external economic benefits and costs
is considered clearly adverse to the host country, as compared to the more
favorable views on overall economic impact. Another feature of these data is the
smaller spread in the average scores among the groups—0.6, 1.1, and 1.1 on
question E versus 1.6, 1.9, and 1.4 on question D, indicating a greater consensus
among elites.

The differences in responses to questions D and E fit a frequently observed
picture of opinions about foreign investment. The internal economic benefits
from employment gains and inputs of capital and skills are quite widely recognized, though there are substantial differences in the degree of recognition among

groups because of differences in impact on specific interests. Consideration of the external balance of costs and benefits, however, brings into play a different type of thinking on which there is more homogeneity among groups. This thinking apparently incorporates elements of both mercantilistic economics and nationalistic defensive reaction against the drain on national wealth by outsiders.

The responses to question F give some further confirmation to the nationalistic element in the economic appraisals. This question was one of a small set at the end of the questionnaire in which the respondents were asked to look at the effects of companies from their own nation in other countries. The questions were mirror images of those asked earlier in the questionnaire. In all cases, the average scores on question F are distinctly lower than for question E, the differences ranging from 0.5 to 1.6. If the replies to the two questions were based solely on general economic concepts, there should be no difference in them. That is to say, it is hard to conceive some logic that would demonstrate that the receipts of French companies from subsidiaries in Brazil, India, and the like were more equitably related to their economic inputs than were the payments by subsidiaries in France to parent firms in Germany, the United States, and so on. When we find such a position endorsed across the board by all 12 elite groups, therefore, we must assume that something other than logic is at work. The explanation presumably lies in the nationalistic bias of the respondent considering his nation's interest in the benefits received from investments in other countries in question F in contrast to his protective nationalistic reaction against the external drain caused by outside investment in his native country in question E. This line of analysis will be pursued more fully in Chapter 3.

The Control Dimension. Tables 1.5 and 1.6 describe various ways the elites feel about the effects of foreign companies on control of national affairs. The main dimensions of the picture are expectable and quickly stated. The loss of control is seen as a significant problem (somewhere between major and minor in Table 1.5, question G) with the impact of U.S. companies a matter of notably greater concern than that of other firms. Furthermore the effects, if greater control is acquired by foreign firms, are quite worrisome (Table 1.6, question I). Underlying these attitudes are beliefs that when companies are foreign owned their decisions are more often adverse to national interests than when they are domestically owned (Table 1.6, question J) and that the home country loyalty of foreign managers creates a moderate problem (question K).

However, the interesting features of the data are shown by more refined analysis. The major surprise is the score for Canada on question G, Table 1.5. In light of the recent strong public reaction against U.S. control of Canadian industry and the traditional worries in Canada about domination by the "friendly giant" to the south, one would have expected a much stronger adverse score here than for Britain and France—something like 6.0, for example, in contrast to the

TABLE 1.5.   Control Effects Related to Countries

Q.G   To what degree do you feel that the activities of the companies of the following nationalities cause a loss of X control over X affairs? Minor loss of control = 1 ; Major loss of control = 7

Q.H   What effect do you believe the operations of X companies have on the control of national affairs by the nationals of the following countries? Loss of control: Minor = 1 ; Major = 7

(Averages of all elite groups)

Country - Y		Question G: Companies of Country Y in X	Question H: X Companies in Country Y
United States	Br.	4.5	1.8
	Fr.	5.4	1.6
	Can.	4.8	0.9
France	Br.	2.6	2.1
	Can.	2.9	0.7
Britain	Fr.	3.5	2.2
	Can.	3.1	0.8
Canada	Br.	—	2.5
	Fr.	—	2.3
Germany	Br.	2.7	—
	Fr.	4.3	—
	Can.	2.9	—
Holland	Br.	2.8	—
	Fr.	3.5	—
Japan	Br.	2.6	1.8
	Fr.	2.9	1.6
	Can.	3.3	0.8
Brazil	Br.	—	2.6
	Fr.	—	2.8

4.5 and 5.4 for the British and French. But no, the Canadians come in with a relatively mild 4.8. As the data in Table 1.7 show, this pattern holds for all groups. There is actually an indication of greater national consensus in the smaller spread between groups than for the other two countries (0.9 versus 1.2 and 1.5).

There is no apparent simple explanation for this Canadian response. As we saw in Table 1.3, the control question is as important for Canadians as for the other elites. The Canadian reactions to control by companies of other countries (for example, Germany and Japan) are sufficiently within the range of those of the British and French so that one cannot say that there has been a general pattern of lower scoring among Canadians for this whole question. The responses to question I indicate that the Canadians do demonstrate a different degree of concern about future loss of control. But there is quite solid evidence here that, despite all the public uproar, Canadian elites do not in fact look upon the actual loss of control resulting from having 60 percent of their factories foreign owned as any more of a problem than the British, with less than a tenth of their manufacturing sector under foreign control.

How can one explain this Canadian response? For a conservative researcher, the sound answer must be that it is a puzzling matter to which further research

TABLE 1.6. Control

Q.I   What will be the result for X if foreign companies have greater control over policy decisions in X industry? Good = 1 ; Bad = 7

Q.J   How often do you think a typical foreign company operating in X acts in ways contrary to X national interests as compared to a typical X firm? No difference = 1 ; Frequently = 7

Q.K   How frequently do you believe X firms operating abroad act in ways contrary to the national interests of host countries as compared to a typical local firm? No difference = 1 ; Frequently = 7

Q.L   To what degree does the loyalty of a foreign manager in X to his own country have a bad effect for X? Minor problem = 1 ; Major problem = 7

		Leg	PG	Lab	Bus	Ave
Q.I	Br.	5.3	4.6	6.0	5.0	5.2
	Fr.	4.8	5.0	5.8	5.1	5.2
	Can.	6.0	5.8	6.3	5.3	5.8
Q.J	Br.	3.5	3.0	4.1	3.1	3.4
	Fr.	3.7	4.0	4.3	3.0	3.8
	Can.	3.5	3.8	4.0	3.3	3.6
Q.K	Br.	3.2	3.1	3.8	2.4	3.1
	Fr.	3.1	3.5	4.1	2.4	3.3
	Can.	2.7	3.1	3.4	2.7	3.0
Q.L	Br.	3.2	2.6	3.8	2.8	3.1
	Fr.	3.7	3.8	4.7	3.2	3.8
	Can.	4.0	3.8	4.3	3.5	3.9

See note for Table 1.1.

TABLE 1.7. Loss of Control of National Affairs because of U.S. Companies

	Leg	PG	Lab	Bus	Ave
Britain	4.4	3.9	5.4	4.1	4.5
France	5.1	5.6	6.1	4.9	5.4
Canada	4.5	4.9	5.4	4.5	4.8

Note: See Question G, Table 1.5. See note for Table 1.1.

must be directed. But one can advance a few thoughts to which other responses in this survey contribute. The most obvious point is that, in terms of overall national welfare, the elites register a quite consistent and generally favorable appraisal (Table 1.1, question A). Thus it would appear likely that the reaction on the control question is influenced heavily by political psychology, the importance to national independence of control for itself, more than because of tangible results of that control. If this is so, scores may be expected to be influenced more by the character of nationalism in a country than by the actual amount of foreign investment. The reactions to U.S. control are consistent with this line of reasoning in terms of the general character of nationalism in the three countries. The high French score fits with the French preoccupation with retention of political independence vis-à-vis the United States, the European Economic Community (EEC), and so on. An interesting confirmation of this preoccupation appears in the difference between French and British scores on degree of concern over control effects of German firms (4.3 versus 2.7, question G, Table 1.5). The British, even though they have a greater volume of U.S. investment, are less worried about political control. The Canadians, while vocally expressing concern about political identity, in fact are for the most part hard-headed and pragmatic in acceptance of the realities of political interdependence and powerful influence from the United States. These are, it must be emphasized, tentative explanatory thoughts, but they would seem to provide fruitful hypotheses for further work.

The influence of nationalistic attitudes also shows up again in the mirror-image question on control. The responses to questions J and H in Table 1.6 are similar to those to questions E and F in Table 1.4 on economic effects, in that the host elites express a more adverse view of the effects of foreign firms within their own countries than within other countries on identical propositions. One notes, however, an intriguing difference in the degree of bias—score differences of 1.2, 0.7, and 0.7 on the economic question versus 0.3, 0.4, and 0.8 on control. While the pattern is not consistent, there is an apparent tendency toward less bias on the control aspects.

A more complicated but presumably even sounder piece of evidence on the same tack is the scoring of the elites in evaluating the loss of control concerning investment in their own countries (question H, Table 1.5). Here we have two viewpoints on two factual, identical situations. When British elites consider the activities of French companies in Britain, they score the loss of control at 2.6. When the French elite consider these same activities in Britain, they rate the loss of control slightly lower at 2.2. As to the activities of British firms in France, the French rate the loss at 3.5 and the British, much less serious at 2.1.

The details of these differences may involve a complexity of explanation. But, for present purposes, the obvious point is that, in both cases, there is clearly a tendency to see the loss of control as more serious when it is in your own country embodied in foreign entities than when it is a distant problem in which the potential danger sources are your own nationals. These, of course, are just small pieces of evidence in a complex story, but they give credence to the hypothesis that the worry over loss of control of national affairs springs not only from tangible issues but from a deep-seated reaction to foreign pressure in the host society.

Cultural Impact. From the data in Table 1.3, we already know that the elites do not attach major importance to the cultural impact of foreign investment. Table 1.8 gives other dimensions of their views on this impact.

The elites apparently recognize that a moderate degree of change in national life is induced by the activities of the firms (question M), with the British on the low side (3.3) and the Canadians on the high side (4.1). The appraisals of the merits of the effects are all at least slightly favorable, with the one exception of the French union leaders (question N). The even more favorable reaction to management practices of foreign firms (question O) is not unexpected in light of the general respect with which U.S. management is regarded. But the receptivity to foreign ways in personal activities (question P) is stronger than one might have anticipated. Perhaps the most decisive demonstration of the weakness of resistance to cultural penetration is the fact that the proud French have the lowest scores on question P, and that among them, the *hautes fonctionnaires*, the mandarins of their society, along with the French businessmen, are the most receptive of all. While these assorted pieces of evidence do not eliminate cultural impact as an issue, they clearly suggest that it is a much lesser one than the economic and control effects of foreign firms.

Labor. The data in Table 1.9 indicate some distinct differences in the image of various aspects of the labor relations of foreign firms. The responses to question Q affirm the generally observed view that foreign firms pay higher wages than local firms, a point that at least in Britain may not be entirely accurate, according to a study by Gennard.[1] When it comes to other working conditions like job security and handling of grievances (question R), however, the weight of opinion shifts toward a less favorable image overall, and a distinctly negative one with the British and French union leaders.

TABLE 1.8. Cultural Effects

Q.M   To what degree do you believe that the influence of foreign ways of life brought in by foreign companies in X changes the X way of life? Small change = 1; Large change = 7

Q.N   Are the changes in way of life referred to in Question M good or bad? Good = 1; Bad = 7

Q.O   The general effect on X of changes in methods of management caused by introduction of practices of foreign companies is: Desirable = 1; Undesirable = 7

Q.P   In your personal activities, to what degree do you feel it is desirable to adopt ways of life or work brought in by foreign companies? Large degree = 1; Not at all = 7

		Leg	PG	Lab	Bus	Ave
Q.M	Br.	3.5	3.2	3.3	3.2	3.3
	Fr.	3.6	4.5	3.6	3.7	3.8
	Can.	4.3	4.0	4.5	3.7	4.1
Q.N	Br.	3.3	3.8	3.9	3.7	3.7
	Fr.	3.2	3.4	4.3	3.1	3.5
	Can.	3.7	3.9	3.9	3.2	3.7
Q.O	Br.	2.9	2.7	4.2	2.6	3.1
	Fr.	2.7	2.6	4.1	2.4	2.9
	Can.	3.3	2.8	3.9	2.6	3.2
Q.P	Br.	4.5	5.3	4.8	4.7	4.7
	Fr.	3.7	3.4	4.6	3.3	3.8
	Can.	4.9	4.8	4.7	4.6	4.8

See note for Table 1.1.

On the third point, union relations, the results present a quite mixed picture. While the questions are not quite comparable, the data confirm a general impression that in France there is not the same intensity of struggle between unions and foreign firms as in Britain. In Canada, the situation clearly is quite different. It is notable not only that the scores are generally lower, but that the union leaders themselves rate the foreign firms as more tractable than domestic companies.

TABLE 1.9.   Labor Relations

How do you believe the treatment of workers by foreign companies in X compares with that by X firms in respect to wages and other working conditions (job security, handling of grievances, etc.)?

Q.Q   Wages: Foreign firms   Better = 1 ; Worse = 7

Q.R   Other Conditions: Better = 1 ; Worse = 7

Q.S   Do you believe that foreign companies in X are more *or* less willing to recognize trade unions than X firms are? (Fr. Q - Disposees ... a s'entendre avec les syndicats) More willing = 1 ; Less willing = 7

		Leg	PG	Lab	Bus	Ave
Q.Q	Br.	2.6	3.3	3.5	2.8	3.1
	Fr.	2.9	2.7	3.2	3.1	3.0
	Can.	3.3	3.4	3.3	3.3	3.3
Q.R	Br.	3.5	3.8	4.5	3.6	3.8
	Fr.	3.8	3.5	4.8	3.8	4.0
	Can.	3.7	3.8	3.6	3.5	3.6
Q.S	Br.	4.9	4.3	5.6	4.3	4.7
	Fr.	3.8	3.6	5.0	4.0	4.1
	Can.	3.3	3.4	3.4	3.1	3.3

See note for Table 1.1.

The Joint Venture Syndrome

From Japan to Canada to Peru, the most popular host-nation desire seems to be that multinational firms subordinate their role by investing in local enterprises on a minority ownership basis. A set of six questions in the survey was designed to shed some light on elite attitudes on this subject. The respondents were asked to rate the effects of a foreign firm owning less than 50 percent of a national company compared with its owning 100 percent for the six aspects of national interests listed in Table 1.10. Two main conclusions are suggested by the pattern of responses.

First, although the attitudes are clearly favorable to joint ventures, they are not as strongly so as the prevalence of stated opinions and the character of some government policies would lead one to expect, especially in Britain and France. The second point is the modest degree of differentiation shown in the European data at the bottom. In reality there are major differences in the effects. For example, joint ventures are often less productive because of technology communications problems (indicated by a score of 2 or 3), while host-nation investors almost always benefit (for instance, a score of 6). The survey shows that the Canadians make such significant distinctions, but the British and French tend to regard joint ventures as all-purpose devices that will help them fairly uniformly in many ways.

Summary

Among the four major subjects examined, the control and economic impacts stand out as being most important and having the most questionable results in the eyes of the elites. The loss of control over national affairs is clearly considered adverse, while the economic appraisals are mixed, generally favorable in overall terms but unfavorable when external payments are considered. The effects on workers are also considered quite important and, while the appraisals are varied, the general picture is favorable to the foreign firms. The opinions on cultural effects indicate that criticism of business influences leading to the Americanization of Canada and Europe are of doubtful significance. The elites rated this criterion distinctly lower than the others and were generally favorable in their judgments of the cultural impact of the firms.

TABLE 1.10. Attitudes on Joint Ventures

	Average Scores of All Elites		
	Britain	France	Canada

Effects of foreign minority ownership as compared to 100% foreign ownership rated as worse (1) to better (7) for each factor.

Opportunities for X managers	5.0	4.5	5.6
X control of national affairs	4.9	4.4	5.3
X balance of payments	4.9	4.4	5.3
X national income	4.7	4.7	4.8
Opportunities for X investors	4.9	4.6	5.6
X industrial productivity	4.4	5.0	4.2
Average	4.6	4.6	5.1

Average of differences between lowest and highest ratings for the six host-nation interests by each respondent.

Legislators	1.8	1.9	3.0
Government officials	1.6	1.9	2.6
Heads of firms	1.6	2.2	2.8
Labor leaders	1.9	1.9	2.5

Since the assessments on the two most important criteria (control and economics) tend toward the adverse side, it is notable that most respondents expressed a favorable overall opinion on the effects of the foreign firms. While there may be diverse, specific factors affecting this overall view, it seems quite likely that, for many respondents, it represents a gut feeling, a synthesis of assorted factual and emotional inputs into the mind. Thus, it would appear that there is among most of them an intuitive view that the foreign firms are beneficial, which balances the somewhat negative views that one might compute by adding up their thoughts about the specific effects weighted by the importance attached to them.

The data also provide small but reinforcing evidences of the underlying nationalistic emotions which affect appraisals. In both the control and economic questions, it is clear that the judgments of the elites were not based entirely on tangible facts or basic logics. Thus the influence of nationalist reaction to external control and drain on national wealth, which can be hypothesized from concepts of nationalism, seems to be confirmed by the data.

Putting the evidences of intuitive overall appraisal and nationalist reaction together, we have an interesting combination of attitudes. It would appear that, among the developed nations, there is a generally receptive overall environment for foreign firms. However, always simmering beneath the surface are basic nationalistic views, which are adverse to the firms and which are closely related to the two specific issues on which negative views are most evident—loss of control of national affairs and economic outflow. Recurring resistance to the firms based on this combination of specific issues and nationalist reaction is a natural expectation, therefore, despite the basically favorable overall appraisal.

Variables Affecting Elite Attitudes

A wide variety of economic, political, social, and cultural factors, some rational, some emotional, are regularly advanced as contributing to reactions to MNCs. The great diversity of opinions in the survey data encourages the search among these factors for explanatory variables. Toward this end, the next section examines three sets of possible explanatory factors: attitudes on general and specific effects, general attitudinal and experience factors, and personal characteristics.

Correlations of Attitudes on Various Effects

A logical starting point for this exploration is the presumption that a person's general attitude toward foreign firms is based on specific effects of the firm on the host nation. Table 1.11 presents data pursuing this presumption. Most of the questions in the survey could be classified under four main categories of effects on the host nation: control, economics, culture, and labor. The most useful ones for this purpose are questions G, I, J, L, D, E, N, O, P, Q, and S

TABLE 1.11. Correlations of Attitudes on Selected Effects of Foreign Firms with Attitudes on Overall Effect

	Britain					France					Canada				
	Leg	PG	Lab	Bus	Total	Leg	PG	Lab	Bus	Total	Leg	PG	Lab	Bus	Total
Number	61	59	82	50	252	55	78	92	52	277	45	81	72	62	260
Control															
Q.G Present															
1. U.S. firms	.20	.34	.21	.09	.29	-.06	.25	.56	.27	.35	-.11	.36	.26	.30	.36
2. British	.16	.18	-.08	.13	.13	.31	.06	.48	.18	.33	.24	.11	.00	.03	.18
3. German	.22	.15	-.14	.24	.13	.10	.11	.55	.28	.34	.19	.06	.04	-.13	.05
4. French	.16	.11	-.08	.14	.09	.21	.18	.55	.30	.39	.16	.05	.07	-.04	.06
5. Japanese	.06	.41	.36	.30	.36	.40	.31	.49	.41	.45	-.02	.12	.04	-.10	.04
Q.I Future	.50	.33	.08	.24	.34	.45	.35	.57	.16	.47	-.11	.40	.48	.34	.46
Q.J National interest	.25	.36	.09	.27	.29	.21	.40	.60	.26	.49	.48	.48	.31	.38	.46
Q.L Manager loyalty											.64	.48	.46	.23	.49
Economics															
Q.D General impact	.32	.36	.36	.09	.39	.25	.33	.58	.38	.53	.52	.49	.60	.23	.57
Q.E Balance of payments	.11	.40	.47	.18	.35	.23	.11	.53	-.04	.43	.44	.28	.33	.30	.45
Culture															
Q.N Way of life	.30	.49	.29	.52	.37	.29	.43	.62	.26	.53	.62	.42	.56	.54	.53
Q.O Management methods	.05	.20	.49	.38	.39	.47	.48	.70	.28	.64	.21	.42	.10	.20	.44
Q.P Personal life	.21	.32	.34	.23	.25	.26	.33	.37	.31	.40	.23	.09	.23	-.20	.11
Labor															
Q.Q Wages	.22	.15	.02	-.02	.13	-.04	.08	.49	.11	.27	.13	.26	.30	-.11	.19
Q.S Union recognition	.03	.04	.24	-.05	.19	-.11	.14	-.25	.09	.03	.21	.26	.22	-.10	.25
Minimum correlation at .05 significance level	.25	.25	.22	.28	.12	.27	.22	.21	.27	.12	.30	.22	.24	.25	.12

See note for Table 1.1.

(see Tables 1.4, 1.5, 1.6, 1.8, and 1.9). The data show the correlation coefficients for each question with the overall appraisal question A (see Table 1.1).

The data in Table 1.11 are informative but far from conclusive in the search for explanatory variables. There are a number of relatively high correlation coefficients, but no single question or set of questions stands out as dominant or fully consistent in the strength of relationships demonstrated. The three general control questions (I–L) and the economics and culture groups seem roughly equal by such general measures as are appropriate for this type of data. For example, a count of the number of coefficients above .30 for the four elite groups in the three countries for each question gives these sums: I = 9, J = 9, and L = 6; economics, D = 9 and E = 6; and culture, N = 9, D = 6, and P = 5. One might lean toward control as a greater influence on this basis. But scanning the columns vertically we find an economics effect has the highest correlation in the total data for one country (D in Canada), a cultural effect in one country (O in France), and one economics and one cultural effect are equal in the third (D and O in Britain). And taking another vertical look one notes that for 7 of the 12 elite groups the highest correlations are in the culture group. Likewise, Question N, effects on way of life, is the only one in which the coefficients all exceed .25. It appears to be the closest approximation to a pervasive or consistent influence, all of the other questions having one or more quite low figures.

All in all, therefore, the data seem to say that culture, control, and economic effects are all significant factors, with a slight indication that the rank of importance is in that order. The apparent importance of culture in this picture is confusing since it scored relatively low when the respondents were asked to rank criteria for judging the value of foreign firms on another set of questions discussed in the previous section.[2] In that case control and economic effects came out essentially as equal in the top ranking by virtually all groups. The heart of the confusion presumably lies in determining what the correlation coefficients are indicating. A high coefficient may mean that the variable is a strong factor influencing the overall appraisal; or that it is a weak factor on which views tend to follow the overall appraisal; or that views on it tend to parallel the overall appraisal without particularly influencing it or being influenced by it. And it may be that to some degree all three possibilities are present. So this analysis must end inconclusively with the minimum conclusion: simply that culture, control, and economics are all significant candidates as important influences.

The data for the other two groups of questions, the control set under G and the labor effects, are generally low and so disparate that they would not seem significant as explanatory variables. This outcome is surprising for question G, as one might expect the current control effects would be just as important as those raised in questions I, J, and L. The presumption must be that the introduction of specific countries affected the responding context in such a way that direct statistical relationships of answers changed from that of the other questions. The nature of the effect, however, is not clear and may be a fruitful direction for future study.

The only immediately useful evidence from the data is the indication of the relative importance of firms from each country in attitude formation. Expectedly, the U.S. firms show the greatest number of high correlations; more interesting, however, are the low and in two cases negative figures for U.S. firms. All three groups of legislators, for example, show higher correlations for companies from some other country than the United States. It is inconceivable that the Canadian legislators' views on foreign investment in general are influenced more by the control effects of British than of U.S. firms. Interpretation of such data would tend to confirm the alternate types of explanations noted above. In this case, as with the cultural impact, it may be that the attitudes on the control effects of British companies happen to parallel or are influenced by the general feelings about foreign companies more than by those about U.S. companies, rather than being themselves actually stronger influences.

The two labor questions, on the other hand, appear to be quite out of the picture as candidates for explanatory variables. With many low figures and seven negative signs among them, they have little statistical force. There is no departure from the general scheme such as the introduction of country differentiation as in question G. Thus, one must assume that opinions about the labor management practices of foreign firms are relatively independent of general attitudes on the effects of the firms. A somewhat extreme illustration in support of this conclusion are the responses of the French labor union leaders. This group, with a heavy Communist component, was strongly negative on virtually all points. Yet it judged the foreign firms quite favorably on union relations, this accounting for the large negative correlation on question S. While generalizing from the labor figures is dubious, there is at least a suggestion here that general attitudes on foreign firms are more likely to be related to other broad factors (control, economics, and culture) than to specific effects like labor conditions.

Stepping back to take a broad look at the data, one is led in quite a different direction from the natural search for a few variables of relatively greater or stronger influence. The roughly similar range of correlation coefficients among the main control, economic, and cultural questions interspersed with distinctly low figures; the disparate pattern in question G where the underlying influences are surely as great as in questions I, J, and L; and the appearance of a few high figures even in the labor group suggest a different pattern of explanatory analysis. It would appear that a substantial number of influences are at work in attitude formation about foreign firms and that the weighting of the influences varies substantially among individuals, groups, and countries. In other words, we are dealing with a complex attitudinal process whose analysis requires breadth of comprehension of many variables, rather than a narrowing to fix on limited explanatory influences.

Experience and Internationalism

The five questions shown in Table 1.12 were designed to explore the relation between attitudes toward foreign firms, and experience, knowledge of

TABLE 1.12. Experience and Internationalism of Respondents

Distribution of Responses (number)

	Britain					France					Canada				
	Leg	PG	Lab	Bus	Total	Leg	PG	Lab	Bus	Total	Leg	PG	Lab	Bus	Total
Q.U Contact															
Little	19	34	36	11	100	12	26	27	9	74	12	26	14	6	58
Moderate	23	14	21	15	73	30	27	48	26	131	19	28	25	14	86
Frequent	19	11	23	24	77	13	22	16	16	67	13	27	33	39	112
Q.V Satisfaction															
Satisfactory	20	23	8	22	73	8	8	9	16	41	15	32	25	36	108
Middle	27	22	52	23	124	38	56	65	31	190	26	39	29	18	112
Unsatisfactory	5	1	7	3	16	2	3	8	2	15	–	5	9	5	19
Q.W Knowledge															
Intensive	13	13	11	10	47	10	9	4	7	30	10	25	22	21	78
Middle	29	17	33	24	103	21	29	46	22	118	22	34	26	26	108
General	19	29	37	16	101	22	36	41	21	120	12	22	23	12	69
Q.X International economic activity															
More	47	48	46	33	174	41	65	52	47	205	25	52	37	53	167
Middle	13	11	24	16	64	13	10	27	4	54	15	24	24	9	72
Less	1	–	11	–	12	1	1	13	–	15	4	3	11	–	18
Q.Y Noneconomic ties															
Increase	35	22	27	16	100	15	15	29	28	87	21	21	15	18	75
Middle	16	35	28	31	110	28	45	21	17	111	15	48	23	41	127
Decrease	9	2	26	2	39	12	15	41	6	74	8	11	34	3	56

Note: Questions:

Q.U Please indicate the extent of your direct contact with foreign firms in X (for example, in labor negotiations, business arrangements, etc.). No contact = 1; Frequent = 7

Q.V If you have had direct contact with foreign firms, to what extent have they satisfied your objectives? Satisfactory = 1; Unsatisfactory = 7

Q.W The responsibilities of people vary in requirements of knowledge of the activities of foreign firms in X. Please indicate the amount of knowledge which your situation has required along the range from intensive investigation to information only from general sources like newspapers. Intensive investigation = 1; General information = 7

Q.X Overall do you believe X's general policy should be to favor more *or* less international economic activity including exports, imports, and foreign investment? More = 1; Less = 7

Q.Y What attitude should X take toward noneconomic international ties like NATO? Decrease ties = 1; Increase ties = 7

See note for Table 1.1.

the subject, and general attitudes on international matters. In each case the questions were structured in a manner similar to the rest of the questionnaire with a 1 to 7 scale. To provide convenient statistical groups the responses are combined in Table 1.12 into three subsets: 1 = scores of 1 and 2; 2 = scores of 3 to 5; and 3 = scores of 6 and 7. The subsequent correlation coefficients are derived from the basic data, not these subsets.

The responses to six questions on attitudes toward foreign firms have been used in the correlation analysis summarized in Table 1.13 to obtain as far as possible a composite measure of the attitudes of the respondents. They include the overall appraisal question B and the following from Tables 1.4, 1.5, 1.6, and 1.7: control, questions G and I; economics, questions D and E; and culture, question N.

Contact with Foreign Firms. The first two sets of data in Table 1.13 concern the possibility that the attitudes toward foreign firms might be affected by the extent of contact people had with them and the degree of satisfaction derived from these contacts.

The correlations in the first set of data are so erratic that one must conclude that there is no relation between degree of contact and attitudes. There is an indication of significant correlations among a few groups, for example, the British and Canadian businessmen, but the pattern is so inconsistent and weak that they are interesting only as suggestions of possible relationships for further exploration.

The second set of data has a more pronounced pattern, which is consistent with expectations. In many groups, especially in Canada, those who have had the most satisfactory contacts with foreign firms appear to be the ones who are most favorable to them. There are substantial exceptions, however, especially among the French where little or no correlation is evident. An interesting point here is the portion of respondents in each subset in Table 1.12. The "satisfactory" group is larger than the "unsatisfactory" group in all cases, and in most the margin is substantial. We also note that for Canada a greater degree of contact is reported and that the portion reporting satisfaction in contacts is greater. This substantial body of pragmatically satisfactory experience with foreign firms would appear to be a strong factor in the direction of favorable judgments.

Knowledge. The next question concerned the degree of knowledge of foreign companies. The phraseology of this question was troublesome. Asking people to rate their own degree of knowledge on a subject is in general not likely to give very accurate results. The alternative used here was to ask about the extent to which knowledge had been sought and to relate the process to job requirements, thus removing some subjective elements. The results are probably still of uncertain validity but were considered the only practical approach and useful for exploratory purposes.

The data do not indicate any general correlation between degree of knowledge and attitudes. There is some indication of the tendency toward less favorable attitudes among those who are better informed indicated by the fact that there are six significant negative correlations versus two positive ones among the elite groups and a 2 to 0 ratio in the totals. But on the whole the pattern is so weak and mixed that little case can be made for any relationship. The apparent conclusion from this, taken along with the results on the degree of contact question, must be that it makes little difference in attitudes on this subject whether a person is well or poorly informed.

Internationalism. The final two sets of data concern the extent to which the degree of general economic and noneconomic internationalism of an individual bears on attitudes toward foreign firms. These questions were also troublesome. Some Canadians found it impossible to answer the first one because they wanted to increase trade but to reduce investment and were unable to arrive at any composite position on a general policy of degree of economic internationalism. Most, however, understood the basic intent of the question and took a position. The inclusion of NATO (North Atlantic Treaty Organization) in the second question aroused doubts in the minds of some advisers in preparation of the survey because it is such a strong political issue, especially in France. But this factor was clearly intended in its use. The intent was to get the emotional reaction of the respondent to the idea of ties representing some loss of sovereignty and joint action among governments, which NATO involves. The distribution of numbers of responses on this point in Table 1.12 seems consistent with the general image of thinking in these countries, with the French on balance positive but less so than the elites of the other countries. It is also interesting to see the strong negative tendency of labor leaders in all countries, and that the business leaders are apparently those most strongly favoring internationalism.

The pattern of correlations is quite strong and consistent with expectations. Both sets of data indicate that those who are most favorable to general internationalism tend to be the more favorable to foreign firms. There appear to be some significant exceptions among groups, notably the British on the second question, which may be clues to something interesting. The weak correlation among all British groups and Canadian officials on both questions and the Canadian businessmen on the noneconomic ties suggests that these groups may be more inclined to see foreign investment as a distinctive issue to be judged on its own merits as distinguished from seeing it as a component of the total subject of international relations. However, the evidence is suggestive, not conclusive.

General. While the data in Table 1.13 suggest significant relations between attitudes toward foreign firms and the satisfaction and internationalism factors, these correlations need to be considered in the same broad perspective as those in the previous section. The coefficients appearing for these questions in Table 1.13 are for the most part weaker and more disparate than those for the questions in Table 1.11. This fact is not surprising, since one would expect that these influences would be weaker than the views on specific effects of foreign firms. The more important point is that in a fair number of cases the coefficients are

TABLE 1.13. Correlations of Experience and Internationalism with Attitudes on Effects of Foreign Firms

	Britain					France					Canada				
	Leg	PG	Lab	Bus	Total	Leg	PG	Lab	Bus	Total	Leg	PG	Lab	Bus	Total
Contact															
B Overall effect	-.24	.49	-.08	-.13	-.07	-.18	.16	-.05	.00	-.05	-.22	.07	-.04	.06	-.01
G Control: U.S. firms	-.15	.11	.22	.22	.09	.05	.04	.00	.17	.02	-.16	-.08	.20	.11	.00
I Future	.03	-.03	.18	-.01	.07	.08	.08	-.14	-.04	-.04	.20	.08	.03	.40	.04
D Economy: general	-.17	.03	.22	-.33	-.02	-.29	.19	-.13	.10	-.08	-.31	.05	-.05	-.06	-.01
E Balance of payments	-.11	-.01	.25	.20	.09	.21	.07	.05	.20	.05	-.43	-.15	.00	.22	.00
N Culture	-.11	-.04	.12	-.14	-.11	-.04	.16	-.07	-.17	-.04	-.05	-.07	.06	.23	-.02
Satisfaction															
B Overall effect	.37	.25	.25	.02	.29	.20	.00	.19	.13	.17	.24	.26	.23	.56	.45
G Control: U.S. firms	.00	.22	.20	.10	.18	.42	-.16	.18	.14	.17	.08	.13	.37	.38	.33
I Future	.01	.28	.16	.14	.21	.04	.05	-.01	.11	.07	.34	.03	.19	.41	.30
D Economy: general	.12	.16	.09	.07	.17	.22	-.16	.29	.20	.18	.29	.18	.29	.13	.33
E Balance of payments	-.18	.06	.19	.08	.09	.33	-.09	.32	.09	.22	.31	.03	.18	-.04	.23
N Culture	.17	.21	-.05	.24	.12	-.13	.08	.20	.04	.12	.23	.18	.37	.37	.39
Knowledge															
B Overall effect	.03	-.43	-.21	.06	.00	.17	-.06	-.35	-.08	-.08	-.22	-.08	-.26	-.05	-.13
G Control: U.S. firms	.03	-.03	-.27	.14	-.07	-.03	.01	-.03	.19	.06	.12	.01	-.19	-.02	-.11
I Future	.08	.12	-.16	-.08	.02	.08	.15	-.04	.13	.10	.12	.03	-.11	.18	-.05
D Economy: general	.16	.14	-.21	.26	.07	.33	-.20	-.25	.05	-.02	-.05	-.10	-.22	-.12	-.12
E Balance of payments	.11	.02	-.15	.01	.00	.02	-.12	-.22	.08	-.07	-.08	.19	-.11	-.34	-.09
N Culture	.01	-.05	-.16	.33	.00	.06	-.08	-.20	.05	-.03	-.04	.14	-.23	-.20	-.04

26

International economic activity

B Overall effect	.18	-.17	.33	.32	.34	.48	.28	.64	.19	.57	.33	.12	.44	.37	.42
G Control: U.S. firms	.30	.15	.24	.06	.28	.08	-.19	.26	.07	.17	.19	-.14	.11	.26	.11
I Future	.23	.24	.09	.22	.26	.14	.03	.27	.02	.23	.14	-.07	.30	.21	.23
D Economy: general	.38	.28	.35	.18	.39	.06	-.05	.38	.25	.35	.40	.21	.27	.20	.35
E Balance of payments	.16	.21	.14	.01	.18	.18	-.08	.42	.05	.36	.18	.00	.16	.08	.22
N Culture	.32	.24	-.03	.20	.15	.38	.29	.51	.07	.45	.39	-.10	.27	.24	.19

Noneconomic ties

B Overall effect	.08	.10	.19	.07	.20	.27	.20	.65	.01	.45	.44	.18	.34	-.20	.29
G Control: U.S. firms	.26	.17	.24	-.08	.25	.38	-.06	.44	.20	.30	-.06	.11	.08	.10	.15
I Future	.12	-.02	.19	.15	.18	.49	.28	.42	.09	.36	.04	.15	.10	-.05	.14
D Economy: general	.28	.15	.06	.07	.22	.18	-.03	.53	-.02	.33	.64	.11	.36	-.03	.32
E Balance of payments	.26	.08	.26	.15	.26	.27	-.12	.66	-.01	.42	.22	-.03	.35	-.03	.36
N Culture	.12	.00	.20	.18	.17	.31	.34	.57	.15	.44	.42	.03	.38	-.24	.22
.05 Significance level	.25	.25	.22	.28	.12	.27	.22	.21	.27	.12	.30	.22	.24	.25	.12

Note: See Questions U–Y, Table 1.12 vs. Questions B, G, I, D, E, and N, Tables 1.1, 1.4, 1.5, 1.6, and 1.8. See note for Table 1.1.

quite high but that the pattern is very mixed. Thus, the general observation made in the previous section is amplified and reinforced. The satisfaction and internationalism elements clearly must be added to the complex mix of factors influencing attitude formation, and the scattering of high correlations in even the contact and knowledge questions suggests that in some cases they also play a part.

Personal Characteristics

The third area in which explanation of attitudes is sought is an assortment of background and situational factors. The questionnaires were precoded according to certain types of information about the respondents that might be relevant to their attitudes. Table 1.14 presents the various subgroups and the deviations of the average scores for each subgroup from the average of its general group. A minus deviation indicates that the subgroup showed a more favorable attitude (lower score) than the full group.

Only a few of the subgroupings showed statistically significant patterns of scores, so it is not fruitful to comment on each in detail. Therefore, the discussion here will be limited to describing the nature of the subgroupings and commenting only on those for which significant opinion patterns are evident.

National Legislators. The breakdown by political parties is self-explanatory. In each country the parties have been listed in a rough spectrum from more conservative-capitalistic philosophies to the more socialist views.

Legislators in these three countries generally consider their elected function as a part-time responsibility and to some degree continue in regular careers. Thus from their biographies one can quite readily identify them with nonpolitical career categories. To achieve reasonably large statistical groups, three categories were used. The business group includes all those with ownership or managerial responsibility. Workers are those with blue collar backgrounds or with union careers associated with blue collar work. Professional and miscellaneous is largely composed of lawyers and others with high intellectual training plus a hodge-podge of housewives, farmers, and the like.

Only for Britain and Canada was information on the education of the legislators available. Oxbridge indicates graduates of Oxford or Cambridge, Britain's eminent status universities. The other categories are self-explanatory, as are the age groups.

The only major difference showing clear statistical significance among the legislator subgroups is among the parties in Canada where the NDP (New Democratic Party) and other minor groups record the strongly antiforeign investment position that they have adopted. The differences among the major political groups are not statistically significant, so one must conclude that there are no meaningful differences in basic attitudes toward foreign investment among the dominant political groups.

There are suggestions of patterns among the other subgroups, including some oddities like the low score for British M.P.s with labor backgrounds. However, the small differences and the limited samples in some subgroups result in lack of statistical significance for these patterns. As confirmation of this lack of significance, it should be noted that when the scores for five other questions on economic, control, and cultural effects were compared, the M.P.s with labor backgrounds on balance were less favorable than those with business careers. Thus we may only note from these three sets of subgroups as suggested leads for future research the indications, for example, that noncollege and older legislators are inclined to be more favorable to foreign firms.

Permanent Government Officials. The ministries were placed in three groups according to perceived similarity of outlook toward foreign investment: those concerned with international commerce and foreign affairs interested in economic and political relations with the world; the industry and finance people responsible for national development; and ministries concerned with health, education, and other general affairs. The characterizations of these groups are, of course, of only limited value in the case of a specific individual whose responsibilities may result in a quite different concern from that assumed for his general group.

The officials were divided into three groups according to their status in the official hierarchy, with 1 being the highest level. The third breakdown of officials was by the nature of their work. The policy group was the senior ministerial civil servants including all of the group 1 men and a few others. The operations group was people with responsibility for some functional phase of ministerial work, while the staff people were generally economic, technological, or management experts in an advisory or service position. The French policy advisers were members of the cabinet of each ministry, a role somewhat superior to that of the staff people in the previous group but still not in the upper policy-making position.

The differences among the government-official groups are not sharp enough to justify any substantial conclusions. It is true that for all countries the scores for the commerce and foreign affairs people are somewhat less favorable than the industry and finance scores, but the differences are small. The fact that the general group is consistently the most unfavorable is more interesting. There is an indication here that those who are closest to the realities of the effects of foreign investment are more favorable while those with only a general knowledge who may be influenced more by less rational influences are less favorable.

The patterns of data by level and position are somewhat mixed but, taken together, they show some indications that those in higher, policy-type positions are more likely to be favorable to foreign firms than those lower in the bureaucratic hierarchy.

Labor Union Leaders. One might expect that labor in fields in which foreign firms were prominent would have different attitudes on foreign investment from those found in fields with few or no foreign firms. The first set of data was

TABLE 1.14. Opinions on Overall Effects of Foreign Firm by Groups (average scores)

	Britain	Scores		France		Scores		Canada		Scores	
	Number	Group Average	Deviation from Group		Number	Group Average	Deviation from Group		Number	Group Average	Deviation from Group
Legislators	61	3.2			55	3.1			45	3.5	
Party											
Conservative	23		0	Progress et Democratic, Modern, & Republicains Independents	18		-.4	Conservative	16		-.4
Labour	28		0					Liberal	21		-.5
				Gaullist	24		+.1	New Dem.	5		+2.1
				Socialist, Radicals, & Independents	13		+.3	Misc.	3		+1.8
Career											
Business	22		0		22		-.2		18		-.2
Prof./misc.	29		+.2		32		+.1		23		+.1
Worker	10		-.6		1		–		2		–
Education											
Oxbridge	20		+.1								
Other college	25		0						28		+.2
No college	16		-.1						17		-.6

Age						
Over 50			23	0	24	0
35–50			25	+.1	18	-.2
Under 35			3	+.2	3	+.8
Government Officials	59	2.8	78	3.1	81	3.2
Ministry						
Ind. & Fin.	27	-.4	45	-.1	38	-.3
Comm. & For. Af.	13	+.2	12	0	14	-.1
General	20	+.4	20	+.2	29	+.4
Level						
1 High	7	-.4	9	-.3	3	+.5
2 Middle	26	-.1	34	0	27	-.1
3 Low	27	+.1	35	+.2	50	0
Position						
Policy	19	-.6	11	-.3	12	-.1
Policy adviser			16	+.1		
Operations	20	-.1	32	+.2	37	0
Staff	21	+.5	17	-.2	32	0
Labor Leaders		4.0	92	4.3	72	4.2
Industry/For. Inv.						
Affected	37	+.2	45	-.5	25	-.2
Not affected	44	-.1	29	+.2	22	+.4
Position						
Nat. Hdq.	18	-.2	20	+.3	17	+.3
Union Sec. Gen.	38	0	41	0	26	-.2
Union Council	26	+.2	30	-.5	29	0

(continued)

TABLE 1.14 (continued)

	Britain — Scores			France — Scores			Canada — Scores		
	Number	Group Average	Deviation from Group	Number	Group Average	Deviation from Group	Number	Group Average	Deviation from Group
Union Group									
CGT				30		+2.0			
FO				19		–1.1			
CFDT				8		–.1			
CGC				35		–1.3			
Businessmen									
Industry/For. Inv.	50	2.9		52	2.8		62	2.6	
Affected	17		–.6	16		0	22		0
Not affected	25		+.2	36		0	29		+.1
Mixed							11		–.3
Size									
Top 100	11		–.2				18		0
101–300	25		+.2				28		+.1
301–500	16		0				16		–.1
Ownership									
100% Canadian							46		+.1
51–99% Canadian							7		–.6
50% or less Canadian							9		+.1

Note: See Table 1.1 for question.

32

designed to explore this possibility. The "affected" industries include vehicles, electronics, chemicals, and others where multinational firms are strong. The "not affected" are those in which foreign investment is a small factor, like food and basic materials (such as steel), and those where it is not present, like government employment. The total response for each country here is less than the total labor union figure at the top because national headquarters officers could not be assigned to an industry sector. The second set of data was used to explore the possibility that the level of a leader in the union hierarchy might affect his attitudes.

In France, labor is divided nationally into four major groups with quite distinct characteristics. The largest group is the Confédération Générale du Travail (CGT), which is dominated by Communists. Next in size and strength is the Force Ouvrière (FO), which split off from the CGT when it came under Communist control. It is smaller but has the same broad coverage of fields. Third largest is the Confédération Française Démocratique du Travail (CFDT), which broke off from the CGT earlier than the FO and has a strong Catholic orientation. The Confédération Générale des Cadres (CGC) is politically neutral serving the technical, professional, and supervisory employees.

The data by industry and position categories show such mixed and minor differences that no general conclusions from them are possible. The only strong distinction among the labor leaders therefore is for the French union groups. Clearly the CGT leaders take a much more negative view of foreign firms than those in the other groups. It should be noted that this was not the result of an indiscriminate condemnation across the board. As noted earlier, when asked if they felt foreign firms were more or less willing to deal with unions than were French firms, the CGT scores were distinctly more favorable to the foreigners than those of the FO and CGC. So it is clear that on the central attitudes of foreign investment the CGT reflect a strong ideological bias distinguishing them from the other union groups. Among the latter there are also differences. The higher level workers in the CGC appear to be the most favorably disposed toward foreign firms, perhaps due again to the ideological factor. The difference between the FO and CFDT is not readily explained by ideological or political distinction; it is of moderate magnitude and may not be significant, especially in light of the small CFDT response.

Heads of Business Firms. Like the union leaders, the heads of business firms were grouped according to the degree of foreign investment in their field so that it might be determined whether compettitve or other effects influence their attitudes. The lists of companies used for France and Canada gave data that permitted selecting a sample with a size range. The companies were selected from three groups, the 100 largest industrial firms in the country, the next 200, and those ranked 300-500.

Ownership breakdowns are given only for Canada. The basic purpose of this survey was to identify the attitudes of national leadership groups, which for the business sector in countries like Britain and France means the heads of the larger local national firms. Thus the survey in those countries did not include heads of subsidiaries of foreign firms even though a few of them might be considered part of the national business elite by virtue of their personal qualities. Canada presented a problem for this approach, however. With 60 percent of its manufacturing foreign controlled, including most of the larger firms, it would have been difficult and misleading to limit the survey to 100 percent Canadian firms. In the reality of Canadian national decision making, the Canadians heading major foreign units are a strong influence and thus clearly part of the elite. Therefore, the survey did include a number of Canadian firms in which there was foreign ownership.

There is no discernible significant pattern to the data for the industry and size groups. However, this fact should not be interpreted to mean that competitive or other experience with foreign firms is not an influence on business leader attitudes. It simply indicates that aggregations such as this do not demonstrate any such relationship.

There is a major difference between the 51-99 percent and 50-0 percent groups in Canada, with the 100 percent group falling in the middle. One might theorize that the 51-99 percent range, which presumably results in strong Canadian control, results in a happier situation for the Canadian chief executive than the subordinate position presumed to exist when control lies in foreign hands. However, the middle position of the heads of 100 percent Canadian firms does not support this thesis, and the small size of the non-100 percent groups makes drawing conclusions from their comparison dubious in any case. Thus, it seems best to observe only that the data do not provide any clear indication that degree of ownership of a firm affects the attitude of its senior officer.

Conclusions

This exploration of possible explanatory variables affecting elite attitudes toward foreign firms leads to two types of concluding comments: a recapitulation of the specific items and a broad assessment.

The first set of variables examined produced the strongest correlations. Opinions on the control, economic, and cultural impacts of foreign firms all showed strong correlations in the same general range of magnitude. The correlations of the general attitudes on internationalism in the second set were also close to the same magnitude, with personal satisfaction in contacts with foreign firms having lower but still significant correlations. Among the personal characteristics, the strongest correlations were related to political extreme groups (NDP in Canada and CGT labor leaders in France) and the business-labor differences among legislators. Some differences were also noted in the age-status area, with the younger legislators and lower level government officials more adverse to foreign firms.

On the other hand, a number of variables showed little or no correlation with the attitudes. Views about labor relations of foreign firms, extent of contact with the firms and knowledge of them, and distinctions among the main political parties, education, types of ministries, types of industries, and size and ownership of firms seemed to have no general relevance as explanatory variables.

These results suggest two observations in a broader perspective. First, the strong correlations seem to be at the extreme on a spectrum of generalization versus direct personal concern. Most of the high correlations involve very broad issues, such as control, internationalism, and ideology. The relationships weaken progressively in more specific areas like labor relations, types of industries, and nationalities of companies, where some fairly explicit personal observations might be expected. However, the in-close point of personal satisfaction in contacts shows high correlation. It is possible that the weakness in the middle area is due to the complexity and mixed character of the experiences that disguise relationships in the present study. On the other hand, there would seem to be logic in the indication that attitudes are most heavily influenced by broad considerations and direct personal experience. In any case, the indications here provide a good basis for pursuing that as a hypothesis for further research.

The second observation is drawn from the very mixed pattern of correlations found throughout the data. Several variables have high correlations, but in each of them the strength varies from group to group, sometimes drastically. And even among variables showing generally weak correlations, there are enough high figures to suggest that they have some influence in attitude formation. All of this leads to the conclusion that attitudes toward multinational firms are based on quite a complex variety of factors. It is to be expected that the character and force of these factors will vary from group to group and individual to individual, making for a very mixed pattern of attitudes. Thus the exploration for explanatory variables, which started with reference to the diversity of attitudes, ends with a fuller picture of the influences but still very much of an open field for future research in studying the assortment of factors that lie behind that diversity.

BUSINESS STUDENT AND MANAGEMENT PROGRAM SURVEYS

The analysis of the business student and management program surveys essentially follows the pattern employed for the elite data but with more limited scope consistent with the quality of information. For comparative purposes, data for the heads of firms from the elite studies are included in this section. The analysis is presented under three main headings: rank order of criteria for judging foreign firms, mean scores on key subjects, and correlations among scores.

TABLE 1.15. Criteria for Evaluating Foreign Firms (computed rank order; 1 = most important)

	Business Students							Managers					Heads of Firms			Average of All Groups
			Philip-			Canada					Canada					
	Japan	Korea	pines	Britain	France	McGill	UWO	Japan	Britain	France	McGill	UWO	Britain	France	Canada	
Number	35	54	71	42	61	31	49	115	41	28	64	84	50	52	62	
Response Rate				100%							32%	45%	25%	30%	25%	
Control over national affairs	3	4	3	1.2 (2.6)	1.0 (3.0)	1.0 (1.7)	1.0 (2.0)	1	1.1 (2.8)	1.2 (3.2)	1.0 (2.0)	1.0 (2.1)	1.3 (3.1)	1.5 (2.9)	1.2 (2.6)	1.15
Effect on balance of payments	6	2	2	1.1	1.2	2.3	1.6	4	1.0	1.0	1.5	1.4	1.1	1.4	1.1	1.18
Effect on X national income	5	1	1	1.0	1.5	1.5	1.6	2	1.3	1.0	1.2	1.4	1.0	1.0	1.2	1.27
Opportunities for X managers	1	5	5	1.4	1.0	1.9	1.7	3	1.4	1.3	1.4	1.3	1.6	2.1	1.0	1.47
Benefits for X workers						2.4	1.7		1.5	1.3	1.1	1.4	1.1	1.9	1.3	1.59
Role of X in the world					2.9	2.3	2.2		2.1	1.4	2.4	1.6	1.3	1.7	1.2	1.87
Opportunities for X investors	4	2	3	2.3	1.8	3.5	2.4	6	2.3	1.4	2.1	1.5	2.0	1.8	1.2	2.00
Changes in X way of life	2	6	6	2.6	2.3	2.3	1.6	5	2.4	1.5	3.1	2.6	2.4	2.1	2.4	2.17

Note: X = British, French, and so on.

Basis: Japan, Korea, and Philippines—Question: What relative importance should the following considerations have in judging the value of foreign companies operating in X? Mark 1 by the most important, 2 by the second most important, etc.

Other countries—see Table 1.3 for question and explanation of scores.

Rankings of Criteria for Foreign Firm Performance

The results of the questions on the importance attached to the various types of impact of foreign firms are summarized in Table 1.15. In the four Asian surveys, the questions simply asked that six criteria be ranked numerically, with the average results shown in Table 1.15. This approach proved troublesome for some of the respondents who had not been confronted by such questions before. Therefore, in the other surveys the questions were rephrased to conform to the general scheme of the questionnaire as described in the elite data analysis.

The most obvious feature of Table 1.15 is the great diversity of rankings. Four of the eight criteria are ranked highest by one or more group, and one criterion, changes in way of life, covers the span from second to bottom. So one must conclude that there are substantial differences among groups in importance attached to various effects.

However, there are some general tendencies apparent in the data. The criteria have been arranged in Table 1.15 according to the average of all of the scores, except for the first four Asian groups. This average has no statistical significance but it is a rough guide to the overall importance of each criterion. The first three, effects on control of national affairs, balance of payments, and national income, stand out at the top with great consistency. With only a few exceptions, they are so close that there is no statistically significant difference among them. The only major departures from this pattern are in the Japanese business students and, as noted above, there were some indications that enough of them were confused by the question so that the data may be inaccurate. Thus it appears that basic control and economic considerations are of more or less equally dominant importance in appraising foreign firms.

The next two criteria, effects on managers and workers, also fall roughly into a unit, though with substantial variations among them. The respondents in many cases give quite high ratings to these tangible human considerations. But still they run distinctly lower in the general pattern than the broad national factors. The pattern becomes even more erratic among the bottom three criteria. In a few cases they have relatively high scores. On the whole, however, the vague concept of contribution to role in the world, the benefits for investors, and the impact on national way of life appear to be relatively of much less importance than those higher on the list.

Examining the data horizontally, one is struck by the substantial degree of similarity among both nations and groups. There are a few interesting deviations, however. One is the relatively high rating of opportunities for investors in the two less developed countries (LDCs) compared to most of the developed countries. One may readily speculate that the former perceive this factor as a broad national matter relating to the desires to build a strong indigenous industry. Most of the respondents in developed countries, on the other hand, probably perceived it entirely in the narrower context of helping individual investors. The quite high rankings by the Canadian heads of firms for this criterion could be viewed in the same way because of the great desire there to build national industry to balance the large degree of foreign ownership (for example, 60 percent of manufacturing). However, the Canadian middle managers do not confirm this ranking.

There is also an indication that the economic criteria are relatively more significant for the LDCs compared to control of national affairs, the reverse of the tendency among the developed countries. While the differences here are too small to be significant, they offer an interesting hypothesis for future research. A lesser but intriguing point is the wide variation in responses to the question on the effect of foreign firms on the global role of the host nation. This question was suggested to the author during his work in France in the closing days of the de Gaulle era. In fact among the groups in Table 1.15 the French give no greater and in some cases less relative importance to this than to other criteria, though in the elite survey it did rank next to the top for French national legislators (see Table 1.3).

Despite these interesting variations, the dominant overall features are the consistency of the broad patterns, notably the high rating of control and economic factors, the low rank of the cultural impact, and the erratic pattern of individual variations. The apparent inference is that there is substantial commonality of host-national thinking on the relative importance of major criteria but that specific points of view are susceptible to considerable variety according to particular country and group characteristics.

Attitudes on Effects of Foreign Firms

Table 1.16 shows the average scores for responses to the key questions on the overall effects of foreign firms and control, economic, and cultural impact. While a number of interesting variations may be found among these figures, a few broad patterns are most conspicuous.

The replies to question B show a consistently favorable appraisal of the overall impact of foreign firms on the host society, all of the scores falling in the favorable range below 4.0. This appraisal is clearly in contrast to the general tendency among the judgments on specific points in the other questions, except under culture. Both the control and economics questions for the most part evoked strong to moderately negative reactions. It is unlikely, especially in light of the low ranking in Table 1.15, that the favorable attitudes on cultural effects would outweigh the feelings about control and economic effects. The conclusion must therefore be that these groups, like other elites, have an overall "gut feel" about the beneficial impact of foreign investment, which overrides the net sum of adverse views on specific points, or that other influences are strongly at work that were not measured in the data at hand.

Looking at the major subject areas, one finds other general patterns. Not surprisingly, the responses to question G on loss of control of national affairs show a marked variation according to the nationalities of the foreign firms. In

TABLE 1.16. Attitudes on Selected Effects of Foreign Firms (average scores)

	Business Students					Canada		Managers			Canada		Heads of Firms		
	Japan	Korea	Philip-pines	Britain	France	McGill	UWO	Japan	Britain	France	McGill	UWO	Britain	France	Canada
General															
Q.B Overall impact	3.5	3.4	3.5	2.7	3.5	3.9	3.6	3.2	3.5	3.3	2.9	3.2	2.8	2.8	2.6
Control															
Q.G															
1. U.S. firms	4.6	4.4	6.1	4.9	5.5	5.4	5.4	4.8	5.0	5.4	5.2	5.0	4.2	4.9	4.6
2. British	3.0	3.3	3.7		5.3	3.0	3.3	3.0		3.5	3.6	3.5		3.7	3.2
3. German				3.0	4.0	2.6	3.0		3.2	4.2	3.3	3.5	2.5	3.5	3.0
4. French	3.0	4.4	2.9	2.4		2.5	3.0	2.9	3.1		3.5	3.5	2.3		3.6
5. Japanese		5.7		2.5	2.5	2.8	3.7		3.1	3.0	3.9	4.1	2.5	2.7	4.0
Q.I Future control	5.7	5.8	5.9	4.5	5.2	6.0	5.8	5.6	5.0	5.5	5.8	6.0	5.0	5.1	5.2
Q.J National interest	3.5	5.2	5.0	3.8	3.7	3.9	3.6	3.9	4.0	3.3	3.8	3.6	3.2	2.9	3.4
Q.L Manager loyalty	4.3	4.9	4.9	3.5	4.5	4.5	4.1	4.1	3.7	4.1	3.6	4.3	2.8	3.3	3.7
Economics															
Q.D General impact	4.2	5.2	5.3	3.6	4.4	4.8	4.1	4.3	4.1	4.4	3.9	4.5	3.4	3.3	3.9
Q.E Balance of payments	4.7	5.0	5.8	4.2	4.5	4.7	4.8	5.0	4.6	4.2	4.6	4.9	4.2	4.2	4.4
Culture															
Q.N Way of life	3.1	3.5	3.2	3.6	3.5	4.1	3.8	3.4	3.7	3.5	3.4	3.1	3.7	3.1	3.0
Q.O Management methods	2.6	2.4	2.0	2.2	1.7	2.9	2.8	2.8	3.2	2.6	3.0	3.0	2.6	2.4	2.5
Average, all questions except G2–5	4.0	4.4	4.6	3.7	4.1	4.5	4.2	4.1	4.1	4.0	4.0	4.2	3.5	3.6	3.7

Korea, it is the Japanese who evoke the greatest concern, while the scores for U.S. firms are strikingly high in the Philippines. (By an unfortunate oversight, Japanese firms were not included in the Philippine questionnaire. From other information, one may speculate that anti-Japanese feelings would have resulted in a score like that for U.S. firms.) In general, it is clear that the threat to control of national affairs is identified most strongly with U.S. firms.

In the economics area, the distinctive general pattern is the significantly more unfavorable response to question E than to question D. With but a few exceptions, the respondents see the balance of payments impact of foreign firms as distinctly more disadvantageous than their overall economic role. These data confirm the general impression noted in the elite data analysis that the internal economic utility of multinational firms is more readily accepted than the fairness of the external cost-benefit calculus.

The favorable view of the impact of foreign firms on host-national ways of life shown in question N also reinforces the elite survey findings as solid evidence to diminish concern aroused by widely publicized attacks on the Americanization of this culture and that. At least among the business-oriented groups surveyed here, that would not seem to be a serious problem. The even more favorable view of the value of foreign management methods is consistent with expectations for these groups.

Scanning the data horizontally shows some other interesting general patterns. Question B and figures at the bottom of the table summarize the considerable similarity of the business student and manager groups in contrast to the slightly more favorable attitude of the heads of firms. The pattern is not uniform, but it does appear that the senior men are generally inclined to see more benefit in the activities of multinational firms than those lower in the business hierarchy. Whether this is a function of age or of other factors cannot be determined. Perhaps more interesting is the notable similarity among the managers and among heads of firms across national lines. Among the student groups there is some greater adverse reaction from the two less developed country groups and the Canadians, for whom the large volume of foreign investment is a conspicuous national issue. However, the differences even here are not as great as one might expect. That is to say, the major antiforeign investment thrust in many LDCs, in contrast to the mild approach in developed countries, might lead one to expect much more unfavorable opinions from the LDC groups. Likewise, the restrictive Japanese policies on foreign investment would lead to a similar expectation. It should be emphasized that we are dealing with business groups who may be expected to have an internationalist outlook, but still it is interesting that the differences among them are not greater.

It should be noted, however, that there are greater differences among the countries on specific questions. On questions G and I, which pose the loss of control issue most directly, the students in the more developed countries seem at least as concerned as those from the less developed nations, and a similar bias in the LDCs is suggested in the culture impact question. On the other hand, the

LDC scores on the economic questions are somewhat more unfavorable than for the developed countries. The evidence here is too slim to draw conclusions, but it suggests interesting hypotheses for future study.

Correlation Analysis

Table 1.17 shows the correlation coefficients of the responses to the questions in Table 1.16 with responses to question B, the overall appraisal of the effects of foreign firms. As in the previous sets of data, these figures are notable for their diversity; no single factor stands out either with full consistency of high correlations or in magnitude above the others. Still there are some patterns that seem to have meaning.

Four of the six coefficients above .50 appear by question N, effect on way of life. If we take .30 as a cut-off point, question N is again high with 8, though the highest with 9 is question I, concern about future control. And the second question under the culture heading has 6, as much as any other except I and N. This pattern is essentially the same as that found in the analysis of the elite data. It therefore affirms as an intriguing area for further research the possibilities that the view of the cultural impact is a strong factor influencing the overall attitude, a weak factor that follows the overall attitude, or an independent element that tends to parallel the overall appraisal, neither influencing nor being influenced by it.

By the same measures of magnitude and frequency of high correlation figures, the factors under the control heading, notably I, future control, and L, manager loyalty, are more significant than the economics factors. But the full meaning of the data is certainly perplexing. With respect to control effects, it was noted previously that the U.S. companies were the dominant factor. Yet correlations in this part of question G are for the most part quite low compared to many of those for other questions on the table. Similarly there is no apparent reason why the national interest question should show lower correlations than the apparently lesser question of manager loyalty for 11 of the 16 groups. Considering such facts as these, one is led to conclude that the influences forming overall attitudes toward foreign firms are probably complex and varied. The lack of consistency and the erratic pattern of high correlation coefficients throughout Table 1.17 confirm this conclusion. The mix of attitudes and dominant influences would appear to vary greatly from group to group and country to country.

Adding to this dimension of the subject is the range in frequency of high correlations within survey groups. For the Japanese business students there is only one figure over .30 while there are six in the British student list, with other groups ranged between these extremes. The lack of strong correlations among a group would suggest that the attitude influences are disparate. One thinks of the Japanese as a relatively homogeneous society in which uniformity of attitude patterns would be expected to be greater than in a country like Britain. Yet the

TABLE 1.17. Correlation of Attitudes on Selected Effects of Foreign Firms with Attitudes on Overall Effect (Question B)

	Business Students					Canada		Managers			Canada		Heads of Firms		
	Japan	Korea	Philip-pines	Britain	France	McGill	UWO	Japan	Britain	France	McGill	UWO	Britain	France	Canada
Number	35	54	71	42	61	31	49	115	41	28	64	84	50	52	62
Control															
Q.G															
1. U.S. firms	.19	.03	.23	.06	.28	.38	-.06	.02	.33	-.01	.20	.28	.09	.27	.30
2. British	.33	-.05	.06		-.10	.05	.08	.06			.09	.27		.18	.03
3. German			-.09	.09	-.13	-.03	.06	.10	.16	-.06	.06	.18	.13	.28	-.13
4. French	.29	-.05		.28		.14	.02		.06	.12	.00	.12	.24		-.04
5. Japanese		.33		.33	-.03	-.04	.30	.20	.14	.34	-.04	.13	.14	.30	-.10
Q.I Future control	.25	.04	.21	.53	.39	.16	.33	.20	.07	.30	.39	.33	.30	.41	.34
Q.J National interest	-.09	.18	.28	.23	.14	.24	.34	.01	-.02	.17	.34	.33	.24	.16	.38
Q.L Manager loyalty	.21	.26	.30	.34	.30	.34	.23	.23	.27	-.18	.19	.23	.27	.26	.23
Economics															
Q.D General impact	.02	.24	.31	.37	.19	.21	.25	.05	.32	.17	.16	.57	.09	.38	.23
Q.E Balance of payments	.16	.12	.33	.19	.22	.15	.26	-.06	.28	-.08	.13	.34	.18	-.04	.30
Culture															
Q.N Way of life	-.09	.41	.23	.52	.31	.22	.36	.31	.13	.52	.11	.07	.52	.26	.54
Q.O Management methods	-.08	-.18	.29	.47	.25	.32	.29	.34	.20	.37	.35	.14	.38	.28	.20
.05 Significance level	.33	.26	.23	.31	.25	.36	.28	.19	.31	.37	.25	.22	.28	.27	.25

opposite is apparently true. So we have yet another question that adds to the agenda for future research.

Conclusions

Stepping back from the specifics of the preceding analysis, one may draw a few broad observations from the data.

First, it appears from the internation comparison that there is substantial similarity among groups with only moderate differences. Groups in the less developed countries seem more concerned about the economic impact of foreign firms, while those in developed countries focus more on control effects. However, the differences are not great. There are also some indications of a consistent rank-age difference cutting across countries, the heads of firms taking a more favorable view of foreign firms than those lower in the hierarchy.

The other consistent pattern is the somewhat confusing relevance of feelings about cultural impact. While it falls low in the explicit ranking of criteria, it stands out as strongly as any factor in the correlation analysis. This finding identifies a key problem for future research both in substantively examining the role of this specific influence and methodologically determining whether high correlations in these data reflect causation, parallel attitudes, or halo effect.

The final observation stems from the substantial diversity throughout the data. Even the two pairs of essentially similar Canadian groups (students and managers) show quite significant differences on some scores and correlations. It is natural and useful to try to narrow down the analysis to a limited number of important factors, key differences among countries, and the like. But the most useful outcome of this research may take just the opposite direction. The indications from the diversity of the data are that attitudes toward multinational firms are significantly related to quite a number of factors and that the nature and importance of those factors varies substantially from country to country, from group to group, and, presumably, from individual to individual. The data at hand give us some instructive leads as to the direction and dimensions of these varied influences and open up ample avenues for further research on them.

REFERENCES

1. John Gennard, *Multinational Corporations and British Labour*. London: British North-American Committee, 1972, p. 30.

2. John Fayerweather, "Attitudes of British and French Elite Groups toward Foreign Companies," *MSU Business Topics*, Winter 1972, p. 15.

2

BELIEFS ABOUT THE MULTINATIONAL ENTERPRISE: A FACTOR ANALYTICAL STUDY OF BRITISH, CANADIAN, FRENCH, AND MEXICAN ELITES

Peter R. Sugges, Jr.

Is the multinational enterprise (MNE) doomed to the same fate as the dinosaur?[1] This is a question that seems to be implicit in much that is written about the MNE. The answer to it appears to depend on whether the chief executive officers (CEOs) of these behemoths are able to change their perceptions from a unidimensional view that these institutions they command are purely economic entities to a recognition that they have social and political dimensions as well. If this change in perception can be made, we will find the CEOs of MNEs acting more like heads of government than heads of business. In this role the CEOs will need to secure the trust, confidence, and good will of the public wherever they do business. In order to do so they will have to resort to many of the techniques employed by politicians to gain access to the concerns of their constituencies. The CEOs will have to pay close attention to the opinions of those individuals who have the power to either legislate or influence legislation that affects the MNEs in the countries where they do business.

In recent years politicians have made increasing use of opinion polls to guide them in developing their political strategies. It now seems in order to suggest that CEOs of MNEs do likewise. Fayerweather[2] has used a popular and inexpensive strategy to gather information about the concerns of selected elites regarding the operations of MNEs within their countries. He developed an anonymous mail-questionnaire in 1970 which he subsequently used in three countries—Britain, Canada, and France—to systematically sample the opinions of selected local interest groups about the operations of foreign companies operating within their country.

PURPOSE OF THIS STUDY

This study is an extension and refinement of Fayerweather's investigation. It was undertaken to add to the Fayerweather data-bank and to improve upon the methods of data analysis that he used. In particular, the questionnaire and survey methodology used by Fayerweather in his earlier studies were taken to Mexico to gather data that would allow comparisons to be made of the opinions found in developed countries with those from a developing country (which in the case of Mexico is one where there is a single dominant political party).[3] The method of data analysis involved factor analysis rather than the item-by-item form of analysis performed by Fayerweather.[4] The factor analytic technique was chosen because it makes it possible to infer whether there are a small number of underlying factors that appear to be responsible for the opinions expressed on a larger number of items included in the questionnaire.

DEFINITIONS

In this study we are dealing with beliefs about the MNE. What do we mean by beliefs and how do we distinguish them from opinions and attitudes? Opinions are the responses that people provide when they are asked to reply to a question; Rokeach suggests that an opinion is a "verbal expression of some belief, attitude, or value."[5] People may change their opinions rather freely but not their beliefs, attitudes, or values. The problem for a researcher is to determine which more deep-seated belief, attitude, or value is responsible for the opinion expressed. In an attempt to avoid influencing a person's response by situational factors, recourse is frequently taken to anonymous questionnaires.

A distinction that is frequently made between belief and attitude is that beliefs have only cognitive components while attitudes have both cognitive and affective components.[6] This seems to be a spurious distinction, with which Rokeach disagrees.[7] The position taken in this study is that beliefs provide us with a way of operationally describing an attitude, just as aptitudes provide us with a way of operationally describing intelligence. Therefore attitude and intelligence are conceptually more abstract summary constructs than belief or aptitude. Rokeach defines a belief as

> any simple proposition, conscious or unconscious, inferred from what a person says or does, capable of being preceded by the phrase "I believe that." The content of a belief may describe the object of belief as true or false, correct or incorrect, evaluate it as good or bad, or advocate a certain course of action or a certain state of existence as desirable or undesirable.[8]

One point of possible confusion about the above definition is that it is frequently assumed that people will show a positive or negative preference for something because they cognitively evaluate it as good or bad.[9] The evidence for categorically accepting this point of view does not seem to be completely persuasive and Rokeach offers the follower demurrer against it:

> The two dimensions of like-dislike and goodness-badness need not necessarily go together. In speaking of the "pro-con" dimension, often said to be the defining characteristic of attitude, we do not know whether the preferential response of approach or avoidance is due to the fact that it is liked or disliked or because it is seen to be good or bad. It is possible to like something bad, and to dislike something good.[10]

Thus one is advised to consider evaluative beliefs as cognitions. Their relationship to the affective component of attitude appears to depend upon how the evaluation impinges upon a more central belief that is defined as a value.[11] In the absence of any knowledge about a person's underlying value system, one has no basis for inferring a directional relationship between evaluative beliefs and the affective component of attitude. In this study we have no such information and therefore we take the evaluative beliefs expressed in two of the questions as cognitive and remain agnostic about their possible connection with the affective component of attitude.

DESCRIPTION OF THE STUDY

An initial premise of this study was that the questionnaire used in earlier studies could not be modified except as was required for sensible translation and administration in Mexico. This resulted in a block consisting of the first 35 questions, which were the same in all countries except for questions 6 through 10, which were systematically adjusted to preserve an alphabetical arrangement in the language of each of the countries.[12]

Stratified samples of approximately 200 individuals were drawn from each of four groups in each country. These four groups were: 1) elected government officials (national legislators), 2) permanent government officials (high-level civil servants), 3) labor union leaders, and 4) heads of business firms. These elite groups were chosen, in preference to others that might have been selected, because of the role they play in creating or influencing national policies and laws that regulate the operation of MNEs within the country. The number of questionnaires sent to each group and the number returned are shown in Table 2.1.

The response rates varied considerably from group to group within a country and between countries. The particularly poor response in Mexico was apparently due to the suspicious nature of the Mexicans as well as to their unfamiliarity with mail questionnaires (even where anonymity is guaranteed).[13] In addition, the returns from all groups in Mexico except for the businessmen were insufficient to meet the sample size requirement of the factor analytic technique.

TABLE 2.1. Sample Size and Response Rates

		Britain	Canada	France	Mexico
Elected government officials	S[a]	200	199	209	273
	R[b]	61	45	55	3
Percent response		30.5	22.6	26.3	1.1
Permanent government officials	S	202	200	201	209
	R	59	81	78	12
Percent response		29.2	40.5	38.8	5.7
Labor union officials	S	200	241	219	201
	R	82	72	92	9
Percent response		41.0	29.9	42.0	4.5
Heads of business firms	S	196	201	215	210
	R	50	62	52	42
Percent response		25.5	25.9	24.2	20.0
Total	S	798	841	844	893
	R	252	260	277	66
Percent response		31.6	30.9	32.8	7.4

[a]S = sent.
[b]R = returned.

Another problem associated with nonresponse is bias: how do those who did not respond differ from those who did respond or, perhaps more to the point, would the inclusion of the nonrespondents' responses have changed the results in a statistically significant way?

In an attempt to determine how different the respondents' opinions were from those of the nonrespondents, a sample of 30 Canadian Members of Parliament (M.P.s) was drawn and a research assistant was engaged to interview them in person to ascertain whether they had returned the questionnaire and also to solicit their response to question 2; that is,

In your opinion what is the overall effect on Canada of the activities of foreign companies in Canada?

Good   1   2   3   4   5   6   7   Bad

Despite all of his attempts, the research assistant was able to interview only 36 out of the 39, or 92.3 percent, of the selected sample.[14] The results are shown in the following tabulation.

Answered Original Questionnaire	Good 1	2	3	4	5	6	Bad 7	Total
Yes	1	3	5	1	0	0	0	12
No	7	5	8	4	2	0	0	24
								36

A contingency table form of analysis, where cells 1 and 2 are aggregated and 3 through 7, yields $\chi^2 = 0.109$ with 1 degree of freedom.[15] The probability of occurrence of such a value is very high (there is a 75 percent chance of exceeding this value by chance alone), and therefore the data contain insufficient evidence to suggest that the views of the respondents and nonrespondents differ from each other.

While it would be desirable to have similar data for each question and for each elite group, this was impractical. Although this is only limited evidence from which to infer that the inclusion of data from the nonrespondents would not affect the results of this study, such inference is made. However, any generalizations must be considered tentative in view of the fact that this possible opportunity for bias was not more thoroughly investigated.

The reliability of an instrument should be calculated for each population to which it is administered. The reliability coefficient provides a measure of the amount of true variance as a percent of the total variance. When one has only a single set of measurements of a sample drawn from a population, the best way of estimating the coefficient of reliability is by means of a two-way analysis of variance.[16] The reliability for each of the population samples in this study is shown in Table 2.2. Although none of these coefficients is particularly high, the F ratio for individuals is significant at the 0.01 level and therefore the coefficients are significant. This fact does not eliminate the need to consider why these coefficients are not higher. Three observations can be made about the size of the reliability coefficients. First, we are attempting to measure a factorially complex concept, and an instrument designed to measure that concept can be

TABLE 2.2. Reliability Coefficients of the Questionnaire for Each Sample

	Britain	Canada	France	Mexico
Elected government officials	0.52	0.44	0.64	*
Permanent government officials	0.65	0.45	0.39	*
Labor union officials	0.66	0.55	0.57	*
Heads of business firms	0.55	0.60	0.63	0.47

*Reliability was not calculated due to small number of responses.

made more valid by introducing additional common factors that are included in the concept, thus increasing validity; but in so doing we lower the internal-consistency reliability.[17] Second, the F ratio for items is significant at the 0.01 level. And third, an examination of the intercorrelations of the 35 items reveals both a low average correlation and great variation in the size of the intercorrelations of the items.

These observations indicate that the questionnaire is measuring more than a single attribute and that some of the items on the questionnaire are ambiguous; that is, they are being interpreted differently by different individuals. Given this situation, it is not at all surprising that the questionnaire has only modest reliability. There are two possibilities available to a researcher in such a case: first, eliminate those items that appear to be ambiguous; and, second, add items to the questionnaire that are of an equal kind and quality as those items that are not ambiguous. Since this is an exploratory research project, which has an objective of providing a methodological improvement over that used by Fayerweather, these two steps were not taken in this study and our conceptual findings are therefore weaker than they would be if these steps had been taken. They should of course be taken in any future work using this questionnaire.

All items on the questionnaire deal with perceptions (beliefs) about MNEs. However, the questionnaire appears to contain clusters of items that are highly interrelated with each other but not particularly related to other items on the questionnaire. Upon reflection, this is not surprising since study has found that intelligence is not a unitary concept, and similarly it appears that cognitions about MNEs are not unitary in nature.

There appear to be a number of beliefs about MNEs which when taken together are what we mean when we speak of the cognitive component of the attitude concept. Whether it really makes sense to talk of a single cognitive component is open to debate since it raises the question of how one combines these beliefs. Therefore our concern will be with identifying the beliefs about MNEs that underlie the questionnaire. The technique used to accomplish this is factor analysis.

Nunnally[18] is critical of this use of factor analysis. He argues that constructing tests on the basis of factor analysis is not as wise as investigating the factorial composition of tests after they are constructed. His reasons are that such analyses are seldom highly successful and that the analysis of test items is extremely laborious.[19] He also recommends that "to prevent taking advantage of chance, a minimum standard (not an ideal) in a factor analysis is that there be at least ten times as many subjects as variables." In our case that is a minimum of 350 respondents per group—a number we unfortunately do not come close to meeting. The problem one may encounter by ignoring Nunnally's recommendations is that the factors found will not stand up in subsequent studies.

There is no reason to assume that the structure of beliefs identified for any one group is identical with those of another group. It is of interest to know how similar they are, however. Harman suggests that the coefficient of congruence be used to make comparisons for a fixed set of variables and different samples.[20] This method of comparison should be of value in corroborating the names selected for factors.

In this study we have several sets of measurements from different populations for a collection of variables. Factor analysis will be used on each set of measurements to summarize the interrelationships among the variables by providing us with mathematically defined constructs that can be used to reproduce the intercorrelations between the variables.[21] We shall also investigate the similarity of the constructs derived from each of the data sets.

COMPUTER PROGRAM USED IN THIS STUDY

The factor analyses for this study were carried out on New York University's IBM 370/145 using the subprogram FACTOR contained in *SPSS: Statistical Package for the Social Sciences.*[22]

Each group in each country was factored separately.

Each data set was composed of 35 variables. OPTION 2 was invoked, which made pairwise deletions where missing data were encountered during the calculation of the data product-moment correlation coefficient matrix.

PA2 (principal factoring with iteration) was the method used to extract the initial orthogonal factor matrix. The number of iterations was limited to 25 or a difference of 0.001 between two successive sets of communality estimates.

Only those factors with an eigenvalue greater than or equal to one were retained for the final rotated solution.

An OBLIQUE[23] rotation was made with $\delta = 0$.

SUMMARY OF RESULTS

The space constraints of this paper allow us to provide only those results upon which we wish to focus. The interested reader is referred to the author's dissertation for a complete presentation and discussion of the findings.[24] The results of this study are presented in Tables 2.3 and 2.4.

Table 2.3 deals with the "belief about the loss of national sovereignty due to the operation of MNEs from countries other than the United States" and Table 2.4 deals with the "belief about the importance of the economic effect of the MNE on the host country." In each of these tables is shown the pattern of coefficients (factor loadings) for each of the variables that were used in defining the nature of the factor in each of the groups in each of the countries included in this study. Because of the poor response rate in Mexico in all of the groups except for the businessmen, they are the only ones for which factors were derived.

The phrases shown in Tables 2.3 and 2.4 reflect the essential nature of the actual questions. Tables 2.5 and 2.6 list translations of the actual questions which were asked.

TABLE 2.3. Summary of Pattern Coefficients Defining Belief about the Loss of National Sovereignty Due to the Operation of MNEs from Countries Other than the United States

Home of MNE	Britain				Canada				France		Mexico
	MPs	PGs	LUOs	BUS	MPs	PGs	LUOs	BUS	MPs	BUS	BUS
Britain	—	—	—	—	.89	.78	.65	.74	—	.90	1.01
France	.92	.73	.83	.87	.90	.97	.76	.89	—	—	.89
Germany	.93	.93	.99	.90	.96	.95	.95	.96	.70	.88	.88
Japan	.83	.97	.91	.84	.77	.81	.82	.87	—	—	.62
United States	—	.60	—	—	—	—	—	—	.64	.73	—
Netherlands	.67	.83	—	.72	—	—	—	—	.83	—	—

Notes: MPs = elected government officials, PGs = permanent government officials, LUOs = labor union leaders, and BUS = heads of business firms.
For British PGs, French MPs, and French BUS the definition of this factor did not exclude U.S. MNEs.
For French PGs and LUOs, the definition of this factor was too poor (pattern coefficients were less than 0.3) to list pattern coefficients.

51

TABLE 2.4. Summary of Pattern Coefficients Defining Belief about the Importance of the Economic Effect of the MNE on the Host Country

	Britain				Canada				France				Mexico
	MPs	PGs	LUOs	BUS	MPs	PGs	LUOs	BUS	MPs	PGs	LUOs	BUS	BUS
Opportunities for host-country investors	—	—	—	—	—	—	.45	.79	—	—	—	—	—
Control over national affairs	—	.56	—	—	—	—	.66	—	.87	—	—	.30	—
Benefits for host-country workers	.84	.65	—	—	.51	.64	.71	—	.62	—	.74	—	.30
Effect on balance of payments	.78	—	—	.91	—	.61	.55	.57	—	.53	.78	.64	.52
Opportunities for host-country managers	—	—	—	—	—	.45	.45	—	—	—	—	—	—
Effect on host-country national income	.87	—	—	.76	.84	.65	.91	—	—	.58	.87	.98	.34
Role of host country in the world	.36	.37	—	—	.62	—	.67	—	.85	.32	.65	.38	—
Host-country balance of payments	—	—	—	.39	—	—	—	—	—	—	—	—	—
Economic result of MNE operation in host country	—	—	—	—	—	—	—	.46	—	—	—	—	—

Notes: MPs = elected government officials, PGs = permanent government officials, LUOs = labor union leaders, BUS = heads of business firms.
There are two different items dealing with impact of MNE on host-country balance of payments.
The British MPs and LUOs, Canadian LUOs, and French MPs, LUOs, and BUS groups defined this factor as "politico-economic effect" rather than simply "economic effect."
For the British PGs the definition of this factor was too poor (pattern coefficients were less than 0.3) to list pattern coefficients.

52

TABLE 2.5. Translations of Actual Questions Used to Define the Factor Labeled: a belief about the loss of national sovereignty due to the operation of MNEs from countries other than the United States

To what degree do you feel that the activities of the companies of the following nationalities cause a loss of Mexican control over Mexican affairs?

Companies	Major loss of control						Minor loss of control
British	1	2	3	4	5	6	7
French	1	2	3	4	5	6	7
German	1	2	3	4	5	6	7
Japanese	1	2	3	4	5	6	7
United States	1	2	3	4	5	6	7

DISCUSSION OF THE RESULTS

The purpose of the surveys reported on herein was to identify the beliefs that host-country policy-influencing elites have about MNEs. The potential value of this knowledge is that it can provide a basis for making predictions about the kinds of pressures that might be brought to bear on MNEs. While the results of these surveys of individual groups in each of the countries may be of particular interest to those involved with those groups in the countries covered by these surveys, of more general or international concern is how similar are the beliefs expressed by elite groups from the different countries, both within and among the countries.

Before going into the cross-group and cross-country similarities, it is important to point out that there are several limitations in these studies that should be kept in mind as one attempts to use these results. The first is that the mail survey method of gathering the data produced a poor response rate in each of the countries. A limited attempt was made in Canada to ascertain the degree of similarity between the respondents and nonrespondents. While no statistically significant difference was found between the responses of the two groups for the one question checked, this is not to say that such a difference might not be found between respondents and nonrespondents for every question and for every group. This alone requires that we label these results as tentative, pending further studies in the area. A second limitation is that good practice in factor analysis requires more subjects than were obtained. This allows us to capitalize on chance and to identify as factors what might in fact be artifacts caused by sampling error. Factors that hold up in repeated studies of a domain are more likely to be "real" than are those that are found to exist only for a single group.

TABLE 2.6. Translations of Actual Questions Used to Define the Factor Labeled: a belief about the importance of the economic effect of the MNE on the host country

How important should the following considerations be in judging the value of foreign companies operating in Mexico?

Importance	Major						Minor
Opportunities for Mexican investors	1	2	3	4	5	6	7
Control over national affairs	1	2	3	4	5	6	7
Benefits for Mexican workers	1	2	3	4	5	6	7
Effects on balance of payments	1	2	3	4	5	6	7
Opportunities for Mexican managers	1	2	3	4	5	6	7
Effect on Mexican national income	1	2	3	4	5	6	7
Role of Mexico in the world	1	2	3	4	5	6	7

Consider two possible forms of ownership of a Mexican firm:

☐ A—A foreign firm owns 45% of the Mexican firm and Mexicans, 55%.
☐ B—The foreign firm owns 100% of the Mexican firm.

What will be the effects for the following Mexican interests?

	A worse than B				B worse than A		
Mexican balance of payments	1	2	3	4	5	6	7

What do you believe is the net economic result of the operations of foreign companies in Mexico?

	They take more than they give				They give more than they take		
	1	2	3	4	5	6	7

Therefore, only those factors that emerged in several groups will be considered to be of significance; the other factors will require further empirical verification.

A third limitation is the low reliability coefficients for each group. This is not an unexpected result of using a single questionnaire to map a factorially complex domain. Since each derived factor has less than the desired number of marker variables per factor, the question of whether or not each set of defining variables is reliable is unanswerable until additional defining variables are added. The application of factor analysis to this questionnaire has, however, provided a starting point for the construction of reliable psychometric scales for measuring beliefs about MNEs. A final limitation is that which is inherent in labeling any construct. Have we appended the correct labels to the facts that we have derived?

Despite the fact that repeated studies of a domain have provided us with the same set of defining variables, different researchers may choose to attach different labels to the same set of variables. The only way out of this difficulty is to wait and see whether the research community chooses one label in preference to others that might be suggested. Thus the labels offered as names for the factors derived in this study are tentative.

Kerr et al.[25] presented their findings in three categories which appear useful to adopt for this study. They suggested that certain things appear to be universal, that is, characteristic of all groups; others are relative in that they are found to exist in only several groups; and finally the remainder are idiosyncratic to particular groups. Thus we can summarize the results of these studies by showing what beliefs about MNEs are universally held, which are limited to a subset of the universe, and finally which are unique to individual groups.

There are only two factors that emerged so consistently that they can be called universally held beliefs about MNEs. The first is:

a belief about the loss of national sovereignty due to the operation of MNEs from countries other than the United States.

This belief was found in all groups except the British permanent government officials (BPGO) group and all four of the French groups. In the BPGO, French Members of Parliament, and the French heads of business firms groups the belief existed that there is a loss of national sovereignty due to the operation of MNEs within their borders without regard to which country they are from. As for the French permanent government officials and the French labor union officials, the definition of the factors was too poor to posit their existence as a finding of this study. However, the fact that this belief exists in 11 of the 13 groups studied leads us to suggest that a more reliable scale would permit their identification in these two groups as well and probably in the more diffuse manner that was found in the other two French groups.

The fact that there is a generally defined belief about MNEs causing a loss of national sovereignty should not be construed as meaning that the belief, which is scaled from "minor" to "major," is at the same level in each group and in each country.

Fayerweather in his earlier item analysis of the data from Britain, Canada, and France concluded that the loss of control over national affairs, or what is herein referred to as loss of national sovereignty, was of major significance to the groups studied. The same finding in Mexico supports the contention that this is a matter of universal concern. Vernon, in his book entitled *Sovereignty at Bay*,[26] has also suggested that the loss of sovereignty is a matter of universal concern. Gabriel, in his review of Vernon's book, stated that "not national sovereignty but the multinational corporation itself is 'at bay.'"[27] Though this may be so, it does not seem to be the belief of the groups included in this study.

What about the "belief about the loss of national sovereignty due to the operation of MNEs from the United States"? This did not emerge as a separately defined belief in the study except for the Canadian labor union officials group, possibly because there were not enough variables to define this factor. If there had been, this factor might have separated itself from the more general factor that was found to exist in France. Of course one could argue that the reason this factor did not emerge is that such a factor does not exist. One can only respond to this by saying that if the loss of sovereignty caused by MNEs from countries other than the United States is of concern to these groups then the fact that there are more U.S. MNEs than there are MNEs from all of the other countries combined logically requires that such a factor, as has been postulated, exists, and that the only reason it was not found was that there were not sufficient marker variables in the questionnaire to allow its identification in this study.

The second universal belief, not nearly as well defined as was the first, is:

a belief about the importance of the economic effect of the MNE on the host country.

This belief was defined by three or more marker variables in every group except for the British permanent government officials group. As has been pointed out in the discussion of the first universal belief where two of the French groups failed to display a definition of that factor, it is possible that this second belief does in fact exist for the BPGO group but that the kinds of variables included in this questionnaire were not of sufficient number to enable this factor to be defined in accordance with the ground rules used. Since the second belief was found in 12 of the 13 groups in this study, it is likely that such a belief does exist for the BPGO group and that it would be found in a study expressly designed to elicit such a belief.

Several of the groups displayed not simply a belief about the importance of the economic effect of the MNE on the host country but instead "a belief about the importance of the politico-economic effect of the MNE on the host country." This latter belief was found to exist in the following groups: British M.P.s and labor union officials; Canadian permanent government officials and labor union officials; all four French groups. The Canadian M.P.s and heads of business firms and the Mexican heads of business firms have factors that are labeled "belief about the importance of the economic effect of the MNE on the host country"; however these factors were not found to be highly congruent with each other. These observations cause us to question whether all groups are in fact speaking of the same economic issues when asked to express their concern about the importance of the economic effect of the MNE on their country. It appears that they are not. This finding suggests that further study is required to more adequately define the salient economic concerns of these groups that are impacted by the MNEs operating within their respective countries.

Fayerweather found in his earlier item analysis of the data from Britain, Canada, and France that each of the groups believed that the economic effect of the MNE on their country was of considerable importance.[28] That this same concern was found in the added Mexican data seems to support the contention that this factor is a matter of universal concern. Two points, however, require emphasis. First, despite the similarity of the label used on the factors derived for each of the groups, the economic issues that each group used in making its judgment are likely to be different from those other groups used, and therefore anyone who asks a person or group about this matter without clarifying what economic issues are relevant can be easily misled about what is meant by the respondent when he says that "he believes that the MNE has an important economic effect on his country." The second point is that this belief is scaled from "major" to "minor" and the level of concern expressed on this factor in each of the groups in each of the countries is not necessarily the same as in other groups.

In the opening paragraph of his *Sovereignty at Bay*, Vernon states that national sovereignty and national economic strengths are two concepts about which host-country nationals are concerned. This study provides empirical social-psychological evidence of their belief that MNEs operating within their borders do have an impact on these concepts. In their book *Global Reach: The Power of Multinational Corporations,*[29] Barnet and Muller express a concern about the effect MNEs have on national sovereignty and their importance in affecting the economic condition not only of those countries where they do business but in the world at large because of the interdependence of the national economies. While one cannot know for sure, one wonders whether the ideologists who write books like these are raising the consciousness of individuals in groups such as those that have been surveyed, or whether they are merely reflecting ideas that they sense to be abroad. It is possible that neither is the whole answer but that both are causal and mutually self-reinforcing. Whatever the initial source of these ideas, there does seem to be abroad a universal concern over the effect that MNEs have on national sovereignty and also a concern about the importance of the role of the MNEs in affecting the economic conditions of countries.

In the foregoing discussion the point made was that the empirically determined beliefs were found to exist in each of the countries surveyed and in virtually all of the groups in each of these countries. When we begin an examination of the remaining beliefs that emerged in our factor analysis of the responses, we find that some of the beliefs that emerged can be given the same label, which initially leads one to suppose that these, too, are universal beliefs. However when these beliefs are checked for congruence with each other we find that the coefficients of congruence turn out to be low for many of these comparisons. The reason for this finding seems to lie in the recognition that what causes the belief varies from group to group. Thus, for example, there seems to be a general concern in many of the groups about how the degree of foreign ownership of local firms affects the host economy, but there does not seem to be any general agreement as to what things in the economy are influenced and to what degree. Also, of course, the level of concern is not necessarily the same for each group.

These kinds of beliefs that were identified, and there were several of them, are classified as "relative beliefs," meaning that they were found to exist in more than a single group but not in all groups—at least in the same form.

The remaining beliefs are idiosyncratic in nature; that is, they are uniquely associated with a single group. The coefficient of congruence between each of these factors and all of the others is too low to claim any relationship between them. The labels applied to each of these idiosyncratic factors are also unique, thus reinforcing the conclusion that the factors are in fact idiosyncratic. Despite the fact that there is no evidence that would allow these idiosyncratic beliefs to be generalized beyond the groups from which they were derived, they did emerge as valid, identifiable factors, from the methodology of this study. Because of space limitations, no report will be made herein of either the relative beliefs or the idiosyncratic beliefs.[30]

IMPLICATIONS FOR MNE POLICY MAKERS

In his book entitled *International Business Management: A Conceptual Framework*, John Fayerweather states that, although an MNE is led toward a strategy of fragmentation because of the large number of countries that it does business in, there is a natural tendency toward integration and uniformity.[31] Thus the executives responsible for developing MNE policies must choose between fragmenting certain corporate activities while generally trying to follow a strategy of unification. The difficulty in making these decisions lies in "the ill-defined environmental forces to which strategies must be directed."[32]

This study provides a definition of some of these ill-defined environmental forces. In particular, it has been shown that there are a small number of universally held beliefs about MNEs that can be dealt with through a unified strategy, including a "belief that MNEs cause a loss of national sovereignty" and a "belief about the importance of the economic effect of the MNE on the host country." Therefore it would be prudent for MNE policy makers to adopt strategies that minimize the likelihood that host nationals might conclude that MNEs are reducing the sovereignty of those countries where they operate. Since increases in income tend to enhance one's freedom of action, it might be possible to overshadow the sovereignty issue by emphasizing the positive economic contribution that MNEs make to the host countries where they operate. For any real chance of success, it is probably best to avoid strategies involving self-serving statements about the issues of sovereignty and economic contribution and to concentrate instead on taking actions that evidence a real attempt to deal with these issues in a meaningful way.

This is by no means an easy thing to do because it conflicts with the MNEs' tendency to centralize certain decisions, which inevitably leads to the belief that MNEs cause a loss in national control over internal affairs since key industrial decisions are being made outside the country's boundary. MNEs are also concerned with the economic contribution that foreign operations make to them rather than the economic contribution that their foreign operations make to the countries where they operate.

The results of this study suggest that to the extent that MNEs ignore the concerns of host nationals about the loss of national sovereignty caused by MNEs and the importance of the economic effect of the MNE on the host country, they are likely to find their freedom of action circumscribed by regulatory or retributory actions by host governments. Canada's "Foreign Investment Review Act"[33] and Mexico's "Law to Promote Mexican Investment and to Regulate Foreign Investment"[34] are but two examples of legislation that governments have enacted in an attempt to ensure that MNEs operating within their national boundaries contribute to local development.

Besides the universally held beliefs, a number of relative and idiosyncratic beliefs were found. The existence of these beliefs suggests that it is necessary for MNE decision makers to follow a strategy of fragmentation because the concerns vary from country to country. The best that can be attained in most areas of corporate operations is unification of policies over a small cluster of countries wherein there are similar general concerns about the way that MNEs affect the host country. Even here, though, because the specific concerns tend to differ, fragmentation, rather than unification, will be the norm. Thus the conclusion is that, while unification may be a highly desirable strategy because of the potential economies and efficiencies of an integrated system, it will be necessary to fragment corporate operations in order to address the specific concerns that differ among countries and groups within countries.

NOTES

1. This particular question was suggested by Irving Kristol's article, "The Corporation and the Dinosaur," *The Wall Street Journal*, February 14, 1974, p. 20.

2. See Chapter 1.

3. Mexico's dominant political party is the Partido Revolucionario Institucional (PRI). This party traces its origins back to the 1910 Mexican Revolution and is referred to as the revolutionary party. For more details on the Mexican system of government the reader is referred to standard sources, such as Robert E. Scott, *Mexican Government in Transition* (Revised Edition, Urbana: University of Illinois Press, 1964).

4. William A. Scott, "Attitude Measurement," *Handbook of Social Psychology*, Vol. II: Research Methods, ed. by Gardner Kindsey and Elliot Aronson (2nd ed.; Reading, Mass.: Addison-Wesley Publishing Company, 1968), p. 211, explains why a technique such as factor analysis is preferred to item-by-item analysis: "Multiple-item assessment (factor analysis) may be preferred for a number of reasons: that single items are subject to too much random response error, that any single item necessarily reflects attributes other than the one in which the investigator is interested, that a composite score constructed from multiple items yields a better representation of the intended attitude, that any inference from a measure to a construct requires multiple measures."

5. Milton Rokeach, *Beliefs, Attitudes, and Values: A Theory of Organization and Change* (San Francisco: Jossey-Bass, Inc., Publishers, 1968), p. 125.

6. For example, see Martin Fishbein and Bertram H. Raven, "The AB Scales: An Operational Definition of Belief and Attitude," *Human Relations*, Vol. 15 (1962), pp. 35–44.

7. *Op. cit.*, pp. 115–6.

8. *Ibid.*, p. 113.

9. Charles E. Osgood and Percy H. Tannenbaum, "The Principle of Congruity in the Prediction of Attitude Change," *Psychological Review*, Vl. 62 (1955), pp. 42–55.

10. *Op. cit.*, p. 121.

11. "Values are generalized moral beliefs to which members of a group subscribe . . . it is important to distinguish between two sets of values which are often linked together and treated as though they were the same. These are (1) pragmatic values and (2) ideal values. Pragmatic values . . . condemn those kinds of actions that threaten to undermine the unity of the group (e.g., dishonesty, violence against fellow members, etc.) and encourage those actions that enable the group to satisfy its needs (e.g., hard work, honesty, etc.). Ideal values define how the ideal man should act . . . (e.g., the Christian Church has always taught that men should love their neighbors as themselves)." Excerpted from Gerhard Lenski, *Human Societies: A Macrolevel Introduction to Sociology* (New York: McGraw-Hill Book Company, 1970), p. 46.

12. A copy of the English version of the questionnaire is available, upon request, from the author.

13. A poorer response was anticipated in Mexico for the reasons mentioned. In conversations with several Mexicans, the point was made that the individuals would very likely have provided the desired information through an interview (provided they were favorably disposed toward the interviewer and the research project). The reason offered is that Mexicans prefer to be treated as individuals rather than as mere statistics. See Samuel Ramos, *Profile of Man and Culture in Mexico*, trans. by Peter G. Earle (Austin: University of Texas Press, 1972), passim, for support for this view.

14. The mail questionnaire was responded to by 22.6 percent of the M.P.s. Thus the response rate was quadrupled by employing a direct interview approach, but 53 of the 54 questions had to be sacrificed. In addition the research assistant devoted over one hour for each M.P. to obtain the desired information even though the M.P.s were centrally located. This anecdote lends some perspective to the difficulties involved in surveying elites, and it also shows the trade-off between the amount of information obtained and the response rate.

15. It is necessary to aggregate the data so that the expected value in each cell is 5 or greater.

16. The criterion used to determine the best method is that of least squares. For a discussion of how the analysis of variance technique is used to estimate the reliability coefficient, see Cyril Hoyt, "Test Reliability Estimated by Analysis of Variance," *Psychometrika*, Vol. 6, No. 3 (June 1941), pp. 153–60.

17. J. P. Guilford, *Psychometric Methods* (New York: McGraw-Hill Book Company, Inc., 1954), p. 389.

18. Jum Nunnally, *Psychometric Theory* (New York: McGraw-Hill Book Company, 1967), pp. 255–8.

19. When we are dealing with an item pool constructed for the measurement of attitudes, Nunnally relaxes his criticism against using factor analysis initially. In fact he states "there is nothing wrong with factor analyzing the (attitude) item pool initially." *Ibid.*, pp. 534–5.

20. Harry H. Harman, *Modern Factor Analysis* (2nd ed. revised; Chicago: University of Chicago Press, 1967), pp. 169–71.

21. There are other reasons for using factor analysis besides this one.

22. Norman H. Nie, Hadlai Hull, Jean G. Jenkins, Karin Steinbrenner, and Dale H. Bent, *SPSS: Statistical Package for the Social Sciences* (2nd ed., New York: McGraw-Hill Book Company, 1975).

23. Direct oblimin.

24. Peter R. Sugges, Jr., "Beliefs About the Multinational Enterprise: A Factor Analytic Study of British, Canadian, French, and Mexican Elites" (Unpublished Ph.D. dissertation, New York University, 1976).

25. Clark Kerr, John T. Dunlop, Frederick Harbison, and Charles A. Myers, *Industrialism and Industrial Man* (New York: Oxford University Press, 1964).

26. Raymond Vernon, *Sovereignty at Bay: The Multinational Spread of U.S. Enterprises* (New York: Basic Books, Inc., 1971).

27. Peter P. Gabriel, "The Multinational Corporation on the Defensive (if Not at Bay)," *Fortune*, Vol. 85, No. 1 (January 1972), pp. 119–24.

28. *Op. cit.*

29. Richard J. Barnet and Ronald E. Muller, *Global Reach: The Power of Multinational Corporations* (New York: Simon and Schuster, 1974).

30. Those interested in these beliefs as well as more details concerning this entire study are referred to the author's doctoral dissertation, *op. cit.*

31. John Fayerweather, *International Business Management: A Conceptual Framework* (New York: McGraw-Hill Book Company, 1969), p. 133.

32. *Ibid.*, p. 167.

33. This act has been widely publicized; for example, see David Barrows and Peter Lyman, "Foreign Ownership and Corporate Behavior in Canada," *MSU Business Topics*, Vol. 23, No. 2 (Spring 1975), pp. 13–20.

34. Rosemary Werrett, "Mexico: Drawing in the Reins on Foreign Investment," *Columbia Journal of World Business*, Vol. 9, No. 1 (Spring 1974), pp. 88–97.

3

THE EFFECT OF NATIONALIST BIAS ON ATTITUDES TOWARD FOREIGN COMPANIES

John Fayerweather
Katherin Marton

The questionnaire used by Fayerweather in the survey of British, Canadian, and French elites described in Chapter 1 contained questions that could be used to identify the presence of nationalistic bias affecting attitudes toward foreign companies. Analysis of the data on these questions is presented in this chapter.

The questions used, as shown in Table 3.1, were of two types. One set consisted of six "mirror-image" questions in which the respondents evaluated identical cultural, economic, and national interest effects by foreign firms on their own country and by MNCs of their country on other countries. The former appeared in Part I of the questionnaire and the latter in Part II. The hypotheses proposed were:

1. Evaluation of foreign companies' effects on one's own nation will be more negative than the evaluation of effects of one's own nation's foreign companies on other countries; that is, there will be a negative bias against foreign investment as it appears in one's own country.
2. There will be a correlation between the degree of negative bias and the degree of adverse appraisal of the effect of foreign companies on one's own nation.

The second set of questions shown at the bottom of Table 3.1 asked for

Richard Dunie assisted in the computer analysis of data for this chapter.

TABLE 3.1. Items in Questionnaire Used to Identify Nationalistic Bias

A. Mirror Image Questions (British set shown as example)

1   How often do you think a typical foreign company operating in UK acts in ways contrary to British national interests as compared to a typical British firm? (frequently . . . no difference)

2   In relation to their economic contribution, the dividends and other payments which foreign companies receive from their overseas operations in Great Britain are (too small . . . too large).

3   Are the changes in life brought about by foreign companies good or bad?

4   How frequently do you believe a typical British firm operating abroad acts in ways contrary to the national interest of host countries as compared to a typical local firm? (frequently . . . no difference)

5   Do you feel that the magnitude of the receipts from British overseas operations in relation to their contribution is (too small . . . too large)?

6   Are the changes in life brought about by the operation of British companies abroad good or bad?

B. Justness of Treatment of Foreign Companies

42–47.   How justly do you believe foreign companies as compared with local firms are treated by the governments of these countries?

		Justly						Unjustly
(42)	Brazil	1	2	3	4	5	6	7
(43)	Canada	1	2	3	4	5	6	7
(44)	France	1	2	3	4	5	6	7
(45)	Great Britain	1	2	3	4	5	6	7
(46)	India	1	2	3	4	5	6	7
(47)	Japan	1	2	3	4	5	6	7
(48)	United States	1	2	3	4	5	6	7

appraisals of the justness with which foreign firms were treated by the respondent's country and by other countries. The hypotheses proposed were:

3. The treatment accorded by one's own nation would be perceived as more just relative to that accorded by other countries; that is, there will be a bias in favor of the actions of one's own nation.
4. There will be a correlation between the bias with respect to treatment of foreign companies and the attitude toward the effects of foreign companies.

ANALYSIS

Mirror-image Questions

The basic data for analysis of the first set of hypotheses were determined by subtracting each respondent's score on the corresponding mirror-image questions and dividing the results into three categories:

a. Respondents evaluating the impact of foreign companies as having less beneficial effects on their own nation than the foreign operations of companies of their own nation on other host nations.
b. Respondents evaluating the impact of foreign companies on their own nation as more beneficial than the impact of companies of their own nation on other host countries.
c. Respondents evaluating the impact of foreign companies on their own nation as equal to the impact of companies of their own country on other host nations.

Table 3.2 shows the percentage distribution of respondents in the three categories. The data indicate that in all three countries a significantly larger proportion of the respondents evaluated their own nation's foreign companies as acting less contrary to the interests of the foreign nation compared to the foreign investors in their own nation. The largest portion is in the Canadian sample where 58 percent rated foreign investments as more harmful to the Canadian economy than Canadian foreign investments in other countries, with only 7.9 percent rating the foreign investors more positively than the Canadian investors abroad, and 34 percent perceiving no difference.

Respondents evaluating the impact of foreign companies on their own nation more positively than that of their own firms abroad ranged in France from 4.2 percent to 30.7 percent on the economic and cultural impacts respectively. On the average, about one-third of the sample evaluated the impact of foreign investments as having the same effect as their own investments on the foreign country.

The difference between respondents' evaluations of the impact of their own nation's foreign companies on a foreign country and that of foreign investors on

TABLE 3.2. Relative Opinions on the Impact of Investments by Foreign Companies on Own and Other Host Countries

Impact of foreign companies on own nation considered in relation to impact of own nation's companies on other host nations considered to be	Type of Impact (percent)		
	Economic	National Interest	Culture
United Kingdom			
a. more negative	50.2	46.7	41.0
b. more positive	9.0	25.8	18.9
c. no different	40.8	27.5	40.2
France			
a. more negative	45.8	44.1	34.5
b. more positive	4.2	28.1	30.7
c. no different	50.0	27.8	34.4
Canada			
a. more negative	58.2	52.8	—*
b. more positive	7.9	26.6	—
c. no different	33.9	20.6	—

*This mirror-image question was not included in the Canadian questionnaire.

their own nation state is consistent with the theory of nationalism. The superior evaluation of the own nation is inherent in the concept of nationalism and this negative difference in the mirror-image questions supports hypothesis 1 based on the definition of nationalism. Thus, nationalism distorts the evaluation of foreign investment on the nation and has a biasing effect on the attitudes toward foreign investments.

While the existence of a negative bias for the majority of the sample is consistent with the literature on nationalism, we could not identify the theoretical explanation for the existence of the positive bias shown by a significant minority. A practical explanation may lie in their perception of the relative magnitudes of the two types of investment, for example, the huge role of foreign companies in Canada in contrast to the small volume of Canadian investment abroad.

The relationship between the negative nationalism bias and attitudes toward foreign investments were measured by correlation analysis. As shown in Table 3.3, all three biases, that is, economic, national interest, and cultural, showed a strong association, ranging from .51 to .75, with the evaluation of attitudes of

TABLE 3.3. **Relationship between Nationalistic Bias and Evaluation of Economic, National Interest, Cultural, and Overall Impact of Foreign Companies on Own Country (Pearson correlation coefficients)**

Bias shown in mirror-image questions on	Evaluation of impact of foreign companies on own nation in	United Kingdom	France	Canada
Economic impact	Economic impact	.51[b]	.58[b]	.61[b]
National interest impact	National interest impact	.54[b]	.52[b]	.57[b]
Cultural impact	Cultural impact	.61[b]	.75[b]	
Economic impact	Overall impact[a]	.12[c]	.05	.20[b]
National interest impact	Overall impact[a]	.16[b]	.01	.12[c]
Economic impact	Bias on national interest impact	.19[b]	.11[c]	.26[b]

[a] "In your opinion what is the overall effect on Canada (France or Great Britain) of the activities of foreign companies in Canada?" Good = 1, Bad = 7.

[b] Significant at the 0.01 level.

[c] Significant at the 0.5 level.

of related opinions of effects. As the scales were transformed for computational purposes, the interpretation of this finding indicates that a negative bias tends to be associated with negative attitudes toward effects of foreign investments.

When the measures of bias were correlated with the respondents' appraisals of the overall effects of foreign firms on their own country, the relationships as shown in Table 3.3 were found to be distinctly weaker. The coefficients for France are not statistically significant. Those for the United Kingdom and Canada are significant at the .05 level, but the coefficients are relatively low.

As a further test of relationships, the intercorrelation of the bias indicators for the two categories of questions used in all three countries (economic and national interest impacts) were determined as shown at the bottom of Table 3.3. For all three countries the coefficients are significant at the .05 level, though again they are not as high as the first set of relationships.

Overall these findings confirm our hypothesis 2 though they suggest that its scope is limited. Where a person is nationalistically biased on a specific aspect of MNC impact, there is a high frequency of adverse views about that aspect of impact on the respondent's nation. However, it is much less common that the biases on specific types of impact are associated with adverse overall appraisals of effects of foreign firms.

Fairness of Treatment of Foreign Firms by Host Governments

In all three countries of the study the treatment of foreign companies by the French, British, and Canadian governments was rated. These responses allowed a comparison of the evaluation of the treatment of foreigners by each nation's own government and as perceived by the nationals of the two other countries as well as by themselves.

Table 3.4 shows the frequency distribution of comparative appraisals of fairness. Bias is indicated by comparison of the figures for appraisals for the two countries shown in each set. For example, in the first set 76.7 percent of British respondents felt their country was more just in treating foreign companies than

TABLE 3.4. Bias Evident in Comparative Appraisal of Justness of Treatment of Foreign Companies by Host Governments

Portion of respondents in country considering treatment of foreign companies (percent)	Country of Respondents		
	Britain	France	Canada
by British government *more just* than by French government	76.7	14.0	48.4
by British government *less just* than by French government	1.3	56.8	6.0
no difference	29.2	29.2	46.6
by British government *more just* than by Canadian government	42.4	45.5	4.7
by British government *less just* than by Canadian government	8.3	17.4	78.4
no difference	49.3	37.0	16.4
by Canadian government *more just* than by French government	64.0	42.0	76.3
by Canadian government *less just* than by French government	4.8	11.8	3.0
no difference	31.1	46.1	20.7

was the French government, while only 14.0 percent of French respondents rated the British government as more just than their own. The 56.8 percent to 1.3 percent comparisons of favorable ratings of the French versus the British government treatment is the converse of the same pattern of views. Thus the British and French appear to be substantially biased in their views toward the relative justness of the treatment accorded by their respective governments.

The pairs of comparative figures in the Britain-Canada and France-Canada sets show a similar pattern. The British and Canadians have strongly opposed appraisals of each other. The contrast is not so strong in the France-Canada set, a substantial portion of the French respondents giving a more favorable rating of the Canadian government than of their own. Still, a significantly greater number of Canadians give this favorable assessment (76 percent) than Frenchmen (42 percent).

These data confirm our hypothesis 3. It appears that a nationalistic bias is reflected in a tendency to view the treatment given by one's own government as more favorable than that by other nations. However, it is also apparent that the extent of the bias can vary greatly. The lesser bias evident in the France-Canada comparison than in the other two suggests that the bias here may reflect underlying nationalistic feelings toward specific countries. That is a possibility that would have to be tested by further research, however.

In hypothesis 4 we proposed that there would be a correlation between the bias reflected in views of the justness with which foreign firms were treated and attitudes about the impact of the firms. To test this hypothesis an indicator of the fairness bias was determined for respondents of each country: British—score for treatment by Britain minus that for France; French—score for treatment by France minus that for Britain; and Canada—score for treatment by Canada minus that for Britain. These indicators were then correlated against the questions asking views on overall, economic, and national interest impact of foreign firms. Only one significant correlation was found, that for the Canadian bias indicator against the appraisal of overall impact of foreign firms (coefficient .27, significant at .001 level). Although the bias indicated in Table 3.4 for this comparison was strong, there is no apparent reason for a more significant correlation in this case and one positive correlation is not adequate to support the hypothesis.

To explore the significance of the justness bias indicators further we also ran a correlation of them with the mirror-image question bias indicators. The results were completely negative.

Thus the analysis does not support hypothesis 4. It appears that while the presence of bias in appraising government treatment of foreign firms is demonstrable (hypothesis 3), this bias is not associated with the other types of bias found in this study nor with adverse-favorable dimensions of views about the impact of foreign firms.

SUMMARY

Derived from the theory of nationalism, which implies a superior evaluation of one's own nation compared to other nations, the hypothesis was established that nationalism is manifested in the negative evaluation of the impact of foreign companies on one's own nation compared with the impact of one's own nation's companies in other host countries. Foreign investments were evaluated in terms of their impact on the national interest, the economic welfare, and the culture of the nation. To allow comparison of the evaluation of the foreign companies with the companies of the own nation, the mirror-image question technique was used. Analysis of the difference on the mirror-image questions indicated that on all three dimensions and in all three countries the majority of the respondents evaluated the impact of foreign companies more negatively than that of their own nation's companies. This difference between individuals' evaluation of the impact of their own nation versus that of the foreign investors was regarded as a negative bias factor. Relationship between the negative bias and attitudes toward foreign investments showed a close association, which is consistent with Marton's findings reported in Chapter 5.

Comparison of the justness of treatment of foreigners by their own versus foreign governments was consistent with the findings on attitudes toward foreign investments. The own government's treatment of foreigners was rated as more positive than that by other governments in all three countries of the sample.

4

ATTITUDES TOWARD FOREIGN INVESTMENTS: A CASE STUDY OF THE CANADIAN BLUE COLLAR WORKER EMPLOYED BY FORD CANADA

Katherin Marton

While the multinational corporation (MNC) is not a new phenomenon, its strongly increasing expansion since World War II has rendered it a significant international power. It has become a major actor in the institutional transformation of economy, with distinct effects not only on domestic and international industrial and financial organizations but relatedly on the manner in which the nation-state and the world political economy behave. The capacity of the MNC to exercise transnational control regardless of national boundaries potentially contributes to the erosion of the integrity of indigenous decision making by nation-states.

The operation of the MNC is based on technological determinism, which requires centralized planning of production and distribution on a global scale. The assumption of the absolute legitimacy of power of the sovereign nation-state is presently not adequate to accommodate the MNC without the creation of considerable tension. Thus the perceived danger of loss of national sovereignty and resistance to the increasing role of foreign investors have been expressed in nationalism in the host country. Nationalism and the potential restraints imposed on the operations of the MNC have led to a view in the investor countries that is expounded by Rolfe: "the conflict of our era is between ethnocentric nationalism and geocentric technology" (Rolfe, 1968). Similarly, George Ball argues that "the structure of the MNC is a modern concept designed to meet the require-

This chapter is based on a doctoral dissertation at New York University and research for which financial support was received from the Scaife Foundation.

ments of a modern age; the nation state is a very old fashioned idea and badly adapted to serve the needs of the present world" (Ball, 1967).

Economists and political scientists have conducted research on the adaptation of the MNC to the host nation, and numerous studies have investigated the costs and benefits of the MNC to the host nation (Behrman, 1969, Vernon, 1971, Caves, 1974). Legal and political implications of the MNC were studied extensively by Litvak and Maule (1971), Behrman (1969), and Barnet and Muller (1974). However, systematic study on the evaluation of foreign investments and of their determinants as well as on the relationship between rising nationalism and foreign penetration in the host economy has been given little research attention.* Given the increasing trend of foreign participation in the host nations, this neglect is somewhat surprising. Governments' awareness of their constituents' evaluation of the MNCs could result in more responsive policy making towards MNCs.

OBJECTIVE OF THE STUDY

The purpose of this chapter is to look at those criteria that contribute to the attitude formation of the respondents in the host nation toward foreign investments. Due to the scope of the research and the methodological problems involved in studying attitudes for a heterogeneous population, the work is confined to the case study of the Canadian blue collar worker employed at Ford Canada.

Using Fishbein's theory of formation and measurement of attitudes, beliefs that have an impact on the evaluation of foreign investments will be identified. From the relevant beliefs an "attitudes toward foreign investment" scale will be constructed and then, by way of multiple regression analysis, tested for content validity and predictive ability. Findings from the blue collar worker sample will be compared with the Canadian elite group, previously studied by Fayerweather (1972). Similarities and differences between the importance ranking of the beliefs about foreign investments will be used to explain the differential evaluation process of the two groups.

Research findings indicate that nationalism tends to arise if foreign intervention in the self-determination of the nation is perceived. Thus the proposition is established that nationalism is inversely related to attitudes toward foreign investments, that is, negative evaluation of foreign investments is associated with strongly nationalist feelings. The proposition will be tested by measuring the extent and direction of association of the two phenomena.

In addition to the main proposition of the study, variables with assumed relationship to the evaluation of foreign investments will be examined. On the

---

*Reference to studies of Fayerweather, Sugges, Truitt and Blake, and Blake and Driscoll, Chapters 1, 2, 6, and 8, respectively.

basis of past research in the area of the adaptation process of the MNC and host nation studied by Fayerweather, and Litvak and Maule (1971), the variables of economic ideology and job satisfaction of the worker employed at the foreign company seemed relevant for inclusion.

THE CONCEPT OF NATIONALISM

The concept of nationalism has been used to describe diverse phenomena that relate to a particular form of political and cultural grouping of individuals. Nationalism has been conceived as "social value" (Silvert, 1963), "school of thought" (Hertz, 1951), "motivation" (Krech and Crutchfield, 1948), "ideology" (Ariely, 1966), "process or movement" (Doob, 1962), and "expression of class struggle" (Marx, 1885). A review of the literature shows that "definitions of nationalism are almost as numerous as nations" (Whitaker, 1961). However, most treatments of the subject consider one or both of the following elements: Belief in the national cause and goal to act in national self-interest and self-determination; national consciousness and an aspiration to preserve national identity and unity of the nation.

Thus, the characteristics most commonly attributed to nationalism are a belief in and pursuit of the national cause of self-determination. The devotion to the nation is based on the conviction that the nation has the right to be autonomous in its economic and political decision making. This desire for autonomy may be accompanied by a tendency to feel animosity toward and to distrust those other nations that are felt to threaten the self-interest and self-determination of one's own nation. Nationalism in this sense is defined by Kedourie as a "doctrine of national self-determination" (Kedourie, 1960).

METHODOLOGY

Sample

At the Ford plant in Oshawa, Southern Ontario, a random sample of 100 blue collar workers was surveyed. The questionnaire shown in Appendix 4.A was personally administered to the sample. The rationale for the selection of Canada was the current salience of the issue of foreign investment there. In 1971, when the survey was undertaken, 60 percent of the manufacturing industry was foreign owned, with a particularly high concentration in Southern Ontario.

So that variation resulting from socioeconomic variables would be minimized, the sample was confined to one occupational class, the blue collar worker. Further, it seemed of interest to consider how different socioeconomic position and access to information might influence the criteria of attitude formation toward foreign investments through comparison of the blue collar workers with the elite studied by Fayerweather.

Non-Canadian citizens, including recent immigrants working in low-skill-level jobs, were excluded from the sample because their nationalism score might have introduced a bias.

Questionnaire

Evaluative Beliefs or Attitudes toward Foreign Investments

Evaluative beliefs related to the issue of foreign investments were obtained following the methodology of Fishbein (1969). In the pilot study, open-ended questions were asked about the benefits and disadvantages of the impact of foreign investments on Canada. In this elicitation process the following issues related to the impact of foreign investments on Canada ranked highest:

influence on the way of life
future influence on Canada
depletion of natural resources
contribution to the economic growth of the country
political influence
recognition of trade unions
working conditions offered
payments to the worker

These issues overlapped to a large extent with the evaluative beliefs used in Fayerweather's study of the elite groups. While the elite questionnaire consisted of 36 items related to the evaluation of foreign investments, factor analysis revealed the political, economic, cultural, and working condition factors as major dimensions. Thus the major issues tended to be consistent for both groups. From the elicited beliefs a nine-item "attitudes toward foreign investments" scale was constructed using the seven-point semantic differential evaluation form developed by Osgood et al. (1957).

Measurement of Nationalism

An analysis of previously constructed nationalism scales revealed their inappropriateness for the present study. Historically and culturally bound, their definition of nationalism is invalid for the present purpose.

Most of these measures tapped a rightist, ethnocentric dimension. For example, one of the most recent studies on South Tyrolians measured nationalism as an incitement to action (Doob, 1962). Bjerstadt's scale measures militaristic national aspirations and tendencies to view other nations in terms of black-white stereotypes (Bjerstadt, 1960). Some of the scales in past research were related to certain political events or ideologies such as communism or fascism (Klineberg, 1950; Ferguson, 1942), inapplicable to the concept of nationalism defined by this study.

For the purpose of this study, Terhune's nationalism scale was selected for the following reasons: Terhune's definition of nationalism is based on the concept of self-determination of the nation, which corresponds with the definition of this study; it is not time-bound, as it is not related to specific politicoeconomic events or national institutions; it is less culture-bound than previous scales by virtue of not referring to any specific country or ideology such as the "white" or "Christian Americans"; and a fairly high degree of validity and reliability of the scale were shown in his cross-cultural research (Terhune, 1965).

Measurement of Attitudes toward Big Business

The average size of U.S. subsidiaries in Canada is larger than that of the domestic firms in the same industry, and these subsidiaries tend to be in highly concentrated industries with substantial oligopolistic market power. The salience of the issues of big business associated with U.S. companies was frequently elicited in the exploratory phase of the research. This assumed relevance of the relationship between attitudes toward foreign companies and attitudes toward big business was supported by Fayerweather's previous findings: in the comparison of the attitudes of four French elite groups, the socialist-oriented labor leaders of CGT (Confédération Generale du Travail) rated the impact of foreign investments below those of other groups. Thus, as an indicator of broad concepts of economic ideology, attitude toward big business was measured using Wilke's scale (Wilke, 1934).

Measurement of Job Satisfaction

According to the functional theory of attitude formation, the positive or negative experience resulting from the interaction of the individual with the stimulus significantly influences attitudes toward the stimulus. Thus, for assessment of the influence of a worker's immediate experience with a foreign company on his or her overall evaluation of foreign investments, job satisfaction was measured according to P. Smith's Job Description Index (JDI) (Smith, 1969).

FINDINGS

Salience of Evaluative Beliefs of Attitudes toward Foreign Investments

The multiple correlation coefficient between the "overall" attitude measurement (question 1, Appendix 4.A) and the nine evaluative beliefs of the scale was .85. In order to determine which of the items of the scale has the closest association with the "overall" evaluation, holding the impact of the other items constant, we performed correlation analysis. Table 4.1 shows the coefficients in descending order.

TABLE 4.1. Correlation of the Overall Evaluation of Foreign Investments and the Items of the "Attitude toward Foreign Investments" Scale

Item	Question	Correlation Coefficient with Question 1, Appendix A r
5	Influence on way of life	.78
8b	Working conditions in foreign-owned companies	.65
8a	Wages paid by foreign-owned companies	.63
7	Foreign companies willingness to recognize trade unions	.60
6	Payments received by foreign companies	.56
3	Foreign companies take out more from the country than they give	.54
9	Future effects of more control by foreign companies	.45
4	Foreign companies cause a loss of control over national affairs	.38
2	Compared to Canadian firms foreign companies in Canada act more frequently in ways contrary to Canadian national interests	.36

Note: N = 100. All variables are significant at 95 percent confidence level.

The item with the highest coefficient measure is foreign investment's "influence on way of life." Because of the salience of this variable in the evaluation of the blue collar worker, semantic clarification of the concept seemed necessary. During the exploratory stage of the study, respondents frequently referred to the perceived impact of foreign companies on the Canadian way of living. The influence was described as a generally faster pace of life imposed on the Canadian life style; the influence on and suffocation of Canadian cultural endeavors created by the inundation of Canada with U.S. movies, periodicals, and the U.S. takeover of publishing houses. The general sense of this feeling was expressed by Perry's description of the "Coca-colanization" of Canada (Perry, 1971).

The three work-related variables showed the second highest correlation with the evaluation of foreign investments. The degree of closer association of the evaluation of working conditions in foreign-owned companies compared with the lower importance of the broader political and economic impacts on the nation indicates the salience of those issues for workers that have immediately perceivable effects in their everyday lives.

Comparison of the Salience of Evaluative Beliefs of the Blue Collar Worker with Those of the Elite Group

Table 4.2 shows that the Canadian elite group surveyed by Fayerweather expressed significantly more positive evaluation of foreign investments. A detailed analysis of the relationship between evaluative beliefs and overall attitudes is discussed by Fayerweather in Chapter 1. In this chapter only the major differences are indicated. While the item "influence on way of living" by foreign companies showed high correlations for both groups, significant differences were found for the other scale items. For the elite group the questions measuring the economic and political control impacts of foreign investments had higher correlations than working conditions, which had the second highest correlations for the blue collar worker.

The low salience of the general economic and political control factors for the blue collar workers might be explained by their lower level of information on the politicoeconomic system in general, which predisposes them toward anchoring attitudes on the more concretely perceivable phenomenon of the immediate working conditions.

TABLE 4.2. Overall Evaluation of Foreign Investments by the Blue Collar Worker and the Elite Group

Rating Scale	Percentage Distribution of Responses	
	Blue Collar Worker[a]	Elite[b]
1 (bad)	39	3
2	12	12
3	5	17
4	13	10
5	20	18
6	6	28
7 (good)	5	12

[a] $n = 100$.
[b] $n = 260$.

The Predictive Ability of the Evaluative Belief

A multiple regression analysis was applied to measure the degree of explained variances of the "overall evaluation of foreign investments." The nine evaluative beliefs gave the following equations:

$$A_0 = -.85 + .05X_1 + .35X_2 + .20X_3 + .28X_4 + .42X_5 + .17X_6 + .06X_7 + .25X_8 + .18X_9 \tag{1}$$

Notation:

A_0 = Overall evaluation of foreign investments

X_1 = Foreign companies operating in Canada act more frequently in ways contrary to Canadian national interest

X_2 = Foreign companies take out more from the Canadian economy than they give

X_3 = Foreign companies cause a loss of control over Canadian national affairs

X_4 = Foreign companies influence the way of living

X_5 = Payment received by foreign companies

X_6 = Willingness of foreign companies to recognize trade unions

X_7 = Wages in foreign-owned companies

X_8 = Other working conditions in foreign-owned companies

X_9 = Future effects of more control by foreign companies

The multiple correlation coefficient of the nine independent variables with the overall evaluation of foreign investments was .85, explaining 72 percent of the variance. However, from the computed t-values only the variables X_2, X_4, and X_5 were significant at the 95 percent confidence level.

As the evaluative beliefs were strongly intercorrelated a new regression analysis was performed including only the three significant variables, with the following result:

$$A_0 = -.80 + .20X_2 + .58X_4 + .29X_5 \tag{2}$$

This reduction of variables from nine to three lowered the multiple correlation coefficient only by .05 and thus lowered the coefficient of determination to .66.

The stepwise regression analysis corroborated the findings on the salience of the evaluative beliefs. Table 4.3 shows that 60 percent of the variance is explained by the variable "influence on way of living." The contribution of the succeeding variables is only minimal.

TABLE 4.3. Stepwise Regression Analysis of the "Attitude toward Foreign Investment" Scale Items with the "Overall" Evaluation of Attitudes

Step Number	Variable in Equation	Multiple Correlation Coefficient	r^2
1	X_4	.78	.60
2	X_4, X_5	.80	.61
3	X_4, X_5, X_2	.81	.64
4	X_4, X_5, X_2, X_6	.83	.68

Findings from the regression analysis are important for two reasons. There is a lack of a theoretical foundation relating to the behavioral manifestation of attitudes toward foreign investments that would allow for testing the construct validity of the "attitude toward foreign investment" scale. The assumption that an individual with negative attitudes would not work for a foreign-owned company is contradicted by the empirical findings of this study. Thus, the high explanatory power of the evaluative beliefs indicates that the beliefs were sampled from the universe of attitudes toward foreign investments. Secondly, it is interesting to note that Zajonc's finding that evaluation of objects, subjects, and ideas is usually based on three to four major evaluative criteria. This is also relevant to the evaluation of foreign investments (Zajonc, 1954).

Relationship between Nationalism and
Attitudes toward Foreign Investments

The distribution of nationalism scores is strongly skewed to the extreme values, with 18 percent "slightly," 30 percent "moderately," and 52 percent "strongly" nationalistic feelings. Responses to the scale items tended to cluster at extreme poles of the scales, indicating strongly bipartisan attitudes related to the issues of political independence and national self-determination.

Table 4.4, which presents the direction and magnitude of association between the nationalism score and attitudes toward foreign investments, supports the proposition of the study. Of all the items, the variable "foreign companies' influence on way of life" showed the closest association with the nationalism score. This is consistent with findings by Krech and Crutchfield (1948) that underlying the nationalism feeling is a desire to maintain the national identity, which, in Canada's historical development, has been of particular concern. A somewhat lower but significant relationship was found between the impact of foreign investments on political independence and the economic welfare of the nation. While the issue of political independence taps the nationalism dimension, thus expressing the desire for self-determination, the item related to the depletion of national resources (question 3) expresses the feeling of "sentimental attachment to the soil of the home country" cited by Ariely (1966). The items measuring the impact of foreign investments on the working conditions showed a statistically significant but low correlation with nationalism.

The preceding ranking of the variables indicates that items encompassing a broader scope of attitudes show a closer relationship to nationalism than those variables related to more specific issues, such as working conditions.

Relationship between Attitudes toward Foreign Investments and Attitudes toward Big Business

Correlation analysis between the overall attitudes toward foreign investment and toward big business scales was .81, indicating that positive evaluation of foreign investments tends to be associated with positive attitudes toward big business and, similarly, negative ratings of foreign investments and negative evaluation of big business are positively related. Due to the cross-sectional nature of the data neither a causal relationship nor the question as to whether respondents generalize the two phenomena as one issue can be identified.

TABLE 4.4. Correlation between the Items of the "Attitude toward Foreign Investment" Scale and the Nationalism Score

Item	Question	Correlation Coefficient r
1	Overall evaluation of foreign investments	.55
5	Influence on way of life	.62
9	Future effects of more control by foreign companies	.44
3	Foreign companies take out more from the country than they give	.40
2	Foreign companies act against Canadian national interests	.38
4	Foreign companies cause a loss of control over national affairs	.37
8b	Working conditions in foreign-owned companies	.17
8a	Wages paid by foreign companies	.12
7	Foreign companies' willingness to recognize trade unions	.10

*Relationship between Attitudes toward Foreign Investments
and Job Satisfaction*

The rationale for including job satisfaction in the study was to establish whether the worker's experience in a foreign-owned company has a significant impact on his overall evaluation of foreign investments. The low correlation of .11 between the JDI score and overall attitude toward foreign investments shows that respondents did not generalize from their experience with the company to all foreign investments. This finding suggests that factors other than their immediate work experience contribute to the image formation process of the worker.

METHODOLOGICAL LIMITATIONS
OF THE FINDINGS

Empirical evidence from attitude measurement suggests that in situations where the object to be evaluated is not well known in all characteristics to be evaluated or when those characteristics "are unclear in behavioral expression," the operation of the "halo effect" will bias the responses (Guilford, 1942).* Given the complexity of evaluating the impacts of foreign investments on the nation, the presence of a halo effect was investigated.

While the findings can be of only a tentative nature, the high intercorrelation of the overall evaluation of foreign investments with the item "foreign companies influence on way of life" suggests the presence of a halo effect. This implies that in rating the attitude toward foreign investment scale respondents tend to rate most of the scale items in terms of the foreign companies' overall impact on their life. If they perceive that foreign investments have a particular effect on their life they tend to rate the other items of the scale similarly.

The presence of the halo effect implies that the rating of the scale items is biased. Practically, this means, as Ash stated, that the "object is viewed as more homogeneously good or bad, than it can be shown to be when his characteristics are independently measured" (Ash, 1946). In terms of prediction of attitudes toward foreign investments this results in an overestimation of the regression coefficients of the items, a tendency that gives a correspondingly lower accuracy for the predicted values.

---

*"Halo effect" occurs when "a particular rater (J) tends to rate a particular ratee (O) similarly on all traits" (Guilford, 1942). Also according to experimental research by Wells, "judges tended to rate subjects and objects on several traits in terms of general impression of goodness or badness and that this introduced a spuriously high correlation into their ratings" (Wells, 1907).

CONCLUSION

While classical and neoclassical economic theories propose that free flow of foreign capital on a world scale will benefit all the economies, the MNC has not been successful in maintaining this image for all segments of host nations. The assessment of economic efficiency and of impact on the political decision making of the country by the MNC is far too inaccessible for an objective evaluation; yet the majority of the sampled blue collar workers evaluated these impacts significantly lower than the elite groups (Fayerweather, 1972).

The empirical analysis of the Canadian blue collar worker supports the a priori assumption of the inverse relationship between nationalism and attitudes toward foreign investments. Due to the lack of longitudinal data on nationalism and attitudes toward foreign investments, no etiological explanations can be provided on the nature of the relationship. Present findings are amenable to three interpretations:

(a) An inherent nationalistic feeling tends to bias the individual to a negative perception of the impacts of the MNC on the nation. This assumption is consistent with research on attitudes toward foreign investments of the Canadian, British, and French elite, where usage of the mirror-image technique as an indirect measurement method of the nationalism bias led to similar conclusions. Nationals in all three countries evaluated the impact of their own foreign investments on the host nation more positively than those by foreign investors in their country (Chapter 4). While the differential evaluation might in certain cases underlie some objective criteria, the consistency of findings suggests the presence of a nationalistic bias.

(b) An alternative explanation of the relationship between nationalism and attitudes toward foreign investments can be provided by using the framework of the sociology of knowledge. According to the central theories of sociology of knowledge (Marx, 1939; Scheler, 1926; Mannheim, 1936), beliefs, social ideas, that is, knowledge in a broader sense, are not immanently determined but rather are determined through a relationship with the existential basis. This would imply that the perceived threat of the loss of self-determination elicits latent nationalistic feeling.

(c) The most plausible explanation is that nationalism and attitudes toward foreign investments underlie several common dimensions. While nationalism is a broader, more abstract concept related to the maintenance of national self-determination, the evaluation of the MNC is conceptualized in a more concrete way, using the cultural, political, and economic dimensions of the overall self-determination syndrome. This interpretation is supported by the high degree of association between the items of the foreign investment scale and the nationalism score.

The nature of this study was exploratory; causality between nationalism and attitudes toward foreign investments could not be established, though a high degree of association was identified. Given that the role of foreign investments will persist in the host economy, major adaptations will be required on the part of the MNC. Presently, despite MNCs' adoption of efforts to be "good corporate citizens" in the host nation, there exists indigenous concern for regaining self-determination and control of the nation's own cultural, economic, and political life.

REFERENCES

Ariely, Y. (1966), *Individualism and Nationalism in American Ideology*, Baltimore: Penguin Books.

Ash, S. E. (1946), "Forming Impressions of Personality," *Journal of Abnormal and Social Psychology*, No. 4, pp. 258-290.

Ball, G. W. (1967), "The Promise of Multinational Corporation," *Fortune*, Vol. 75, No. 6, p. 80.

Barnet, E., and Muller, R. (1974), *Global Reach*, New York: Simon and Schuster.

Behrman, J. (1969), *Some Patterns in the Rise of the Multinational Enterprise*, Chapel Hill: U. of North Carolina Press.

Bjerstadt, A. I. (1960), "Ego-Involved World Mindedness," *Journal of Conflict Resolution*, No. 4, pp. 185-192.

Caves, R. (1974), "Multinational Firms, Competition and Productivity in Host Country Markets," *Economica*, Vol. 41, pp. 121-129.

Doob, L. W. (1962), "South Tyrol: An Introduction to the Psychological Syndrome of Nationalism," *Public Opinion Quarterly*, No. 26, pp. 172-184.

Fayerweather, J. (1972), "Elite Attitudes toward Multinational Firms," *International Studies Quarterly*, Vol. 16, No. 4, pp. 472-490.

Fayerweather, J., and Marton, K. (1975), The Effect of Nationalistic Bias on Attitudes toward Foreign Companies, unpublished working paper.

Ferguson, L. W. (1942), "The Isolation and Measurement of Nationalism," *Journal of Social Psychology*, Vol. 16, pp. 189-213.

Fishbein, J. (1969), "The Source of Beliefs, their Saliency, and Prediction of Behavior," *Journal of Social Psychology*, No. 4, pp. 67-74.

Hertz, F. (1951), *Nationality in History and Politics: A Psychology and Soci-*

ology of National Sentiment and Nationalism, London: Routledge and Kegan Paul.

Horowitz, E. L. (1940), "Some Aspects of the Development of Patriotism in Children," *Sociometry*, No. 3, pp. 329-341.

Kedourie, E. (1960), *Nationalism*, London: Hutchinson and Co.

Klineberg, O. (1950), *Tensions Affecting International Understanding*, New York: Social Science Research Council.

Krech, D., and Crutchfield, D. (1948), *Theory and Problems of Social Psychology*, New York: McGraw-Hill.

Litvak, I., and Maule, D. (eds.) (1971), *Foreign Investment: the Experience of Host Countries*. Special Studies in International Economics and Development, New York: Praeger.

Mannheim, K. (1936), *Ideology and Utopia*, New York: Harcourt and Co.

Marx, K. (1885), *Der Achtzehnte Brumaire des Louis Bonaparte*, Hamburg.

—— (1939), *The German Ideology*, New York: International Publishers.

Osgood, E. C., Suci, P., and Tannenbaum, P. (1957), *The Measurement of Meaning*, Urbana: U. of Illinois Press.

Perry, R. (1971), *Galt, U.S.A.*, Toronto: Macmillan Press.

Rolfe, S. (1968), "Up Dating Adam Smith," *Interplay*, Vol. 2, pp. 15-19.

Scheler, M. (1926), *Versuch zu einer Soziologie des Wissens*, Muenchen: Duncker and Humbold.

Silvert, K. H. (ed.) (1963), *Expectant Peoples: Nationalism and Development*, New York: Random House.

Smith, P. (1969), *The Measurement of Satisfaction in Work and Retirement*, Chicago: Rand McNally.

Terhune, K. W. (1965), Nationalism among Foreign and American Students: an Exploratory Study, unpublished dissertation, U. of Michigan.

Vernon, R. (1971), *Sovereignty at Bay: the Multinational Spread of U.S. Enterprises*, New York: Basic Books.

Whitaker, E. (1961), *Nationalism and International Progress*, San Francisco: Chandler.

Wilke, W. H. (1934), "An Experimental Comparison of the Speech, the Radio, and the Printed Page as Propaganda Devices," *Arch. Psychology*, pp. 169-184.

Zajonc, R. (1954), Structure of the Cognitive Field, unpublished doctoral dissertation, U. of Michigan.

APPENDIX 4.A

Questionnaire

ATTITUDES TOWARD FOREIGN INVESTMENTS SCALE

Please, indicate your opinion by circling the number on the scale which comes closest to your opinion:

1. What is the overall effect on Canada of the activities of foreign companies in Canada?

   good   1   2   3   4   5   6   7   bad

2. Compared to Canadian firms, foreign companies operating in Canada act more frequently in ways contrary to Canadian national interests

   agree   1   2   3   4   5   6   7   disagree

3. Foreign companies take out more from the Canadian economy than they give

   agree   1   2   3   4   5   6   7   disagree

4. The activities of foreign companies cause a loss of Canadian control over Canadian national affairs

   agree   1   2   3   4   5   6   7   disagree

5. Do you believe that the influence of foreign ways of life brought in by foreign companies in Canada are

   good   1   2   3   4   5   6   7   bad

6. In relation to their economic contributions, the dividends, royalties, and other payments which foreign companies receive from their operations in Canada are

   too small   1   2   3   4   5   6   7   too large

7. Do you believe that foreign companies in Canada are more *or* less willing to recognize trade unions than Canadian firms are

   more willing   1   2   3   4   5   6   7   less willing

8. In respect to wages and other working conditions (job security, handling of

grievances, etc.) the treatment of workers by foreign companies in Canada compared with that by Canadian firms is:

a. Wages: foreign firms   worse   1   2   3   4   5   6   7   better
b. Other conditions: worse   1   2   3   4   5   6   7   better

9. What will be the result for Canada if foreign companies have greater control over policy decisions in the Canadian industry?

good   1   2   3   4   5   6   7   bad

NATIONALISM SCALE

		Agree						Disagree

1. It is only natural that my country should put its own interests first — 1 2 3 4 5 6 7

2. To the degree possible, my country should be both economically and politically independent of other nations — 1 2 3 4 5 6 7

3. My country should guard against nations which try to push it around — 1 2 3 4 5 6 7

4. The best way for my people to progress is to maintain themselves as a distinct and independent nation — 1 2 3 4 5 6 7

5. My country must seek to control its own destiny — 1 2 3 4 5 6 7

6. My country should guard against other nations altering its identity and national way of life — 1 2 3 4 5 6 7

7. In making decisions in the national interest my country's leaders should not be influenced by "world opinions" — 1 2 3 4 5 6 7

8. Until other countries can be trusted, my country should protect its welfare by reserving the right to accept or reject any decisions of the United Nations — 1 2 3 4 5 6 7

ATTITUDES TOWARD BIG BUSINESS SCALE

		Agree						Disagree

1. It is contrary to the interests of the people of Canada to permit the concentration of capital in a few large companies   1 2 3 4 5 6 7

2. If 10 percent of the companies owns 90 percent of the country's total manufacturing assets it is because the most able rise to the top   1 2 3 4 5 6 7

3. We should encourage the development of big business as vitally necessary to supply the large amount of capital for a modern industrial society   1 2 3 4 5 6 7

4. What is essential for Canada is to break the present degree of overwhelming private corporate power and redistribute it   1 2 3 4 5 6 7

5. We have no true democracy in this country, because only large business has economic opportunity   1 2 3 4 5 6 7

JOB SATISFACTION SCALE

The following words relate to different aspects of your job. Please indicate with Yes or No which comes closest to your mind.

WORK	SUPERVISION
——— Fascinating	——— Asks my advice
——— Routine	——— Hard to please
——— Satisfying	——— Impolite
——— Boring	——— Praises good work
——— Good	——— Tactful
——— Creative	——— Influential
——— Respected	——— Up-to-date
——— Hot	——— Does not supervise enough
——— Pleasant	——— Quick tempered
——— Useful	——— Tells me where I stand

—— Tiresome
—— Healthful
—— Challenging
—— On your feet
—— Frustrating
—— Simple
—— Endless
—— Gives sense of accomplishment

—— Annoying
—— Stubborn
—— Knows the job well
—— Bad
—— Intelligent
—— Leaves me on my own
—— Lazy
—— Around when needed

PAY

—— Income adequate for normal expenses
—— Satisfactory profit sharing
—— Barely live on income
—— Bad
—— Income provides luxuries
—— Insecure
—— Less than I deserve
—— Highly paid
—— Underpaid

PROMOTIONS

—— Good opportunity for advancement
—— Opportunity somewhat limited
—— Promotion on ability
—— Dead end job
—— Good chance for promotion
—— Unfair promotion policy
—— Regular promotions
—— Infrequent promotion policy
—— Fairly good chances for promotions

5

SOURCES OF FOREIGN INVESTMENT ATTITUDES: A STUDY OF CANADIAN EXECUTIVES

John A. Smetanka

In recent years, foreign direct investment has become increasingly problematic for many countries. Technological dependence, economic exploitation, infringement of national sovereignty, cultural distortion, and political interference head the list of concerns that advanced industrial and underdeveloped societies have raised with respect to foreign multinational corporations operating within their national boundaries (Blake and Walters, 1976:91-97). These concerns have been addressed in an extensive literature on the political and economic impacts of multinational corporate investment.[1] In addition, a number of researchers have investigated these issues in opinion surveys of host-national attitudes toward foreign investors. These surveys have been cited by policy makers as indicators of public mood and have been used to legitimate national policies implemented to control foreign investment (Keenleyside, LeDuc, and Murray, 1976).

The author is an assistant professor of sociology at the State University of New York at Buffalo and a research associate of the University of Windsor's Institute for Canadian-American Studies. The research presented in this study was conducted while the author was a research associate of the Center for International Affairs, Harvard University. The financial assistance of the University Consortium for World Order Studies (James P. Warburg Fellowship) and the Center for International Affairs is gratefully acknowledged. The author would also like to thank Charles Judd, Richard Wanner, and James Meeker for their statistical advice on aspects of the data analysis; William Busching for his consummate typing of Appendix B; and John Feather, Gloria Heinemann, and Thomas Koenig for their insightful comments on earlier drafts of this study.

Depending on their purpose and the sample surveyed, foreign investment opinion surveys can be placed into one of four categories. Large-scale national opinion polls comprise the first category. These surveys have been conducted either by polling agencies such as Gallup (Sigler and Goresky, 1974) or by university research institutes to investigate public attitudes on various issues related to foreign investment and to monitor feelings of economic nationalism. Most notable are the efforts of the University of Windsor's Institute for Canadian-American Studies, which for the past ten years has conducted an annual survey of Canadian opinion on U.S. investment in Canada (Keenleyside, LeDuc, and Murray, 1976; LeDuc and Murray, 1977; Murray and Gerace, 1972; Murray and LeDuc, 1975a, 1975b, 1976a, 1976b, 1976-77, 1978; Murray, 1973).

A second category includes studies of select publics—business and political leaders, other opinion setters, local communities—conducted by business research organizations with the expressed purpose of informing multinational corporate policy (Blake and Driscoll, 1977; LaPalombara and Blank, 1976; Truitt and Blake, 1976).

A third major investigative effort has been directed toward examining dimensions of nationalist sentiment and attitudes toward foreign investment among various national groups: executives and other employees of foreign and national corporations, labor leaders, and elected officials at the national and state-provincial levels (Fayerweather, 1972; Hilton, 1976; Marton, 1973; Province of Ontario, 1974; Stevenson, 1974). Studies in this category have also focused on attitudes toward governmental regulation of foreign firms (Stevenson, 1974) while others have had direct input into the formation of regulatory policies (Province of Ontario, 1974).

Finally, nationalist and Marxist critics of multinational corporations have conducted studies of political and economic attitudes among national business elites (Faria, cited in Evans, 1972; Johnson, 1972; Petras and Cook, 1973a, 1973b). These studies have been designed to provide support for a major critical proposition: that nationals employed by foreign corporations are members of a comprador class that is favorable to foreign investment and that identifies with the interests of international capitalism over those of the nation (Bodenheimer, 1971; Clement, 1975; Sunkel, 1973).

In addition to outlining the parameters of foreign investment opinion, researchers in each of the above categories have also attempted to describe differences of opinion in terms of such variables as the age and education of respondents, national regional differences, and familiarity with foreign firms. In several of the studies—particularly those in the last category—investigators have focused on possible differences in attitudes between executives who work for independent national firms and those who are employed by the affiliates of foreign corporations. More often than not, however, little difference in opinion has been observed from the data.

With respect to this latter issue, concentration in the research on the single variable of ownership glosses over several other distinctions between executives and corporations that might have an impact on foreign investment attitudes. Differences may emerge when a firm's involvement in international trade is taken into account in conjunction with its ownership structure. Executives in both foreign affiliates and domestic firms that service a number of international markets may feel less threatened by foreign competition than those whose interests are tied to a domestic national market. Further, as Bauer, Pool, and Dexter (1972) observed in their study of attitudes toward trade liberalization, opinion may vary according to the division in which an executive works and the kinds of experiences he encounters in the exercise of his corporate responsibilities. Finally, the age of an executive, his educational level, and his socioeconomic background may also affect his foreign investment attitudes.

Given these considerations, the purpose of the present study is twofold. Its first aim is to present a particular approach for analyzing the foreign investment attitudes of host-country executives. This approach takes into account characteristics of the firm for which an executive works, characteristics of an executive's position in the firm's organizational structure, and an executive's personal background characteristics. Second, the adequacy of the framework and the insights it may provide are examined with a case study of Canadian automotive and automotive-parts executives and their attitudes toward U.S. investment in Canada.

FOREIGN INVESTMENT ATTITUDES AND HOST-COUNTRY EXECUTIVES: A FRAMEWORK FOR ANALYSIS

The proposed framework for studying executive attitudes toward foreign investment is presented in Figure 5.1. The first set of variables considered in the model encompasses two characteristics of an executive's corporation: corporate ownership and market structure. In addition, the interaction between these two variables is included to check whether the impact of ownership on investment attitudes is affected by the extent to which a corporation is involved in international trade.

The second set of variables refers to selected characteristics of an executive's position in the corporate organization: the frequency of an executive's contact with foreign businessmen, work responsibilities that are international in content (for example, dealing with import-export activities), familiarity with the operations of foreign firms required by an executive's position, an executive's rank in the corporate hierarchy, and the work area or department in which an executive works.

As indicated in Figure 5.1, it is expected that the frequency with which an executive interacts with foreign businessmen and the extent to which his job requires familiarity with foreign firms will depend on the international scope of his work responsibilities. It is also postulated that required familiarity with

FIGURE 5.1. **Proposed Framework for Analyzing Foreign Investment Attitudes among Host-Country Executives**

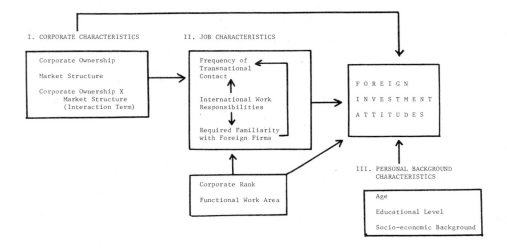

the operations of foreign firms will, in turn, serve as an additional source of transnational contact. Further, these three characteristics of an executive's role are expected to depend on his rank and work area. International work responsibilities, for example, could be expected to vary from lower to middle to upper management, as well as from department to department (for example, marketing as opposed to personnel) in both foreign and domestic corporations. Certain positions and corporate functions are more susceptible to transnational concerns than others, and this proposition can be established on an empirical basis.

In addition, it can be argued that aspects of corporate structure will determine characteristics of an executive's work experience. Executives employed by foreign-owned affiliates and by firms that produce for export markets can be expected to have frequent contact with foreign business nationals, international work responsibilities, and knowledge about the activities of foreign firms.

We can also predict an interactive relationship between the ownership and market variables with respect to an executive's work experience. We would expect executives in independent national firms to be increasingly similar to their counterparts in foreign affiliates in terms of transnational contact, international work responsibilities, and familiarity with foreign firms, depending on the extent to which their firms are involved in international trade.

In sum, Figure 5.1 indicates that interrelated characteristics of an executive's work experience can directly affect his foreign investment attitudes. In addition, we may find that the relationship between corporate characteristics and investment attitudes is not a direct one but a relationship mediated by the experiences circumscribing an executive's job—given that an executive's work experience is expected to be directly determined by the kind of corporation for which he works. This possibility has not been addressed in any of the literature cited previously.

Finally, three personal background characteristics of an executive—age, level of educational attainment, and socioeconomic background—are included in the framework as a third set of factors that could influence his foreign investment attitudes.

THE CANADIAN CASE

The framework outlined in the previous section was used in a questionnaire survey of executives in the Canadian automotive and automotive-parts industry. These industrial sectors were selected for a number of reasons. They comprise the most important manufacturing industry in the Province of Ontario with a combined estimated value of shipments of $9,967 million in the first three quarters of 1978. Total Canadian employment in the auto manufacturing and parts sectors in 1976 was 94,409 persons, of whom 85,175 or 90.2 percent were in Ontario, representing over 10 percent of the province's manufacturing labor force (Brunt, 1975). Further, the automotive and automotive-parts industry figures substantially in the balance of payments and trade relationship between Canada and the United States. In 1978, for example, over 90 percent of Canada's import and export trade in automotive products was with the United States. The industry has also achieved some prominence in other political-economic relations between the two countries, such as the issues surrounding the 1965 Automotive Trade Agreement (Beigie, 1970) and the extraterritorial application of U.S. laws (Leyton-Brown, 1974; Litvak and Maule, 1969). The Canadian automotive and automotive-parts industry, therefore, is an important and visible sector of the Canadian economy—one that is particularly attuned to both national economic policy and the political economy of Canadian-U.S. relations.

Two characteristics of the firms that comprise the automotive and auto-motive-parts industry are also important from the standpoint of the present study. Ninety-seven percent of the capital employed in the industry is controlled by U.S. corporations (Litvak and Maule, 1970). The automotive sector is completely owned and controlled by the "Big Four" U.S. auto companies: Chrysler, Ford, General Motors, and American Motors. Although the parts sector is also largely controlled by U.S. firms, it still contains a number of independent Canadian suppliers. With respect to participation in international (regional) trade, the automotive subsidiaries manufacture primarily for export to the United States while the parts companies, both U.S.- and Canadian-owned, vary in the ratio of their domestic to export sales. Thus, by using the Canadian automotive and parts industry, we can demonstrate the relative impact of a firm's ownership as well as its market structure on an executive's attitudes toward foreign investment.

Sample and Research Procedures

The distribution of questionnaires and the collection of data for the study proceeded in two stages. The first involved executives in the automotive subsidiaries, and the second, executives in the automotive-parts companies. In the first stage, extensive cooperation was received from the Canadian subsidiaries of Chrysler, Ford, and General Motors.[2] Each corporation agreed to distribute 50 to 60 questionnaires through its intracompany mail service to executives in a number of functional work areas. The executives returned their completed questionnaires to the author by mail.

The second stage of the data collection involved executives from the Canadian automotive-parts sector in both U.S.-owned and Canadian-owned firms. Since many more companies, relative to the automotive subsidiaries, comprise the parts industry and since they are geographically spread across southern Ontario and are found, to a lesser extent, in other provinces as well, a mail survey was chosen as the major data-gathering technique for this phase of the data collection.

Two sources were used to obtain the names and addresses of executives in the automotive-parts firms. The first source was the 1975 *Directory of the Automotive Parts Manufacturers' Association (Canada).*[3] This source listed all of the association's member firms including the names of the firms' representatives and alternates to the association. The membership of the APMA can be considered a fairly representative sample of the Canadian automotive-parts suppliers as a whole. All of the representatives and alternates to the APMA from U.S.-owned and Canadian-owned automotive parts producers were sampled. Additional names and firms were sampled from the 1972 *Canadian Automotive Parts Directory* published by the government's Department of Industry, Trade, and Commerce.[4]

In total 617 executives representing 286 establishments were contacted. The three automotive subsidiaries distributed 173 questionnaires to their managerial personnel of which 71.7 percent or 124 were returned. Questionnaires were sent to 211 executives in 113 U.S.-owned parts firms and 254 executives in 169 Canadian-owned parts firms. The response rates for these two groups were, respectively, 30.8 percent or 65 respondents representing 48 companies and 30.5 percent or 71 respondents representing 66 companies. With all three groups combined, an aggregate response rate of 42.1 percent or 260 executives representing 117 firms was achieved.

The modal executive profile (see Table 5.1) that emerges from a consideration of the sample's characteristics is that of a middle-aged male with at least some university education from either a middle-class or, to a slightly lesser extent, working-class background. The executive is a Canadian citizen by birth who lives in the province of Ontario and who has voted in the federal and provincial elections prior to the survey. He more than likely is a member of the Progressive Conservative party and places himself along the conservative side of

TABLE 5.1. Biographical Data of Executive Sample

	Total Sample	Corporate Ownership U.S.-Owned Firms	Canadian-Owned Firms
Sex			
Male	100%	100%	100%
N	260	189	71
Age			
Mean	47.3 years	47.4 years	47.0 years
N^b	258	188	70
Education			
Some secondary	3.1%	1.6%	7.1%
Graduated secondary	13.5	12.7	15.7
Some university	29.7	29.1	31.4
Graduated university	31.3	33.3	25.7
Postgraduate	22.4	23.3	20.0
N^a	259	189	70
Social class origins			
Upper middle class[f]	17.4%	20.0%	10.3%
Middle class[g]	33.2	30.8	39.7
Working class[h]	48.2	48.7	47.1
Other	1.2	.5	2.9
N^e	253	185	68
Location			
Ontario	94.6%	97.9%	85.7%
Prairies	1.9	.5	5.7
Quebec	3.5	1.6	8.6
N^c	257	187	70
Canadian citizen by birth			
Yes	80.3%	83.1%	72.9%
No	19.7	16.9	27.1
N^a	259	189	70
Political party preference			
Yes	78.0%	76.7%	81.4%
No	22.0	23.3	18.6
N^a	259	189	70
Specific political party for those who stated a preference			
New Democratic	1.5%	2.1%	—
Liberal	32.0	34.4	26.3%
Progressive Conservative	62.6	58.9	71.9
Mixed[i]	3.9	4.8	1.8
N	203	146	57

(continued)

TABLE 5.1 (continued)

	Total Sample	Corporate Ownership	
		U.S.-Owned Firms	Canadian-Owned Firms
Vote in last federal election			
Yes	96.1%	96.8%	94.3%
No	3.9	3.2	5.7
N[a]	259	189	70
Vote in last provincial election			
Yes	93.8%	94.2%	92.9%
No	6.2	5.8	7.1
N[a]	259	189	70
Ideological self-categorization[j]			
Far left	—	—	—
Left-center	11.0%	10.7%	11.4%
Center	26.2	22.3	35.7
Right-center	62.1	66.1	51.4
Far right	.8	.5	1.4
Mean	4.7	4.8	4.6
N[d]	256	186	70

[a]Missing observations = 1.

[b]Missing observations = 2.

[c]Missing observations = 3.

[d]Missing observations = 4.

[e]Missing observations = 7.

[f]Father's profession: professional, top manager.

[g]Father's profession: self-employed businessman, governmental white-collar, nongovernment white-collar.

[h]Father's profession: nongovernmental blue-collar, farmer.

[i]Checked more than one of the above, indicating a preference for one party at the provincial level and another at the federal level. The above preferences should be taken as preferences at the federal level.

[j]Using a seven-point scale where 1 = far left and 7 = far right. Scale values of 2 and 3 are represented by the left-center category; scale values of 5 and 6, right-center; and 4, center.

the ideological spectrum. This profile is characteristic of executives from both U.S.-owned and Canadian-owned firms with relatively few minor differences.

Variable Measures

The variables in the conceptual framework were operationalized in the following manner:

1. *Ownership (OWNSHP)* is employed as a dummy variable in the analysis with U.S.-owned firms coded as 1 and Canadian-owned firms as 0.

2. *Market structure (MKT)* refers to the extent to which a company's products are manufactured for an export, relative to a domestic, market. Using the following scale, the executives were asked to indicate the market for their company's products: 1 = completely domestic market, 2 = mostly domestic market with some exports, 3 = mostly exports with some domestic market, 4 = completely exports. The sample does not include executives from firms that are solely export-oriented. MKT, therefore, takes only the first three values of the above scale.

3. *Frequency of transnational interaction (CONTACT)* refers to the frequency with which a Canadian executive interacts with U.S. businessmen: 1 = almost never, 2 = a few times a year, 3 = several times a year, 4 = a few times a month, 5 = once a week or more.

4. *International work responsibilities (IWR)* gauges the extent to which an executive's work responsibilities are geared to Canadian-U.S., relative to only Canadian, concerns: 1 = only domestic Canadian issues, 2 = primarily domestic Canadian issues, 3 = Canadian-U.S. issues and domestic Canadian issues receive roughly the same working time, 4 = primarily Canadian-U.S. issues related to exports, procurement, subsidiary operations, and so on.

5. *Required familiarity with U.S. firms (FAMLR)* reflects the extent to which a Canadian executive's business role requires familiarity with the activities of U.S. firms operating in Canada. The executives were asked to indicate the amount of familiarity with U.S. firms their job required on a 7-point scale where 1 = very little and 7 = very much.

6. *Corporate rank (RANK)* is an ordinal variable and refers to an executive's rank in the corporate hierarchy. The title of an executive's current position was used as an indicator of his corporate rank. A title of supervisor, engineer, sales representative, or superintendent was classified as lower management and coded as 1; a title of general manager, manager, or assistant manager was classified as middle management and coded as 2; and a title of president, vice-president, chairman of the board, director, secretary-treasurer, or comptroller was classified as upper management and coded as 3.

7. *Functional work areas* were coded using an effects coding procedure (Cohen and Cohen, 1975:188-195). This coding scheme was used in order to compare each functional work area with the entire set of work areas rather than with one selected work area, which would follow from a dummy coding procedure. In the multiple regression analyses that follow, "effects coding takes as its point of reference for each of the [work areas] *all* of the [work areas] taken as an equally weighted aggregate. The partial coefficients thus reflect the effect of 'eccentricity' of each [work area] relative to the others" (Cohen and Cohen, 1975:194). Six work areas are considered in the analyses: personnel (PERSONNEL); production (PRODUCTION); accounting and finance (ACCT/FIN); marketing, sales, and purchasing (MKT/SALES); organization and administration

TABLE 5.2. Effects Coding of Functional Work Areas

	Variable Names					
Work Areas	Personnel	Production	Acct/Fin	Mkt/Sales	Organi- zation	Exec Ldrshp
Personnel	1	0	0	0	0	0
Production	0	1	0	0	0	0
Accounting and finance	0	0	1	0	0	0
Marketing, sales, and purchasing	0	0	0	1	0	0
Organization and administration	0	0	0	0	1	0
Executive leadership	0	0	0	0	0	1
Other	-1	-1	-1	-1	-1	-1

(ORGANIZATION); and executive leadership (EXEC LDRSHP). Executives were assigned a value of 1 for their particular work area and a value of 0 for all others. Executives in a seventh category—that of "other," which includes advertising, communications and transportation, corporate legal responsibilities, and computer analysis—were assigned a value of -1 (as required by effects coding) and are not represented in the analyses. The effects coding scheme for the functional work areas is summarized in Table 5.2.

8. *Socioeconomic background (SES)* is employed in the analyses with father's occupation used as an indicator. This variable was dummy coded. Executives whose fathers held white-collar positions (professional, top manager, self-employed businessman, government white-collar, nongovernmental white-collar) were assigned a value of 1; those with fathers in blue-collar positions (nongovernmental blue-collar, farmer), a value of 0.

9. *Education (EDUC)* describes an executive's level of educational attainment: 1 = some elementary school, 2 = completed elementary school, 3 = some secondary school, 4 = graduated secondary school, 5 = some university, 6 = graduated university, 7 = postgraduate education.

10. *Age (AGE)* refers to an executive's age at the time of the survey.

Dimensions of Executive Foreign Investment Attitudes

Despite a climate of economic nationalism, the Canadian executives in the study do not perceive U.S. investment as Canada's most pressing problem

TABLE 5.3. General Executive Opinion on U.S. Investment in Canada

1. Most important issue facing Canada (1975–76):[d]

	Most important	Total mention[e]
Inflation	78.3%	96.5%
Taxation	6.6	41.1
Energy	4.3	50.8
English/French relations in Canada	3.9	22.9
Provincial/federal relations	3.5	18.6
Unemployment	1.6	42.6
Environment and pollution	.8	12.4
U.S. investment in Canada	.8	12.4
Government spending/ imposition of bilingualism[f]	.4	1.2
N[a]	258	

2. As you know, a lot of Canada's development has been financed by U.S. money. Do you think this has been beneficial to Canada in the past, in the present, and will continue to be so in the future?[g]

	Very beneficial	Uncertain	Very harmful	Mean	SD	N[a]
In the past	96.5%	.8%	2.7%	6.21	.94	258
In the present	74.9	16.7	8.5	5.24	1.23	258
In the future	51.5	12.8	35.7	4.40	1.75	258

3. What form of American investment in Canada would you personally prefer?[h]

Few or no conditions on American investment in our economy	9.7%
Equal participation with Canadian firms in mixed enterprises	36.2
Predominance of Canadian firms in mixed enterprises	41.2
Limit American investors to providing loans, credits, and/or licensing agreements	12.1
Elimination of all American investment in Canada	.8
N[b]	257

(continued)

TABLE 5.3 (continued)

4. Many people feel that the Canada-U.S. Automotive Trade Pact has been beneficial to overall Canadian well-being, while others feel that it has not worked out to Canada's advantage. What is your opinion?[g]

Very beneficial	81.6%
Uncertain	7.4
Very harmful	10.9
Mean	5.52
Standard deviation	1.41
N[c]	256

5. Would you like to see more "Trade Pacts" in other industries between Canada and the U.S.?[i]

Yes	37.2%
No	8.5
Depends on industry	51.2
No opinion	3.1
N[a]	258

Note: N = number of responses.

[a]Missing observations = 2.

[b]Missing observations = 3.

[c]Missing observations = 4.

[d]Adapted from Murray and LeDuc (1975a).

[e]Total of first, second, and third choices. Up to three responses were permitted.

[f]Added to questionnaire choices by four respondents.

[g]A 7-point scale was used. For the purposes of this table, very beneficial = 5, 6, 7; uncertain = 4; very harmful = 1, 2, 3. The higher the mean, the more beneficial an item is evaluated. Question 2 was adapted from Sigler and Goresky (1974).

[h]Adapted from Petras and Cook (1973a).

[i]Adapted from Murray and LeDuc (1976a).

(Table 5.3, Question 1). Inflation, taxation, energy, unemployment, and national unity (that is, English-French and provincial-federal relations) are all ranked higher than U.S. investment by the executives as the more important issues facing Canada. This primary concern with internal economic and political problems parallels general Canadian opinion as documented in a number of national surveys by Murray, LeDuc, and their colleagues (1975a, 1975b, 1976a, 1976b, 1976–77, 1978; Keenleyside, LeDuc, and Murray, 1976; LeDuc and Murray, 1977; Murray, 1973).

The question of economic nationalism did come into play, however, when the executives were asked directly about the impact of U.S. capital in Canada.

Overwhelmingly they mention its beneficial consequences for Canada in the past (Table 5.3, Question 2) but indicate a growing sense of uncertainty and harmfulness about such investment in the present and in the future. Although the executives would not like to see the elimination of U.S. investment altogether (Table 5.3, Question 3), very few on the other hand are willing to support its unfettered presence in the Canadian economy. Most would prefer joint ventures, preferably with Canadian firms in positions of majority control.

The Canada-U.S. Auto Pact has also been the subject of controversy in recent years (Beigie, 1970; Brunt, 1975), but the automotive and automotive-parts executives perceive it as being beneficial to Canada despite the fact of a declining trade balance in the parts subsector (Table 5.3, Question 4). However, the executives are not willing to support an unconditional extension of such trade pacts to other industrial sectors but prefer an industry-by-industry analysis before such agreements are negotiated (Table 5.3, Question 5).

On the whole, the executive opinions just reviewed—while not extremely nationalistic—do indicate a cautious and qualified assessment of U.S. investment and Canadian-U.S. economic relations.

Having discussed the general context of executive attitudes, we now turn to two sets of specific questions that were used to assess executive opinion on U.S. investment in Canada. These items are also used in the development of major dependent indices for the analyses that follow in the next section. The first set of items consisted of ten criteria for evaluating U.S. firms operating in Canada. These evaluational criteria, eight of which were originally used by Fayerweather (1972) in his cross-national study of elite attitudes toward foreign investment, are presented in Table 5.4. The Canadian executives and managers were asked to indicate their assessment of the importance of each of these criteria using a seven-point scale where the end-points were defined as "minor importance" and "major importance."

As shown in Table 5.4, the executives are much more concerned with the possible economic and industrial benefits of U.S. investment than with its impact on Canadian culture or control over national affairs. Nevertheless it should be noted that each of the criteria for evaluating U.S. firms was considered important by more than half—and in most cases, by more than two-thirds—of the executive sample.

These evaluation items were factor analyzed using an iterative principal-factors method, and the initial principal-factor matrix was rotated to an orthogonal solution, which is presented in Table 5.5. This procedure was followed to investigate possible underlying themes of the evaluative criteria and to reduce the number of items to a set of independent (orthogonal) dimensions which could be used as dependent variables in further analyses. A decision on the number of factors or dimensions to extract in the analysis was based on three criteria: (1) the general meaningfulness and interpretability of the factors, (2) the conventional criterion of eigenvalues (latent roots) greater than or equal to unity, and (3) Cattell's scree-test for the number of factors (Gorsuch, 1974:

TABLE 5.4. Executive Opinion on Criteria for Evaluating U.S. Firms in Canada

	Major Importance	Uncertain	Minor Importance	Mean	Standard Deviation	N[a]
1. Effect on Canadian national income[b]	91.4%	5.1%	3.6%	5.87	1.15	256
2. Benefits for Canadian workers	89.5	4.7	5.8	5.77	1.25	257
3. Effect on balance of payments	88.3	8.6	3.2	5.81	1.13	256
4. Industrial efficiency	85.9	9.8	4.3	5.84	1.22	256
5. Transfer of skills and technology	81.7	10.2	8.3	5.61	1.38	256
6. Opportunities for Canadian managers	78.6	10.5	10.9	5.49	1.46	257
7. Opportunities for Canadian investors	74.7	10.4	13.5	5.23	1.54	256
8. Control over national affairs	70.4	11.7	17.9	5.20	1.87	257
9. Changes in Canadian way of life	59.0	20.7	20.3	4.79	1.67	256
10. Role of Canada in the world	55.0	20.4	24.7	4.63	1.66	255

[a] Missing observations range from 3 to 5 per item.
[b] A seven-point scale was used for these items. For the purposes of this table, major importance = 5, 6, 7; uncertain = 4; minor importance = 1, 2, 3. The higher the mean, the more importance is attached to a certain criterion.

TABLE 5.5. Varimax Rotated Factor Matrix of Evaluative Criteria Items

Evaluative Criteria	Factor Loadings			
	I	II	III	h^2
Effect on Canadian national income	.788	.029	.082	.477
Benefits for Canadian workers	.664	.183	.161	.458
Effect on balance of payments	.616	.080	.102	.395
Opportunities for Canadian managers	.492	.155	.295	.366
Changes in Canadian way of life	.078	.845	.043	.380
Role of Canada in the world	.222	.573	.167	.354
Control over national affairs	.030	.472	.124	.252
Transfer of skills and technology	.070	.226	.868	.453
Industrial efficiency	.288	.081	.618	.424
Opportunities for Canadian investors	.312	.327	.352	.319
Eigenvalues (unrotated matrix)	3.50	1.53	1.15	
Percentage of total variance	35.0	15.3	11.5	61.8
Percentage of common variance	61.8	22.0	16.2	100.0
Factor variable name	EVAL1	EVAL2	EVAL3	

Note: N = 245.

152-156). A variable loading of .400 was used to place individual items on a particular dimension.

Three evaluative themes emerged in the analysis. The first dimension incorporates four of the initial ten criteria that refer to an evaluation of U.S. firms in terms of the socioeconomic benefits they provide: their effect on Canadian national income and balance of payments, and the benefits and opportunities they provide for Canadian workers and managers. The items that comprise the second factor refer to criteria for evaluating U.S. firms in terms of their impact on national sovereignty and culture. The third factor describes criteria for judging U.S. firms in relation to the industrial benefits they provide: transfer of skills and technology and industrial efficiency. These three dimensions of criteria for evaluating U.S. firms mirror not only general Canadian concerns and expectations (see Government of Canada, 1972) but also reflect concerns most host countries have expressed with respect to foreign investment within their national boundaries (Behrman, 1970; Fayerweather, 1972; LaPalombara and Blank, 1976; Vernon, 1971).

In addition to the evaluation items, the Canadian executives were also asked a number of specific questions related to the political, economic, and cultural consequences of U.S. investment in Canada. These questions, 12 of which were used in the Fayerweather study (1972) cited earlier, are presented in Table 5.6. Table 5.6 reveals that a sizable proportion of the Canadian executives evaluate the economic consequences of U.S. direct investment and its impact on control over national affairs in negative terms even though their overall evaluation is generally favorable.[5] However, in one economic area—the wages and working conditions in U.S. companies—U.S. firms are perceived as equal to if not better than Canadian companies.

With respect to cultural impact, U.S. firms fare much better. A majority of the executives feel that Canadian life is influenced by U.S. culture transmitted through the operations of U.S. firms but evaluate this influence favorably, particularly in the area of business culture and management methods. However, more so than on the other issues considered, a greater sense of uncertainty exists among many executives in their evaluation of the cultural impact of U.S. firms in Canada.

Finally, the role the multinational corporation has played in the extra-territorial application of parent-country laws has been a sore point and source of tension for Canada (Government of Canada, 1972; Leyton-Brown, 1974; Litvak and Maule, 1969; Rotstein and Lax, 1972) and for other countries, as well, which host foreign investors (Behrman, 1970; Blake and Walters, 1976). The executives in this study, however, are more likely to view the U.S. company in Canada as an autonomous corporate actor rather than as an extension of U.S. foreign and domestic policy.

The investment attitude items were also factor analyzed, using the same procedure followed for the evaluative criteria items, and the results are presented in Table 5.7. These results indicate that, for all practical purposes, the structure of executive opinion on U.S. investment is unidimensional. The various issues considered—economic and cultural impact, control, and extraterritoriality—did not separate into distinct opinion areas in the analysis. Almost all of the items loaded on the first factor with those items related to the issues of economic impact and control loading most highly. This finding reveals the relative consistency of executive opinion on U.S. investment. Executives who view U.S. firms in positive economic terms are also likely to evaluate the cultural impact of U.S. companies positively and to feel that such companies do not threaten Canadian ability to control national and industrial policies. Only wages and working conditions emerged as issues on the second factor independent of the rest.

Some additional observations on the results of the factor analyses warrant further consideration at this point. First, one evaluation item—opportunities for Canadian investors—and two investment opinion items—the relation of U.S. companies to U.S. policy and the degree to which U.S. companies affect the Canadian way of life—did not load significantly on any of the dimensions of the

TABLE 5.6. Executive Opinion on the Impact of U.S. Firms Operating in Canada

Overall Evaluation:[c]

1. In your opinion, what is the overall effect on Canada of the activities of American companies in Canada?
(Scale: Bad = 1, 2, 3; Uncertain = 4; Good = 5, 6, 7)

Bad	13.6%	Mean	5.26
Uncertain	3.9	Standard Deviation	1.28
Good	82.6	N^b	258

Economic Impact:

2. What do you believe is the net economic result of the operations of American companies in Canada?
(Scale: They give more than they take = 1, 2, 3; Give equals take = 4; They take more than they give = 5, 6, 7)

They give more than they take	32.0	Mean	4.25
Give equals take	21.2	Standard Deviation	1.49
They take more than they give	46.7	N^a	259

3. In relation to their economic contributions, the dividends, royalties, and other payments which American companies receive from their operations in Canada are:
(Scale: Too small = 1, 2, 3; Equal = 4; Too large = 5, 6, 7)

Too small	6.9%	Mean	4.73
Equal	39.1	Standard Deviation	1.05
Too large	54.3	N^b	258

Cultural Impact:

4. To what degree do you believe that the influence of American ways of life brought in by American companies changes the Canadian way of life?
(Scale: Small change = 1, 2, 3; Uncertain = 4; Large change = 5, 6, 7)

Small change	33.2%	Mean	4.24
Uncertain	11.2	Standard Deviation	1.62
Large change	55.7	N	260

5. Are the changes in way of life referred to in the above question good or bad?
(Scale: Very bad = 1, 2, 3; Uncertain = 4; Very good = 5, 6, 7)

Very bad	23.2%	Mean	4.27
Uncertain	35.1	Standard Deviation	1.11
Very good	41.7	N^a	259

(continued)

TABLE 5.6 (continued)

6. The general effect on Canada of changes in methods of management caused by the introduction of practices of American companies is:
(Scale: Very undesirable = 1, 2, 3; Uncertain = 4; Very desirable = 5, 6, 7)

Very undesirable	17.4%	Mean	4.72
Uncertain	19.7	Standard Deviation	1.34
Very desirable	62.9	N^a	259

The Issue of Control:

7. To what degree do you feel that the activities of American companies in Canada cause a loss of Canadian control over Canadian affairs?
(Scale: Major loss of control = 1, 2, 3; Uncertain = 4; Minor loss of control = 5, 6, 7)

Major loss of control	48.5%	Mean	3.89
Uncertain	12.3	Standard Deviation	1.61
Minor loss of control	39.3	N	260

8. What will be the result for Canada if American companies have greater control over policy decisions in Canadian industry?
(Scale: Bad = 1, 2, 3; Uncertain = 4; Good = 5, 6, 7)

Bad	76.9%	Mean	2.57
Uncertain	11.5	Standard Deviation	1.47
Good	11.6	N	260

9. Compared to Canadian firms, American companies operating in Canada act more frequently in ways contrary to Canadian national interests.
(Scale: Strongly disagree = 1, 2, 3; Uncertain = 4; Strongly agree = 5, 6, 7)

Strongly disagree	41.5%	Mean	4.00
Uncertain	15.4	Standard Deviation	1.71
Strongly agree	43.1	N	260

10. To what degree does the loyalty of an American manager in Canada to his own country pose a problem for Canadian policies?
(Scale: Minor problem = 1, 2, 3; Uncertain = 4; Major problem = 5, 6, 7)

Minor problem	50.4%	Mean	3.63
Uncertain	13.8	Standard Deviation	1.64
Major problem	35.8	N	260

(continued)

TABLE 5.6 (continued)

The Issue of Extraterritoriality:

11. On this continuum, where would you locate the nature of the American corporation operating in Canada?[d]
    (Scale: Instrument of parent government policy = 1, 2, 3; Uncertain = 4; Autonomous actor pursuing corporate objectives = 5, 6, 7)

Instrument of parent government policy	32.7%	Mean	4.43
Uncertain	11.5	Standard Deviation	1.71
Autonomous actor pursuing corporate objectives	55.8	N[a]	259

Wages and Working Conditions:

How do you believe the treatment of workers by American companies in Canada compares with that of Canadian firms with respect to wages and other working conditions?

12. Wages: (Scale: Much worse = 1, 2, 3; Equal = 4; Much better = 5, 6, 7)

Much worse	6.5%	Mean	4.55
Equal	49.6	Standard Deviation	.99
Much better	43.8	N	260

13. Other working conditions: (Scale: Much worse = 1, 2, 3; Equal = 4; Much better = 5, 6, 7)

Much worse	14.6%	Mean	4.35
Equal	48.5	Standard Deviation	.98
Much better	37.0	N	260

[a] Missing observations = 1.
[b] Missing observations = 2.
[c] All of the following items, except for Question 11, were adapted from Fayerweather (1972).
[d] Adapted from Carleton University's *Canadian International Image Study*. The questionnaire and interview schedule were provided to the author by Professor Peyton Lyon.

factor analyses. These results do not cast doubt on the substantive importance of or indicate lack of opinion on these items. Rather they suggest either the autonomy of these items vis-à-vis the dimensions that emerged in the analysis or the ambiguity or multiple interpretations that could be attached to these items by the respondents. These issues need clarification if the items are to be included in further research efforts.

Second, when the factors that emerged in the analyses are correlated, the low magnitudes of the coefficients (see Table 5.8) provide empirical support

TABLE 5.7. Varimax Rotated Factor Matrix of Investment Impact Questions

Question Number*	Question Category	Factor Loadings		
		I	II	h²
7	Issue of control	.711	.010	.456
3	Economic impact	-.703	-.152	.505
9	Issue of control	-.698	-.179	.472
1	Overall evaluation	.664	.195	.449
2	Economic impact	-.625	-.151	.402
8	Issue of control	.618	.228	.408
10	Issue of control	-.567	-.032	.317
5	Cultural impact	.563	.151	.340
6	Cultural impact	.495	.307	.321
13	Wages and working conditions	.208	.771	.425
12	Wages and working conditions	.032	.735	.357
11	Issue of extraterritoriality	.306	-.034	.116
4	Cultural impact	-.176	-.033	-.079
Eigenvalues (unrotated matrix)		4.75	1.45	
Percentage of total variance		36.5	11.2	47.7
Percentage of common variance		80.8	19.2	100.0
Factor variable name		IMPACT1	IMPACT2	

Note: N = 252.
*Question numbers refer to questions in Table 5.6.

TABLE 5.8. Correlation Matrix for Evaluative Criteria and Foreign Investment Opinion Dimensions

	EVAL1	EVAL2	EVAL3	IMPACT1	IMPACT2
EVAL1	—				
EVAL2	23	—			
EVAL3	.27	.28	—		
IMPACT1	.17	-.14	.15	—	
IMPACT2	.04	-.09	.06	.32	—

Note: N ranges from 247 to 256. See text for definition and measurement of variables, Tables 5.5 and 5.7.

108

for considering "criteria for evaluating the operations and contributions of American firms" as distinct from "opinions related to the consequences and impact of American firms in Canadian society." Further evidence of this distinction is suggested by the fact that even though the executives were able to express definite opinions on the control issue (Table 5.6), they did not consider this issue as important as socioeconomic and industrial benefits for evaluating U.S. subsidiaries (Table 5.4).

Given the results of the factor analyses, factor scores were computed for each executive, representing a weighted sum of standardized scores for the items that loaded on a particular attitudinal dimension. The larger an executive's factor score on a particular dimension, the more likely he is to consider certain criteria as important in judging the activities of U.S. firms in Canada or to evaluate the impact of U.S. corporations positively. These factor scores serve as dependent variables in the analyses that follow.

SOURCES OF FOREIGN INVESTMENT ATTITUDES: AN EMPIRICAL ASSESSMENT

Previously, it was proposed that a host-country executive's attitudes toward foreign investment could be considered functions of characteristics of his firm, job-related characteristics, and personal background. In addition, aspects of an executive's job—namely, frequency of transnational contact, international work responsibilities, and required knowledge of foreign firms—were considered to be determined by certain properties of the firm for which he works—a company's ownership and market structure—as well as by his rank and work area in the corporate organization. Using multiple regression techniques, we shall assess these propositions with data from the Canadian executive survey.[6] We shall focus first on characteristics of an executive's job and then turn to an analysis of foreign investment attitudes.

Frequency of Transnational Contact

As predicted, the results of the initial regression analyses (see Table 5.9, Equation 9-1) indicate that Canadian executives who work for the U.S. automotive and automotive-parts subsidiaries are more likely to interact frequently with U.S. businessmen than are their counterparts in Canadian-owned parts firms. It was also found that executives in firms involved in international trade are more likely to have frequent cross-national business contacts than are executives who work for firms oriented to a domestic market.[7]

In addition, the analyses reveal that ownership and market structure do not act independently of one another, since a significant interaction effect was found between these two variables. In other words, both the ownership and market structure of a firm must be known in order to predict accurately the expected

TABLE 5.9. Multiple Regression Statistics for Variables Predicting Frequency of Transnational Interaction (CONTACT)

Independent Variables	Eq. 9-1	Eq. 9-2	Eq. 9-3
OWNSHP	2.29[c]	1.65[b]	1.65[b]
	(1.04)	(.75)	(.74)
MKT	1.06[a]	.86[a]	.86[a]
	(.60)	(.49)	(.51)
OWNSHP X MKT	-.85[a]	-.59[c]	-.58[c]
	(-1.12)	(-.78)	(-.76)
IWR		.15[c]	.13[c]
		(.14)	(.13)
FAMLR		.11[a]	.11[a]
		(.21)	(.20)
RANK			-.00
			-.00
Work area			
PERSONNEL			-.07
			(-.02)
PRODUCTION			.03
			(.01)
ACCT/FIN			-.09
			(-.04)
MKT/SALES			-.04
			(-.02)
ORGANIZATION			-.02
			(-.01)
EXEC LDRSHP			.09
			(.05)
Intercept	1.59	1.12	1.18
Multiple R	.43	.50	.50
R^2	.19	.25	.25
Overall F	19.46	16.80	6.90
df	3/256	5/252	12/244
Significance level	<.001	<.001	<.001

Note: Unstandardized regression coefficients are presented in this table. Standardized regression coefficients are presented in parentheses. See text for definition and measurement of variables.

[a]Significant at the .001 level.
[b]Significant at the .01 level.
[c]Significant at the .05 level.

110

degree of cross-national contact for an individual executive. In order to determine the nature of this interactive relationship, the predicted values of transnational contact were calculated and are plotted in Figure 5.2.[8]

Figure 5.2 clearly illustrates that Canadian executives employed by U.S. subsidiaries are very similar to each other in their frequency of contact with U.S. businessmen, regardless of the extent to which their firms are engaged in either export or domestic markets. Canadian executives who work for Canadian-owned firms that manufacture primarily for export markets appear to be similar to their multinational counterparts where crossnational contact is concerned. The group that appears to have the least amount of business contact with Americans is, not unexpectedly, executives who work for Canadian-owned firms that manufacture solely for a domestic Canadian market.

FIGURE 5.2. Predicted Values of Frequency of Transnational Interaction (CONTACT)

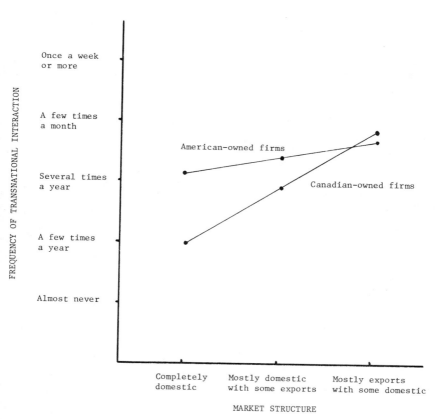

Consistent with the relationships posited in Figure 5.1, further analyses reveal that an executive position that involves international work responsibilities and requires familiarity with the operations of foreign firms also increases the possibility of transnational business contact—as indicated by the significant positive coefficients for these two variables (IWR and FAMLR) in Equation 9-2.

TABLE 5.10. Multiple Regression Statistics for Variables Predicting International Work Responsibilities (IWR)

Independent Variables	Eq. 10-1	Eq. 10-2
OWNSHP	1.92^b (.90)	2.09^a (.98)
MKT	$.86^a$ (.51)	$.83^a$ (.49)
OWNSHP X MKT	$-.84^a$ (-1.15)	$-.86^a$ (-1.18)
RANK		.20 (.11)
Work area PERSONNEL		$-.59^b$ (-.23)
PRODUCTION		$.71^a$ (.37)
ACCT/FIN		-.12 (-.05)
MKT/SALES		-.14 (-.08)
ORGANIZATION		-.18 (-.07)
EXEC LDRSHP		$.29^c$ (.16)
Intercept	.67	.11
Multiple R	.27	.47
R^2	.07	.22
Overall F	6.65	7.11
df	3/255	10/247
Significance level	<.001	<.001

See notes for Table 5.9.

FIGURE 5.3. Predicted Values of International Work Responsibilities (IWR)

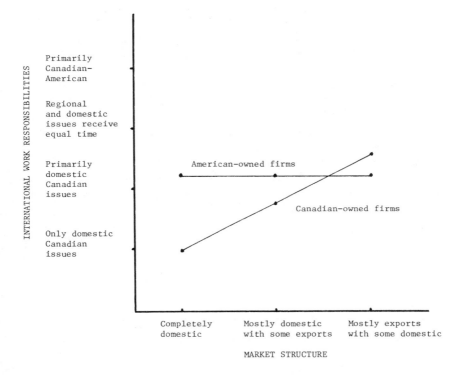

Nothing in the way of explained variance is gained, however, by considering an executive's rank or work area as predictors of transnational contact (Equation 9-3). It appears that such contact is determined more by corporate characteristics and other aspects of an executive's work experience.

International Work Responsibilities

Similar to the findings for transnational business contact, Canadian executives with international work responsibilities are found in the U.S.-owned auto and auto-parts firms and in both U.S.-owned and Canadian firms that manufacture for an export market (Table 5.10, Equation 10-1). As expected, a significant interaction between ownership and market structure was also found for international work responsibilities (see Equation 10-1).

When the values for international work responsibilities are plotted (Figure 5.3), the resulting configuration is very similar to that found for cross-national contact.[9] Multinational executives, irrespective of their firm's market structure, are very similar to each other in the international content of their work responsibilities. Executives in Canadian-owned firms with export activity are similar to multinational executives in this regard. The executives who have the least amount of international content in their work responsibilities, once again, are those in Canadian–owned firms that service only a domestic Canadian market.

Unlike transnational business contact, however, the inclusion of rank and work areas in determining international work responsibilities adds a significant 15 percent to the portion of variance explained by the corporate organizational variables alone (see Equation 10-2). In particular, executives in the work areas of production and executive leadership are substantially higher and personnel executives substantially lower in international work responsibilities than those in the other work areas considered. The standardized coefficients reveal that international work responsibilities, which involve Canadian-U.S. issues for our sample, can be found to a greater extent among production executives than among those in executive leadership positions. This finding clearly underscores the position of the production executive as an important transnational link in the North American automotive and automotive-parts industry.

Required Familiarity with Foreign Firms

At first glance, required familiarity with foreign firms follows the same pattern as that set for transnational business contact and international work responsibilities (Table 5.11, Equation 11-1). More familiarity with U.S. firms in Canada is required of executives in the subsidiaries of U.S. auto and auto-parts manufacturers and in firms that service an export market, although the latter variable (MKT) is not statistically significant. A significant interaction between ownership and market also emerged in this initial analysis.

Further analyses indicate, however, that the impact of corporate characteristics on required familiarity is channeled through an executive's international work responsibilities, given the significant positive coefficients for this variable (IWR) in Equations 11-2 and 11-3 and the parallel decline in the magnitudes and significance levels of the corporate variables in these equations. In other words, executive positions that involve international work responsibilities require greater knowledge about the operations of U.S. firms in Canada than those positions without such responsibilities, and these types of positions can be found primarily in U.S. auto and parts subsidiaries and in Canadian-owned parts suppliers that manufacture for an export market.

International work responsibilities were also shown, in previous analyses, to be concentrated among executives in the work areas of production and executive leadership and to be less prevalent among personnel executives. We can expect, therefore, to find job-related familiarity with U.S. firms distributed among these three work areas in particular.

TABLE 5.11. Multiple Regression Statistics for Variables Predicting Required Familiarity with Foreign Firms (FAMLR)

Independent Variables	Eq. 11-1	Eq. 11-2	Eq. 11-3
OWNSHP	3.16^b	2.51^c	1.88
	(.77)	(.61)	(.46)
MKT	.62	.34	.24
	(.19)	(.10)	(.07)
OWNSHP X MKT	-1.18^c	−.91	−.62
	(−.83)	(−.64)	(−.44)
IWR		$.30^b$	$.26^c$
		(.16)	(.13)
RANK			−.16
			(−.05)
Work area			
PERSONNEL			−.34
			(−.07)
PRODUCTION			.09
			(.02)
ACCT/FIN			−.43
			(−.10)
MKT/SALES			.38
			(.12)
ORGANIZATION			−.28
			(−.06)
EXEC LDRSHP			$.64^c$
			(.18)
Intercept	3.43	3.31	3.75
Multiple R	.17	.22	.29
R^2	.03	.05	.08
Overall F	2.41	3.26	6.57
df	3/255	4/253	10/246
Significance level	.067	.013	.025

See notes for Table 5.9.

Equation 11-3 also indicates that, relative to all other work areas, executives in top-level corporate positions (EXEC LDRSHP) are required to be more familiar with the operations of U.S. firms in Canada.[10] This result suggests that in addition to their international responsibilities—which are controlled for in Equation 11-3—other sources exist for corporate leadership's knowledge about U.S. firms. One such source is the nature of the Canadian automotive and automotive-parts industry itself. Since the industry is formally integrated on a continental basis, the decline or expansion of a subsidiary may affect not only several aspects of its own operations but also other U.S. subsidiaries as well as parts suppliers who are sensitive to the vitality of both Canadian and U.S. markets. In this type of interdependent environment, it is not surprising that top executives in both U.S.-owned and Canadian firms need to keep abreast of the range and conditions of U.S. subsidiary operations in Canada.

Foreign Investment Attitudes: Criteria for Evaluating U.S. Firms

Prior analyses revealed three dimensions of criteria for evaluating U.S. firms in Canada: socioeconomic benefits they may provide, industrial benefits, and impact on national sovereignty and culture. The executives' factor scores for each of these dimensions were regressed on the corporate, job, and background variables designated in Figure 5.1, the results of which are presented in Tables 5.12, 5.13, and 5.14.

As shown in Table 5.13 (Equations 12-2, 12-3, and 12-4), neither job-related nor personal background characteristics serve to differentiate between executives in terms of the importance of socioeconomic benefits as criteria for evaluating U.S. firms. Rather, corporate-level characteristics were found to be the important variables (Equation 12-1). The significant coefficient for ownership indicates that executives in U.S.-owned auto and auto-parts firms attach more importance to socioeconomic benefits than do those in Canadian-owned firms. This finding is qualified, however, by the significant interaction between corporate ownership and market structure. The nature of this interaction can be seen in Figure 5.4 where the predicted values for Equation 12-1 are plotted. As illustrated in this figure, major concern with socioeconomic benefits that U.S. firms may provide can be found among those executives in U.S.-owned parts firms supplying a domestic Canadian market, most likely the U.S. auto subsidiaries. The least concerned are those executives in Canadian-owned parts firms that also produce for a domestic market. It appears, therefore, that Canadian executives in U.S. subsidiaries, in general, and those in subsidiaries tied to a domestic market, in particular, attach greater priority than do executives in Canadian-owned firms to such criteria as income, workers' benefits, opportunities for Canadian managers, and the impact of U.S. firms on Canada's balance of payments—items that comprise the socioeconomic benefits dimension.

TABLE 5.12. **Multiple Regression Statistics for Variables Predicting the Importance of "Socioeconomic Benefits" as Criteria for Evaluating U.S. Firms in Canada (EVAL1)**

Independent Variables	Eq. 12-1	Eq. 12-2	Eq. 12-3	Eq. 12-4	Eq. 12-5
OWNSHP	1.42^c				1.25
	(.74)				(.65)
MKT	.31				.25
	(.20)				(.16)
OWNSHP X MKT	$-.51^c$				-.47
	(-.76)				(-.71)
CONTACT		.01	.02		-.00
		(.01)	(.02)		(-.00)
IWR		.09	.12		.09
		(.10)	(.13)		(.10)
FAMLR		.30	.05		.05
		(.06)	(.10)		(.10)
RANK			.01		.03
			(.00)		(.02)
Work area:					
PERSONNEL			.14		.15
			(.06)		(.07)
PRODUCTION			-.15		-.11
			(-.09)		(-.06)
ACCT/FIN			.20		.23
			(.10)		(.11)
MKT/SALES			-.02		-.06
			(-.01)		(-.04)
ORGANIZATION			-.12		-.14
			(-.05)		(-.06)
EXEC LDRSHP			-.22		-.21
			(-.13)		(-.13)
SES				-.04	.01
				(-.02)	.00
EDUC				.01	-.03
				(.01)	(-.04)
AGE				.01	-.00
				(.02)	(-.01)
Intercept	-.81	-.43	-.54	-.11	-.85
Multiple R	.17	.13	.21	.03	.25
R^2	.03	.02	.04	.00	.06
Overall F	2.42	1.45	1.07	.06	.91
df	3/242	3/240	10/232	3/240	16/224
Significance level	.067	.229	.388	.983	.563

See notes for Table 5.9.

TABLE 5.13. Multiple Regression Statistics for Variables Predicting the Importance of "Industrial Benefits" as Criteria for Evaluating U.S. Firms in Canada (EVAL3)

Independent Variables	Eq. 13-1	Eq. 13-2	Eq. 13-3	Eq. 13-4	Eq. 13-5
OWNSHP	.29				.22
	(.14)				(.11)
MKT	−.06				.02
	(−.03)				(.01)
OWNSHP X MKT	−.13				−.12
	(−.19)				(−.16)
CONTACT		−.11	−.12		−.11
		(−.12)	(−.13)		(−.12)
IWR		.04	.07		.07
		(.04)	(.07)		(.07)
FAMLR		.09[b]	.09[c]		.08[c]
		(.18)	(.18)		(.16)
RANK			.02		.01
			(.01)		(.00)
Work area:					
PERSONNEL			.03		.05
			(.01)		(.02)
PRODUCTION			−.15		−.16
			(−.08)		(−.09)
ACCT/FIN			.14		.15
			(.06)		(.07)
MKT/SALES			.08		.09
			(.05)		(.05)
ORGANIZATION			−.31		−.33
			(−.13)		(−.14)
EXEC LDRSHP			.01		−.00
			(.00)		(−.00)
SES				−.01	−.13
				(−.05)	(−.07)
EDUC				.09	.09
				(.11)	(.10)
AGE				−.00	−.00
				(−.01)	(−.04)
Intercept	.20	−.10	−.15	−.40	−.36
Multiple R	.10	.20	.25	.12	.28
R^2	.01	.04	.06	.01	.08
Overall F	.76	3.17	1.48	1.06	1.20
df	3/242	3/240	10/232	3/240	16/224
Significance level	.520	.025	.149	.365	.267

See notes for Table 5.9.

TABLE 5.14. Multiple Regression Statistics for Variables Predicting the Importance of "Impact on National Sovereignty and Culture" as Criterion for Evaluating U.S. Firms in Canada (EVAL2)

Independent Variables	Eq. 14-1	Eq. 14-2	Eq. 14-3	Eq. 14-4	Eq. 14-5
OWNSHP	.29				.49
	(.15)				(.25)
MKT	.27				.27
	(.17)				(.17)
OWNSHP X MKT	−.13				−.19
	(−.19)				(−.28)
CONTACT		.03	.03		.01
		(.03)	(.03)		(.01)
IWR		.03	.04		.01
		(.03)	(.05)		(.01)
FAMLR		−.18	−.00		.02
		(−.04)	(−.01)		(.04)
RANK			−.08		−.02
			(−.05)		(−.01)
Work area:					
PERSONNEL			.38[c]		.47[c]
			(.16)		(.20)
PRODUCTION			.04		.00
			(.02)		(.00)
ACCT/FIN			.04		.03
			(.02)		(.01)
MKT/SALES			−.17		−.16
			(−.11)		(−.10)
ORGANIZATION			.25		.18
			(.11)		(.08)
EXEC LDRSHP			−.11		−.07
			(−.06)		(−.04)
SES				−.03	−.06
				(−.02)	(−.04)
EDUC				−.12[c]	−.14[c]
				(−.15)	(−.17)
AGE				−.01	−.01
				(−.13)	(−.13)
Intercept	−.65	−.11	.02	1.29	.70
Multiple R	.12	.06	.23	.17	.30
R^2	.01	.00	.05	.03	.09
Overall F	1.13	.25	1.30	2.38	1.40
df	3/242	3/240	10/232	3/240	16/224
Significance level	.336	.865	.230	.070	.143

See notes for Table 5.9.

119

**FIGURE 5.4.   Predicted Values of Importance of "Socioeconomic Benefits"
as Criteria for Evaluating U.S. Firms in Canada (EVAL1)**

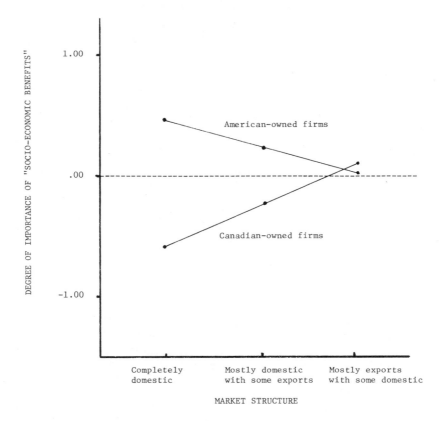

The industrial benefits of U.S. firms—transfer of skills and technology, industrial efficiency—are high-priority criteria among executives whose positions require familiarity with the operations of U.S. firms in Canada (see Table 5.13, Equations 13-2, 13-3, and 13-5). Familiarity, in turn, depends on an executive's international work responsibilities, which again brings us back to executives in U.S.-owned and Canadian export-oriented firms and also to those executives in the work areas of production and executive leadership. Knowing more about U.S. firms may inform an executive not only of how much such firms can provide but also of the gap between how much they can and how much they actually do provide in the way of industrial benefits. This interpretation was nicely illustrated in an interview with an auto-subsidiary vice-president who lauded the parent corporation's plan to build a new Canadian truck-manufacturing plant while at the same time indicating a sense of frustration about the subsidiary's minimal research and development activities.

Finally, the extent to which U.S. firms should be accountable for their impact on Canadian national sovereignty and culture is a concern that is inversely related to an executive's level of education (see Table 5.14, Equations 14-4 and 14-5). In other words, the more education an executive has, the less he is concerned about matters of sovereignty and control. Neither corporate nor job-related characteristics were found to be influential in this regard (Equations 14-1 and 14-2). In addition, personnel executives were found to be more concerned about sovereignty issues than were executives in other work areas (Equations 14-3 and 14-5). Reasons for the uniqueness of this group are not readily apparent from the available data. We might conjecture, however, that the seemingly nationalist stance of personnel executives may be due to the fact that their positions require the least amount of transnational business contact, international work responsibilities, and familiarity with U.S. firms relative to other corporate work areas. Personnel executives, as a result, would be less involved in international business issues and more insulated from sources of influence and information that might mitigate nationalist sentiments. This interpretation is only tentative at this point, however, and needs to be examined further.

Foreign Investment Attitudes: Evaluating the Impact of U.S. Firms

In addition to criteria that should be applied in evaluating U.S. firms, two dimensions emerged in previous analyses that gauge the actual opinions of executives on U.S. firms operating in Canada: the socioeconomic impact of U.S. firms in Canada and the extent to which they infringe on Canadian control and national interests, and the wages and working conditions of U.S. firms relative to Canadian companies. As in the analysis of the criteria dimensions, the executives' factor scores for these two dimensions were used as dependent variables in a series of regression analyses with the corporate, job, and background characteristics as independent variables.

The initial results in Table 5.15 (Equation 15-1) indicate that executives in U.S.-owned automotive and automotive-parts firms evaluate the socioeconomic and control impact of U.S. firms more favorably than do those in Canadian-owned firms. Executives in export-oriented firms are also more favorable to U.S. investment than those in firms that supply a domestic market. The significant interaction term for ownership and market structure in Equation 15-1 indicates that the locus of support for U.S. investment is found in U.S.-owned and Canadian export-oriented firms, with the least amount of support being generated from executives in Canadian-owned firms that service a domestic market. Further analyses (Equations 15-2, 15-3, and 15-5), however, provide strong support for international work responsibilities as the link between favorable attitudes toward U.S. firms and the type of firm for which an executive works. In addition, executives in production and executive leadership positions can be expected

TABLE 5.15. Multiple Regression Statistics for Variables Predicting Attitudes toward U.S. Investment in Canada: Evaluation of Socioeconomic and Control Issues (IMPACT1)

Independent Variables	Eq. 15-1	Eq. 15-2	Eq. 15-3	Eq. 15-4	Eq. 15-5
OWNSHP	1.62[b]				.92
	(.77)				(.43)
MKT	.53[c]				.30
	(.31)				(.17)
OWNSHP X MKT	−.65[c]				−.37
	(−.90)				(−.51)
CONTACT		.04	.03		−.01
		(.04)	(.04)		(−.01)
IWR		.24[a]	.25[a]		.24[a]
		(.25)	(.26)		(.24)
FAMLR		.02	.01		−.00
		(.03)	(.03)		(−.00)
RANK			.15		.18
			(.09)		(.11)
Work area:					
PERSONNEL			.04		−.01
			(.02)		(−.01)
PRODUCTION			−.05		−.01
			(−.03)		(−.01)
ACCT/FIN			−.11		−.10
			(−.05)		(−.05)
MKT/SALES			.07		.07
			(.04)		(.04)
ORGANIZATION			−.21		−.18
			(−.09)		(−.07)
EXEC LDRSHP			−.08		−.07
			(−.04)		(−.04)
SES				−.03	.01
				(−.02)	(.01)
EDUC				.14[c]	.11[c]
				(.16)	(.13)
AGE				−.00	−.01
				(−.01)	(−.04)
Intercept	−1.22	−.85	−1.19	−.67	−2.10
Multiple R	.17	.27	.30	.16	.35
R^2	.03	.07	.09	.03	.12
Overall F	2.49	6.19	2.36	2.03	1.90
df	3/242	3/240	10/232	3/240	16/224
Significance level	.061	<.001	.011	.110	.021

See notes for Table 5.9.

122

TABLE 5.16. Multiple Regression Statistics for Variables Predicting Attitudes toward U.S. Investment in Canada: Evaluation of Wages and Working Conditions (IMPACT2)

Independent Variables	Eq. 16-1	Eq. 16-2	Eq. 16-3	Eq. 16-4	Eq. 16-5
OWNSHP	-.31				-.19
	(-.16)				(-.10)
MKT	.11				.14
	(.07)				(.09)
OWNSHP X MKT	.17				.12
	(.25)				(.18)
CONTACT		.39	.29		-.03
		(.05)	(.03)		(-.03)
IWR		.04	.04		.03
		(.04)	(.04)		(.03)
FAMLR		-.06^c	-.05		-.06
		(-.13)	(-.12)		(-.13)
RANK			.08		.10
			(.05)		(.06)
Work area:					
PERSONNEL			.46^c		.29^c
			(.20)		(.13)
PRODUCTION			.18		.01
			(.01)		(.01)
ACCT/FIN			-.21		-.24
			(-.10)		(-.12)
MKT/SALES			-.15		-.10
			(-.10)		(-.07)
ORGANIZATION			-.19		-.07
			(-.08)		(-.03)
EXEC LDRSHP			-.05		.07
			(-.03)		(.04)
SES				-.07	-.09
				(-.04)	(-.05)
EDUC				.14^b	.15^b
				(.18)	(.18)
AGE				.01	.01
				(.09)	(.07)
Intercept	-.39	.03	-.11	-1.17	-1.42
Multiple R	.17	.13	.23	.17	.32
R^2	.03	.02	.05	.03	.10
Overall F	2.48	1.36	1.33	2.46	1.60
df	3/242	3/240	10/232	3/240	16/224
Significance level	.061	.257	.213	.064	.071

See notes for Table 5.9.

123

to be especially supportive of U.S. investment due to their international work responsibilities.

Further, an executive's level of education also appears to influence his evaluation of U.S. investment. The positive coefficient for education in Equation 15-4 implies that the more education an executive has the more likely he is to evaluate the operations of U.S. firms in Canada positively.

An executive's evaluation of the wages and working conditions of U.S. firms was also found to be a function of his level of education; that is, more positive evaluations were associated with higher levels of educational attainment (Table 5.16; Equations 16-4 and 16-5). With increased education an executive gains occupational mobility. He may have worked for both U.S. and Canadian companies in his career and thus may have acquired some basis for comparison (63 percent of the executives in the sample have worked for two or more companies exclusive of the firms in which they are currently employed). We must not rule out the possibility, however, that since education appears to be negatively associated with nationalist sentiment, an executive's positive evaluation of the wages and working conditions of U.S. firms may be a spillover from favorable attitudes toward such firms in general.

The results in Table 5.16 (Equations 16-3 and 16-5) also indicate that personnel executives are particularly favorable in their evaluation of the wages and working conditions of U.S. firms. Even though their positions may require less familiarity with U.S. firms in general, we would expect wages and working conditions to be areas of particular knowledge and expertise among personnel executives.

One additional aspect of the findings in Table 5.16 needs to be mentioned at this point. In Equation 16-2—where only job-related characteristics are considered—a significant effect for familiarity with U.S. firms was found. However, the significance of this variable (FAMLR) becomes negligible when executive work areas are controlled for in Equations 16-3 and 16-5.

Summary

An overview of the research findings is provided below. A summary listing of the results can be found in Table 5.17.

1. In our initial concern with the nature of an executive's work experience, *frequent contact with U.S. businessmen* was found primarily among Canadian executives in the subsidiaries of auto and auto-parts firms and among executives in Canadian-owned parts firms that are extensively involved in international trade. The extent to which an executive's position involves international work responsibilities and requires familiarity with the operations of U.S. firms in Canada serve as additional, job-related sources of transnational business contact. Although executives in various work areas differ in their frequency of transnational business interaction, work area was not as important as corporate and job-related characteristics in determining such contact.

TABLE 5.17. Summary of Research Findings

Issue Area	Level of Findings and Significant Variables	Direction of Findings
I. Characteristics of Executive Position		
1. Transnational business contact	Corporate characteristics Ownership Market structure Ownership/market interaction	 U.S. firms Export-oriented
	Job-related characteristics International work responsibilities Required familiarity with foreign firms	 Positive Positive
2. International work responsibilities	Corporate characteristics Ownership Market structure Ownership/market interaction	 U.S. firms Export-oriented
	Work area Personnel Production Executive leadership	 Negative Positive Positive
3. Required familiarity with foreign firms	Job-related characteristics International work responsibilities	 Positive
	Work area Executive leadership	 Positive
II. Criteria for Evaluating U.S. firms		
1. Socioeconomic benefits	Corporate characteristics Ownership Ownership/market interaction	 U.S. firms
2. Industrial benefits	Job-related characteristics Required familiarity with foreign firms	 Positive
3. National sovereignty and culture	Work area Personnel	 Positive
	Personal background characteristics Level of educational attainment	 Negative
III. Foreign Investment Attitudes		
1. Socioeconomic and control impact	Job-related characteristics International work responsibilities	 Positive
	Personal background characteristics Level of educational attainment	 Positive
2. Wages and working conditions of U.S. firms	Work area Personnel	 Positive
	Personal background characteristics Level of educational attainment	 Positive

2. *International work responsibilities* were also found among executives in U.S.-owned subsidiaries and in Canadian export-oriented companies. In addition, personnel executives were significantly lower and executives in production and executive leadership significantly higher in international work responsibilities than their counterparts in other work areas, irrespective of the type of firm for which they worked.

3. The extent to which an executive's position requires *familiarity with the operations of U.S. firms in Canada* depends on the international content of his work responsibilities. International work responsibilities, then, play a mediating role between corporate organizational variables and work areas, on the one hand, and required familiarity with U.S. firms, on the other. Executive leadership roles, particularly, were found to require more familiarity than the other work areas considered in the research.

4. *Socioeconomic benefits* were cited as important criteria for evaluating U.S. firms in Canada more by executives in U.S.-owned subsidiaries than by those in Canadian-owned firms, in general. In particular, executives in U.S. parts subsidiaries that manufacture for a domestic market were the most concerned about socioeconomic benefits while those in Canadian parts firms that service a similar market were the least concerned.

5. Executives whose positions require more familiarity with the operations of U.S. firms are more likely to consider *industrial benefits* as important criteria for evaluating U.S. firms than those whose jobs require little knowledge about U.S. investment.

6. The *impact of U.S. firms on Canadian national sovereignty and culture* is an evaluative criterion raised more by personnel executives than by those in other work areas. Level of educational attainment is also important here—highly educated executives being less concerned about national sovereignty and cultural impact than others.

7. Executives with international work responsibilities are more *favorable toward U.S. investment (on socioeconomic and control issues)* than those with less international content to their job responsibilities. Again, it should be recalled that internationally oriented executives are employees primarily of U.S. subsidiaries and Canadian export-oriented firms and are found especially in the work areas of production and executive leadership for our sample. The analysis of this issue area also revealed that highly educated executives are more positive toward U.S. firms in Canada.

8. Personnel executives and more highly educated executives evaluate the *wages and working conditions* of U.S. firms as equal to if not better than those of Canadian companies.

THE RESEARCH FINDINGS IN PERSPECTIVE

Without further investigation, it would be hasty to overgeneralize from the results of the present research. However, several aspects of the research findings corroborate and, at the same time, suggest modifications in arguments made by Canadian nationalists regarding U.S. investment. The findings also indicate directions for further research on host-country executive attitudes toward foreign investment in general.

Foreign Investment Attitudes and the Canadian Nationalist Argument

In recent years, Canadians have registered concern not only about the amount of control U.S. corporations exert over sectors of their economy but also about the role U.S. multinationals play in increasing Canada's dependence on the United States. Nationalist critics maintain that Canada's dependent status is not only externally imposed but also furthered by internal social forces (Clement, 1975; Levitt, 1970). One such force is the existence of a managerial class that represents, supports, and benefits from the interests of U.S. multinationals in Canada. According to the critics' argument, this class is composed of executives who work either for U.S.-owned subsidiaries or for Canadian firms that are dependent on the operations of U.S. firms.

The research presented in this study supports one major premise of the critics' argument. If we consider the socioeconomic impact of U.S. firms on Canada and their impact on Canadian national control, we find that Canadian executives who work for U.S. auto and auto-parts subsidiaries are relatively favorable in their evaluation of these issues. Limits to the critics' argument, however, are also apparent from the research findings. Not all executives in the Canadian-owned parts firms—whose firms are dependent on the auto industry and who would also supposedly favor U.S. investment—are as favorably inclined as their subsidiary counterparts. Only those executives in Canadian parts firms that manufacture products for a regional market (that is, international trade activity) are similar to subsidiary executives in their positive evaluation of U.S. investment. Ownership *and* market structure emerge as the two interrelated variables necessary for the prediction of executive attitudes. Further debate and discussion, then, must be ready to address issues surrounding international business (or international capitalism) that includes U.S.-owned as well as Canadian "international" firms.

The research evidence also suggests that functional work areas must be considered in determining the locus of favorable attitudes toward U.S. investment. International work responsibilities, which were found to be the immediate precursors of positive attitudes toward U.S. firms in Canada, not only were linked to a firm's ownership and market structure but also were found to a greater extent among production and top-level executives and to a lesser extent among personnel executives. We would expect, therefore, that foreign investment attitudes would vary accordingly. Thus, it is not executives as a group but a group of executives in particular work areas with international work responsibilities who are the important transnational links in the chain of dependence.

In addition, the significance of an executive's international work responsibilities and required familiarity with U.S. firms at various junctures of the research underscores the importance of job-related characteristics as mediators between macro-level corporate characteristics and micro-level foreign investment attitudes. What is indicated with these findings—but is beyond the scope of the present study—is the development of a critical theory of class in conjunction with a critical theory of organization to describe the crucial aspects of an executive's job-related activities that are in line with the interests of foreign investment. We might ask, for example, what particular interests or class identifications are developed with international work responsibilities, irrespective of a firm's ownership or market structure, which lead an executive to look favorably on various aspects of foreign investment.

Additional observations are worth noting at this point. In considering criteria for evaluating the operations of U.S. firms in Canada, we found more importance attached to the socioeconomic benefits such firms may provide among executives in U.S.-owned and Canadian export-oriented firms. Industrial benefits were cited as important criteria by executives whose jobs required familiarity with the operations of U.S. firms. Such familiarity was found to hinge on an executive's international work responsibilities, which lead, once again, to executives in U.S. subsidiaries, in Canadian export-oriented firms, and those in production and executive leadership roles. It appears, then, that these executives not only are more favorable to U.S. investment but also demand more from it.

The findings also indicate that a Canadian executive's educational background has an impact on his foreign investment attitudes. Highly educated executives are less concerned about the impact of U.S. investment on national sovereignty and culture. They are more favorable than those with less education in their evaluation of U.S. investment, in general, and of wages and working conditions of U.S. subsidiaries, in particular. Several reasons for these findings can be suggested. It may be that most of the executives have been educated in U.S. universities, which would account for their favorable attitudes. However, close to 80 percent of the executives were, in fact, educated in Canadian universities. Nevertheless, most Canadian business schools—86 percent of the executives majored in business or engineering—are strongly influenced by U.S. methods and ideas, which could predispose executives favorably toward U.S. investment. In addition, for our sample, education is inversely related to an executive's age ($r = -.29$). Thus, the younger, highly educated executive's favorable attitudes may be indicators of a perception of U.S. multinationals as instrumental to his occupational mobility and material gain. It appears, then, that there are forces generated from within Canadian society, unrelated to corporate affiliation or job-related experiences, which increase the receptiveness of Canadian executives to U.S. investment—a point that should be addressed in further research.

Limitations of the Findings and
Suggestions for Further Research

The research findings must also be considered with a view to their limitations. In the analyses of the evaluative criteria and investment impact dimensions, significant effects emerged for a number of the variables presented in the analytical framework (see Figure 5.1), but these variables accounted for a relatively small portion of the variance in the dependent variables. The findings were strongest for the investment impact dimensions in which between 10 percent and 12 percent of the variance, overall, was explained by the variables considered, and weakest for the evaluative criteria dimensions in which between 6 percent and 9 percent of the variance was explained. Although these percentages are reasonable for attitude research, they do create some concern about measurement error variance. This would be the case particularly for the evaluative criteria and investment impact indices since, as shown in Tables 5.5 and 5.7, they are composed of attitude items with low to moderate communalities. Thus, the development of more reliable indices, in which random error variance is reduced as much as possible, is needed. Estimates of explained variance may also be increased by the development of better indicators for such variables as international work responsibilities and required familiarity with the operations of foreign firms. Knowing in more detail what types of responsibilities are involved and what kind of knowledge is required may allow us to account more precisely for certain dimensions of foreign investment attitudes.

The problem of self-selection must also be considered. Executives may choose to work for a particular company—a prestigious multinational subsidiary, for example—because it represents certain values and orientations already acquired through channels of influence and socialization unrelated to business. Thus, we may find differences in attitudes between executives in different types of firms due to a prior self-selection process rather than to job-related variables such as international work responsibilities and required familiarity with foreign firms. Although there is no way to dismiss this problem conclusively in the present research, informal interviews with a number of executives indicated that their decision to work for a certain firm was based on practical reasons related to salary, benefits, and availability of employment rather than to ideological concerns. In order to address the issue of bias and self-selection more concretely, it would be necessary to study executives from their initial entrance into a firm and to explore their reasons for choosing a particular firm. It would be interesting to assess their attitudes toward foreign investment at this initial point and to follow any changes that may occur through various points in time.

A replication of the research in other sectors of the Canadian economy would also seem to be appropriate. The Canadian automotive and automotive-parts industry in some ways represents a special case since it is formally integrated on a regional basis. Production, for example, has usually been thought of as a particularly domestic area. It is interesting, therefore, that executives in this work area were found to have significantly more international work responsibilities than those in most other work areas. This finding is a reflection of the reorganization of the 1965 Auto Pact after which Canadian executives in production found themselves much more involved in Canadian-U.S. issues than they had been previously, particularly in maintaining production schedules for auto lines and parts designated for the United States. Executives in other work areas became more responsible for the Canadian end of their operations and, as a result, more oriented to the Canadian domestic market. Research in other industries and sectors (that is, resource extractive and service in addition to manufacturing) may reveal work areas, different from those in the auto and parts industry, with significant international work responsibilities. Such responsibilities were found to be particularly important links to favorable attitudes toward U.S. investment in Canada. Research in other sectors should also indicate which aspects of the framework (Figure 5.1) can be generalized across industrial sectors, as well as those relationships that are specific to a given industry.

Finally, the relationship between attitudes and behavior would be an especially important topic to pursue. To what extent, we may ask, are foreign investment attitudes related to executives' actions as corporate decision makers and citizens of a particular nation? How do executives make national policy makers aware of their opinions on foreign investment, and to what extent do executive opinions actually filter into the policy-making process? What is the effect, if any, of executive foreign investment attitudes on corporate policy—in both foreign-owned subsidiaries and independent national firms? Answers to these and other questions dealing with the relationship between attitudes and actions may provide some insight into the future evolution of international business and the linkages between business and governmental policy making.

In conclusion, the research findings suggest several important issues that should set the tenor for further discussion of foreign investment attitudes among host-country executives. In the introduction to this study, it was pointed out that several research efforts had focused on attitudinal differences between executives in foreign-owned and domestic firms with inconclusive results. The findings of the present research indicate that differences may emerge when a company's market structure is taken into account. Thus, a wider perspective is mandated in further studies of executive attitudes toward foreign investment, one that focuses on aspects of international, rather than just multinational, business. The findings also indicate that a sharper perspective should be taken to identify executives with certain corporate functions and job-related experiences. The inclusion of these variables may lead to an understanding of how corporate characteristics are translated into foreign investment attitudes, which functional work areas are more sensitive than others to certain concerns, and what aspects of functional work areas—such as, international work responsibilities or required familiarity with foreign firms—may be important in explaining an executive's attitudes. Finally, the findings indicate that sources external to corporate and job-related characteristics—education was particularly important for our sample—must also be incorporated into further explorations of executive foreign investment attitudes. In sum, our initial proposition that host-country executive attitudes toward foreign investment must be assessed from the combined perspective of corporate, job, and personal background characteristics has proved to be a useful heuristic in guiding the present research. Further theoretical elaboration and empirical research should prove fruitful from this vantage point.

NOTES

1. Excellent reviews of this literature are provided in Biersteker (1978) and Hanson (1976).

2. American Motors (Canada) Ltd. was also contacted to participate in the study. However, after an initially favorable response and the delivery of questionnaires to be distributed to the Canadian headquarters office, the corporation reneged on its initial commitment. The minor level of operations and the fact that the other automotive corporations had participated were cited as reasons for the refusal.

3. This Directory was provided by Patrick Lavelle, president of the Automotive Parts Manufacturers' Association (Canada), hereafter referred to as the APMA.

4. The 1972 Directory was used since the 1975 version unfortunately was not available at the time of the study. The use of the 1972 version, however, introduced the possibility that executives either had left the firms or had changed positions and work areas by early 1976 when the questionnaires were mailed. There was no way to prevent this problem, and the author did receive an indication that more questionnaires were undelivered than those that were returned as such. Thus, to a certain extent the response rate is a conservative estimate of those executives who had returned the completed questionnaire in relation to those who actually received it.

5. A point about the internal consistency of executive responses can be made here. Note that the mean and standard deviation for the overall evaluation item, Question 1, Table 5.6, are practically identical to the executives' evaluations of present U.S. capital in Canada in Question 2, Table 5.3.

6. A summary listing of variables used in these analyses can be found in Appendix 5.A.

7. This analysis and all of the other analyses that follow were also performed including corporate size—using number of employees as an indicator—in the estimations, along with its interaction with the ownership and market variables. In all cases, nonsignificant, zero effects were found for the size variable.

8. Calculated from Equation 9-3 with all other variables held constant.

9. Calculated from Equation 10-2 with all other variables held constant.

10. It is possible that the statistical nonsignificance of ownership (OWNSHP) in Equation 11-3 may be an artifact of a loss of degrees of freedom due to sample size and the number of variables in the equation. To check this possibility, a regression was computed that included only the variables for ownership, international work responsibilities, and executive leadership. The analysis confirmed the statistical significance of the latter two variables but not that of ownership.

REFERENCES

Bauer, R. A., de Sola Pool, I., and Dexter, L. A. *American Business and Public Policy: The Politics of Foreign Trade*. Chicago: Aldine Publishing Co., Second Edition, 1972.

Behrman, J. N. *National Interests and the Multinational Enterprise*. Englewood Cliffs, N.J.: Prentice-Hall, 1970.

Beigie, C. E. *The Canada-U.S. Automotive Agreement: An Evaluation*. Washington and Montreal: Canadian-American Committee, 1970.

Biersteker, T. J. *Distortion or Development? Contending Perspectives on Multinational Corporations*. Cambridge: M.I.T. Press, 1978.

Blake, D. H. and Driscoll, R. E. *The Social and Economic Impacts of Transnational Corporations: Case Studies of the U.S. Paper Industry in Brazil*. New York: Fund for Multinational Management Education, 1977.

Blake, D. H. and Walters, R. S. *The Politics of Global Economic Relations*. Englewood Cliffs, N.J.: Prentice-Hall, 1976.

Bodenheimer, S. Dependency and imperialism: The roots of Latin American underdevelopment. In K. T. Fann and D. C. Hodges (Eds.), *Readings in U.S. Imperialism*, Boston: Porter Sargent, 1971, 155–181.

Brunt, R. *The Automotive and Automotive Parts Industry: Sector Analysis*. Ontario: Ministry of Industry and Tourism, 1975.

Clement, W. *The Canadian Corporate Elite: An Analysis of Economic Power*. Toronto: McClelland and Stewart, Ltd., 1975.

Cohen, J. and Cohen, P. *Applied Multiple Regression/Correlation Analysis for the Behavioral Sciences*. Hillsdale, N.J.: Lawrence Erlbaum Associates, 1975.

Evans, P. B. National autonomy and economic development: Critical perspectives on multinational corporations in poor countries. In R. O. Keohane and J. S. Nye, Jr. (Eds.), *Transnational Relations and World Politics*, Cambridge: Harvard University Press, 1972, 325–342.

Fayerweather, J. Elite attitudes toward multinational firms: A study of Britain, Canada, and France. In G. Modelski (Ed.), *Multinational Corporations and World Order*, Beverly Hills: Sage Publications, 1972, 70–88.

Gorsuch, R. L. *Factor Analysis*. Philadelphia: W. B. Saunders Co., 1974.

Hanson, E. C. (with the assistance of R. Mandel). Theoretical perspectives on the multinational corporation: A synthesis. Paper presented at the Seventeenth

Annual Meeting of the International Studies Association, Toronto, February, 1976.

Hilton, A. C. Perceptions of foreign investment in Nigeria. In K. P. Sauvant and F. G. Lavipour (Eds.), *Controlling Multinational Enterprises: Problems, Strategies, Counterstrategies*, Boulder: Westview Press, 1976, 145–158.

Johnson, D. L. The national and progressive bourgeoisie in Chile. In J. D. Cockroft, A. G. Frank, and D. L. Johnson (Eds.), *Dependence and Underdevelopment: Latin America's Political Economy*, Garden City, N.Y.: Anchor Books, 1972, 165–217.

Keenleyside, T. A., LeDuc, L., and Murray, J. A. Public opinion and Canada-United States economic relations. *Behind the Headlines*, December, 1976.

LaPalombara, J. and Blank, S. *Multinational Corporations and National Elites: A Study in Tensions*. New York: The Conference Board, 1976.

LeDuc, L. and Murray, J. A. Canadian nationalism: Pause or decline? Paper presented at the Conference of the World Association for Public Opinion Research, Oslo, August, 1977.

Levitt, K. *Silent Surrender: The American Economic Empire in Canada*. New York: Liveright, 1970.

Leyton-Brown, D. The multinational enterprise and conflict in Canadian-American relations. *International Organization*, 1974, *28*, 733–754.

Litvak, I. A. and Maule, C. J. Conflict resolution and extraterritoriality. *Journal of Conflict Resolution*, 1969, *13*, 305–319.

Litvak, I. A. and Maule, C. J. Foreign investment in Canada. In I. A. Litvak and C. J. Maule (Eds.), *Foreign Investment: The Experience of Host Countries*, New York: Praeger, 1970, 76–104.

Marton, K. Attitudes toward Foreign Investments: A Case Study of the Canadian Blue-Collar Worker Employed at Ford Canada. Doctoral dissertation, New York University, 1973.

Murray, J. A. An analysis of public attitudes on the question of U.S. investment in Canada. Paper presented at the Canadian Institute of International Affairs, Carleton University, Ottawa, November, 1973.

Murray, J. A. and Gerace, M. C. Canadian attitudes toward the U.S. presence. *Public Opinion Quarterly*, 1972, *36*, 388–397.

Murray, J. A. and LeDuc, L. A cross-sectional analysis of Canadian public attitudes toward U.S. equity investment in Canada. Toronto: Ontario Economic Council, 1975. (a)

Murray, J. A. and LeDuc, L. Public attitude surveys of Canadians on significant economic, political, and social issues. Windsor: International Business Studies Research Unit, Occasional paper 75-101, 1975. (b)

Murray, J. A. and LeDuc, L. Public opinion on the U.S. influence in Canada: Recent issues and trends. Paper presented at the Bi-Centennial Conference on "Canada and the United States: Towards a New Partnership," Boston, April, 1976. (a)

Murray, J. A. and LeDuc, L. Public attitude surveys of Canadians on significant economic, political, and social issues. Windsor: International Business Studies Research Unit, Occasional paper 76-101, 1976. (b)

Murray, J. A. and LeDuc, L. Public opinion and foreign policy options in Canada. *Public Opinion Quarterly*, 1976-1977, *40*, 488-496.

Murray, J. A. and LeDuc, L. The changing climate for foreign investment in Canada. Paper presented at the Forty-eighth Annual Meeting of the Southern Economic Association, Washington, November, 1978.

Petras, J., and Cook, T. Dependency and the industrial bourgeoisie: Attitudes of Argentine executives toward foreign economic investment and U.S. policy. In J. Petras (Ed.), *Latin America: From Dependence to Revolution*. New York: John Wiley and Sons, Inc., 1973, 143-175. (a)

Petras, J., and Cook, T. Politics in a nondemocratic state: The Argentine industrial elite. In J. Petras (Ed.), *Latin America: From Dependence to Revolution*. New York: John Wiley and Sons, Inc., 1973, 176-192. (b)

Puchala, D. J. International transactions and regional integration. In L. Lindberg and S. A. Scheingold (Eds.), *Regional Integration: Theory and Research*, Cambridge: Harvard University Press, 1971, 128-159.

Rotstein, A. and Lax, G. (Eds.). *Independence, The Canadian Challenge*. Toronto: Committee for an Independent Canada, 1972.

Russett, B. M. and Henson, E. C. *Interest and Ideology*. San Francisco: W. H. Freeman, 1975.

Sigler, J. H. and Goresky, D. Public opinion on United States-Canadian relations. *International Organization*, 1974, *28*, 637-668.

Sjellsbaek, K. The growth of nongovernmental organization in the Twentieth Century. In R. O. Keohane and J. S. Nye, Jr. (Eds.), *Transnational Relations and World Politics*, Cambridge: Harvard University Press, 1972, 70-92.

Stevenson, G. Foreign direct investment and the provinces: A study of elite attitudes. *Canadian Journal of Political Science*, 1974, *7*, 630-647.

Sunkel, O. Big business and 'dependencia.' *Foreign Affairs*, 1972, *50*, 517–531.

Terhune, K. W. Nationalism among foreign and American students: An exploratory study. *Journal of Conflict Resolution*, 1964, *8*, 256–270.

Terhune, K. W. Nationalistic aspiration, loyalty, and internationalism. *Journal of Peace Research*, 1965, *2*, 277–287.

Teune, H. The learning of integrative habits. In P. E. Jacob and J. V. Toscano (Eds.), *The Integration of Political Communities*, Philadelphia: J. B. Lippincott Co., 1964, 247–282.

Thurstone, L. L. *The Measurement of Social Attitudes*. Chicago: The University of Chicago Press, 1931.

Truitt, N. S. and Blake, D. H. *Opinion Leaders and Private Investment*. New York: Fund for Multinational Management Education, 1976.

Vernon, R. *Sovereignty at Bay*. New York: Basic Books, Inc., 1971.

Government Documents

Foreign Ownership: Corporate Behavior and Public Attitudes. Select Committee on Economic and Cultural Nationalism of the Legislative Assembly, Province of Ontario, 1974.

Foreign Direct Investment in Canada. Government of Canada, 1972.

APPENDIX 5.A

Summary Listing of Regression Variables

Variable	Definition	Operationalization and Coding Scheme
OWNSHP	Corporate ownership	1 = U.S.-owned firm 0 = Canadian-owned firm
MKT	Corporate market structure	1 = Completely domestic market 2 = Mostly domestic market with some exports 3 = Mostly exports with some domestic market 4 = Completely exports
CONTACT	Frequency of transnational business contact; business contact with U.S. executives	1 = Almost never 2 = A few times a year 3 = Several times a year 4 = A few times a month 5 = Once a week or more
IWR	International work responsibilities; work responsibilities involving Canadian-U.S. firms	1 = Only domestic Canadian issues 2 = Primarily domestic Canadian issues 3 = Canadian-U.S. issues and domestic Canadian issues receive roughly the same working time 4 = Primarily Canadian-U.S. issues
FAMLR	Required familiarity with operations of foreign firms; with operations of U.S. firms in Canada	Seven-point scale where 1 = Very little and 7 = Very much
RANK	Executive's rank in the corporate hierarchy	1 = Lower management 2 = Middle management 3 = Upper management
PERSONNEL	Functional work area: Personnel and training	Coded as 1
PRODUCTION	Functional work area: Production	Coded as 1
ACCT/FIN	Functional work area: Accounting and finance	Coded as 1

Variable	Definition	Operationalization and Coding Scheme
MKT/SALES	Functional work area: Marketing, sales, and purchasing	Coded as 1
ORGANIZATION	Functional work area: Organization and administration	Coded as 1
EXEC LDRSHP	Functional work area: Executive leadership	Coded as 1
OTHER	Functional work area: Other	Coded as −1 (Not represented in equations)
SES	Executive's socioeconomic background	1 = White-collar 2 = Blue-collar
EDUC	Executive's educational attainment	1 = some elementary school 2 = completed elementary school 3 = some secondary school 4 = graduated secondary school 5 = some university 6 = graduated university 7 = postgraduate education
AGE	Executive's age	Self-report of age at time of survey
EVAL1	Criteria for evaluating U.S. firms in Canada: Socioeconomic benefits	Factor score for first factor in Table 5.5
EVAL2	Criteria for evaluating U.S. firms in Canada: Impact on national sovereignty and culture	Factor score for second factor in Table 5.5
EVAL3	Criteria for evaluating U.S. firms in Canada: Industrial benefits	Factor score for third factor in Table 5.5
IMPACT1	Impact of U.S. firms in Canada: Socioeconomic and control	Factor score for first factor in Table 5.7
IMPACT2	Impact of U.S. firms in Canada: Wages and working conditions	Factor score for second factor in Table 5.7

APPENDIX 5.B

Zero-Order Correlation Matrix for Multiple Regression Variables

Variables	(1)	(2)	(3)	(4)	(5)	(6)	(7)	(8)	(9)	(10)	(11)	(12)	(13)	(14)	(15)	(16)	(17)	(18)	(19)	(20)
1. EVAL1	–																			
2. EVAL2	.23	–																		
3. EVAL3	.31	.29	–																	
4. IMPACT 1	.17	–.13	.16	–																
5. IMPACT2	.03	–.09	.08	.32	–															
6. OWNSHP	.11	.05	–.04	.07	.12	–														
7. MKT	.05	.11	–.09	.08	.16	.52	–													
8. CONTACT	.07	.04	–.06	.11	.03	.27	.35	–												
9. IWR	.11	.03	.05	.26	.03	.07	.18	.27	–											
10. FAMLR	.10	–.01	.16	.07	–.11	.05	–.02	.25	.17	–										
11. RANK	–.00	–.05	.03	.07	.03	–.27	–.21	–.06	.03	.00	–									
12. PERSONNEL	–.03	.17	–.05	–.09	.08	–.03	.02	–.05	–.12	–.06	.04	–								
13. PRODUCTION	–.05	.12	–.09	–.03	–.00	.03	.10	.06	.22	.02	–.23	.38	–							
14. ACCT/FIN	.01	.09	–.02	–.10	–.06	–.07	–.04	–.09	–.06	–.10	.17	.46	.33	–						
15. MKT/SALES	–.02	–.02	.03	–.04	–.10	–.07	–.12	–.04	–.11	.08	–.02	.34	.16	.28	–					
16. ORGANIZATION	–.08	.14	–.11	–.12	–.06	–.20	–.14	–.09	–.06	–.05	.08	.50	.38	.46	.34	–				
17. EXEC LDRSHP	–.08	.03	.00	–.02	–.01	–.30	–.22	–.01	.13	.13	.38	.37	.21	.32	.14	.37	–			
18. SES	–.01	–.05	–.02	.01	.00	–.01	.10	–.04	–.11	.08	.05	.11	–.09	.05	.05	–.02	.11	–		
19. EDUC	.00	–.12	.12	.14	.15	.09	.02	.10	–.01	.16	–.03	.05	–.04	–.02	–.05	–.10	–.05	.22	–	
20. AGE	–.00	–.07	–.04	–.05	.05	.02	.03	.03	–.03	.02	.24	.10	–.13	–.03	.10	–.04	.11	–.02	–.29	–

See text for definition and measurement of variables.

6

OPINION LEADERS
AND PRIVATE INVESTMENT

Nancy S. Truitt
David H. Blake

The role, effectiveness, and even the ability to operate, of multinational corporations are affected by the attitudes of those in positions of influence within the host countries. While this has always been true, significant changes have taken place in the last few decades that have changed the nature of these groups and their basic perceptions of the role that private investment, both national and foreign, should play in their economies. The number of individuals and groups that have a significant role in influencing social decisions has greatly increased with industrialization and the growth of a middle class. At the same time, growing concern about the control and direction of national development has led to heightened nationalism and increased interest in many areas in the role of the state, rather than private investment, as the primary motor of development.

As a result of these changes, private investors in the developing countries face a very different situation today from that of a number of years ago when their contribution to national development goals was less severely questioned and when it was possible to deal with a few influential national leaders to resolve problems. Progress toward the twin goals of democratization and development has brought with it a new external environment in which numerous groups

This chapter is based on a more complete report of the research by the same title published by the Fund for Multinational Management Education, New York, 1976. The field research for the study was done by Elena Valenzuela, Jose Elias A., Carlos Olavarria A., and John R. Pate.

within the society play a role in influencing the conditions under which private investors operate.

It is within this framework of the relationship between influential groups of the society and the effective functioning of private investment that the study discussed here was undertaken. Its basic goals were to determine the attitudes of opinion leaders influential in decisions concerning private investment in manufacturing, both national and foreign, as they make decisions.

The two countries in which the interviews took place were Chile and Venezuela, both members of the same regional group, the Latin American Free Trade Association,[1] but with differing policies toward foreign investment. The study was designed to determine the following:

- The attitudes of the different groups toward four types of private investment in manufacturing: national, U.S. multinational, non-U.S. multinational, and mixed ventures[2];
- Whether their attitudes vary according to the type of investment, or the source of their information on private investment;
- If, and by how much, their perceptions of what companies are doing vary from their expectations as to what they think they should be doing, and, in contrast to both of these, what corporations in reality are doing;
- How opinions vary by country.

METHODOLOGY

The questionnaire for the survey (Appendix 6.A) was structured to elicit information on the issues mentioned above. Respondents were asked to reply with reference to private investment in manufacturing, with the electronics, chemical, and food-processing industries given as examples. Two types of questions were asked. One set dealt with the opinion leaders' perceptions of the general, or overall, impact of the firm in both national and personal terms. These questions covered their perceptions of the general social and economic impact of the different types of firms, the advantages and disadvantages of foreign investment, and what type of firm they would recommend to their sons were they interested in a career in business.

A second set of questions, probing specific aspects of business activity, covered three basic areas: economic impact, social impact, and communications efforts. More specific questions were asked about profits, reinvestment, R&D, exports, employment of foreign nationals, promotion opportunities for nationals, training, public service activities, and communications efforts. Most of these questions were phrased to elicit an idea first of what the respondent thought corporate performance to be and then what he thought it should be, thus providing the basis for comparison between perception and expectation.

The goal of the study was to obtain the opinions of those influential in the area of private investment in the two countries. Thus, those interviewed were clearly designated opinion leaders with either direct or indirect, present or future impact on private investment. Five categories of opinion leaders were selected:

- government officials, consisting of top officials from ministries and agencies involved with investment, such as foreign investment, economics, planning, and the central bank, parliamentarians or, in the case of Chile, ex-parliamentarians, and, in the case of Venezuela, top military officers;
- labor leaders, consisting of the leaders of national labor unions;
- businessmen, consisting of the leaders of national business associations and local businessmen from major national firms;
- intellectuals, consisting of leaders of the media such as newspaper, television and radio editors and commentators who deal with economic and business issues, and deans and professors of university faculties of business, administration, and economics;
- students, consisting of university students in their last year of business, administration, or economics.

A stratified sample was used. The researchers drew up lists of the persons in each of the categories, placed in order of their titles, starting, for example, with ministers, followed by vice ministers, department chiefs, and so on. Interviewers worked down the list, starting first with those on the top. They would move to the next name only when an interview had been completed or could not be obtained. Almost all the interviews were done in person.[3] The response rate for each of the individual questions varied but was considered satisfactory for all those included in this report.

The total number of names on the lists in each country was 300. The final number of interviews obtained in Venezuela was 198, or 66 percent; in Chile it was 170, or 57 percent. These response rates for this type of detailed interview are considered to be highly satisfactory. A detailed list of the number of persons in each category on the original list and the number who completed the interview is shown in Table 6.1. In Venezuela there were problems in obtaining an adequate number of responses from two of the subgroups, labor leaders and media officials. This was attributed by the researcher to the strong feelings about both multinational firms and research projects concerning them on the part of persons in these two subgroups. As a result, the number of labor leaders who answered the questionnaire was considered too small to be discussed as a separate group. It was not possible to obtain any responses from those in the media in Venezuela. Thus cross-country comparisons were possible only for other groups of which government officials, businessmen, and students provided the chief contrasts.

In analyzing the results frequencies of answers were obtained for each country. Cross-tabulations of the answers by primary occupation, source of information on business, and type of business contact were run. The chi-square test was used to determine which variances were statistically significant. A

TABLE 6.1. **Opinion Leaders Survey: Sample and Response**

	Chile		
	Basic[a] List	Interview[b] List	Answered[c] Questionnaire
Intellectuals		80	41
	100		
Students		28	28
Labor Leaders		23	11
	100		
Government Officials		80	35
Businessmen	100	100	55
	Venezuela		
Intellectuals		91	61[d]
	100		
Students		40	40
Labor Leaders		25	5
	100		
Government Officials		125	37
Businessmen	100	86	55

[a] Basic List: the goal in number of interviews for each of the three basic categories.

[b] Interview List: the number of names actually compiled, using the stratified sample requirements in each of the subcategories. Where the number totals more than 100, a supplementary sample listing was used. This list was established using the same criteria.

[c] Answered Questionnaire: the actual number of persons in each of the subcategories who completed the questionnaire.

[d] Those who answered the questionnaire consisted exclusively of academics (deans, rectors, and professors).

comparison of the means using the two-tailed t test was used to determine if the variances by type of firm, between perception of performance and expectation, and between the two countries were statistically significant.

In addition to perception and expectation, the study attempted to establish reality as a third point of reference. This was done in two ways: a limited survey of actual corporate performance was conducted as part of the study, and other research data were used to provide information on the actual impact of foreign investment. Limitations of time and money prevented the type of full-scale, national study that would have been necessary to document fully what the four different types of firms were doing in each of the areas covered on the questionnaire. However, a survey of three types of manufacturing industries in which there has been significant foreign investment, but in which national firms also thrive, was undertaken. Thus, ten companies in chemicals, electronics, or food processing in each country were surveyed to obtain information on their operations and activities in the areas covered in the opinion leaders' survey. When combined with information from other, broader-based surveys such as those of the U.S. Department of Commerce and *Business Latin America*, a basis for establishing actual performance and impact, particularly with regard to U.S. firms, does exist.

INFORMATION AND CONTACT VARIABLES

The questionnaire explored the input variables that might influence the opinions of respondents. They were asked to describe the extent and nature of their contacts with the manufacturing community in their country and how they obtain information about both the domestic and the foreign business communities. The pattern of responses to these questions is shown in Table 6.2. When the responses for these variables were cross-tabulated with the answers to the rest of the questionnaire, no statistically significant differences that could be attributed to type of contact or source of information emerged. Pursuing this question further, sources of information were divided into just two categories—media and nonmedia. When these were cross-tabulated the variations still were not statistically significant. Thus, from the data at hand, it cannot be concluded that the type of contact with, or the source of information about, private business plays a role in influencing the opinions of the groups interviewed.

GENERAL PERCEPTIONS OF PRIVATE INVESTMENT

The general perceptions of the opinion leaders were approached in two ways: by eliciting their attitudes toward the impact of different types of investment in national terms and in personal terms. Their perceptions in both contexts differed primarily with regard to U.S. firms. National firms are considered to be the most beneficial in terms of economic and social impact, followed closely by mixed ventures (Table 6.3). There is a statistically significant difference in both countries between the perceptions of beneficial impact of national firms relative to U.S. multinational corporations—the former thought to have a more positive impact.[4] However, when the context is changed from that of general national welfare to personal opportunity, in terms of what type of firm they would advise their sons to join, the ranking changes and U.S. multinationals come in second to national firms in both countries. (See Table 6.4.)

In both Venezuela and Chile there were statistically significant differences between the answers by occupational groups on the question of economic and social impact (Table 6.5). The Venezuelans varied on both national and U.S.

TABLE 6.2. Contacts and Source of Information (percentages of respondents)

	Chile				Venezuela			
Primary Contact with Domestic Manufacturing Business Community	Government Officials	Businessmen	Students	All Groups	Government Officials	Businessmen	Students	All Groups
Associations (trade, etc.)	6.5	20.8	0	9.3	0	15.0	0	2.8
Business relations (e.g., creditors, customers)	0	22.6	7.7	10.6	2.9	15.0	3.0	8.4
Media	3.2	9.4	19.2	15.2	2.9	0	9.1	4.9
Government functions	45.2	0	0	9.3	14.7	5.0	3.0	4.9
Personal contacts	12.9	9.4	23.1	15.9	8.8	15.0	15.2	9.1
Academic	0	1.9	23.1	10.6	8.8	0	9.1	7.7
Work in a business	25.8	30.2	11.5	21.2	11.8	50.0	21.2	21.7
None	6.5	5.7	15.4	7.9	2.9	0	39.4	39.9
Primary Source of Information about Domestic Business								
Associational sources	10.3	26.0	11.1	16.3	0	46.2	0	4.5
Academic sources	3.4	0	11.1	4.1	0	0	2.8	3.0
Media sources	20.7	24.0	33.3	26.5	46.4	0	63.9	53.7
Government sources	13.8	2.0	3.7	4.8	7.1	7.7	2.8	6.7
Business sources	31.0	24.0	18.5	21.8	10.7	38.5	19.4	16.4
Personal sources	20.7	20.0	22.2	24.5	35.7	7.7	11.1	13.4
None of these	0	2.0	0	1.4	0	0	0	1.5
Don't know	0	2.0	0	0.7	0	0	0	0.7

144

Foreign Business Community

Associational sources	0	2.1	0	0.7	0	7.1	0	0.8
Academic sources	0	2.1	11.1	4.3	0	0	6.1	3.1
Media sources	69.2	61.7	74.1	67.4	48.0	35.7	81.8	63.0
Government sources	3.8	2.1	0	2.1	0	0	0	2.4
Business sources	19.2	21.3	7.4	14.9	20.0	28.6	12.1	14.2
Personal sources	3.8	4.3	7.4	6.4	28.0	28.6	0	11.0
None of these	3.8	6.4	0	4.3	0	0	0	3.1
Don't know	0	0	0	0	4.0	0	0	2.4

TABLE 6.3. **Appraisal of Social and Economic Impact**
(percentages)

	Chile			
	National Firms	U.S. MNCs	Non-U.S. MNCs	Mixed Firms
Very beneficial	45.8	24.8	25.0	40.7
Beneficial	39.2	53.7	53.3	46.6
Neutral	14.2	14.0	15.8	11.9
Harmful	0.8	7.4	5.8	0.8
Very harmful	0	0	0	0
	Venezuela			
Very beneficial	58.2	16.4	16.2	31.0
Beneficial	31.5	52.9	50.0	53.2
Neutral	8.9	17.1	20.0	12.7
Harmful	1.4	8.6	9.2	1.6
Very harmful	0	5.0	4.6	1.6

firms while the Chileans showed statistically significant differences only with regard to U.S. firms. Businessmen in Venezuela are more favorably inclined toward all types of private investment than are the other groups. The extent of feeling toward U.S. multinationals in Venezuela is evidenced by the fact that not a single Venezuelan government official viewed them as "very beneficial." In Chile, with regard to U.S. multinational firms, students are the most favorably inclined, followed by government officials. Clearly, the differences in government policy are reflected in the respective attitudes of government officials.

Respondents were asked to name the advantages and disadvantages of foreign investment. As can be seen in Table 6.6, the overwhelming need of Chile to attract foreign capital in order to rebuild its economy, and the government's decision to do so as witnessed by its liberal foreign investment law, are clearly reflected in the replies of Chilean opinion leaders. The surprising fact, given oil revenues, is that 22 percent of the Venezuelans answering feel that capital is a major advantage of foreign investment.

The disadvantages of foreign investment as perceived by the opinion leaders in both countries are, once again, fairly similar (Table 6.6). Most emphasis is given to the creation of dependence and to the feeling of exploitation, that the company benefits from the investment more than does the nation. However, the divergence over the third answer indicates, again, the concern in Venezuela over issues related to technology transfer, such as payments for licenses and patents, and overpricing of required imports, while the Chileans indicate more concern with changes created in the economic structure by foreign investment.

TABLE 6.4. Firms Recommended for Son's Employment and Reasons for Recommendation (percentages)

	Chile				Venezuela			
	Government Officials	Businessmen	Students	All Groups	Government Officials	Businessmen	Students	All Groups
National	66.7	50.0	45.8	53.0	87.1	64.9	41.7	61.9
U.S. Multinationals	28.6	28.6	20.8	27.0	9.7	24.3	36.1	22.4
Non-U.S. Multinationals	0.0	11.9	8.3	6.1	0.0	5.4	2.8	2.7
Mixed	4.8	9.5	25.0	13.9	3.2	5.4	19.4	12.9
WHY								
More professional opportunities	38.1	56.8	47.8	49.5	36.4	37.0	45.2	40.7
Support of nation and national industry	14.3	24.3	26.1	22.5	54.5	48.1	41.9	45.4
Better opportunities for promotion	19.0	5.4	17.4	10.8	0	0	3.2	2.8

147

TABLE 6.5. Appraisals of National and U.S. Multinational Firms by Occupational Groups (percentages)

Chile

	National			U.S. MNC		
	Government Officials	Businessmen	Students	Government Officials	Businessmen	Students
Very beneficial	47.8	40.5	37.5	36.4	19.0	12.5
Beneficial	43.5	45.2	45.8	45.5	54.8	79.2
Neutral	4.3	14.3	16.7	18.2	19.0	8.3
Harmful	4.3	0	0	0	7.1	0
Very harmful	0	0	0	0	0	0

Venezuela

	National			U.S. MNC		
	Government Officials	Businessmen	Students	Government Officials	Businessmen	Students
Very beneficial	45.2	87.8	22.2	0	32.7	8.8
Beneficial	41.9	10.2	58.3	61.3	59.2	41.2
Neutral	9.7	2.0	16.7	19.4	8.2	20.6
Harmful	3.2	0	2.8	9.7	0	20.6
Very harmful	0	0	0	9.7	0	8.8

TABLE 6.6. Principal Advantages and Disadvantages of Multinationals
(percentages)

	Chile				Venezuela			
	Government Officials	Businessmen	Students	All Groups	Government Officials	Businessmen	Students	All Groups
Principal Advantages								
Brings in capital	43.8	53.1	53.8	48.6	3.0	22.2	32.4	22.4
Brings in technology and training	20.7	22.4	7.7	20.0	39.4	35.6	27.0	31.1
Develops the economy	17.2	10.2	30.8	18.6	48.5	22.2	8.1	24.8
Provides employment	10.3	12.2	7.7	10.0	3.0	0	27.0	9.9
Develops natural resources	0	0	0	1.4	3.0	20.0	2.7	6.8
Principal Disadvantages								
Dependency	22.7	22.5	24.0	24.6	37.0	8.1	40.5	26.7
Company benefits more than country	36.4	20.0	16.0	22.9	22.2	27.0	24.3	26.0
Harmful to economy	18.2	22.5	28.0	20.3	3.7	13.5	8.1	14.4
Negative effect on balance of payments	13.6	7.5	16.0	11.9	22.2	16.2	18.9	16.4
Local competition suffers	0	0	8.0	4.2	7.4	18.9	5.4	9.6
Harms local culture	0	2.5	0	1.7	3.7	13.5	2.7	4.8

149

Statistically significant differences with regard to occupational groups appear only in Venezuela. While students and businessmen rate capital as a major advantage, it is low on the list of government officials. Technology and development of the economy are of primary importance to them, as they are to the businessmen as well. The concern with technology may reflect the strong emphasis the Venezuelan government has placed on controlling and regulating its flow into the country. The greater concern shown by Venezuelan government officials with economic development as an advantage may reflect their positions and responsibilities, as the category covers such areas as diversification of exports, increasing national production, improving the balance of payments, providing competition, and raising the standard of living.

As to disadvantages, again there are statistically significant differences only among the Venezuelans. More students and government officials than others feel that dependency is the primary disadvantage. Interestingly, it hardly figures in the businessmen's perceptions of disadvantages.

Clearly, there are stronger feelings of dependency in Venezuela with regard to foreign investment, particularly among government officials. In contrast, in Chile it is the students and government officials who are most favorably inclined to foreign investment. Finally, it is important to note that a much more general consensus among occupation groups is indicated in Chile than in Venezuela.

A comparison of the answers to the question as to which type of firm they would advise their sons to join indicates that there is no statistically significant difference between Chilean and Venezuelan answers. Opinion leaders in both countries strongly favor national firms, followed by U.S. firms, as indicated in Table 6.4. There are no statistically significant differences between groups in Chile. In Venezuela, however, government officials again illustrate their strong sense of nationalism, as over 80 percent of them would recommend a national firm to their sons. Students, on the other hand, are the least favorably inclined to national firms and the most positive, of all the groups, toward U.S. multinationals. The greatest difference in the reasons for advising their sons to join a particular firm appears in the response concerned with supporting national industries. As such, it provides confirmation of the stronger sense of nationalism in Venezuela.

To summarize, the general answers concerning private investment indicate that national firms are strongly favored in both a national and a personal context, but that a distinction is made with regard to U.S. multinationals. While their economic and social impact is rated well below that of mixed firms, they are recognized for providing desirable personal opportunities. Likewise, although mixed firms are viewed more favorably in national welfare terms, it is not felt that they offer career opportunities as great as those offered by U.S. multinationals.

PERCEPTIONS OF ECONOMIC IMPACT

Profits

On the question of what constitutes a reasonable rate of profits there are statistically significant differences between the countries only with regard to national firms. There are none with regard to U.S. and mixed firms. In Venezuela there are statistically significant differences between the rates of profits Venezuelans feel different firms should receive. As Table 6.7 indicates, Venezuelans favor higher rates of profit for national and mixed firms than for multinational firms. Chileans do not make distinctions that are statistically significant.

Despite the criticism often heard throughout Latin America, and reflected in this study, that foreign companies make excessive profits, it is interesting to note that what is felt to be a reasonable rate of profit (16 percent) is above the average that the firms surveyed reported but quite similar to what U.S. firms as a whole are reported to be making in Latin America. The average profits over the past five years reported by the firms—national, U.S., and non-U.S.—surveyed in Venezuela ranged from 3.2 percent to 19.8 percent, with the overall average being 12 percent. Those reported in Chile ranged from 1.2 percent to 23 percent, with the overall average being 8.8 percent. Figures calculated by the Bureau of Economic Statistics, U.S. Department of Commerce, indicate that profits on investment of U.S. manufacturing subsidiaries in Latin America in 1974 were

TABLE 6.7. **What Do You Think Ought to Be a Reasonable Rate of Profit as a Percent of Investment?** (median responses)

	Chile			
	Government Officials	Businessmen	Students	All Groups
National firms	14.0	14.6	15.3	14.8
U.S. MNCs	14.5	14.9	15.4	14.9
Non-U.S. MNCs	14.6	14.9	15.3	14.9
Mixed firms	13.0	14.9	15.1	14.8
	Venezuela			
National firms	15.3	15.4	19.8	19.5
U.S. MNCs	14.9	14.3	15.0	14.9
Non-U.S. MNCs	14.9	14.0	14.9	14.8
Mixed firms	15.3	14.5	15.4	15.2

TABLE 6.8. What Proportion of Their Profits Do You Think Each of the Following Reinvest Here in an Average Year? What Do You Think the Rate of Reinvestment Ought to Be as a Percent of Profits? (percentages)

	Chile				Venezuela			
	Government Officials	Businessmen	Students	All Groups	Government Officials	Businessmen	Students	All Groups
Average Year								
National firms	78.3	80.0	77.9	79.1	14.3	49.5	51.1	40.1
U.S. MNCs	35.8	39.3	20.4	30.3	12.0	35.0	15.0	19.8
Non-U.S. MNCs	39.3	39.6	25.0	33.5	9.8	39.7	16.0	19.6
Mixed firms	50.0	50.9	40.3	49.9	16.0	39.9	20.7	27.8
Ought To Be								
National firms	71.5	60.2	78.6	69.6	26.5	45.0	50.9	49.8
U.S. MNCs	58.3	58.4	52.2	50.8	15.3	49.4	50.0	49.6
Non-U.S. MNCs	52.5	58.1	52.2	50.7	15.5	50.0	49.9	49.6
Mixed firms	61.3	59.0	65.0	59.6	26.0	49.7	50.2	49.5

14.7 percent,[5] very close to the opinion leaders' estimates of what their profits should be.

Looking now at the opinions of the various occupation groups, differences between the countries are evident. While Venezuelans differ among themselves on national and mixed firms, Chileans differ on multinational firms. Students in Chile feel more than do the other groups that profits should be higher.

Reinvestment

When asked what percent of profits is being reinvested each year, and what it should be, opinion leaders indicate statistically significant differences between perception and expectation in both countries with regard to multinational firms (Tables 6.8). These firms are viewed as reinvesting much less than the opinion leaders feel they should reinvest. On the other hand, national firms are expected in both countries to reinvest more than other types of firms. There is a statistically significant difference in the desired rate of reinvestment between the countries, with Chileans favoring a higher rate. This is to be expected given the much greater need in Chile for investment after the decapitalization that took place under the Allende government.

Perceptions about the extent of reinvestment in Chile do vary somewhat from reality, particularly with regard to multinational firms. According to the survey of manufacturing firms conducted for the study, reinvestment rates over the last five years averaged over 85 percent for both national and U.S. firms. While this is close to what Chilean opinion leaders felt to be the case for national firms, it is well above that felt to be the case for multinational firms. However, the economic situation faced by companies during and after the Allende regime makes drawing conclusions from a five-year average questionable. Given the decapitalization that took place during Allende's years in office, it is logical to expect high rates of reinvestment, as the Chileans do, and as are planned by the firms interviewed. National firms indicated that they expected during the next five years to reinvest almost 100 percent per year. U.S. firms reported a rate closer to 70 percent per year.

In Venezuela, reinvestment rates as reported by the firms interviewed for the last five years are considerably lower: national firms, an average of 45 percent per year; U.S. firms an average of 12 percent per year; and other foreign firms, an average of 27 percent per year. Venezuelan perceptions, in this case, were more accurate for national firms than for U.S. multinational firms whose reinvestment rates were lower than Venezuelan opinion leaders estimated them to be. Rates of reinvestment projected for the next five years by these firms are similar to those for the last five years. This means that what Venezuelan opinion leaders feel multinational firms should be reinvesting is well above what those interviewed project they will be reinvesting. This large difference between what opinion leaders think multinational firms should reinvest and what those

TABLE 6.9. Taxes as a Percent of Gross Income Average for Last Five Years and What Ought to Be (median responses)

	Chile				Venezuela			
	Government Officials	Businessmen	Students	All Groups	Government Officials	Businessmen	Students	All Groups
Last five years								
National firms	36.5	39.8	34.0	34.9	20.3	17.5	15.7	19.8
U.S. MNCs	34.8	39.9	40.0	39.5	29.7	15.5	19.8	20.0
Non-U.S. MNCs	35.0	39.7	40.5	35.5	29.7	16.8	15.6	19.9
Mixed firms	35.7	35.0	25.5	34.9	25.3	17.0	12.5	19.8
Ought To Be								
National firms	30.0	29.6	20.4	25.2	37.8	12.2	15.8	19.5
U.S. MNCs	30.5	29.8	29.7	29.9	42.2	17.6	28.8	29.6
Non-U.S. MNCs	30.5	29.8	29.9	29.9	43.8	16.2	26.9	25.3
Mixed firms	30.5	29.7	25.0	29.7	39.3	15.0	19.6	20.2

154

interviewed say they are planning to reinvest may well reflect a lack of understanding on the part of the opinion leaders of the effects of Venezuela's policies toward foreign investment on those investors.

As a point of comparison, reinvested earnings as a percent of overall earnings of all U.S. affiliates in Latin America in 1974 was some 29 percent.[6] As might be expected, data from the companies surveyed indicate that those in Venezuela fell below this amount while those in Chile were considerably above it.

The more general consensus in Chile is again indicated by the fact that there is no statistically significant difference between the answers of the four groups on what ought to be a reasonable rate of reinvestment. In Venezuela, however, this is not the case. The most striking difference is the feeling evidenced by government officials that the rate of reinvestment for all types of firms should be much lower than other groups think it should be. This is particularly the case for multinational firms. This may be a reflection of adherence to government policy with regard to reduction of foreign investment through fadeout. Of interest, too, is the fact that all groups, except businessmen, feel that national firms should reinvest more than other types of firms should. Businessmen not only feel that national firms should reinvest less than other types of firms should, but they also feel that national firms should invest less than they now believe them to be reinvesting.

Taxes

In the area of taxes, a statistically significant difference emerges between the two countries (Table 6.9). While the Venezuelans feel that the average tax paid on gross income should be higher than they perceive it to be for all but national firms, the Chileans think that it should be lower. Interestingly enough, the feeling as to what the rate should be in both countries is virtually the same for all firms but national ones. It is important to note that opinion leaders in both countries indicated that taxes for national firms should be lower than they are for other types of firms. However, the Venezuelans favor a lower rate for national firms than do the Chileans.

The data collected in the company surveys indicate that the Venezuelans may not be correct in their perception that national firms pay less in taxes than do multinational or mixed firms. In Venezuela the five-year average of taxes reported to be paid by national, multinational, and mixed firms covered in the survey is about the same, ranging from 3.5 percent for food-processing companies to an average of 16-20 percent for electronic firms. In Chile, though, national firms reported paying an average over the last five years of just over 4 percent in all types of taxes, while U.S. multinationals reported paying an average of 24 percent per year. As a final point of comparison, *Business Latin America* in its survey of "Corporate Tax Rates in Latin America"[7] reports that the typical manufacturer's tax load for wholly owned foreign subsidiaries in

Chile is 40 percent and in Venezuela, 31.3 percent. The probable reason for multinational firms reporting much lower taxes than the typical load in Chile is the lowered profits over the five years during which the tax average was taken, that is, those of the Allende regime and immediately after it.

It is interesting to compare the typical tax load for foreign subsidiaries with what the opinion leaders feel it ought to be. In Chile the majority of opinion leaders feel that it should be 33 percent, below what it is—40 percent. In Venezuela, on the other hand, where the typical tax load is 31.1 percent, the opinion leaders feel it should be about 30 percent, close to what it is.

The Chileans again indicate greater consensus, differing only on what the rate for national firms ought to be. Here it is the students who advocate a rate much lower than that favored by businessmen and government officials. In Venezuela, there is much greater divergence of opinion. Businessmen favor a rate much lower than do the others. Businessmen in Chile do not appear to share their feeling. Looking at the other groups, the government officials show greater consistency between types of firms than do students, who would raise taxes for multinational firms well above those for national firms.

Research and Development

Research and development expenditures in the host country are becoming an area of increasing attention in the international debate on the multinational firm as developing countries see them as a means of gaining access to the ability to develop technology. Both the Chileans and the Venezuelans interviewed indicated a statistically significant belief that there is a difference between what national firms are spending on R&D and what U.S. multinational firms are spending, with the latter believed to be spending more (Table 6.10). However, their expectations as to what percent of gross income should be spent are the same for all types of firms. The median answer in both countries is a little over 5 percent.

Among the firms surveyed in Chile, national firms are spending less than multinational firms, as Chileans perceived to be the case. However, the amounts being spent are much less than the respondents believe them to be. Only one firm in Chile reported spending over 1 percent of gross income per year on local R&D, whereas the opinion leaders estimated expenditures to be in the 2-3 percent range.

In Venezuela, of the firms surveyed, very few were spending anything on R&D. The U.S. firms reported no expenditures. One of the national firms reported spending .005 percent of gross income, and one of the foreign firms reported spending 1 percent. Again, these are amounts well below what Venezuelans estimated them to be. Clearly, large differences exist on this issue between perception, expectation, and reality.

Chilean opinion leaders are in general agreement both on what they think is spent on R&D and what they think should be spent. Once again, this is not the

TABLE 6.10. Research and Development: Amount Spent on R&D as a Percent of Gross Income and Amount Ought to Spend (median responses)

	Chile				Venezuela			
	Government Officials	Businessmen	Students	All Groups	Government Officials	Businessmen	Students	All Groups
Do Spend								
National firms	1.3	1.3	2.7	1.3	1.2	1.3	2.0	1.5
U.S. MNCs	5.1	4.9	4.9	4.7	1.4	2.1	4.6	2.4
Non-U.S. MNCs	4.3	4.3	4.9	3.9	1.0	2.0	3.5	2.1
Mixed firms	2.8	2.8	2.9	2.5	2.4	2.0	2.7	2.4
Ought To Spend								
National firms	5.2	5.0	6.5	5.2	5.0	4.6	10.0	6.2
U.S. MNCs	8.5	7.0	9.7	7.3	4.8	4.9	9.7	5.5
Non-U.S. MNCs	8.0	5.3	9.7	6.0	4.8	4.8	9.8	5.5
Mixed firms	5.1	5.1	8.2	5.3	4.9	4.6	10.0	7.0

157

TABLE 6.11. Exports: Percent of Sales Believed Exported and Reasonable Effort to Expand Exports

	Chile				Venezuela			
	Government Officials	Businessmen	Students	All Groups	Government Officials	Businessmen	Students	All Groups
Percent Exported (median responses)								
National firms	9.9	5.0	7.0	5.3	3.5	14.9	10.3	10.1
U.S. MNCs	10.2	10.4	15.5	10.5	5.2	29.7	39.7	29.6
Non-U.S. MNCs	10.5	10.1	14.6	10.5	4.7	29.5	21.0	19.6
Mixed firms	10.1	7.5	10.4	10.0	5.4	20.5	19.9	18.3
Making Reasonable Effort To Expand (percent—Yes)								
National firms	85.2	90.0	92.6	90.0	51.4	64.0	61.5	58.1
U.S. MNCs	72.0	73.5	81.5	72.7	37.8	58.0	64.1	52.9
Non-U.S. MNCs	72.0	70.8	81.5	71.0	29.7	64.6	65.8	53.3
Mixed firms	88.0	85.7	96.3	88.0	55.6	72.9	64.9	66.5

case in Venezuela where businessmen and government officials feel that less is and should be spent than do students.

Efforts to Export

Export promotion is another area on which developing countries are placing increasing emphasis, having been disappointed with import substitution as a means to industrial development. However, current government policy in Chile places greater emphasis on export promotion as a keystone of its economic policy than does that in Venezuela where the emphasis is on developing local capacity in a broad range of industrial endeavors. Respondents in both countries feel that national firms are exporting less than other types and that U.S. multinationals are exporting more (Table 6.11).

However, major differences emerge between respondents in the two countries when queried about the efforts they believe different types of firms to be making to export. Once again, Chileans seem much more satisfied than Venezuelans with the efforts they believe are being made. It should be noted that the Chileans recognize a greater disparity between the efforts of national and multinational firms than do the Venezuelans.

Here, as with expenditures on R&D, perceptions vary considerably from the reality as reported by the manufacturing firms interviewed. In Chile both national and U.S. firms reported minimal amounts of exports (less than 2 percent of sales); in Venezuela only the foreign multinationals reported exports, at a level of 10 percent of sales each. However, national firms in both countries project large increases in exports over the next five years, ranging up to 25 percent. The Chilean belief that significant efforts are being made, particularly by national firms, may be further explained by the fact that the government has implemented a number of policies to increase exports, and nontraditional exports have increased from some 5 percent of total exports in the past to almost 25 percent at present.[8] Neither the Venezuelans nor the Chileans differ by occupation group on the extent of the efforts being made by different types of firms to export.

Summary

In the area of business operations a number of differences exist between the two countries. First, Venezuelans appear to be more nationalistic and less favorably inclined toward foreign investment than do the Chileans. This is particularly evident in the fact that Venezuelans would have national firms earn more in profits than multinational firms. It is reflective of the differences in national policy. Chile's new foreign investment law is founded on two basic tenets: that foreign investment is "indispensable" for rapid economic growth and that foreign investors should not be discriminated against.[9] On the other hand, Venezuela is going through a period of strong nationalistic sentiment in which the primary emphasis is on building national capabilities, as witnessed by implementation of very strict transfer of technology legislation and pursuance of Andean Common Market fadeout requirements.

With regard to what are considered to be reasonable rates of taxes and reinvestment, there are also differences. The Venezuelans feel that the amount of profits to be reinvested each year should be less than the Chileans feel it should be. On the question of taxes, both countries are in agreement on what rates should be, with the exception of those for national firms for which the Venezuelans again favor lower rates than do the Chileans.

As to occupational groups, clearly the students in Chile tend to have more unrealistic images, particularly with regard to profits, than the other groups. In Venezuela both the government officials and the businessmen exhibit clear and consistent attitudes. The businessmen are, quite naturally, strong advocates of national firms, to the point of favoring reduced rates of reinvestment and lower rates for national firms. Government officials, on the other hand, favor higher taxes and much lower rates of reinvestment than do the other groups. These attitudes are consistent with their role in presiding over a government intent on strengthening its role in the economy.

PERCEPTIONS OF SOCIAL IMPACT

The following questions deal with those aspects of a company's activities in a country that are not necessarily a part of its productive operations but which do have a significant social impact on the community. Among these are employment of foreigners and training of national employees, opportunities for advancement for local personnel, involvement in public service activities, and communication with the public.

Employment of Foreigners and Training of Nationals

One of the major issues of concern in the developing countries is the training of nationals, in both managerial and technical positions, to take over jobs previously occupied by foreign nationals. Thus, a number of questions dealt with this area. When asked about the number of foreign nationals they thought were in management positions in multinational and mixed firms over the last 15 years, respondents in both countries clearly indicated a belief that the numbers had diminished considerably (Table 6.12). Such reductions are confirmed in the data on U.S. multinationals from the survey, as well as by studies of employment of both U.S. personnel and third-country nationals abroad. A study of employment in U.S. Latin American subsidiaries showed that the number of U.S. personnel employed in managerial, technical, and professional positions was

4.4 percent of all employed in those categories in 1966.[10] This was a reduction from the number employed in 1957, which was 7.2 percent of the category. A more recent study of 54 U.S. corporations operating internationally indicated that in the last five years employment of U.S. personnel overseas has decreased by 26 percent.[11] In the same period the employment of third-country nationals by these firms increased by 105 percent, indicating an increase in opportunities for individuals who are not from the home country of the corporation.

There are some clear differences between the countries in their perceptions with regard to the employment of foreign nationals. While there is no statistically significant difference between opinion leaders on what the number of foreign nationals employed in managerial positions by U.S. firms should be, there are statistically significant differences on how many are believed to be currently employed. The median answer given by the Venezuelans is that some 29 percent of those in managerial positions are foreigners; the median answer for Chile is only 15 percent. The median answer from both countries for how many foreigners should be employed in these positions is 14 percent. Thus, there is, again, a much greater difference between perception and expectation in Venezuela than in Chile.

There are some very interesting differences among occupational groups on these questions. Students in Chile are willing to accept a much higher number of foreign nationals in managerial positions than are any of the other groups in either country, while the businessmen in Chile are the group who feel that the number of foreigners so employed should be the lowest. The greatest gaps between perception and expectation occur among the businessmen and government officials in Venezuela.

In technical and professional positions there is again a statistically significant difference between the countries in terms of the number of foreigners whom respondents believe to be currently employed, but not of the number that they believe should be employed. As Table 6.12 indicates, the opinion leaders feel that fewer foreigners should be employed in technical and professional positions than in managerial positions. It should also be noted that while Chileans showed no statistically significant differences between the number of foreigners they believe are and should be employed in managerial positions, they do show a difference with regard to technical and professional positions.

Only Venezuela registers a statistically significant difference on the question of how many foreign nationals should be employed in these positions. Here it is the businessmen who favor a higher number than do the other groups. This could be a result of their everyday working familiarity with manufacturing, in which they recognize a need for foreign technicians.

It should be noted that these questions clearly raise some definitional problems: How are the different categories defined? Who is considered to be a foreign national? In addition to these problems, the data available on employees in multinational firms are not directly comparable, since they deal with U.S. citizens employed in U.S. subsidiaries, and not with all foreign nationals. They

TABLE 6.12. Employment of Foreign Managers and Technical Personnel: Percentage Believed Employed in Last 15, 10, and 5 Years and Percentage Should Be Employed in U.S. Multinationals (median responses)

	Chile				Venezuela			
	Government Officials	Businessmen	Students	All Groups	Government Officials	Businessmen	Students	All Groups
Managers								
Last 15 years	53.0	40.5	80.0	50.2	77.5	79.6	50.0	76.0
Last 10 years	40.0	29.9	70.5	39.9	60.0	65.0	39.8	60.0
Last 5 years	30.3	19.8	59.8	29.7	42.0	48.8	20.3	40.4
Should be	10.1	9.9	30.5	10.2	10.0	19.6	10.1	10.3
Technical Personnel								
Last 15 years	39.4	20.3	30.8	29.8	61.3	71.0	49.7	69.6
Last 10 years	29.5	19.6	30.0	20.2	50.5	60.5	40.0	50.4
Last 5 years	18.0	10.1	19.7	10.5	49.8	50.1	20.0	40.3
Should be	9.7	5.2	9.7	9.6	7.2	10.5	5.4	9.8

TABLE 6.13. Why Do You Think Foreign Firms Continue to Rely
on Foreign Nationals in Managerial Positions?
In Professional and Technical Positons?
(percentages)

	Managerial		Professional and Technical	
	Chile	Venezuela	Chile	Venezuela
Firms have more faith in foreigners	37.9	21.7	17.5	14.9
Foreigners are better prepared	17.2	33.7	72.3	73.9
Foreigners put company interests ahead of country	10.3	11.4	1.5	0.6
Foreigners are familiar with the system	18.8	9.0	2.9	5.0
To preserve secrets	7.2	12.0	5.8	1.9

also aggregate the two categories into one. However, even assuming the number of third-country nationals employed was equal to the number of U.S. personnel, and that there had been no further reduction since 1966, there would still be a large gap between what opinion leaders perceive to be the case and what it appears to be. In fact, it would seem that the numbers are much lower than opinion leaders think they should be.

It is interesting to note that in both countries respondents are willing to accept a few more foreign nationals in management positions than in technical and professional positions. The reasons for this become clear in their answers to the question as to why foreign nationals continue to be employed. As indicated in Table 6.13, there are two primary reasons given in both countries for continued reliance on foreigners in management positions: foreign companies have more faith in foreigners, and foreigners are better prepared while nationals lack training. However, the predominant beliefs in the two countries show that Chileans feel the main reason is that foreign companies have more faith in foreigners, while the Venezuelans cite as a main reason lack of national training and that foreigners are better prepared (33 percent). This may help to explain the divergences between perception and expectation with regard to the numbers employed. If the Chileans feel that the primary reason foreign nationals are employed in management positions is that the foreign companies have more faith in them, then there is little Chileans can do to change the situation. Thus,

TABLE 6.14. Evaluation of Training Efforts and Advancement Opportunities (average scores)

	Training Efforts (1 = very much, 5 = very little)				Advancement Opportunities (1 = very good, 5 = very poor)			
	Government Officials	Businessmen	Students	All Groups	Government Officials	Businessmen	Students	All Groups
Chile								
National firms	3.6	3.6	3.9	3.7	1.5	1.8	2.4	1.8
U.S. MNCs	2.3	2.5	2.5	2.5	3.0	3.4	3.2	3.1
Non-U.S. MNCs	2.6	2.7	2.5	2.7	3.1	3.4	3.1	3.2
Mixed firms	3.0	3.1	3.0	3.1	2.2	2.5	2.6	2.5
Venezuela								
National firms	2.4	2.3	2.9	2.6	1.8	1.8	2.1	2.0
U.S. MNCs	2.5	2.5	2.7	2.5	2.7	2.8	3.5	3.0
Non-U.S. MNCs	2.8	2.5	2.8	2.7	2.9	2.6	3.3	3.0
Mixed firms	2.4	2.5	2.7	2.6	2.0	2.3	2.9	2.4

they make no real distinction between what is and what ought to be the number employed. On the other hand, the Venezuelans may show a greater difference between perception and expectation because they believe it is a question of training, which they could obtain, and not simply one of faith, which they could not affect.

With regard to technical and professional positions, there is overwhelming agreement in both countries that the primary reason for employing foreign nationals is that they are better prepared and that nationals lack training.

Pursuing this question of training, respondents were asked to evaluate the training efforts for the country's employees by the various types of firms. Here there are statistically significant differences between the countries only with regard to national firms (Table 6.14). Only 10 percent of the Chilean respondents answered that they thought Chilean national firms were making very much effort at training. In contrast, 47 percent of the Venezuelans felt that their national firms were doing so. However, perceptions of the efforts of U.S. multinationals were very similar, with over 55 percent of the respondents in both countries feeling that the efforts made were strong. What emerges, therefore, is a picture of close to 50 percent of the Venezuelans feeling that all types of firms are making good efforts, while in Chile it is felt that such efforts are only being made by the multinational firms.

Opportunities for Advancement

There are no statistically significant differences between the countries in terms of the way in which they rate opportunities for advancement in the various types of firms (Table 6.14). Both Venezuelan and Chilean opinion leaders view opportunities as being significantly better in national than in U.S. firms. The breakdown by occupational groups shows no statistically significant difference among the Chileans; however, Venezuelans differ on opportunities available in multinational and mixed firms. Students, even though they, more than any of the other groups, would recommend that their sons join a U.S. multinational firm, seem to feel that opportunities for advancement there are poor.

Public Service Activities

A question on public service activities was included in the study to attempt to determine what manufacturing firms are perceived to be doing in this area and what it is felt that they should be doing. The differences in the replies between the two countries shed some light on the perceived needs of the opinion leaders in the two countries. Manufacturing firms are believed to be involved in the following types of public service activities:

Chile		Venezuela	
Type of Activity	Percent of Respondents	Type of Activity	Percent of Respondents
Housing	25	Education	20
Sports and recreation	20	Medical	15
Medical care	13	Social welfare	12
		Housing	12

However, when asked what they feel are the most important voluntary public service projects in which they think the private sector should be involved, the primary importance of education and technical training emerges in both countries:

Chile		Venezuela	
Type of Activity	Percent of Respondents	Type of Activity	Percent of Respondents
Education	23	Education	43
Housing	20	Technical training	14
Technical training	15	Social welfare	10

Thus the total number of respondents interested in education and technical training in Chile is 38 percent while in Venezuela it is 57 percent. The belief that foreign nationals are favored for managerial, technical, and professional positions because they are better prepared is reflected here in the desire for greater assistance in education and technical training. The fact that more opinion leaders in Venezuela than in Chile cite these areas is not surprising given both the much greater illiteracy rate in Venezuela and the stronger feeling that it is training that prevents nationals from occupying positions in multinational firms.

The responses revealed little difference between groups in terms of the types of activities that they perceive companies to be engaged in or what they felt they should be doing. However, groups in Venezuela did vary in their feelings as to why companies engage in public service activities. The majority of businessmen in Venezuela indicated that public service activities are part of an enterprise's function, its social responsibility. Students placed more emphasis on its being done for reasons of public image and public relations. Interestingly enough, few in the government seemed to feel that such activities were part of an enterprise's function, emphasizing instead that they were done for reasons of public image and labor relations. Thus, in Venezuela, there seems to be a feeling in all categories, with the exception of businessmen, that community service activities are engaged in, not because they are part of a business function, but rather in order to gain some advantage, such as improved public image or better labor relations.

In Chile there were no statistically significant differences among groups in their opinions of why companies engaged in public service activities. The primary reason given by all groups was that they were done for public relations reasons; the second reason was that of improved labor relations. Relatively few, compared to Venezuela, felt that public service activities were part of the function of a business enterprise.

After reviewing the activities leaders believe companies should be involved in, it is interesting to take a look at the amounts that the different groups feel should be spent, as a percent of total income, on public service activities. There is a statistically significant difference between the two countries on this issue (Table 6.15). The median answer in Venezuela ranges from 5.4 percent to 8.1 percent for the different firms, while that in Chile is some 4.5-4.6 percent. Once again, the Venezuelans show more significant differences in opinions by occupational group than do the Chileans. It is the businessmen in every case who feel expenditures should be much lower than others think they should be. It is also interesting to note that there is little real distinction made by the groups between types of firms, except for the Venezuelan businessmen who feel that multi-national firms should expend more than national firms.

Effectiveness in Communication

Interviewees were asked how effective they feel the different types of firms to be in communicating their activities and interests. This question was included

TABLE 6.15. Percent of Total Income that Should Be Spent on Public Service (median responses)

	Chile			
	Government Officials	Businessmen	Students	All Groups
National firms	4.5	2.5	4.9	4.5
U.S. MNCs	4.5	2.7	5.0	4.6
Non-U.S. MNCs	4.5	2.8	5.0	4.6
Mixed firms	4.5	2.5	4.9	4.5
	Venezuela			
National firms	9.6	3.3	9.6	5.4
U.S. MNCs	9.8	4.6	9.8	8.1
Non-U.S. MNCs	9.7	4.5	9.7	8.0
Mixed firms	9.7	3.8	9.7	7.5

TABLE 6.16. Evaluation of Effectiveness in Communication
(average scores; 1 = very effective, 5 = very ineffective)

	Chile			
	Government Officials	Businessmen	Students	All Groups
National firms	2.9	3.3	2.9	3.1
U.S. MNCs	2.8	2.7	2.7	2.6
Non-U.S. MNCs	2.9	2.9	2.8	2.8
Mixed firms	2.9	2.9	2.6	2.8
	Venezuela			
National firms	2.7	2.7	2.7	2.8
U.S. MNCs	2.1	2.2	2.3	2.3
Non-U.S. MNCs	2.3	2.3	2.6	2.5
Mixed firms	2.1	2.5	2.7	2.6

in order to permit a comparison between the respondents' general and specific attitudes toward the types of firms, and their perceptions of how effective the firms are in communicating with them. There is a statistically significant difference between the countries on this issue (Table 6.16). In Venezuela more respondents thought that all types of firms were "effective" or "very effective" in communicating than did respondents in Chile.

Thus, an interesting dichotomy with regard to Venezuela is revealed. Given the strong sense of nationalism among Venezuelans and their less positive attitude toward multinational firms, one might have expected that they would not view such firms as communicating well. However, the reverse is the case. Some 64 percent of the Venezuelan respondents replied that U.S. firms were effective or very effective in communicating their activities and interests. Only some 37 percent felt that national firms were "effective" or "very effective." Venezuelan government officials especially appear to feel that non-national firms are much more effective in communicating their activities than are other groups. While Chileans also viewed U.S. multinationals as the most effective, it was not by such an overwhelming amount and there is no statistically significant difference by occupational group.

This raises some questions concerning the results of effective communication. In Venezuela, where firms, particularly U.S. multinationals, are viewed as communicating quite effectively, the general attitude toward them is less favorable than it is in Chile. This may reflect a general questioning of the role of private investment, and particularly foreign investment, in the development process in

Venezuela. In Chile this question has clearly been answered for the present by government policy.

CONCLUSIONS

There are a number of conclusions that emerge from the cross-country comparison of the research results. First, the differences among perception, expectation, and reality are greater in Venezuela than in Chile, particularly in such areas as reinvestment, exports, and employment of foreign nationals. Second, there is much more consensus by occupation group in Chile than in Venezuela. Third, the Chileans exhibit a more favorable attitude toward multinationals, which is reflected in specific issues such as profits. Finally, several issues emerge as of real importance in both countries: the availability of training, particularly technical training, perception of lack of opportunity for advancement in multinational firms, and a desire for much higher expenditures on both R&D and public service activities.

Breaking down the opinions by occupation groups, several trends among them emerge, particularly in Venezuela. Here, for example, students tend to be the least realistic in their estimations of what profits and expenditures on R&D are and ought to be. Venezuelan businessmen exhibit a clear tendency to favor special conditions for national firms over other types of firms. Chilean businessmen do not indicate this tendency. Venezuelan government officials tend to be on the more realistic side in their estimations of what expenditures on R&D and reinvestment are and ought to be, which might be attributed to their positions, which bring them into contact with such information. On the other hand, they appear to overestimate the number of foreigners in managerial positions. They appear to feel less positively than the other groups about the multinationals, as witnessed by their answers to questions on impact, what firm they would recommend to their sons, and what they think rates of reinvestment should be. In contrast, Chilean government officials are among the most positively inclined of the Chilean groups toward multinationals. However, in Chile none of the groups shows the extensive or consistent differences of opinion that are evident in Venezuela.

Thus there emerges a picture of two countries whose opinion leaders generally believe that foreign investment is beneficial, but who differ on how it ought to be treated in the crucial area of profits, reflecting their governments' general policies toward foreign investment. The opinion leaders in the two countries also differ in the amount of divergence between their perceptions, their expectations, and reality, with the greater difference being shown in Venezuela. Thus, while much less frustration and dissonance might be expected in Chile than in Venezuela as a result of the greater convergence of perception, expectation, and reality, future conflict might emerge from the greater difference between general opinion of the impact of foreign investment, which is similar to that in Venezuela, and present treatment, which differs.

NOTES

1. Though Chile was a member of the Andean Common Market at the time this research was conducted, it has since withdrawn from that organization. Venezuela continues to be active in the Andean Common Market.

2. Mixed ventures were defined as those in which there was a minimum of 50 percent national participation.

3. In Chile, 5 of the 170 interviews were conducted by mail. None of the 198 questionnaires in Venezuela was mailed.

4. All differences discussed between types of firms, between perceptions and expectations, and between countries are significant at the .01 level or better. Differences on opinions by occupation group are significant at the .05 level or better.

5. This figure was prepared, on request, by the Bureau of Economic Statistics, U.S. Department of Commerce. Published data on U.S. manufacturing investment and return in Latin America is based on "direct investment" defined as "the net book value of foreign parent's net equity in, and outstanding loans to U.S. affiliates." Thus, it is not comparable to the term used in the question asked of the leaders, which was simply "investment."

6. See note 5.

7. "Comparative Corporate Tax Rates in Latin America," *Business Latin America*, June 4, 1975, pp. 180-181.

8. "Non-traditional Export Boom Helps Chile," *Business Latin America*, March 24, 1976, p. 94.

9. "Chile Issues Flexible Investment Law," *Business Latin America*, July 17, 1974, p. 232.

10. U.S. Investment in the Latin American Economy (1955) and Selected Data on Latin American Manufacturing Enterprises (1966), Office of Business Economics, U.S. Department of Commerce, as printed in: Mason, R. Hal, "The Multinational Firm and the Cost of Technology to Developing Countries," *California Management Review*, Summer 1973, p. 12.

11. "Third Country Nationals," *Innovation in International Compensation*, June 1976, pp. 4-5.

APPENDIX 6.A

Questionnaire for the Opinion Leaders on
Private Investment in Manufacturing

Basic Information

I. Primary Occupation (Academic, Media, Labor, Student, Businessman, Government)
II. Age
III. Please describe the extent and nature of your contacts with the domestic manufacturing business community and with the foreign business community.
IV. How do you obtain information about the domestic business community and about the foreign business community?
V. Which of these is most important?

The Questions

1. What do you think ought to be a reasonable rate of profit as a percent of investment for the following types of firms?
   National
   U.S.
   Non-U.S.
   Mixed
2. What proportion of their profits do you think each of the following reinvest here in an average year?
   National
   U.S.
   Non-U.S.
   Mixed
3. What do you think the rate of reinvestment ought to be as a percent of profits?
   National
   U.S.
   Non-U.S.
   Mixed
4. In the area of taxes, please indicate what you think for the last five years is the average amount of taxes as a percent of gross income paid by each of the following types of firms.
   National
   U.S.
   Non-U.S.
   Mixed
5. What do you think these firms ought to pay in taxes?
   National
   U.S.
   Non-U.S.
   Mixed

6. In the area of employment, please indicate what you think is the average amount of labor costs as a percent of gross income for the following types of firms.
   National
   U.S.
   Non-U.S.
   Mixed
7. In the area of research and development, what do you think is the average percent of gross income spent by the following types of firms in the country?
   National
   U.S.
   Non-U.S.
   Mixed
8. In the area of research and development, what do you think if the percent of gross income which these firms ought to spend in the country?
   National
   U.S.
   Non-U.S.
   Mixed
9. In the area of exports, what do you think is the average percent of sales which is exported by the following types of firms?
   National
   U.S.
   Non-U.S.
   Mixed
10. Do you think these companies are undertaking reasonable efforts to expand exports?
    (yes or no)
11. In the managerial category, what do you think is the average percent of those employed in 1975 who are foreign nationals?
    U.S.
    Non-U.S.
    Mixed
12. What do you believe was the average percentage of foreign employees in managerial positions in the last 15 years, the last 10 years, and the last 5 years?
    U.S.
    Non-U.S.
    Mixed
13. What do you think the percentage of foreign nationals here in the country in managerial positions should be?
    U.S.
    Non-U.S.
    Mixed

14. In the professional and technical category, what do you think is the average percentage of those employed in 1975 who are foreign nationals?
    U.S.
    Non-U.S.
    Mixed
15. What do you believe was the average percentage of foreign employees in professional and technical categories in the last 15 years, the last 10 years, and the last 5 years in each of the following types of companies?
    U.S.
    Non-U.S.
    Mixed
16. What do you think the percentage of foreign nationals employed here as technicians and professionals should be?
    U.S.
    Non-U.S.
    Mixed
17a. Why do you think foreign firms continue to rely on foreign nationals in managerial positions?
17b. Why do you think foreign firms continue to rely on foreign nationals in professional and technical positions?
18. How would you evaluate the following types of firms in their training efforts for the country's employees? (5-point scale—very much to very little)
    National
    U.S.
    Non-U.S.
    Mixed
19. For each of the following types of firms, please evaluate on a 5-point scale from very good to very poor the opportunities they provide for advancement for country personnel into managerial ranks.
    National
    U.S.
    Non-U.S.
    Mixed
20. Many manufacturing firms engage in various types of voluntary public service programs. Please name the type of activities you think they do engage in and identify the one which you feel is most important.
21. In this country, what are the most important voluntary public service projects which you think the private sector should be involved in but is presently not?
22. What do you think is a reasonable average percent of total income that each of the following types of firms should spend on voluntary public service activities?
    National
    U.S.
    Non-U.S.
    Mixed

23. Why do you think the private sector engages in voluntary public service activities?
24. In general, how beneficial or harmful do you consider the social and economic impact of each of the following types of firms to be?
    National
    U.S.
    Non-U.S.
    Mixed
25. Speaking of foreign investment in general, what is its principal advantage for the country?
26. What is the principal disadvantage of foreign investment?
27. How effective are the following types of firms in communicating their activities and interests to you? (5-point scale—very effective to very ineffective)
    National
    U.S.
    Non-U.S.
    Mixed
28. If you had a son interested in a business career, which one of the following types of firms would you recommend that he join?
    National
    U.S.
    Non-U.S.
    Mixed
29. Why would you recommend the firm which you did?

7

TESTING FOR ACCURACY AND NATIONALISM EFFECTS IN CHILEAN AND VENEZUELAN DATA

John Fayerweather

The survey of Chilean and Venezuelan elites described in the previous chapter was designed to provide information on perceptions of specific matters concerning MNCs and other types of firms. However, the results offered opportunities for analysis of sets of questions that showed two types of common characteristics: accuracy of perception and nationalistic orientation. The character of the data was such that analysis of these two characteristics was difficult, but it was desirable, particularly in testing out potentials for future research, to pursue this line of exploration.

ACCURACY OF PERCEPTION

Responses to the economic and social impact questions showed that a substantial portion of respondents had inaccurate perceptions of the magnitude of various measures of MNC activity. This observation led naturally to exploring whether some individuals were consistently either well or poorly informed on varied subjects and, if so, whether degrees of accuracy were associated with degrees of favorableness of perceptions of MNCs.

Analysis of this area was complicated by the lack of a clearcut determination of reality against which the accuracy of perceptions could be measured. In some instances, notably research and development (R&D), for which the reality was apparently close to zero expenditure, a reasonably precise base could be

Richard Dunie performed the computer analysis of data for this chapter.

established. In others, such as the number of foreign managers employed, the reality was very poorly defined. For these subjects the only course available was to define the reality as falling in an approximate range as determined by the survey of companies and other sources noted in the preceding discussion. The analysis was also complicated by the fact that for some questions the reality was an intermediate figure and inaccuracy had to be measured in two directions away from it. For example, the actual rate of taxes was in the 30–49 percent range in Chile and the 20–39 percent range in Venezuela.

As a practical means of working within these complications, the responses for the five most appropriate questions were grouped into four categories, as shown in Table 7.1. A score of 1 was assigned for those responses within the range of apparent reality, with others grouped in categories out to a score of 4 at the least accurate range. The distribution of responses by each category for each question is shown in Table 7.2.

TABLE 7.1. Accuracy of Perception Scaling Code

	Scale Code	Range of Perceptions (percentages)	
		Chile	Venezuela
Rate of reinvestment of profits	1	70 and up	0–19
	2	40–69	20–39
	3	20–39	40–59
	4	0–19	60 and up
Rate of taxation of profits	1	30–49	20–39
	2	20–29, 50–59	10–19, 40–49
	3	10–19, 60–69	0–9, 50–59
	4	9–9, 70 and up	60 and up
Percent of income spent on R&D	1	0–1.9	same as Chile
	2	2–5	
	3	6–10	
	4	11 and up	
Foreign managers as percent of total management staff	1	0–9	same as Chile
	2	10–20	
	3	21–40	
	4	41 and up	
Foreign technical and professional personnel		same as for foreign managers	

TABLE 7.2. Distribution of Accuracy of Perception Responses
(percentages)

	Scale Code			
	1	2	3	4
Reinvestment of profits				
Chile	11.8	29.1	29.1	29.9
Venezuela	45.9	28.9	19.5	5.7
Rate of taxation				
Chile	32.2	27.8	20.0	20.0
Venezuela	35.8	44.6	14.9	4.7
R&D expenditures				
Chile	32.8	32.8	23.2	11.2
Venezuela	35.0	35.0	14.1	14.1
Foreign managers				
Chile	37.0	25.9	14.1	23.0
Venezuela	11.7	25.1	25.1	38.0
Foreign professionals				
Chile	34.1	37.2	14.7	14.0
Venezuela	9.6	35.3	28.7	26.3

With this data base, the possibility of consistent patterns of accuracy among respondents was tested in two ways. First, Pearson correlation matrices were run for each country, the results of which (see Table 7.3) show that there is little relation between the extent of a respondent's accuracy on one question and that on another. The only high and significant correlation is the accuracy of perception of employment by managers and professionals, an area in which lack of consistency would have been very surprising. Otherwise there appears to be no pattern of relationships.

The second approach was to add the scores on the five questions, with resulting frequencies shown in Table 7.4. A high clustering of scores at either the low or high ends would indicate a number of individuals who were consistently well informed or poorly informed respectively. In fact, there is no such clustering, the majority of respondents falling in the middle range which indicates no consistency in degree of accuracy of perceptions. Thus both approaches suggest that individual members of the elites in these two countries tend to be well informed on some subjects and not on others, rather than consistently well or poorly informed on all aspects of MNC activity.

In light of the lack of consistent patterns of accuracy of perceptions, it seemed unlikely that any significant relationship would be found between accuracy measures and attitudes toward MNCs. Nonetheless, correlations were

TABLE 7.3. Cross Correlation of Scaled Indicators of Accuracy of Perception (Pearson correlation coefficients)

	Reinvestment	Taxation	R&D	Foreign Managers
Chile				
Rate of taxation	-0.028			
R&D expenditures	-0.129	0.025		
Foreign managers employed	0.078	0.067	0.100	
Foreign professionals	0.001	0.106	0.238*	0.618*
Venezuela				
Rate of taxation	-0.006			
R&D expenditures	0.089	0.016		
Foreign managers employed	-0.101	-0.175*	-0.064	
Foreign professionals	0.023	-0.068	-0.005	0.477*

*Significant at .05 level.

run for the five indicators developed above and their composite scores against the respondents' attitudes toward the value of MNCs (very beneficial, and so on). The results for four of the indicators (taxes, R&D, managers, and professionals) show no significant correlations. For the reinvestment of profits indicator, the correlation coefficients were both significant at the .05 level: -.197 for Chile and .282 for Venezuela. In considering this result, the opposite signs would seem to be significant. Note that because actual reinvestment rates were very high in Chile and moderate in Venezuela the accuracy scales went in opposite directions for the two countries (Table 7.1). It would appear that the correlation is to the rate of reinvestment rather than accuracy; that is, in both countries firms tended to be rated as more beneficial according to the rate of profits they were believed to be reinvesting rather than the accuracy of that perception. As to the composite accuracy scores, the correlation with the overall appraisal in Chile is low and insignificant, but in Venezuela the coefficient is .146 with a significance of .065. This could be a random and meaningless outcome. On the other hand, it is possible that it is meaningful, that, while accuracy of perceptions on individual issues is not directly related to opinions about MNCs, the overall degree of accuracy of knowledge is in some circumstances (Venezuela versus Chile) related to those opinions. At a minimum the Venezuelan correlation is sufficient to encourage further research on this subject.

TABLE 7.4. Distribution of Aggregate Accuracy Score (percentages of respondents)

Total of Scores on Five Questions*	Chile				Venezuela			
	Government Officials	Businessmen	Students	All Groups	Government Officials	Businessmen	Students	All Groups
6	5.0	0	0	2.2	0	0	0	0
7	5.0	9.1	3.7	5.4	0	0	0	0
8	0	15.2	3.7	6.5	0	0	3.6	0.8
9	5.0	15.2	3.7	8.7	0	2.2	3.6	1.6
10	15.0	6.1	14.8	13.0	3.4	11.1	3.6	6.3
11	30.0	9.1	14.8	15.2	17.2	11.1	14.3	14.8
12	15.0	21.2	29.6	20.7	24.1	24.4	10.7	21.1
13	10.0	0	3.7	4.3	24.1	2.2	17.9	14.1
14	5.0	12.1	3.7	6.5	3.4	15.6	21.4	12.5
15	C	3.0	11.1	6.5	10.3	15.6	3.6	10.9
16	10.0	6.1	3.7	6.5	13.8	6.7	14.3	10.9
17	0	0	0	1.1	3.4	4.4	3.6	3.9
18	0	0	7.4	2.2	0	6.7	3.6	3.1
19	0	0	0	0	0	0	0	0
20	0	3.0	0	1.1	0	0	0	0

*See Table 7.2.

179

NATIONALISM

Throughout the survey, responses to questions could be influenced by the nationalistic feelings of respondents. It was possible, therefore, that patterns of responses could be identified according to the degree of nationalism felt by each individual. To explore this possibility, relations among the results of five questions in which nationalistic influence might be expected to be substantial were analyzed and Pearson correlation coefficients for them determined, as shown in Table 7.5.

The difference in the overall assessment of the value of national firms and U.S. MNCs might be attributed in part to nationalism, an emotional bias against the foreigners and a tendency to see the national firms in a more favorable light. Accordingly, the first indicator shown in Table 7.5 is the score for U.S. MNCs minus that for national firms; for example, a person giving a ."beneficial" rating of U.S. MNCs having a score of 2 minus "very beneficial" for national firms scored 1 would result in +1 for this indicator.

The respondents were asked what rate of profits ought to be reasonable. The responses showed that, at least in the Venezuelan case, the respondents made a distinction, the view being that the reasonable rate of profit for national firms ought to be higher than for U.S. firms. Such a view might be based on nationalism, so it was included in this set of data. The responses for national firms were subtracted from those for U.S. firms.

Responses showed that in both countries national firms were perceived as reinvesting a higher portion of earnings than U.S. firms. It could be hypothesized that this perception was based on the nationalistic feeling that the latter were draining profits out of the country excessively. The third indicator used in Table 7.5 therefore is the response to this question for national firms subtracted from that for U.S. firms.

The study showed a substantial body of opinion that U.S. firms ought to pay higher taxes than national firms, especially in Venezuela. With the hypothesis that nationalistic feelings might have contributed to this view, the responses for U.S. firms were subtracted from those for national firms, providing the fourth indicator.

The hypothesis tested in the final two indicators is that respondents with stronger nationalistic attitudes would be more inclined to feel that U.S. firms should employ fewer foreign nationals in managerial and professional positions.

The data in Table 7.5 do not show sufficient correlations to provide evidence that nationalism is a strong and consistent influence in forming perceptions on the subjects selected here. The correlations are generally weak, the significant ones being either in a haphazard pattern or, in the case of managers versus professionals, due to the inherent similarity of the subjects. One cannot demonstrate from these data that nationalism is not a significant influence on the attitudes since other explanations of the pattern are equally plausible, notably

TABLE 7.5. Cross Correlation of Indicators of Nationalism (Pearson correlation coefficients)

	Benefit U.S. MNCs minus National	Profits	Reinvestment	Taxes	Managers
Chile					
Profits, national firms minus U.S. MNCs	-.174*				
Reinvestment, national firms minus U.S. MNCs	.014	.184*			
Taxes should pay, U.S. MNCs minus national	-.019	-.385*	-.221*		
Foreign managers employed	-.094	-.042	-.101	-.052	
Foreign professionals	-.008	-.065	-.006	-.033	.758*
Venezuela					
Profits	.043				
Reinvestment	-.030	.002			
Taxes	-.018	.035	.027		
Managers	-.002	.022	-.148*	.323*	
Professionals	.053	.037	.073	.050	.580*

*Significant at .05 level.

that other influences are stronger in some or all of the perceptions and that the degree to which each subject involves the nationalistic attitudes of a respondent may vary greatly. The data are therefore useful simply in the methodological exploratory context of research as a demonstration of the difficulty of identifying the ways in which nationalism may affect attitudes on such subjects.

As one further exploratory test in this area, the indicators of nationalism were correlated with the overall appraisal of U.S. MNCs, that is, ratings as very beneficial, beneficial, and so forth. In general, the results showed the same haphazard pattern and lack of significant correlations as in the previous exercise. The only strong correlations were with the data measuring the differences between overall appraisal of U.S. MNCs and national firms, which were .558 for Chile and .759 for Venezuela. But this would be expected on other grounds than nationalism since the two sets of data concern the same basic perception question.

8

PERCEPTIONS OF U.S.
PAPER FIRMS IN BRAZIL

David H. Blake
Robert E. Driscoll

The attitude study reported in this chapter was one phase of an attempt to measure and assess the multiple impacts of foreign pulp and paper companies in Brazil. There were two parts to the research. One part analyzed the economic and social impact of the companies at the local community level, at the state level, and at the national level. In addition, the study sought to inventory and assess the social activities of the companies.

The second part of the study involved interviews with state and local government officials, business leaders, opinion leaders such as teachers, clergy, media, workers, and so on, and employees at various levels about their attitudes toward the companies. The intent was to obtain some measure of how the firms were viewed in general and in specific areas of concern. The results of this second part of the study are analyzed here.

BACKGROUND OF THE COMPANIES

The operations studied were wholly owned subsidiaries of the U.S. firms, Olinkraft and Westvaco. The former, Olinkraft Celulose e Papel Limitada, had a kraft paper plant in Igaras near Lages in the state of Santa Catarina, and a box

This chapter is based on the following book: *The Social and Economic Impacts of Transnational Corporations: Case Studies of the U.S. Paper Industry in Brazil*, by David H. Blake and Robert E. Driscoll. Copyright held by Fund for Multinational Management Education.

TABLE 8.1. Comparison of Eight Leading Brazilian and Foreign Firms in Pulp and Paper Industry in Brazil, 1968 and 1974

	1968				1974*			
	Sales Pulp and Paper		Paper Production		Sales Pulp and Paper		Paper Production	
	% of Total	Rank	% of Total	Rank	% of Total	Rank	% of Total	Rank
Brazilian firms	29.6	1, 2, 3, 7	31	1, 2, 4, 6	20.2	1, 2, 3, 6	29.6	1, 2, 3, 6, 8
Foreign firms	18.3		11.2		12.9		12.3	
Champion (U.S.)	6.3	4	2.9	5	3.6	4	4.2	4
Olinkraft (U.S.)	2.4	8	2.2	7	3.2	5	2.8	7
Rigesa (U.S.)	4.1	6	3.9	3	3.1	7	3.6	5
Pirahy (British)	5.5	5	2.2	8	3.0	8	1.7	9

*The 1974 figures do not reflect the current expansion of Olinkraft and understate Rigesa's production at Tres Barras, which was only beginning in 1974.

plant at Jundiai on the main highway between Campinas and São Paulo. The latter, Rigesa Celulose, Papel e Embalagems Limitada, had a paper mill at Tres Barras, close to Canoinhas in Santa Catarina and a box plant at Valinhos near São Paulo. In both instances the paper plants were in rural sections where the firms owned forest lands, which made the operations self-sufficient in raw material, a significant element in their image since previous Brazilian owners of both operations had not developed such resources. The box plants of both firms were growing operations which were important factors in the moderate-sized industrial cities in which they were located. The economic and social analysis in the study demonstrated that both firms had made strong contributions at the local level in such matters as employment and social services and at the national level, especially to the Brazilian balance of payments in saving foreign exchange. Table 8.1 indicates the status of these firms in the Brazilian industry.

SURVEY RESULTS

The intent of the interviews was to gather data on the perceived impact of the firms on the local community, the state, and the country. Interviews were completed with 196 Brazilians, 88 in communities associated with Olinkraft, 77 in communities with Rigesa plants, and 31 at the state and national level in cities not directly associated with the firms' operations.

The interviews, conducted by a Brazilian research firm,* followed an interview schedule that had both forced choice and open-ended questions on a variety of issues. (A copy of the questionnaire in English is in Appendix 8.A.) The respondents were asked to identify what they thought were the positive and negative effects of the companies after they had indicated on a five-point scale whether the companies' effects had been very positive, positive, don't know, negative, or very negative. In addition, respondents were asked to indicate on a similar scale the effect of the companies on 19 different items like balance of payments, tax payments, fringe benefits, pollution, and so on. The interviews also asked the respondents to express their views, on a five-point scale from much better to much worse, as to how the companies compared with other U.S. firms in Brazil, with non-American but foreign multinationals, and with Brazilian firms in their impact on Brazil. Demographic data were also collected on the age of the respondents, their sources of information about the companies, and their location relative to the major plants of the firms.

The appraisals shown in Table 8.2 reflect highly favorable feelings toward both firms. The effects at the local community level were rated highest with "very positive" responses by 61 percent for Olinkraft and 84 percent for Rigesa. The perception of impact at the national level was not so overwhelmingly

---

*Demanda Instituto de Pesquisas e Estudos de Mercado Ltda.

TABLE 8.2. Impact on Local Community, State, and Brazil
(percentages)

	Very Positive	Positive	Don't Know, Negative, or Very Negative
Olinkraft			
Local community	61.4	37.5	1.1
State	50.2	44.3	5.7
Brazil	28.4	61.4	10.3
Rigesa			
Local community	84.4	14.3	1.3
State	55.8	40.3	3.9
Brazil	45.5	50.6	3.9

supportive but still strong with 90 percent at Olinkraft and 96 percent at Rigesa giving at least a positive rating.

Table 8.3 presents several of the more significant distinctions among different types of respondents on the degree of positiveness toward the impact of the companies. For Olinkraft the differences in appraisal of impact at the local community level suggest that the closer and more involved people are with the company the more positive their response will be. In addition, the urban Jundiai plant was only several years old and had not had the time to have the impact that the rural facility at Igaras had had. Moreover, it probably would never have the same kind of impact because of the essential oneness of the plant in Igaras with the local community. Jundiai was part of the São Paulo industrial complex; Igaras stood alone.

When Rigesa results were analyzed in terms of the influence of various independent variables, only in the case of urban or rural location were there differences of a statistically significant character. The respondents from the urban area of Valinhos were significantly more positive about the effect of Rigesa than were the rural respondents in the Tres Barras area.

Several explanations might be offered for these findings. While Tres Barras had been the site of Rigesa forestry operations for many years, the mill had only been in operation for several years. Undoubtedly the construction and start-up phases, including the influx of new workers, caused some dislocations in the area. In addition, after more than 20 years in Valinhos, the company had had more time to have a significant impact on that community, so the people were more aware of the positive aspects of the firm's activities at all levels.

Table 8.4 shows the responses to an open-ended question asking those interviewed to elaborate on the positive aspects of the companies' activities. The

TABLE 8.3. Attitudes toward Impact of Firms According to Location, Closeness of Following Activities, and Source of News (percentages)

	Number of Respondents	Impact on Community			Impact on State			Impact on Brazil			
		Very Positive	Positive	Don't Know	Very Positive	Positive	Don't Know	Very Positive	Positive	Don't Know	Negative
Location											
Olinkraft:											
Rural	62	67.7	32.3	0	51.6	43.5	4.8	27.4	58.1	11.3	3.2
Urban	26	46.2	50.0	3.8	46.2	46.2	7.7	30.8	69.2	0	0
Rigesa:											
Rural	45	75.6	22.2	2.2	46.7	53.3	0	33.3	64.4	2.2	0
Urban	32	96.9	3.1	0	68.8	21.9	9.4	62.5	31.3	6.3	0
Following activities											
Olinkraft:											
Very closely	46	67.4	32.6	0	45.7	50.0	4.3	21.7	67.4	8.7	2.2
Closely	30	66.7	33.3	0	63.3	33.3	3.3	46.7	43.3	6.7	3.3
Not very closely	12	25.0	66.7	8.3	33.3	50.0	16.7	8.3	83.3	8.3	0
Rigesa:											
Very closely	42	92.9	7.1	0	50.0	47.6	2.4	45.2	50.0	4.8	0
Closely	31	86.6	16.1	3.2	67.7	29.0	3.2	48.4	48.4	3.2	0
Not very closely	4	25.0	75.0	0	25.0	50.0	25.0	25.0	75.0	0	0

TABLE 8.3 (continued)

Source of news

Olinkraft:

Employees	66	66.7	33.3	0	50.0	45.5	4.5	30.3	60.6	6.1	3.0
Other	22	45.5	50.0	4.5	50.0	40.9	9.1	22.7	63.6	13.6	0

Rigesa:

Employees	61	86.9	11.5	1.6	55.7	4.1	3.3	44.3	52.5	3.3	0
Other	16	75.0	25.0	0	56.3	37.5	6.3	50.0	43.8	6.3	0

TABLE 8.4.   Positive Aspects of Companies' Effect on Community

	Number of Times Mentioned
Creates employment	110
Contribution to community life	49
Contribution to industrial development	42
Contribution of taxes and services to government	26
Generates other business	19
Good place to work	14
Brings in and develops technology and employee skills	13
Reforestation activities	9
Provides needed products	8

sample of people interviewed was heavily skewed toward those employed directly or indirectly by the firm; thus it is not surprising that employment ranks so high. This may also reflect the fact that Igaras/Lages and Tres Barras/ Canoinhas, where 53 percent of the interviews were conducted, were very much dependent upon the mills for jobs and income. When asked to elaborate on the negative aspects of the companies' activities, three people mentioned pollution, 24 decried the lack of greater investment by the firms, and 164 had no answer or did not know of any negative aspects.

Regarding the impact on the states, the major benefits are listed in Table 8.5. The respondents were conscious of the importance of generating tax revenues, since most local monies, and therefore services, were financed through taxes paid to the state government, which then returned some of the money to the local units. The authors thought it interesting that reforestation activities were mentioned relatively infrequently at both the state and local level, for both companies

TABLE 8.5.   Positive Aspects of Companies' Effect on States

	Number of Times Mentioned
Generates taxes	97
Creation of employment	49
Contribution to regional development	36
Provides needed products	16
Reforestation efforts	14
Generates other business	12

were quite proud of the fact that they had developed a pulp and paper industry with their own forests, where earlier lumbering activities had essentially eliminated most local supplies of trees. On the negative side, 165 respondents stated no negative effects for the state, and the concerns that were expressed did not cluster in any one area, though three mentioned pollution and three felt that the important decisions were made in the United States.

Table 8.6 presents the opinions of positive impact on Brazil. It should be noted that the federal government had restricted exports of pulp, thereby reducing the opportunity for positive contributions to the balance of payments. The fact, though, that generating exports was mentioned may suggest some lack of knowledge by the respondents. There were only eight negative statements offered by the respondents, three concerned with foreign decision making and two concerned with pollution.

However, responses to a direct question asking respondents to indicate those activities or effects of the companies that had harmed the local community, the states, or Brazil provided more information about the negative aspects of the firms (Table 8.7). Pollution was clearly an important concern, but apparently something that was minor in comparison to the perceived benefits of the firm. While pollution was the important issue, the survey did pick up a number of allusions here and elsewhere in the interviews to specific concerns of some individuals. The Tres Barras housing shortage was mentioned, and a member of the clergy was upset by the fact that one result of the construction crews at Tres Barras was the existence of too many unwed mothers. A few were concerned about the fact that the native Parana pine had been almost totally replaced by the Loblolly pine. Our point is that while there was almost unanimous support for these firms there were some local issues that ought not to be ignored.

TABLE 8.6.   Positive Aspects of Companies' Effect on Brazil

	Number of Times Mentioned
Creation of employment	31
Generates taxes	28
Generally positive	26
Generates exports and reduces imports	25
Contributes to economic development	25
Develops paper industry	23
Provides needed products	22
Human and technical development	18
Helps create a good image for Brazil	12
Generates other business	9

TABLE 8.7. Harmful Effects of Companies on Local Community, States, or Brazil

	Number of Times Mentioned
No harm	91
Pollution	60
Don't know, no answer, or neutral	33
Local problems	7
Only one kind of tree planted	4

Perceptions of impact in certain subjects were selected for more in-depth analysis according to the characteristics of the respondents. The issues on which we now focus are effect on pollution, protection of forestry resources, helping to make the local community a better place to live, creating jobs and businesses for others not working directly for the firms, and political effect. Table 8.8 summarizes the responses on these five issues.

In further analysis of the responses on the pollution issue for Olinkraft, it is interesting to note that urban respondents were more negative than rural respondents, 62 percent of the former and 37 percent of the latter, with chi square significance level of .1. This was a particularly intriguing finding because the plant in Igaras was a far heavier polluter than the clean box plant in Jundiai. A similar finding was that employees and suppliers, those most closely connected with the company, were less concerned about pollution issues than others were: 40 percent of the employees and suppliers responded negatively or very negatively while 69 percent of the others did so. (This result is significant at the .04 level.) Two explanations for these findings can be developed. One is that the rural respondents and the employees and suppliers were more closely linked with the company and felt that the pollution was an acceptable price to pay for the many other contributions of the company. The other explanation was that those more removed from Olinkraft responded essentially to what they had read and heard about pollution, or experienced generally in the São Paulo area, and that this colored their reaction to Olinkraft's pollution.

On the issue of the protection of forestry resources, a somewhat similar pattern emerges. Of the rural respondents, 92 percent felt that Olinkraft's impact was positive to very positive while 77 percent of the urban people responded in the same way (significant at the .1 level). Of those who followed the company's activities closely or very closely, 92 percent of the respondents felt that the company had a positive or very positive effect on the protection of forestry resources. Only 58 percent of the 12 who did not follow the company closely felt that the impact was positive (significant at the .001 level). Again,

TABLE 8.8. **Responses about Companies' Effect on Various Issues
(percentages)**

	Very Positive or Positive	Don't Know	Very Negative or Negative
		Olinkraft	
Pollution	40	16	44
Protection of forestry resources	87	13	
Helping local community	84	16	
Creating secondary jobs and businesses	73	27	
Political effect	47	39	15
		Rigesa	
Pollution	41.6	26	32.5
Protection of forestry resources	90.9	9.1	
Helping local community	83.1	16.9	
Creating secondary jobs and businesses	84.4	15.6	
Political effect	31.2	59.7	9.1

those more removed physically or in terms of knowledge seemed to have less positive opinions.

The same pattern of differences emerged on the issue of creating jobs and businesses for those not working directly for the firm. Seventy-nine percent of the rural respondents were at least positive, while 58 percent of those who did not follow the company closely responded positively or very positively (significant at the .09 level).

This same tendency existed regarding Olinkraft's political effect. Rural respondents and those who followed the company closely or very closely were more likely to be positive about the company's political effect than the urban and less knowledgeable respondents. The implication of this analysis is clear. The more closely linked people are to the firm—geographically and in terms of information—the more positive the reaction to the company's actions on a number of issues. Unfortunately, the sample was not large enough to determine whether the rural variable or the knowledge factor was more important in leading to positive reactions.

At Rigesa further analysis indicated that the urban respondents had more positive feelings about the pollution issue than did the rural respondents (chi square level of .059). A possible explanation for this is that the new mill at

Tres Barras (rural) had brought pollution while the company had significantly reduced pollution levels in Valinhos from what they once were. This had occurred both by greater pollution control efforts and by the phasing out of the more polluting activities.

The only other variable that had any importance was the fact that the youngest respondents, age 17–25, were significantly less positive (only 50 percent of them) than people from other age groups (chi square probability level, .027). An explanation for this might be the lack of experience or understanding on the part of these younger respondents of how Rigesa helped to create jobs in the community.

There was a great deal of concern by the respondents on the pollution issue. In addition, there was a significant amount of "don't know" response on the question of Rigesa's impact on politics. On the three other issues, however, there again was overwhelming support for the beneficial impact of the company.

The responses to the questions on the 19 specific effects on Brazil are listed in Table 8.9, beginning with those receiving the highest positive score. The data are largely self-explanatory. It may be useful to point out, though, that only on the last two issues of political effect and pollution are there more don't know and negative responses than positive ones.

When asked to compare Olinkraft with other kinds of firms, the respondents clearly felt that Olinkraft was better (Table 8.10). In the case of Rigesa, the majority felt that the firm had a more beneficial impact than Brazilian firms had. However, in comparison with other U.S. firms and other foreign companies (not American in origin), the respondents were less certain. Few felt that Rigesa was worse than other firms, but a major portion responded in a don't know fashion.

Further analysis of the Olinkraft data revealed that the respondents who followed the company's activities more closely, those who were employees and suppliers, and those who obtained information from employees, were all more likely to view Olinkraft positively in this comparative rating than those more removed from the firm. (These results are all statistically significant at the .05 level or lower, except for one at the .06 level.) Unfortunately, through interview error, 24 of the respondents were not asked about their age; but we are able to report that on the basis of 64 interviews age did seem to have an effect on the comparison of Olinkraft with other U.S. and non-U.S. foreign firms. Generally, respondents in the 36–45, 46–55, and 56 and older ranges were less likely to rank Olinkraft as being better or much better than those of a younger age.

Analysis of the Rigesa data showed that in the comparison with other U.S. firms the rural respondents were less positive (28.9 percent as opposed to 53.1 percent for the urban respondent, with a chi square significance level of .044). No explanation is offered for this finding. In addition, those who obtained information from employees were more likely to feel that Rigesa had a better impact than Brazilian firms. Of the 61 people obtaining information from employees, 73.8 percent felt that the firm was more beneficial than a Brazilian firm; only 50 percent of those who did not use employee

TABLE 8.9. Effect of Companies on Various Issues
(percentages; N = 196)

	Very Positive	Positive	No Answer Don't Know	Negative	Very Negative
Steady employment	42	53	3	2	—
Tax payments	45	43	12	—	—
Training Brazilians	38	50	9	3	—
Transfer of technology	37	47	12	4	—
Protection of forestry resources	43	40	8	8	1
Economic effect	29	56	14	2	—
Fringe benefits	34	48	13	5	1
Wages	28	53	16	3	1
Nice place to work	27	50	18	6	1
Creating secondary jobs and businesses	22	56	16	6	—
Social effect	24	51	18	8	—
Level of profits	23	47	27	2	1
Helping local community	24	47	21	7	—
Responsive to needs of local community	25	47	21	7	—
Responsive to needs of Brazil	19	47	30	4	1
Balance of payments	17	50	27	6	—
Responsive to needs of states	16	52	28	4	1
Political effect	6	31	52	10	2
Pollution	10	25	24	36	6

Note: Percentages may not equal 100 because of rounding.

194

TABLE 8.10. Comparison with Other Types of Firms
(percentages)

	Better and Much Better	Don't Know	Worse and Much Worse
	Olinkraft		
Other U.S. firms	62	37	1
Non-U.S. foreign	71	28	1
Brazilian	69	23	8
	Rigesa		
Other U.S. firms	39	57.1	3.9
Non-U.S. foreign	37.7	57.1	5.2
Brazilian	68.8	22.1	9.1

sources of information felt that way. (This is statistically significant at the .063 level.) None of the other independent variables had any major bearing on the responses to this set of questions.

Much of the preceding data has been analyzed in terms of the demographic characteristics of the respondents:

1. Age
2. Rural/urban location
3. Geographical closeness to facilities of companies
4. Closeness with which they followed activities of companies
5. Employees and suppliers vs. business leaders, educators, clergy and community leaders, political and government officials, media people
6. Source of information about companies

Rather than report the actual statistics for all the analyses, we will discuss the findings of statistical significance and present the data where they are thought to be particularly useful.

Age was a characteristic that affected the reactions of respondents on some of the issues, but there did not seem to be reasonable theoretical explanations for these effects. However, on the major issues of the impact of companies on local community, state, and Brazil, age was not an important variable. Nor was age an important factor for the comparison with other firms. On the pollution issue and on the protection of forestry resources, the 56 and older category, as well as the 26–35 category, were less positive than other age groups. The 17–25 age group was far less positive than others regarding the creation of secondary jobs. Each of the above findings was statistically significant at the .05 level, but we are unable to provide a plausible explanation for these relationships.

In comparison of the urban with the rural respondent, a much clearer picture emerges. Fifty-five percent of the respondents came from the rural areas of Lages/Igaras and Tres Barras/Canoinhas, while 45 percent came from the urban areas of Blumenau, Florianopolis, Jundiai, Valinhos, and São Paulo. As Table 8.11 shows, on most issues rural respondents were likely to be more positively inclined than urban respondents. The latter, in most cases, also felt strongly that the companies had a positive impact, but they were not as positive as the rural respondents.

The results were also analyzed according to the geographical closeness of the respondents to company facilities. The 165 respondents from Igaras/Lages, Tres Barras/Canoinhas, Jundiai, and Valinhos were all located close to major facilities of the companies. More distant were the 31 respondents from São Paulo, Blumenau, and Florianopolis. This variable of closeness versus distance had an important impact on the attitudes of those interviewed, as is shown in Table 8.12. On all but one issue there was significant difference between those close and those distant, with the former always being more positive. Those living at a

TABLE 8.11. **Rural versus Urban Respondents on Different Issues**
(N = 196)

		Chi Square Level of Significance
Effect on community	Rural respondents more positive	.003
Effect on state	Rural respondents more positive	.06
Effect on Brazil	No significant difference	.4
Effect on pollution	Rural respondents more positive and less negative	.09
Effect on forestry	Rural respondents more positive	.007
Helping local community	Rural respondents more positive	.0006
Creating secondary jobs and businesses	No significant difference	.17
Political effect	Rural respondents more positive and less negative	.0093
Comparison with U.S. firms	No significant difference	.15
Comparison with non-U.S. foreign firms	Rural respondents more positive	.02
Comparison with Brazilian firms	No significant difference	.5

TABLE 8.12. Close versus Distant Respondents on Different Issues
(N = 196)

		Chi Square Level of Significance
Effect on community	Close respondents more positive	.0000
Effect on state	Close respondents more positive	.01
Effect on Brazil	Close respondents more positive	.005
Effect on pollution	Close respondents more positive and less negative	.0002
Effect on forestry	Close respondents more positive	.0000
Helping local community	Close respondents more positive	.0000
Creating secondary jobs and businesses	No significant difference	.89
Political effect	Close respondents more positive	.06
Comparison with U.S. firms	Close respondents more positive	.01
Comparison with non-U.S. foreign firms	Close respondents more positive	.0000
Comparison with Brazilian firms	Close respondents more positive	.0000

distance from the plants were not usually negative about the effects of the companies, but they were much less positive.

The variable concerned with how closely the respondents followed the activities of the companies exhibited a similar pattern as on the geographical closeness versus distance dimension. Those following the company closely or very closely were likely to be significantly more positive and sometimes less negative than those who did not follow the company closely. As might be expected, there was substantial but not total overlap between those respondents located at a distance and those who did not follow company activities closely. Given the small numbers involved, it was not possible to make any meaningful distinction, and thus for all practical purposes, this variable is the same as the geographical closeness one. The results are almost exactly the same.

We also analyzed the results according to the occupational characteristics of the respondents. On the one hand, there were the employees of and suppliers to the companies—67 percent of the 196 respondents. On the other, there were various community and government leaders such as business executives, educators, clergy, government and political officials, media people, and general community leaders, composing 33 percent of the respondents. The results summarized in Table 8.13 show that on most issues the employees and suppliers were

TABLE 8.13. Employees and Suppliers versus Community and Government Leaders (N = 196)

		Chi Square Level of Significance
Effect on community	Employees et al. more positive	.0001
Effect on state	No significant difference	.25
Effect on Brazil	No significant difference	.32
Effect on pollution	Employees et al. more positive and less negative	.0000
Effect on forestry	Employees et al. more positive	.0000
Helping local community	Employees et al. more positive	.0011
Creating secondary jobs and businesses	No significant difference	.87
Political effect	No significant difference	.14
Comparison with U.S. firms	Employees et al. more positive	.002
Comparison with non-U.S. foreign firms	Employees et al. more positive	.0000
Comparison with Brazilian firms	Employees et al. more positive	.0000

more positive about the impact of the companies than the other respondents were. For the most part, these differences are statistically significant.

The preceding analyses provide substantial evidence that the geographical, informational, and occupational closeness of the respondents had a significant effect on attitudes about the positive impacts of the companies. The rural location of the respondent exhibited a similar tendency, but there was substantial overlap in this category with the above three variables. Unfortunately, the interviewing procedure did not provide enough respondents in each category so that the authors could try to isolate through more sophisticated statistical techniques which of the above variables, if any, was most critical. However, these four variables do suggest a multidimensional rippling effect in which those more closely linked to the company—by job, location, or information—are likely to be significantly more positive about the effect of the company than those who are more removed. The relationship can be usefully expressed by a set of concentric circles with those closest to the center associated with positive attitudes toward the companies. Ideally, the configuration in Figure 8.1 should be multidimensional, showing a clustering close to the firm of employees and suppliers, local business, community and government leaders, and persons who follow the firm more closely. Here, the strong tendency is for very positive attitudes. As one moves away from the center on each of these dimensions, the attitudes become somewhat less positive. As one moves away, attitudes are likely to be formed from very indirect information sources, knowledge of the firm will be less, and existing, but nonspecific, predispositions about foreign investment are likely to color one's perceptions.

This multidimensional concept of distance is susceptible to more sophisticated analysis. As a step in that direction we assigned a "closeness" score to each respondent for each dimension shown on Figure 8.1. A score of 1 was given to those close to the firm (employees and suppliers, those living near the operations, and those following them closely) and a score of 2 to those not close in each respect. The sum of these figures was then determined as a composite "closeness" score. Table 8.14 gives the breakdown of respondents by these scores and the distribution of their views of effects of the firms on the community and Brazil. The data show clearly the strong correlation of closeness to degree of favorable assessment of effects on the community and the somewhat less strong relation of views about effects on Brazil. This statistical analysis is relatively crude due to the nature of the data. We would encourage future research in which the various dimensions of closeness would be determined with greater precision and dispersion along measurement scales.

FIGURE 8.1. Effect of Distance on Attitude toward Companies

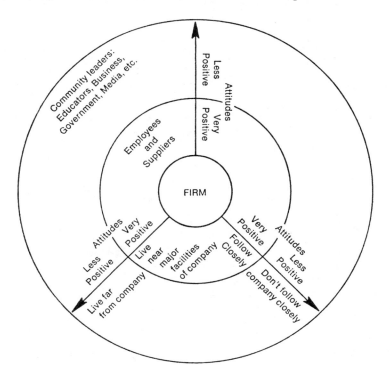

TABLE 8.14. "Closeness" Scores and Attitudes on Effects of Firms on Community and Brazil

Composite "Closeness" Score*	Number of Respondents	Effect on Community (percentages)				Effect on Brazil (percentages)			
		Very Positive	Positive	Don't Know	Negative	Very Positive	Positive	Don't Know	Negative
3	120	75.0	25.0	0	0	38.3	53.3	6.7	1.7
4	41	63.4	29.3	7.3	0	29.3	65.9	4.9	0
5	20	30.0	55.0	15.0	0	30.0	55.0	15.0	0
6	15	13.3	40.0	33.3	13.3	20.0	46.7	26.7	6.7

*3 = Closest; 6 = Most distant.

These findings on the effect of closeness suggest some interesting and important hypotheses for governmental as well as company consideration. It may well be that political pressures and governmental officials located in distant capitals may make policy that is contradictory to that which might be advocated by those who are more immediately and directly affected by the operations of the company. Whether policy decisions, theoretically speaking, are more or less beneficial for the nation as a whole varies from case to case, but the evidence presented here suggests an attitudinal tendency different from that of those close to the firm. From the corporate point of view, the findings imply the need to convey the nature of the firm's impact to those who are more removed from it.

The results reported above were also analyzed according to how the respondents obtained information about these firms. Most of those interviewed, 132, indicated that their information came through the companies as employees or through employees of the companies who were friends. The news media were the major source of information for 23 respondents; commercial sources (business associations, banks, economic surveys, competitors) for 41; government and political sources for 7; and social and community sources for 10. Because of the obvious overlap with the employee occupation category discussed previously, not too much was revealed by this analysis. Generally, though, those relying upon the news media or commercial sources tended to be quite a bit less positive on the 11 issues listed in Tables 8.11, 8.12, and 8.13 than those relying upon employee sources. In some cases, particularly in the comparison with other types of firms, the differences were statistically significant at the .1 level, at least. Once again, closeness to the companies seems to be an important factor.

The data presented in this chapter show immense support for the impact of the Olinkraft and Rigesa firms. The 196 people interviewed generally felt that the firms contributed extensively to the local communities, to the states of São Paulo and especially Santa Catarina, and to Brazil. Of course, the degree of support varied with the issue and with the characteristics of the respondents. However, it is interesting to note that the companies were judged to be beneficial primarily because of the contributions that accompany a successful investment, particularly employment, taxes, local and regional development, and so on. The people interviewed were impressed by the fact that a successful investment brought with it, more or less as a matter of course, significant benefits for Brazil and its people. On the negative side, pollution was singled out as a negative factor of the companies' operations. Clearly, though, the companies were held in high regard in almost all respects by the 196 people interviewed.

APPENDIX 8.A

Questionnaire for Brazilian Survey

I. Background Information
  1. Category of elite

  2. Age

  3. How would you describe your political views?

  _____ _____ _____
  left of center   center   right of center

  4. Please describe the extent and nature of your contacts with the foreign owned paper industry, especially Rigesa and Olinkraft.

  5. Generally, how closely do you follow the activities of this firm (these firms)?

  _____ _____ _____
  very closely   closely not very closely

  6. How do you obtain information about the firm (these firms)? Which information sources are most important to you?

II. Attitudes toward the firm (firms)

In this section I am going to ask you questions about how you evaluate the activities of the company (companies). After telling me generally how you feel, perhaps you can tell me more specifically what you think.

  1. a) The company's (companies') effect on the local community has been generally

  _____ _____ _____ _____ _____
  very positive   positive   don't know   negative   very negative

  b) Please elaborate (both positive and negative aspects)

  2. a) The company's (companies') effect on the state has been generally

  _____ _____ _____ _____ _____
  very positive   positive   don't know   negative   very negative

  b) Please elaborate (both positive and negative aspects)

202

3. a) The company's (companies') effect on Brazil has generally been

very positive	positive	don't know	negative	very negative
————	————	————	————	————

b) Please elaborate (both positive and negative aspects)

4. Please indicate and discuss those activities or effects of the company which have benefited the local community, the state, or Brazil.

5. Please indicate and discuss those activities or effects of the company which have harmed the local community, the state, or Brazil.

6. Listed below are a number of activities or impacts of the company (companies). Please indicate whether the company's (companies') effect has been very positive _____ , positive _____ , don't know _____ , negative _____ , very negative _____ . We are also interested in anything you may wish to say about each one of these areas:

	very positive	positive	don't know	negative	very negative
	————	————	————	————	————
a) Brazil's balance of payments					
b) Profits					
c) Tax payments					
d) Transfer of technology					
e) Providing steady employment					
f) Wages					
g) Training Brazilian workers and managers					
h) Fringe benefits					
i) Nice place to work					
j) Pollution					
k) Protection of forestry resources					

l) Helping to make
the local community
a better place to live

m) Creating jobs and businesses for others not
working directly
for the firm

n) Responsive to needs
and concerns of
local community

o) Responsive to needs
and concerns
of state

p) Responsive to needs
and concerns
of Brazil

q) Economic effect

r) Social effect

s) Political effect

7. As far as being a good corporate citizen and compared with other U.S. firms, do you feel that the company (companies) is—

Much Better Than Other U.S. Firms	Better Than Other U.S. Firms	Don't Know	Worse Than Other U.S. Firms	Much Worse Than Other U.S. Firms

8. Compared with other non-American multinational companies, do you feel that the company (companies) is—

Much Better Than Other Non-U.S. Foreign Firms	Better Than Other Non-U.S. Foreign Firms	Don't Know	Worse Than Other Non-U.S. Foreign Firms	Much Worse Than Other Non-U.S. Foreign Firms

9. Compared with Brazilian owned companies, do you feel that the company is—

Much Better Than Brazilian Firms	Better Than Brazilian Firms	Don't Know	Worse Than Brazilian Firms	Much Worse Than Brazilian Firms

10. Anything you would like to add?

Thank you.

9

PERCEPTIONS OF FOREIGN INVESTMENT IN NIGERIA

Andrew C. E. Hilton

Notwithstanding significant exceptions, it is generally true that, in relatively developed countries, societal cleavages tend to cut across, rather than to reinforce, one another. It is also true that in these more or less homogeneous societies the entry of the MNE does not usually represent a radically new social, political, or economic input. In relatively less-developed countries, on the other hand, ethnic, linguistic, religious, urban-rural, and economic cleavages tend to be mutually reinforcing—with the concomitant results that the political structure is fragile and the circulation of elites is rapid and often violent.[1]

Within these societies—of which Nigeria, with its ethnic fractionalization and history of political instability, is a paradigm case—the MNE, by virtue both of its size and the value-clusters with which it is associated, is bound to have a more profound impact than in societies accustomed to large-scale industry and ostensibly committed to Weberian norms of rationality and bureaucracy.

This chapter, therefore, deals with the position of direct foreign investment in a country deeply divided by ethnic, linguistic, and religious cleavages and which epitomizes the most extreme problems of development. It presents some conclusions, generated by data collected in 1972, and addresses itself to three major points: (1) the levels of awareness of foreign investors shown by respondents, (2) the degree of favorableness shown toward investment by different

This study, data collection for which was made possible by the Danforth Foundation and by a grant from the University of Pennsylvania, should in no way be taken to represent official policy of the International Bank for Reconstruction and Development, with which the author is currently associated.

national groups, and (3) the possibility that hostility toward certain foreign groups might serve a positive function both as a means of securing in-group cohesiveness and as a way of diverting hostility from other potentially more vulnerable expatriate communities.[2]

The question of foreign investment is not of merely academic interest in Nigeria. While the situation of 1949—where indigenous traders controlled only 5 percent of imports and the three largest expatriate companies accounted for 49 percent of all traded items[3]—no longer exists, the 1968 Industrial Survey of 625 manufacturing establishments estimated that, out of a total paid-up capital of $179.8 million, private non-Nigerian sources accounted for almost $126 million—or 70 percent.[4] Of this figure, approximately 51 percent was British, 20 percent was American, and 22 percent was Western European. The remainder—only 7 percent of the total—was divided among such groups as the Lebanese and Indians.[5]

The economic and psychological impact of such a large foreign presence is compounded by the privileged position of expatriates within—or rather parallel to—Nigerian society. In the first place, most Western European and American expatriates are geographically contained within what are essentially white ghettos. Few Nigerians in Lagos can afford the annual house rent of up to $8,400 in Ikoyi, Apapa, or on Victoria Island. Second, the distribution of wealth in Nigeria is highly skewed: of 87,714 employees interviewed in the 1968 Industrial Survey only 2,040 (2.3 percent) were non-Nigerians, yet this expatriate group accounted for 25.1 percent of all wages and salaries, and received 63.4 percent of all "nonmonetary" rewards. Finally, given that at least 56 percent of the indigenous labor force is engaged in small scale agriculture, and the estimates of urban unemployment run as high as 20 to 25 percent, the economic position of the expatriates as a highly privileged and virtually inaccessible elite is further enhanced. After all, the average foreigner earns eight times as much as the most privileged Nigerian—those with jobs.[6]

AWARENESS OF FOREIGN INVESTMENT

Notwithstanding these glaring social and economic inequalities, the tendency for foreigners to both live and work in relatively narrowly defined enclaves, and to interact with the indigenous population only minimally and almost exclusively on a master-servant basis, would seem to make widespread awareness of the extent of foreign investment a priori unlikely. To test this hypothesis, respondents were asked two sets of questions: (1) to ascertain whether certain specific firms were felt to be domestic or foreign, and (2) to assess their ability to link particular companies with their individual national origins.

In the first case respondents were asked whether they thought five well-known, larger firms were "at least 51 percent owned by foreigners." Of those chosen, three were in fact expatriate and two were owned and controlled by Nigerians, but as is illustrated in Table 9.1, four out of the five were assigned correctly by a majority. The sole exception can perhaps best be attributed to

TABLE 9.1. Awareness of Domestic or Foreign Status of Specific Companies

Company	Actual status	Percentage of those choosing each category	
		Foreign	Domestic
Nigerian Breweries	Foreign	55.1	44.9
Henry Stephens and Sons	Domestic	34.1	65.9
West African Breweries	Domestic	72.4	27.6
Kingsway Stores	Foreign	82.6	17.4
Nigerian Tobacco Co.	Foreign	51.0	49.0

the extremely sophisticated market strategy employed by West African Breweries to compete against long-established and very popular foreign-owned beers, such as "Star," "Heineken," and "Guinness"—all of which are bottled by the foreign-owned Nigerian Breweries.

While only 16.6 percent of respondents identified every company correctly, almost 75 percent were able to identify three or more accurately and, even among manual workers and the unemployed, over half made less than two errors. Moreover, there was a clear association between socioeconomic status and level of awareness—for example, 63 percent of respondents earning over $1,960 per annum, and only 44.3 percent of those earning less, identified four or five correctly,[7] but such a correlation is less important than the overall inference of a population highly aware of the presence of foreign investors.

On the second question, when respondents were asked to give the nationality of companies identified to be foreign, in only one case was the modal response not the correct one—a situation shown in Table 9.2. Furthermore, in the case of U.T.C., its Swiss origins might not be apparent even to sophisticated observers.

What is perhaps equally interesting is the perceived dominance of British business and the extent to which the United States has come to be associated with the petroleum sector. Thus, U.T.C.—a Swiss company in the traditionally

TABLE 9.2. Awareness of Foreign Companies by Specific National Origin

Company	Correct origin	Countries listed (percentage of those responding)				
		U.K.	U.S.	France	Switzerland	Nigeria
U.T.C.	Switzerland	67.2	1.4	4.3	15.8	1.5
Lever Brothers	U.K.	85.7	3.1	2.8	0.2	2.9
Total Oil	France	26.7	29.6	31.4	—	1.4
Mobil Oil	U.S.	31.7	56.9	3.4	—	1.1

TABLE 9.3. Percentages Giving Correct Nationality of Selected Foreign Firms

Respondents	Enterprises			
	U.T.C.	Lever Brothers	Total Oil	Mobil Oil
Employment status				
White collar	24.9	89.0	42.9	61.1
Blue collar[a]	10.6	84.2	24.0	56.4
Students	7.6	82.7	22.2	50.7
Education				
Postsecondary	20.0	88.1	37.5	60.5
No further education	13.0	84.3	27.3	54.3
Annual income				
Over $1,960	32.6	93.9	48.0	70.3
$1,960 or less	11.1	83.4	26.6	52.9
Preferred criteria for office holders[b]				
Modern	16.4	87.8	33.6	61.0
Traditional	13.6	78.7	23.5	41.2
Preferred method of farming[c]				
Innovative	18.9	87.3	34.3	58.3
Traditional	5.2	80.5	21.2	52.7

[a]Manual workers, plus those currently unemployed.

[b]Respondents were given a list of four criteria for the appointment of officials, two of which were deemed to be modern and two traditional.

[c]Respondents were asked to comment on a story about the introduction of modern techniques to farming. Their answers were classified as either modern or traditional.

British trading sector—was thought by over two-thirds to be British, and Total Oil was thought by almost 30 percent to be American.

Although the association between higher socioeconomic status and knowledge of corporate nationality is more pronounced in this particular case, one may still legitimately wonder whether, in a "developed" Western society, quota sampling across economic and educational bounds would indicate such general awareness, among even the most deprived groups, as is illustrated in Table 9.3.

AFFECTIVE ORIENTATION TOWARD FOREIGN INVESTMENT

Although if an "attitude" toward foreign investment does indeed exist it does so only as a complex, multidimensional phenomenon, not susceptible to straightforward scaling techniques,[8] disaggregation of investment in Nigeria by origin does generate interesting discrepancies. The first—and perhaps, most surprising—of these findings, is the unequivocal conclusion that, while there is little animosity directed toward most foreign investors, deep hostility is often displayed toward indigenous enterprise. The second conclusion, less surprising but perhaps more important in its implications, is that where antiforeign sentiment exists, it is primarily directed against those expatriate groups closest economically and socially to the Nigerians themselves, irrespective of their economic influence, rather than against the most economically powerful expatriates.

Table 9.4 also shows the general unwillingness to take any kind of "strong" position, either for or against foreign investment. Nevertheless, almost 53 percent of the total responses can be construed as demonstrating support for foreign business and only the item suggesting Britain's right to a privileged economic position evinced a strongly xenophobic response.

Controlling the responses to the questions in Table 9.4 by the tribal affiliation of the respondents presents interesting patterns in view of the ethnic cleavages in Nigeria. In general, the recently defeated Ibos did seem better disposed toward foreigners than the dominant Yoruba. For example, while 20 percent of the Yoruba felt a time might come when foreigners would have to leave, this sentiment was held by less than one in ten Ibos. Even when age and socioeconomic status were controlled, these differences still remained: for instance, among respondents earning under $1,960 per annum, 63.2 percent of the Ibos, compared to only 45 percent of the Yoruba, felt that there was no need for Nigerians to take over all foreign firms. Similarly, among respondents earning less than $1,960 per annum, 54.5 percent of the Ibos, compared to 41.8 percent of the Yoruba, were opposed to such total "Nigerianization."

The significance of this disaggregation would seem to be enhanced by the parallel—though not wholly conclusive—finding that, ceteris paribus, Yoruba respondents tended to be less well-informed of the origin and extent of foreign investment in the country. There exists, therefore, a suggestive relationship between knowledge of and support for foreign businesses.[9]

One relationship that may help explain the differences in the response patterns between the Yoruba and Ibos suggested itself in the questionnaire. Respondents who scored positively on a scale designed to measure their sense of personal efficacy exhibited more negative feelings toward foreign investors than their less effectual compatriots. It may be that negative feelings toward foreign investors require a secure psyche which can simultaneously harbor memories of a psychologically debilitating colonial past. Thus, the politically and socially dominant Yoruba could apparently feel more secure to harbor less favorable sentiment toward foreign investors compared to the relatively disadvantaged Ibos.

The general impression of favorability toward the bulk of foreign investment is strongly reinforced by the results of a sixteen-point semantic differential test, included in the questionnaire, profiles resulting from which are illustrated in Figure 9.1. These profiles do, however, also indicate the ambivalence of

TABLE 9.4. Percentages Responding on Items on Proforeign Sentiment

1. "I don't care who owns a company as long as it provides jobs for Nigerians."

Strongly agree	19.4
Agree	28.9
Indifferent	8.6
Disagree	24.8
Strongly disagree	18.2 (Missing = 2.9%)

2. "For the good of the economy, it is essential that all foreign companies are eventually owned by Nigerians."

Strongly agree	17.7
Agree	22.4
Indifferent	11.6
Disagree	34.6
Strongly disagree	13.7 (Missing = 1.0%)

3. "Because Britain has been associated with Nigeria for so long, it is only fair that the U.K. should be given special privileges which other countries do not enjoy."

Strongly agree	5.9
Agree	16.5
Indifferent	10.8
Disagree	34.7
Strongly disagree	31.9 (Missing = 2.2%)

4. "Do you think that there will ever come a time when all foreigners will have to leave Nigeria?"

Yes	17.7
No	82.1 (Missing = 2.2%)

5. "Foreign companies offer better employment prospects for Nigerians than do indigenous companies."

Strongly agree	28.7
Agree	38.9
Indifferent	9.4
Disagree	15.4
Strongly disagree	7.6 (Missing = 7.4%)

6. "Many people seem to feel that the best way to encourage economic growth in Nigeria is by inviting foreign companies to invest here. Do you agree with them?"

Yes	49.8
No	50.2 (Missing = 4.6%)

7. "Nowadays, foreign companies are no longer interested only in profits—they are beginning to care about their workers and about the development of Nigeria."

Strongly agree	5.4
Agree	31.1
Indifferent	13.9
Disagree	31.3
Strongly disagree	18.3 (Missing = 4.6%)

respondents' orientations toward local firms and their virtually unmitigated hostility toward the Lebanese.[10] It is also interesting to note how much more willing respondents were to advocate an extreme position when the national group and the criterion under consideration were both specific. In fact, out of all responding, an average of almost 52.5 percent chose an extreme position on each item and only 18.2 percent opted for the neutral mid-point. However, significantly, on those items pertaining to Nigerian companies, the comparable figures were 44.8 and 22.5 percent.

From these profiles, it would seem that little differentiation is made between United Kingdom and U.S. companies, which are both generally considered honest, considerate, contributory, and successful. Where such differences exist, however, U.S. firms tend to be the beneficiaries. Thus, for instance, on the criterion of honesty, 38.7 percent of those responding perceived British firms to be "very honest" as against 48.5 percent for U.S. companies. In contrast to these strongly positive orientations, Lebanese and Nigerian companies seem to be perceived in a negative light. Thus, Lebanese firms were considered to be "very dishonest" by 53.1 percent of the respondents and Nigerian companies by 35.7 percent. Similarly, while 50 percent of those responding classed the Lebanese as "very inconsiderate," almost 37 percent did the same for local firms.

The position of Nigerian firms on these semantic-differential tests is consistent with other people's findings on the feelings of depressed self-worth prevalent in Nigeria. Only on the dimension of contribution to the economy—where 42.4 percent perceived them to be "very contributory"—did local firms score well. These response patterns suggest that support for foreign firms and negative perceptions of indigenous business are closely related, perhaps reflecting the same postcolonial psychological insecurity. There is abundant evidence that Nigerians have been unable to compete in many commercial areas.[11] Nevertheless, the willingness to accept much of the blame for this, or to transfer it on to the relatively innocuous Levantines, rather than to direct hostility toward the international enterprises which still dominate the Nigerian market, is indicative of the pervasive debilitation associated with colonization and, at the same time, indicates the immediate security of tenure enjoyed by large-scale foreign corporations.

Comparison of Ibo and Yoruba group responses to these semantic-differential items, however, makes such judgments perhaps too facile. While Ibos had appeared more favorably inclined toward foreigners on the items in the main body of the questionnaire, on the specific questions of the semantic-differential test they were (1) marginally less positive toward U.S. and United Kingdom firms, and (2) markedly more negatively disposed toward Nigerian companies on all criteria except that of business success.

Such findings would seem to imply that dissatisfaction with local business might be simply a symptom of a deeper economic or political malaise. However, with the civil war so recent, it is probably also true that, for most Ibos, the terms "Nigerian" and "non-Ibo" are virtually synonymous. Under such circum-

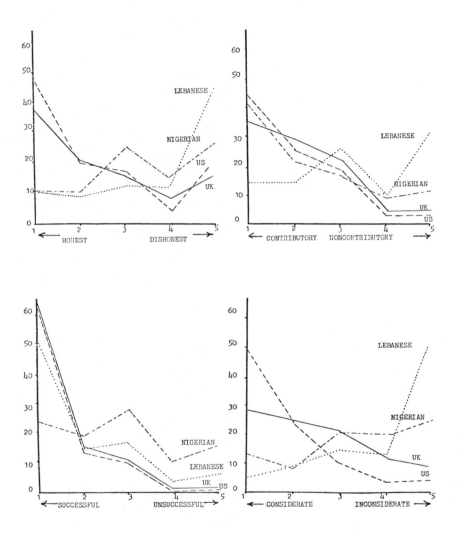

stances, it is perhaps little wonder that they display such marked hostility. What is more surprising is the similar—though less extreme—pattern of rejection displayed even by the Yoruba.

Ibo ambivalence to foreign investment—as shown by contradictory responses on the profiles and in the main questionnaire—may be a function of their historically nationalistic sentiment, allied to recent political reverses. Although, when asked whether they would vote in a future election, affirmative responses were 15 percent higher among Yoruba, such apoliticism among the Ibo is a new phenomenon. Because they lacked the large-scale permanent social systems associated with the Hausa and Yoruba, they sought to achieve the same kind of cohesion through voluntary associations which became both a rudimentary social security system and the basis for political parties such as the NCNC.[12]

Given this history of nationalism, it might be safest to interpret their support for the more general points concerning foreign investment as a corollary to their war-induced antipathy to local, i.e., Yoruba and Hausa, business. Confronted with the specific questions of the semantic-differential test, one might infer that a more deeply-rooted cynicism prevailed.

THE SCAPEGOAT HYPOTHESIS

Nevertheless, whether or not conditions in Nigeria were temporarily biased against local firms, the existence of the Lebanese as a socially sanctioned recipient of nationalist anger might well provide a safety-valve for hostility which might otherwise be directed against the major investors.

The role of the "Cora"[13] in Nigeria is not unlike that of the Indians in East Africa. They constitute an economic and social buffer group between indigenous Nigerians and American and European residents, and one would suggest that the disproportionate hostility which they clearly evince is a function of this position as intermediaries. They have historically been primarily engaged in small-scale retail trade and such technologically unsophisticated sectors as road haulage. Their primary contacts are directly with Nigerians and even in terms of residential patterns, they tend to live—not in the virtually all-white areas of Ikoyi or Victoria Island—but in the marginal, higher density areas of Obalende or Surulere to which the Nigerian middle class already aspires. At the same time, however, their small-scale, family-based business operations tend to reinforce the impression of a homogeneous, essentially endogenous and exclusive alien group.[14]

This economic and social proximity—coupled with a form of ethnic exclusivity—is bound to generate resentment. Indeed, in line with the Berkowitz hypothesis that a "preferred" scapegoat will be one who has in the past provoked justified hostility,[15] this antipathy is not without foundation for it is true that the Levantines' easier access to finance has historically helped to exclude Nigerians from commercial areas eminently within their competence. More important, however, than the validity of anti-Lebanese sentiment is the fact that, by attracting hostility from virtually all ethnic and socioeconomic groups, Levantines and Indians appear to shield other expatriate groups from resentment commensurate with their real economic power. Their presence, therefore, allied with negative perceptions of local enterprise and deep divisions within Nigerian society, works to counter the potentially destabilizing impact of the very high awareness levels prevalent among all groups.

Should the position of the "Cora" within the Nigerian economy be radically altered—perhaps by their expulsion but, more likely, as a corollary to the "Nigerianization" of technologically less-advanced sectors—it is possible that this awareness could translate itself into a markedly more hostile environment for foreign investors from the major trading nations.[16] For the moment, however, with a scapegoat readily available, it is clear that, even in a situation where a very high proportion of modern sector employment is dependent—directly or contingently— on a relatively small number of expatriate concerns, it is not legitimate to infer that widespread awareness will be associated with a parallel antipathy. Indeed, currently, the converse holds true. Greater awareness, associated as it is with higher socioeconomic status and education, would seem to be correlated with generally more positive orientations toward foreign business.

NOTES

1. See S. M. Lipset and S. Rokkan, "Cleavage Structure, Party Systems, and Voter Alignments," in *Party Systems and Voter Alignments: Cross-National Perspectives*, ed. Lipset and Rokkan.

2. Data were collected while the author was a research associate at the Nigerian Institute of International Affairs, and were gathered through distribution of questionnaires to 680 adult male respondents in the Lagos area. Respondents were chosen on a quota basis, to reflect the ethnic, socioeconomic, and educational heterogeneity of the city. Lagos was selected as the site since, as the national and state capital, and as the country's largest city, it houses over 70 percent of the headquarters of foreign industrial companies and attracts about 33 percent of total foreign investment entering the country. Moreover, population density on Lagos was about 112,000 per square mile in 1960 and is undoubtedly much higher today, reflecting both the difficulties of institution building and the remarkable ethnic mixture represented in the town. Finally, the passage of free primary education acts in the old Western Region, and the existence of a highly developed and relatively sophisticated communications network based on the Lagos-Ibadan axis, make functional literacy rates and political awareness considerably higher than elsewhere in the country.

3. Peter Kilby, *Industrialization in an Open Society, Nigeria 1945-1966*, p. 62.

4. *Industrial Survey of Nigeria, 1968*, Federal Office of Statistics, Lagos, 1970. While there is no reason to believe that the sample set used by the government was representative of the manufacturing industry in the country as a whole, the figure of 70 percent for foreign control of the Nigerian economy is widely accepted among the elite and frequently cited in the press.

5. "Economic and Financial Review," *Central Bank of Nigeria, Lagos*, June 1968, p. 77.

6. The *1966 Industrial Survey*, Federal Office of Statistics, Lagos, 1969, gave average annual wages of non-Nigerians as $7,000, professional and managerial Nigerians as $843, skilled and semi-skilled workers as $510, and unskilled workers as $308 per annum.

7. All such response distributions produce chi-squared values significant at or above the 0.05 level.

8. Such a conclusion is based upon results generated when the 24 items administered as part of the questionnaire, related to respondents' sentiments toward foreign investment, were binarized and subjected to factor analysis.. The orthogonally rotated factor pattern matrix resulting was such that the first four factors explained 15, 9, 9, and 8 percent of the total variance, respectively—an aggregate of just under 42 percent. When the sixteen semantic-differential items were excluded, the first three factors of the orthogonal solution still explained only 47 percent of the total variance.

9. This conclusion is reinforced by a fairly clear association between socioeconomic status and favorability to the MNE. Thus, for example, while in general almost 56 percent of respondents earning $1,960 per annum or less felt foreign companies to be interested solely in profit-making, theirs was an opinion shared by only 41 percent of those in the higher income bracket.

10. Lebanese firms were chosen because, while they probably do not account for more than 5 percent of total foreign investment, they tend to be small-scale, family-based businesses, heavily concentrated in the retail and textile trades.

11. In fact, in 1972 the writer found no locally-owned firm operating in Lagos which could trace its identity back to as late as the 1940s.

12. R. L. Sklar and C. S. Whitaker, Jr., "The Federal Republic of Nigeria," in *National Unity and Regionalism*, ed. Gwendolyn Carter.

13. The term "Cora" is used to denote not only Lebanese but also Syrian and even Indian traders. Its usage is itself indicative of how effective an "out-group" they constitute. Although "European" is used also to connote Americans, no similar derogatory or pejorative epithet has as yet emerged to encapsulate the major foreign investors.

14. For instance, the 1972 Annual Conference of the Nigerian Institute of Management, which attracted representatives of over 450 companies, listed no Levantine names among its participants.

15. Leonard Berkowitz, "Aggression," in *International Encyclopaedia of the Social Sciences*. A problem of causality clearly exists here. From the immediate evidence it is not clear whether the "Cora" are disliked *sui generis*, or whether hostility is in fact directed mainly at small-scale family-owned businesses—of which many happen to be owned by Levantines. Nevertheless, the combination of close socioeconomic contact and discernible ethnic difference, allied with an acceptance by the Lebanese of their role as an "out-group," makes them a preferred target for "syncretism"—the compounding of several prejudices onto one set of individuals.

16. *Nigerian Enterprises Promotion Decree, 1972*, Decree no. 4, Official Gazette, March 1972.

10

CHANGING ATTITUDES TOWARD FOREIGN INVESTMENT IN CANADA

J. Alex Murray
Lawrence LeDuc

Much of the current debate over the multinational enterprise is due to the large amount of foreign investment in Canada. For 1972, over 75 percent of Canadian rubber, automobile, chemical, and electrical apparatus manufacturing industries were owned by foreigners. These types of statistics have provided fuel for nationalists who favored tighter regulation of multinational corporations headquartered outside of Canada.

At the same time, the high degree of interdependence between Canada and the United States is jointly responsible for the popular feeling that offshore companies were headquartered in a friendly domain. And, given the small size of the Canadian population and the geographical spread of Canadian markets, Canadians usually felt that national control over the economy was something to be dealt with at the federal level, with only passing attention being given to it by provincial or local governments. It was not until the strong nationalist sentiment was raised by Walter Gordon and a number of his followers that Canadians began to formulate opinions toward specific public policies dealing with regulation of incoming foreign investment. In this vein, the contribution of public opinion to the formation or maintenance of specific foreign investment policies was very problematic. In the area of foreign policy, for instance, it is generally conceded that the contribution of public opinion is more marginal, and shifts in public opinion are often seen to follow rather than precede changes in government policy on such issues.[1] Often, foreign affairs are seen as preoccupations of an elite. Nevertheless, in certain areas where foreign policy touches directly on the domestic affairs of the country, or when international issues assume greater salience for the general public, the impact of public opinion in the policy process may be greater. This is not to suggest that under such circumstances public opinion will of itself determine the direction of policies, but rather that democratic governments must of necessity be responsive over time to changes in public moods. It is most interesting to note that public opinion in Canada has shifted over time, and the changes in these shifts are being noted by foreign policy decision makers and observers alike. As a result, a close linkage can be seen between the recent government policies affecting multinational corporations and foreign investment generally, and changing public attitudes over the past decade. Most recently, the question of Quebec separatism has added a new dimension to internal Canadian politics, and of nationalism, for the multinational corporation. How critically current issues will affect previous investment decisions is yet to be seen. In this chapter, however, with the aid of national opinion survey data, we will explore the shifting patterns of public attitudes toward foreign investment in Canada, and the relationship between changing climates of opinion and shifts of government policy in this area.[2]

THE RISE OF CANADIAN NATIONALISM

In the decade of the 1950s and early 1960s government policies generally tended to reflect (or vice versa) the public's favorable view of close relations with the United States, particularly in the economic sphere. There was, in this period, little evidence of public concern over the extent of U.S. economic influence in Canada. From 1948 until the mid-1960s, for example, public opinion polls generally indicated that at least half of those surveyed did not think that the Canadian way of life was being influenced too much by the United States.[3] In 1956, 63 percent of those surveyed by the Canadian Institute of Public Opinion (CIPO) felt that there was not too much U.S. influence, while only 27 percent expressed concern (Figure 10.1). Forty-eight percent of a national sample in 1963 felt that Canadian dependence on the United States was basically a good thing.[4] With respect to trade relations, a 1956 government report cited a poll showing that 68 percent of those surveyed supported the idea of free trade with the United States.[5]

It was not until the publication in 1958 of the report of the Royal Commission on Canada's Economic Prospects (The Gordon Commission) that signs of government concern with the then existing state of Canadian-U.S. relations began to arise. Although the Diefenbaker government talked of transferring some 15 percent of Canada's trade with the United States to Britain, little came of such proposals. Most government efforts in the area of Canadian-U.S. relations in that period were intended to emphasize Canada's political independence from the United States, and the Canadian posture during the Cuban missile crisis and at the United Nations began to reflect this attitude. There were, however, limited moves toward restricting foreign ownership in television broadcasting (1958) and restrictions placed on the granting of oil and gas leases in territories under federal jurisdiction (1960) during this period.

FIGURE 10.1. Percent Indicating that There Is "Too Much U.S. Influence in the Canadian Way of Life," 1956–74

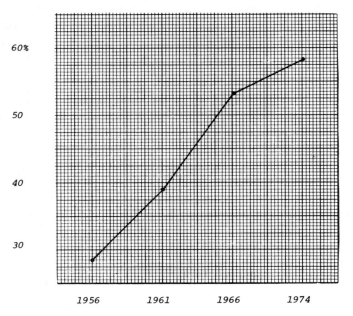

Sources: CIPO, *The Gallup Report*, May 25, 1974; and John H. Sigler and Dennis Goresky, "Public Opinion on United States-Canadian Relations," *International Organization*, XXVIII (1974), p. 658.

With the return of the Liberal Party to power in 1963, the first major initiative directed at the problem of foreign ownership of Canadian business was undertaken. Walter Gordon, then finance minister, introduced a 30 percent "takeover tax" to be levied on the value of shares of Canadian firms acquired by nonresident corporations, but the tax was withdrawn under strong pressure from the financial community and the suggestion of an absence of widespread public support.

Public attitudes toward U.S. economic influence in Canada were however gradually changing during the late 1950s and early 1960s, and these changes began to accelerate by the middle of the decade. The late 1960s and early 1970s were marked by a growing volume of literature critical of the Canadian-U.S. relationship. George Grant, Donald Creighton, Walter Gordon, Karl Levitt, Mel Watkins, Abraham Rotstein, and Gary Lax were among those who wrote books critical of U.S. economic influence in Canada during this period.[6] A radical wing of the New Democratic Party began to advocate the nationalization of foreign firms as the only way for Canada to regain control over its economy. And in 1970 a Committee for an Independent Canada was organized as a broadly based interest group to press for a reassertion of Canadian control in both economic and cultural affairs.

These developments were accompanied by a number of government initiatives in selected areas. In 1968, a special task force created by the federal government issued a report (the Watkins Report) which put forward several policy proposals intended to enhance Canadian economic independence. In 1972 the Trudeau government tabled a long awaited report on foreign direct investment (the Gray Report), which recommended a plan for dealing with foreign investment by means of a government screening agency.

All these events led to increased media attention throughout the late 1960s and early 1970s on the state of Canadian-U.S. relations, particularly in the economic sphere. The cumulative effect of the growing awareness of this area of Canadian public policy was a body of public opinion increasingly more critical of the Canada-U.S. relationship. Thus, while in 1956 only 27 percent of the respondents in the CIPO poll cited earlier felt that there was "too much American influence," the figure climbed steadily to 57 percent by 1974 (see Figure 10.1). The 48 percent who in 1963 felt that Canadian dependence on the United States was basically a good thing was down to 34 percent by 1972.[7] Forty-six percent who felt that there was enough U.S. capital in Canada in 1964 climbed to 67 percent in 1972.[8] In that same year, while the discussion of an agency to screen foreign investment was under discussion, 69 percent were found in a CIPO poll to favor the creation of such an agency.[9]

With respect to Canada-U.S. trade relations, there was not the same shift of opinion over this period that is discernible in the other data. For example, the 54 percent of a CIPO sample who had been found in 1953 to favor a free trade arrangement with the United States had remained virtually constant at 56 percent when the CIPO last asked this question in 1968.[10] A 1965 CIPO survey found Canadians equally divided between more and less trade with the United States, as did our own 1974 survey, which examined attitudes toward the Canada-U.S. auto agreement.[11]

Paralleling shifting public attitudes toward U.S. economic influence in Canada was a modest flow of new policies growing out of the various government studies and reports mentioned earlier. Until 1972 the approach was highly selective, designed primarily to protect specific sectors of the Canadian economy from undue foreign influence. Amendments to the Insurance and Loan and Trust Companies Act, restrictions on the tax deductibility of advertising in newspapers and magazines, and the blocking of the sale of a large uranium mine (Dennison) to a U.S. corporation are examples of the types of specific initiatives taken during this period. Perhaps because of the unhappy experience with the proposed takeover tax in 1963, more comprehensive measures to deal with U.S. economic influence were not considered. Then, in 1972, the government introduced legislation to create a Foreign Investment Review Agency (FIRA), which was to make all new foreign direct investment in Canadian companies subject to government review. This legislation was passed in 1973, and was hailed as a significant new initiative in attempting to confront the problem of foreign investment in the Canadian economy.

At about the same time, significant initiatives were also being taken in the foreign policy sphere. Mitchell Sharp, then secretary of state for external affairs, released a paper entitled "Canada–U.S. Relations: Options for the Future," which sought to identify three options that the country might pursue vis-à-vis the United States. These were identified as (1) maintenance of the existing relationship with the United States with a minimum of policy adjustments; (2) movement toward closer economic integration with the United States; and (3) the reduction of Canada's dependence on the United States through the cultivation of closer ties with other countries and the development of a comprehensive strategy to develop and strengthen the Canadian economy. The paper, together with the discussion that followed, left little doubt that the last of these, or the "third option" as it came to be identified, was the one favored by the government.[12] Slowly the third option attained the status of official government policy, a position finally made explicit by Sharp's successor, Allan MacEachen, in 1975. Over the past two years, however, the level of commitment of the government to a third option policy appears to have waned somewhat.

It is impossible to discern exactly the role of public opinion either in the development of a comprehensive foreign investment policy or in the evolution of the "third option." That both of these developments were accompanied by an escalating public concern for Canadian economic independence, however, is evident from the survey data. It also seems reasonable to argue that the government was slow in adopting a comprehensive policy until it was convinced that public opinion was supportive, perhaps because of the negative experience with the 1963 takeover tax. There is in addition some specific evidence of government awareness of the climate of public opinion with respect to the proposed third option. In his initial paper, Sharp cited the "growing public awareness of concern" about the trend of Canadian-U.S. relations, and stated that the public was prepared to "contemplate and support reasonable measures." In announcing the third option as official government policy, MacEachen referred specifically to trends in public opinion, even citing the polls.

> This new feeling of being Canadian is reflected very sharply in the economic field. The issue is our economic independence. I have already cited figures showing the degree to which we are dependent on the United States in trade and investment. A cross section of various polls taken in Canada in 1972 indicated that 88.5% of Canadians thought it important to have more control over our economy, and that two out of every three Canadians considered the level of American investment in Canada too high.[13]

FOREIGN INVESTMENT: SOME RECENT TRENDS

Just as the adoption of the Foreign Investment Review Act and the third option were accompanied by an increasingly nationalistic climate of public opinion, the last two years have seen a shift both in opinion and in the posture of the government. A national magazine recently charged that the Foreign Investment Review Act was "falling apart in the face of corporate obstinacy and government indifference."[14] A new Trade Minister, Jean Chrétien (now finance minister), was thought by many observers to have been less aggressive than his predecessors in the enforcement of FIRA. At the same time, surveys monitoring the level of public concern about the foreign investment issue have registered a leveling off and then a sharp decline. Over a nine-year period, our surveys on this topic show the percentage of Canadians who view U.S. investment in Canada as a "bad thing" peaking in 1973-74 (see Figure 10.2), and declining to an eight-year low in the most recent survey. For the first time since 1969, Canadians who feel that U.S. investment is basically a good thing outnumber those viewing foreign investment in more negative terms. The largest overall shifts of opinion over

FIGURE 10.2. **Percent of National Sample Who Believe that U.S. Investment in Canada is a "Bad Thing": 1969-77**
   (excludes "no opinion" and "qualified" answers)

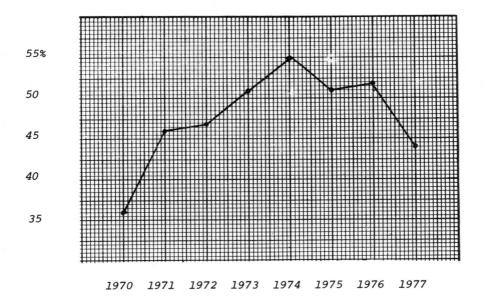

TABLE 10.1. **Percent of National Sample Who Believe that U.S. Investment in Canada Is a Good or Bad Thing for the Country, by Region, 1976-77 (1975-76 shown in parentheses)**

	Atlantic	Quebec	Ontario	Prairies	British Columbia	Total Canada
Good thing	44	46	51	47	48	48
	(38)	(35)	(43)	(40)	(41)	(39)
Bad thing	41	40	39	38	41	39
	(41)	(46)	(40)	(44)	(41)	(42)
Qualified	4	7	5	5	6	6
	(7)	(8)	(7)	(6)	(9)	(9)
No opinion	11	7	5	10	5	7
	(14)	(11)	(10)	(10)	(9)	(10)
N (1976-77) =	384	1,090	1,418	668	429	3,989

1976-77 appear to have occurred in Quebec and in the prairie provinces, although the percentage of respondents who see U.S. investment as a good thing for Canada has also increased sharply in Ontario (see Table 10.1). As in previous surveys, young persons are among those more likely to express negative attitudes toward foreign investment, 46 percent of the respondents under 30 years of age in the most recent survey rating U.S. investment in the economy a bad thing in contrast with 36 percent of those over 50 years expressing a similar opinion. Women (42 percent) are slightly more likely than men (37 percent) to feel that U.S. investment is bad for Canada, and there are modest relationships between socioeconomic status and attitudes toward this issue, with the lowest income groups expressing more strongly positive attitudes toward U.S. investment (51 percent). Opinion among higher income groups is evenly divided. There are also, as might be expected, relationships between opinions on this issue and more fundamental political attitudes, with supporters of the New Democratic Party expressing the highest proportion of negative attitudes (49 percent) toward U.S. investment. Both Liberals and Conservatives are strongly positive (52-37 and 53-36 respectively). The overall pattern of these sociodemographic correlates is not appreciably different from that of previous surveys, suggesting a fairly uniform shifting of opinion on this issue with some regional variation as noted earlier.

The distribution of reasons given by respondents to support their position on the foreign investment issue has not changed appreciably over the period during which this question has been asked in the annual surveys (Table 10.2). Respondents who feel that U.S. investment in the Canadian economy is basically a bad thing tend to give general nationalistic reasons ("Canada should control its own affairs," "Canada should be more independent," and so on) and to cite the extent of U.S. influence ("too much U.S. control," for example). On the other hand, those who feel that U.S. investment in Canada is basically a good thing strongly tend to cite economic growth and development as the reason behind their attitude. Nearly half the respondents in this group give answers relating specifically to employment or unemployment, and many more mention reasons

TABLE 10.2. Reasons for Believing that U.S. Investment Is a Good or Bad Thing for the Canadian Economy (multiple response)

Good Thing[a]	Percent	Bad Thing[b]	Percent
Creates more employment/ helps alleviate unemployment (1)[c]	46	Too many takeovers/ Canada should control own affairs (1)	37
Expansion/develop resources (2)	20	Profits leave country/ U.S. benefits (2)	35
Brings money into Canada (3)	15	Canada can go it alone, should be more independent (4)	17
Improves living standards (4)	13	Discrimination, unequal trade, unfair advantage (8)	4
Canadians too cautious, not willing to invest (5)	13	Taking jobs, business away from Canadians (5)	4
Good experience in past/need U.S. help/interdependence (7)	7	Canadians should invest, keep capital here (3)	4
Promotes friendship/ cooperation (8)	6	Loss of identity, Americanization (7)	4
More products/markets/ helps exports (6)	4	Too much foreign control/ discourages Canadian investment (6)	4
Other, miscellaneous	1	Other, miscellaneous	1

[a]N = 1,490.
[b]N = 1,283.
[c]Denotes rank order in 1970 survey.

such as resource development or the improvement of living standards. There is a strong suggestion, therefore, that the shift of attitudes toward foreign investment, which is evident in the survey data over the past two years, may be related to the lackluster performance of the economy and perhaps more specifically to the high levels of unemployment of recent years. This argument is also reinforced by the fact that, as noted earlier, persons in the lowest income groups are the most positive toward U.S. investment.

The foreign investment issue has generally not been a significant source of political conflict in Canada, particularly among the general public. No political party attempted to make foreign investment an explicit issue in the 1974 federal election, and a national survey conducted at the time of that election found very few respondents mentioning foreign investment as an issue.[15]

There has also been some uncertainty among the Canadian public as to the exact meaning and understanding of the foreign investment issue. Although it is possible to elicit opinions on various aspects of foreign investment in Canada, Canadians differ in the meaning that they impart to the term foreign investment. Only 17 percent of the 1974 national election sample (Table 10.3) related the foreign investment question specifically to the United States in response to an

TABLE 10.3. Some Descriptions of the Meaning of Foreign Investment
(1974 national half sample)

	Percent
General reference to one country investing in another	12
General reference to foreigners investing in Canada	12
References to foreigners investing in Canada in	
Natural resources	3
Manufacturing	1
Other and combinations	1
Reference to U.S. investing in Canada in	
General reference	13
Natural resources	2
Manufacturing	2
Other specific countries investing in Canada	1
Multinational corporations investing in Canada	1
Foreign trade	3
Canada investing abroad; Canadian foreign aid	11
Other responses, miscellaneous	13
No answer, no opinion	24

Note: N = 1,241.

Source: Harold Clarke, Jane Jenson, Lawrence LeDuc, and Jon Pammett, *Political Choice in Canada* (McGraw-Hill Ryerson, 1978).

FIGURE 10.3. Percent of National Sample Who See Foreign Investment as a Serious Problem at the Present Time: 1974-77

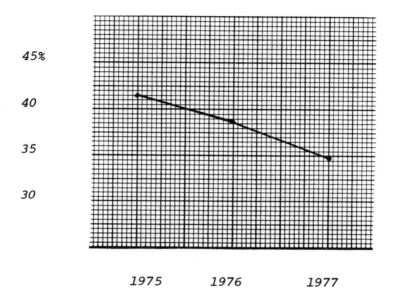

open-ended question that attempted to determine what Canadians thought of when the term foreign investment was mentioned.[16] Much larger numbers responded to this question in more general terms, or were unable to give any response. Some 11 percent responded in terms of Canadian investment abroad, reversing the usual political meaning of the term in Canada.

The responses to open-ended questions, together with the directional trend of opinion noted earlier (Figure 10.2) would tend to suggest that control of foreign investment in Canada, although frequently mentioned in public debate, has not been a problem high on the national agenda. In fact, our annual surveys indicate that the proportion of Canadians who see foreign investment as a "problem" with which the country must deal has declined in each of the last two surveys from the level registered in 1974-75. This question, which was introduced the year following the implementation of the Foreign Investment Review Act, asked respondents to indicate whether they saw control of foreign investment as "a serious problem" and (if so) what action they favored to deal with it. This sequence was asked in each of the 1974-75, 1975-76, and 1976-77 surveys.

The findings for the period studied closely parallel the trends evident on the directional question. The percentage of respondents who define foreign investment in the economy as a serious problem has declined in each of the past three surveys, from 42 percent in 1974-75 to 35 percent in 1976-77 (Figure 10.3). The regional pattern is similar to that noted earlier, although the largest year to year increases in the percentage stating that foreign investment was not a problem

TABLE 10.4. Percent of National Sample Who See Foreign Investment
as a Serious Problem, by Region, 1976-77
(1975-76 shown in parentheses)

	Atlantic	Quebec	Ontario	Prairies	British Columbia	Total Canada
Yes, a serious	27	40	34	32	36	35
problem	(36)	(43)	(39)	(34)	(40)	(39)
No, not a problem	34	25	35	31	33	31
	(25)	(21)	(26)	(27)	(23)	(24)
Maybe in future	30	30	25	30	25	28
	(26)	(29)	(25)	(27)	(29)	(27)
No opinion	9	5	6	7	6	6
	(13)	(7)	(10)	(12)	(8)	(10)
N (1976-77) =	384	1,090	1,418	668	429	3,989

occur in British Columbia, Ontario, and the Atlantic provinces. However the trend is essentially the same in all parts of the country, with Quebec, as in previous surveys, showing the largest proportion of respondents identifying foreign investment as a problem (Table 10.4).

It should be noted that, in spite of the similarity of the overall trends, there are some significant differences between the two survey questions. While the percentage defining foreign investment as a problem has been declining, still only 31 percent of the 1976-77 sample actually state that foreign investment is not a problem, an increase of 7 percent from a year earlier. A large percentage of the respondents concede that foreign investment might be a developing problem, and the percentage who identify this issue as a future problem has remained nearly constant over the surveys. Although one cannot be certain from independent, cross-section surveys, there is some hint that a fairly constant proportion of the public may be waiting and watching, not seeing foreign investment as an immediate problem to be dealt with but rather as one that might become more serious over time.

A clearer picture of the relationship between these two attitudinal items, and a more accurate measure of the most genuinely concerned proportion of the population, is obtained from a cross-tabulation of the two sets of survey responses. As is seen in Table 10.5, not all respondents who feel that U.S. investment is a bad thing also identify it as an immediate problem. While there is clearly a relationship between the two sets of responses, there is also some degree of independence. Only 21 percent of the 1976-77 national sample identified foreign investment as a bad thing *and* as a serious problem. An intriguing

11 percent of the sample feel that it is basically a good thing, but nevertheless agree that it must be controlled.

The recognition of foreign investment as either a present-day or future problem has not been accompanied by widespread public support for direct government action. In previous surveys, only a minority of those who identified foreign investment as a problem were found to favor direct government regulation such as FIRA, although some favored selective controls in certain industries. More supported incentives for Canadian business, or alternate investment schemes such as the Canada Development Corporation. In the 1976-77 survey, the level of support for comprehensive government regulation further decreased, with only 27 percent of those identifying foreign investment as a problem favoring this solution (Table 10.6).

Again, it would be improper to attempt to specify cause and effect here. But it is apparent that the decline in the identification of foreign investment as a problem, and in public support for government regulation, has been accompanied by a decrease in the number of takeovers or new investment proposals disallowed by the agency, and a shift in the general posture of FIRA.[17]

TABLE 10.5. Correlation between Feeling toward U.S. Investment as a Good or Bad Thing and Identification of Foreign Investment as a Serious Problem, 1976-77 National Sample
(diagonal percentages with row percentages shown in parentheses)

| | Foreign Investment a Problem | | | | |
U.S. Investment	Yes, a serious problem	No, not a problem	Maybe a future problem	No Opinion	N
Good	11 (23)	20 (42)	14 (30)	2 (5)	1,909
Bad	21 (53)	7 (18)	10 (25)	2 (4)	1,566
Qualified	2 (32)	2 (26)	2 (36)	* (6)	245
No opinion	1 (13)	2 (32)	2 (25)	2 (30)	269
					3,989

Note: V = .24; p < .001.
*Less than 1 percent.

TABLE 10.6. Proposed Solutions to Foreign Investment Problem, 1976-77 and 1975-76 National Samples (percentages of respondents indicating foreign investment as a problem only)

	1976-77[a]	1975-76[b]
More support for Canadian business	31	34
Government regulation	27	31
Canada Development Corporation	17	17
Selected industry controls	11	14
Diversification of investment	9	7
All other	3	2
No opinion	2	2

Note: Multiple responses possible.
[a] N = 1,390.
[b] N = 1,556.

THE THIRD OPTION

The third option strategy proposed by Sharp in 1972 and embraced by MacEachen in 1975 likewise seems to have undergone some change in the next two years, both in terms of the position of the government and with respect to public opinion. Following the publication of the Sharp paper, the concept of foreign policy options received a large amount of discussion and commentary, both supportive and critical.[18] In the first public opinion survey that we conducted on this topic in 1973-74, 31 percent of the public were found to favor a third option type of policy, although a larger percentage (42 percent) favored the status quo. Only 18 percent of those sampled were in favor of a policy of closer relations with the United States than then existed.[19]

Since that time, however, the proportion of respondents in the annual national surveys expressing a preference for the third option has declined significantly, while the percentage favoring closer relations with the United States has increased steadily. The largest year to year decrease in public support for the third option occurred in the 1975-76 survey, followed by a large year to year increase in the percentage favoring closer relations with the United States in the 1976-77 poll (Figure 10.4). In the most recent survey, 30 percent of the national sample favored closer relations with the United States, a five-year high, while only 23 percent favored a Canadian foreign policy oriented more toward Europe or Asia. Forty percent of the respondents favored a policy of maintaining existing relationships with few adjustments.

Breakdowns of the data by province and region reveal that the greatest increases in public support for a foreign policy oriented more toward the United States have occurred in British Columbia, Quebec, and Ontario (Table 10.7). In previous surveys, British Columbia and Quebec have generally been the provinces most supportive of the third option policy, with 34 percent and 32 percent of the respondents in those two provinces respectively favoring closer ties with Europe in a 1974-75 survey.

It would be intriguing to relate the shift in opinion in Quebec particularly to the victory of the separatist Parti Québécois in the November 1976 election in that province. However, the interviewing for the survey was carried out only a very short time following that election (and prior to Premier René Lévesque's visit to New York), and there is no reason to believe that the shift in Quebec opinion is related to specific events. It may be, however, that some Québécois feel that a stronger economic position for Quebec in North America is a precondition for independence. On the other hand, the shift in Quebec is not appreciably different from that in other parts of the country. As with the foreign

FIGURE 10.4. Percent of National Sample Favoring a Change in Canadian Foreign Policy: 1973-77

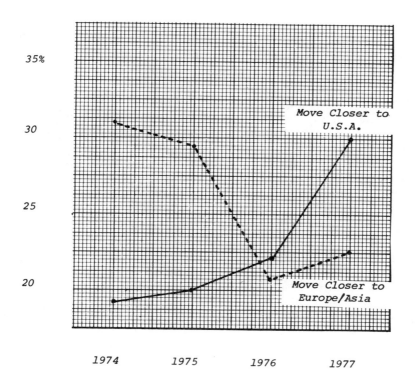

TABLE 10.7. Preference of National Sample for Three Foreign Policy Options, by Region, 1976-77
(percentages; 1975-76 shown in parentheses)

	Atlantic	Quebec	Ontario	Prairies	British Columbia	Total Canada
Stay as we are	51 (59)	40 (39)	40 (52)	36 (42)	32 (39)	40 (46)
Move closer to U.S.A.	25 (21)	33 (23)	29 (20)	30 (25)	31 (20)	30 (22)
Move closer to Europe/Asia	14 (12)	20 (24)	24 (19)	26 (22)	25 (31)	23 (21)
No opinion	10 (8)	7 (14)	7 (9)	8 (11)	12 (10)	8 (11)
N (1976-77) =	384	1,090	1,418	668	429	3,989

investment issue, it may be that the shift of opinion toward a policy of closer relations with the United States is related more generally to the weakness of the economy. Support for maintenance of the status quo, although commanding a plurality of the national sample, has not increased over the past year in any part of the country. In Ontario, it has fallen off sharply from a year earlier.

The sociodemographic correlates of attitudes toward the third option policy have generally been similar to those for the foreign investment issue. Younger persons have generally been more favorable toward the third option than other groups, with 27 percent of those under 30 in the most recent survey favoring this policy and only 25 percent favoring closer relations with the United States. Thirty-three percent of the respondents over 50 favored closer relations with the United States, while only 17 percent of this group preferred the third option. Men (33 percent) are slightly more favorable toward closer ties with the United States than are women (27 percent), a pattern similar to that of previous surveys. There are no significant relationships between socioeconomic status variables such as income or occupation and attitudes toward the third option.

The most visible element in the government pursuit of the third option policy since 1975 has been the attempt by Prime Minister Pierre Trudeau to negotiate a contractual link with the European Common Market. But government policy in this area has maintained a very low profile. David Humphreys recently observed that:

Neither the Government nor the Opposition in Canada appears to rate foreign policy high on its scale of priorities. Our leading politicians make few speeches with the intention of enlisting support for foreign policy initiatives. There has yet to be a full dress debate in the Commons on the Contractual Link, and rarely in recent years has there been discussion of any other aspect of foreign policy.[20]

It may well be, however, that, if public opinion is a considered element of government policy making in this area, the "go slow" policy that has been followed is the best that could be expected in the face of weak or declining public support.

CONCLUSION

Although the causes of the decline in support for the third option over the past few years and the decline of public concern about the foreign investment issue detailed earlier are undoubtedly related, attitudes toward these two issues are surprisingly independent of one another. Only 30 percent of those respondents in the national sample who felt that U.S. investment in the Canadian economy was basically a bad thing also support the third option (Table 10.8). Twenty-one percent of this group actually favor closer ties with the United States. Similarly, only 40 percent of those who rate U.S. investment in Canada as a good thing are favorable toward closer ties. Or, viewed differently, these two groupings comprise respectively only 12 percent and 19 percent of the national sample.

TABLE 10.8. Correlation between Attitudes toward Foreign Investment in Canada and Support for Changes in Canadian Foreign Policy, 1976-77 National Sample (diagonal percentages with row percentages shown in parentheses)

U.S. Investment	Status quo	Closer to U.S.A.	Closer to Europe/Asia	No Opinion	N
Good	17	19	9	3	1,909
	(36)	(40)	(18)	(6)	
Bad	17	8	12	3	1,566
	(42)	(21)	(30)	(7)	
Qualified	3	2	2	*	245
	(40)	(25)	(24)	(11)	
No opinion	3	1	*	2	269
	(45)	(20)	(10)	(25)	
					3,989

Note: V = .24; p < .001.
*Less than 1 percent.

TABLE 10.9. Most Important Issues Facing the Country: 1976-77 (1975-76 shown in parentheses)

	Most Important	Total Mentions*
	(percentage of respondents)	
Inflation	39 (59)	76 (86)
Unemployment	20 (14)	65 (65)
Environment and pollution	12 (12)	33 (38)
English-French relations	9 (2)	28 (13)
Provincial-federal relations	6 (2)	23 (16)
Energy	5 (3)	30 (28)
Taxation	4 (4)	28 (30)
U.S. investment	4 (4)	15 (18)

Note: N (1976-77) = 3,989.

*Totals to more than 100 percent because multiple mentions were permitted in the survey.

The pattern of attitudes on these several issues suggests that for many Canadians attitudes toward issues such as foreign investment in the economy or the orientation of the nation's foreign relations are based not on emotions but on more practical considerations. Often, issues involving elements of nationalism might be expected to be highly emotional and related to more deeply held feelings. Undoubtedly there are many Canadians who are nationalists in this sense. But there appear to be more who are characterized by a highly pragmatic attitude toward such issues. Just as there are substantial numbers of people who recognize foreign investment as a problem but nevertheless consider it a good thing (Table 10.5), there are significant numbers who favor closer ties with the United States in general terms in spite of a negative attitude toward U.S. investment specifically. The fact that a number of combinations exist in itself suggests that such attitudes are not unidimensional in character, and the fact that opinion has been shifting in both areas in recent years suggests that much of the public may be more heavily influenced by short-term policy considerations than by deeply held beliefs or emotions that are, by definition, more resistant to change.

Earlier we speculated that the apparent decline in public support for government regulation of foreign investment and of public support for a third option in foreign policy might be related to the slackening of the Canadian economy and more specifically to growing unemployment. Certainly the same surveys that have documented the trends in opinion on these two policy issues have also disclosed that economic considerations occupy a much higher priority for most Canadians than do issues such as foreign investment or the contractual link with the EEC (Table 10.9). In particular, the last three surveys have detected a reawakening concern of the Canadian public about high unemployment, even as unemployment rates have steadily risen. It is understandable then that much of the public may see these issues in economic terms, and that a more favorable attitude toward foreign investment or toward closer ties with the United States may be seen by some as necessary in a period of economic slowdown. Chrétien, the minister previously responsible for the enforcement of FIRA, recently was quoted as putting these tradeoffs succinctly in stating that "a continuing inflow of direct investment from abroad is an essential condition of continuing economic progress in Canada."[21]

The broader question of the relationship between policy making and public opinion in this area is somewhat more problematic. These are issues that are not by themselves highly salient to much of the public although they are bound up with larger economic policy questions that are. Thus, on the one hand, a government may have considerable freedom of action in an area such as foreign policy at one particular point in time, but may have to subordinate its initiatives in this area to other shorter term considerations at another. It would be going beyond the limitations of the data reported here, however, to infer that on issues such as FIRA or the third option the Canadian government has retreated in the face of unfavorable public opinion, or alternatively that changes in government policy themselves have had an effect on public opinion. Rather, it seems more likely that at least part of the change in public opinion is accounted for by an overriding concern for the health of the economy and that the government, like the public, has simply had its attentions focused elsewhere, at least temporarily. As Humphreys has noted, the government has made no real attempt to "sell" the contractual link with the EEC to the Canadian public as yet, and its pursuit of the third option has been extraordinarily low-key of late. But an attempt to enlist public support behind such a policy, or to strengthen FIRA, could well be decisive, particularly if such action were initiated in an improved or improving economic climate.

NOTES

1. For a general discussion of the linkages between public opinion and foreign policy, see James N. Rosenau, *Public Opinion and Foreign Policy* (New York, 1961). See also Barry Farrell, *The Making of Canadian Foreign Policy* (Toronto, 1969), Bruce Thorardson, *Trudeau and Foreign Policy: A Study in Decision Making* (Toronto, 1972), and John Holmes, "The Impact of Domestic Political Factors on Canadian-American Relations," *International Organization* 38 (1974), pp. 611-36.

2. The data reported in this chapter have been obtained from surveys conducted annually by Elliott Research Corporation (Toronto, Ontario), and the International Business Studies Research Unit at the University of Windsor (Windsor, Ontario). Interviewing takes place in November of each year, with reports issued shortly after the first of the year. In this chapter, data collected in November 1976 are shown as a "1976-77" result, indicating the year-end nature of the studies. The surveys are based on national quota samples of approximately 4,000 respondents, controlled for province, rural-urban location, age, and sex. Some reports that have utilized data from past surveys in this series are J. Alex Murray and Mary C. Gerace, "Canadian Attitudes Toward the U.S. Presence," *Public Opinion Quarterly* 36

(1972), pp. 388-97; J. Alex Murray and Lawrence LeDuc, *Canadian Public Attitudes Toward U.S. Equity Investment in Canada*, Ontario Economic Council Working Papers Series, 1975; Lawrence LeDuc and J. Alex Murray, "Public Attitudes Toward Foreign Policy Issues," *International Perspectives*, May-June, 1976, pp. 38-40; Terence A. Keenleyside, Lawrence LeDuc, and J. Alex Murray, "Public Opinion and Canada-United States Economic Relations," *Behind the Headlines* 35 (1976), No. 4; and J. Alex Murray and Lawrence LeDuc, "Public Opinion and Foreign Policy Options in Canada," *Public Opinion Quarterly* 40 (1976), pp. 488-96.

The following table of 95 percent confidence limits may be employed in interpreting percentages reported in this chapter. For a discussion of quota sampling and the reporting of error for such samples, see F. Stefan and P. McCarthy, *Sampling Opinions* (New York, 1958), ch. 10.

	For Percentages of Approximately				
Size of Base (N)	10% or 90%	20% or 80%	30% or 70%	40% or 60%	50%
100	(±) 9	12%	13%	14%	15%
300	5	7	8	8	8
500	4	5	6	6	7
700	3	4	5	5	6
1000	3	4	4	5	5
1500	2	3	3	4	4
3000	2	2	2	3	3
4000	2	2	2	2	3

3. John H. Sigler and Dennis Goresky, "Public Opinion on United States-Canadian Relations," *International Organization* 28 (1974), pp. 656-59. See also Terence A. Keenleyside, Lawrence LeDuc, and J. Alex Murray, "Public Opinion and Canada-United States Economic Relations," *Behind the Headlines* 35 (1976), No. 4, pp. 8-10.

4. CIPO, *The Gallup Report*, August 26, 1972.

5. As quoted in Mitchell Sharp, "Canada-U.S. Relations: Options for the Future," *International Perspectives*, Autumn, 1972 (special issue), p. 11. See also Sigler and Goresky, op. cit., pp. 652-55.

6. George Grant, *Lament for a Nation* (Toronto, 1965); Donald Creighton, *Canada's First Century* (Toronto, 1970); Walter Gordon, *A Choice for Canada* (Toronto, 1966); Kari Levitt, *Silent Surrender* (Toronto, 1970); D. Godfrey and M. Watkins (eds.), *Gordon to Watkins to You*; and Abraham Rotstein and Gary Lax (eds.), *Independence the Canadian Challenge* (Toronto, 1972).

7. CIPO, *The Gallup Report*, August 26, 1972.

8. CIPO, *The Gallup Report*, February 12, 1972.

9. Ibid.

10. CIPO, *The Gallup Report*, May 18, 1968.

11. CIPO, *The Gallup Report*, January 29, 1969. See also, Keenleyside, LeDuc, and Murray, op. cit., pp. 20-22.

12. Sharp, op. cit., p. 17. See also Denis Smith, "Nationalism and the Third Option," paper presented to the Conference on Canada-U.S. Relations, Department of External Affairs, February, 1975.

13. Department of External Affairs, Ottawa, *Statements and Speeches*, no. 75-1.

14. Ian Urquhart, "FIRA: Watchdog or Lapdog?" *MacLeans*, July 11, 1977, pp. 18-20.

15. Less than 1 percent of the national sample mentioned foreign investment in response to an open-ended question asking respondents to identify the "most important issues." This survey was conducted following the 1974 election by Harold Clarke, Jane Jenson, Lawrence

LeDuc, and Jon Pammett, and its findings are reported in *Political Choice in Canada* (Toronto, 1978).

16. The sequence of questions was as follows:

I would like to get your opinions on an issue that has been important for some time now in Canadian politics, not just in this election. That issue is foreign investment. What do you usually think of when foreign investment is mentioned?

How do you feel about foreign investment?

Which party is closest to you on this issue?

This sequence was asked of *half* the respondents in the 1974 national sample. See *Political Choice in Canada*, op. cit., ch. 8.

17. Ian Urquhart, op. cit.

18. See, among others, Dale C. Thomson, "Option Three; What Price Tag?," Louis Balthazar, "Achieving a Stronger Identity," Harry G. Johnson, "The Advantages of Integration," Abraham Rotstein, "Shedding Innocence and Dogma," and Jeremy Kinsman, "Pursuing the Realistic Goal of Closer Canada-EEC Links," all in *International Perspectives*, January–February, 1973, pp. 3-13 and 22–27. Some reactions to the proposals and additional commentary may also be found in "Canada-U.S. Relations: Options for the Future," no. 1, "American Reaction," and no. 2, "Canadian Reaction"; *Behind the Headlines* 32 (February and April, 1973). Some more recent discussion and analysis of the third option may be found in Alex Inglis, "A New Approach to the Discussion of Canadian-American Relations," and Christopher Young, "End of an Era or a Constant in Political Vocabulary," both in *International Perspectives*, March-April, 1975, pp. 3–15.

19. J. Alex Murray and Lawrence LeDuc, "Public Opinion and Foreign Policy Options in Canada," *Public Opinion Quarterly* 40 (1976), p. 491.

20. "Canada's Link with Europe Still Not Widely Understood," *International Perspectives*, March–April, 1976, p. 33.

21. As quoted in Urquhart, op. cit., p. 18.

11

DEVELOPED COUNTRIES AND MULTINATIONAL CORPORATIONS: THREAT PERCEPTION AND POLICY RESPONSE IN FRANCE AND THE UNITED KINGDOM

Norman A. Graham

INTRODUCTION

An important goal of studies of elite and mass attitudes toward multinational corporations (MNCs) is an effort to discover and explain the sources of these attitudes. This chapter seeks progress toward this goal but also seeks to begin to determine the impact of such attitudes and perceptions on governmental policy responses.

Presenting data drawn from a larger inquiry into the impact of external threats on national foreign and domestic policy decisions,[1] the chapter explores British and French elite attitudes, perceptions of threat, and policy preferences related to MNCs. The data used in the quantitative analyses to follow were collected by means of an elite mail survey. The quantitative analysis of attitudes is supplemented with an effort to trace government policy in the two countries since the early 1960s, as decision makers responded to concern about MNCs.

CONCEPTUAL FRAMEWORK

The starting point in our consideration of the impact of attitudes on governmental policy responses is a proposition put forward by Ernst Haas: "A helpful

The author would like to acknowledge the advice and kind assistance provided by John Fayerweather, Jean Kime, Wilfrid L. Kohl, Donald J. Puchala, Susan J. Rod, and Glenda G. Rosenthal during several stages in the preparation of this article. Fellowship support for field research from the Inter-University Consortium for World Order Studies and the Georges Lurcy Foundation is also greatly appreciated.

but by no means indispensable, condition (for international unification) is the existence of an external threat, real or imagined."[2] Accordingly, in a simple stimulus-response model ($S \rightarrow R$) it is hypothesized that external threats provide a stimulus for a state to engage in international cooperation. However, this model is too simple and general. We need to specify the variety of factors that mediate, inhibit, or encourage this relationship. We therefore need to move toward a much more complex mediated stimulus-response model:

$$S \rightarrow X \rightarrow R$$

where X represents the intervening or mediating variables. For the purposes of this specification, the variables of the model can be divided into four groups: 1) the independent variable—the external threat involved; 2) variables relating to the process of threat perception and the process of bringing the threat to the attention of the relevant decision makers; 3) variables that intervene between the point of elite threat perception and the point of cooperative or noncooperative policy implementation; and 4) the dependent variable—the type of cooperation (or noncooperation) selected to deal with the external threat. We might thus designate the model as follows:

$$S \rightarrow P \rightarrow I \rightarrow R$$

where   S represents the external threat;
           P represents the elite threat perception process;
           I represents subsequent intervening variables; and
           R represents the international cooperation.

This is still rather simple, but we can add complexity as we explore the data.[3]

Effectively testing the above model is a complex undertaking, requiring reliance upon several sources and forms of data. The remainder of the chapter presents and discusses the results of survey and case study analyses designed to meet this need. The data for the analyses were collected by a combination of elite interviewing, archival research, and a mail survey.

THE SURVEY ANALYSIS

Procedures

To discuss the procedures followed in the elite survey, it is necessary to begin with the construction of the questionnaire. The survey was designed and conducted according to procedures utilized in Fayerweather's study of British, Canadian, and French elite attitudes toward MNCs (see Chapter 1). The same questions asked in the Fayerweather survey were in some instances utilized in this survey to replicate the earlier findings and to provide some possibility for examining the stability of the attitudes through time. Other questions were designed solely for this survey. Information gained through a documentary and press search and through elite interviewing was used in the question construction, particularly in suggesting alternative responses.

The questions (including the French translation) were submitted to evaluation and criticism by several knowledgeable researchers, and the questionnaires were pretested on a group of nongovernment nationals in each country. After needed modifications were made, the questionnaires were sent to 50 members of the British House of Commons as a pilot study. The pilot study revealed no problems in procedure or comprehension, so the questionnaires were then sent in turn to the total sample of British M.P.s and civil servants. One follow-up letter was used to encourage further responses. The same procedure (including the pilot study) was followed for the French members of the National Assembly and civil servants.

A stratified, systematic random sample was drawn from the universe of British M.P.s and high civil servants (at the undersecretary and deputy secretary levels in the ministries of defense, energy, foreign and commonwealth affairs, industry, overseas development, trade, and treasury) and of French National Assembly members and high civil servants (at the directeur, directeur général, directeur général adjoint, directeur adjoint, and sous-directeur levels in the ministries of affaires étrangères, commerce, coopération, défense, économie et finances, and industrie et recherche). The British portion of the survey was conducted from May 5 to July 3, 1975, and the French portion was conducted from June 18 to August 21, 1975. Each respondent was coded as to the postmark date of the response, so that the effects of intervening events might be examined.

Approximately 200 questionnaires were sent out for each of the four subgroups in order to ensure a large enough sample. The resulting response rates were similar to those obtained by the Fayerweather study conducted in late 1970: British M.P.s, 32.0 percent (64 of 200); French M.P.s, 32.5 percent (65 of 200); British civil servants, 19.6 percent (36 of 184); and French civil servants, 30.1 percent (61 of 200). While higher response rates would certainly have been preferable, those obtained were probably about the best that could be expected for a mail survey (the only practical means available for the study) of preoccupied political and bureaucratic elites. Moreover, a comparison of the number of responses obtained from various subgroups (according to background variables and affiliations) with the proportions of members of those subgroups in the universe of the study revealed no apparent systematic bias at work. For example, the percentage of British M.P. responses received from each of the major political parties almost exactly duplicated the proportions of party members present in the House of Commons as a whole at the time that the survey was conducted.

However, two points of concern should be noted. First, the response rate for British civil servants was significantly lower than for the other three main groups. Judging by notes of explanation sent by some of the civil servants to whom questionnaires were sent, this was largely due to a view that reporting their views (even anonymously) on the questions involved would in their minds violate the impartial, nonpolitical traditions of the British civil service. No similar claims were made by French civil servants who did not complete the questionnaire. In general, however, the responses received from British civil servants were divided proportionally to the numbers surveyed in each ministry of the government, and the number of British civil servant respondents obtained (36) was large enough to permit statistical analysis.

Second, no responses were received from French M.P.s who were affiliated with the Communist party of France. While no notes of explanation were received, it appears that some uniform suspicion as to the motives or potential uses of the research was present.

Findings

Table 11.1 presents the results to the first question seeking to investigate threat perceptions. Here the focus was on possible sources of threat to the two countries. Uniformly and by a large margin over other possibilities, the Soviet Union was viewed as posing the greatest threat to security. The problems associated with Northern Ireland ranked next for the British respondents, and the Organization of Petroleum Exporting Countries (OPEC) ranked third for the British and second for the French respondents. Other possible sources of threat were cited with a low frequency.

TABLE 11.1. **British and French Elite Perceptions of Sources of Threat (percentages)**

(Question: Which of the following is the greatest threat to Britain's [France's] security at the present time?)

Source of Threat	British MPs	British Civil Servants	French MPs	French Civil Servants
U.S.S.R.	54.7	38.9	38.5	45.9
Northern Ireland	10.9	13.9	—	—
OPEC	3.1	13.9	13.8	6.6
PLO	1.6	0.0	3.1	3.3
People's Republic of China	0.0	0.0	3.1	0.0
United States	0.0	0.0	3.1	0.0
West Germany	1.6	0.0	0.0	0.0
Developing countries	0.0	0.0	0.0	0.0
Other	4.8	11.2	4.6	1.6
No threat	23.3	22.1	35.9	42.9
N	64	36	65	61

A rather significant percentage of the respondents felt that there was no threat to the country's security at the present time, but national differences in perceptions are evident here, with the number of French respondents for both groups who perceived no threat nearly doubling the corresponding British figures.

If we focus on kinds of threats, expanding the concept of threat to include domestic problems, we can evaluate their perceived relative importance and place foreign threats in the context of other areas of elite concern. Table 11.2 represents an effort to provide such an analysis, and from this it is immediately clear that domestic economic problems occupy a primary position. For all four groups, domestic economic problems received a ranking as the most serious kind of threat or problem facing the two countries by more than a majority of the respondents. As one might expect, this concern was more frequently cited in the United Kingdom than in France. Indeed, it was ranked first by more than 80 percent of the responding British M.P.s and civil servants. In contrast to the British, a significant percentage of French M.P.s and civil servants (approximately 20 percent) perceived foreign economic threats to be the most serious kind facing the country. It should perhaps be noted that in neither country did the percentage of respondents who perceived foreign military threats as the most serious kind reach 5 percent.

In an attempt to further specify kinds of threats or problem areas, the respondents were asked to cite the most serious foreign economic threats facing their country. As Table 11.3 shows, world inflation and the related OPEC oil

TABLE 11.2. **British and French Elite Perceptions of Kinds of Threat (percentages)**

(Question: What is the most serious kind of threat or problem facing Britain [France] at the present time?)

Kind of Threat	British MPs	British Civil Servants	French MPs	French Civil Servants
Domestic economic problems	85.9	83.3	52.3	60.7
Foreign economic threat	1.6	0.0	18.5	21.3
Domestic political instability	6.3	8.3	1.5	4.9
Foreign political pressure or threat	1.6	0.0	7.7	4.9
Foreign military threat	3.1	0.0	4.6	1.6
Terrorism	0.0	0.0	6.2	0.0
Separatism	0.0	0.0	0.0	0.0
Other	1.6	8.3	6.2	6.6
No answer	0.0	0.0	3.1	0.0

Note: N = 226.

TABLE 11.3. British and French Elite Perceptions of Foreign Economic Threats (percentages)

(Question: What are the most serious foreign *economic* threats facing Britain [France] at the present time?)

Foreign Economic Threat	British MPs	British Civil Servants	French MPs	French Civil Servants
World inflation	18.8	19.4	46.2	52.5
OPEC oil price increases	46.9	52.8	18.5	16.4
Foreign MNCs	7.8	0.0	18.5	3.3
U.S. economic competition	0.0	0.0	4.6	14.8
Trade imbalances	7.8	2.8	6.2	1.6
Currency speculation	7.8	0.0	3.1	4.9
Demands of the developing countries	0.0	2.8	0.0	1.6
Japanese economic competition	0.0	2.8	1.5	0.0
Other	6.3	19.4	1.5	3.3
No answer	3.1	0.0	0.0	4.9

Note: N = 226.

TABLE 11.4. British and French Elite Perceptions of the Overall Effect of MNCs (percentages)

(Question: In your opinion, what is the overall effect on Britain [France] of the activities of foreign-owned multinational companies in Britain [France]?)

	Good						Bad	
	1	2	3	4	5	6	7	NA*
British MPs	14.1	23.4	25.0	4.7	15.6	12.5	3.1	1.6
British civil servants	16.7	50.0	27.8	5.6	0.0	0.0	0.0	0.0
French MPs	1.5	6.2	18.5	24.6	16.9	20.0	12.3	0.0
French civil servants	0.0	6.6	23.0	29.5	26.2	11.5	3.3	0.0

Note: N = 226.
*NA = no answer.

241

TABLE 11.5. British and French Elite Perceptions of the Net Economic Result of MNC Operations (percentages)

(Question: What do you believe is the net economic result of the operations of foreign-owned multinational companies in Britain [France]?)

	They take more than they give				They give more than they take			
	1	2	3	4	5	6	7	NA
British MPs	6.3	17.2	10.9	26.6	20.3	7.8	9.4	1.6
British civil servants	0.0	2.8	5.6	19.4	27.8	36.1	8.3	0.0
French MPs	12.3	26.2	21.5	26.2	10.8	3.1	0.0	1.6
French civil servants	3.3	18.0	29.5	32.8	13.1	3.3	0.0	0.0

See notes for Table 11.4.

price increases were cited most frequently by far. Foreign MNCs were ranked third, with the French respondents, especially the M.P.s, citing them more frequently.

Turning directly to perceptions of threat relating to foreign-owned MNCs, several questions were posed in order to investigate different dimensions of

TABLE 11.6. A Comparison of the Fayerweather and Graham Findings (expressed as mean scores)

	Overall Effect of MNCs (Good = 1; Bad = 7)	Net Economic Result (Give More Than Take = 1; Take More Than Give = 7)
Fayerweather 1970 Survey:		
British MPs	3.2	3.8
British civil servants	2.8	3.2
French MPs	3.1	4.1
French civil servants	3.1	3.8
Graham 1975 Survey:		
British MPs	3.3	4.0
British civil servants	2.2	2.9
French MPs	4.6	4.9
French civil servants	4.2	4.6

TABLE 11.7. **British and French Elite Perceptions of the Threat to Business Independence (percentages)**

(Question: The independence of business throughout Europe—not just in Britain [France]—is being threatened by American take-over.)

	Strongly Agree						Strongly Disagree	
	1	2	3	4	5	6	7	NA
British MPs	3.1	10.9	26.6	14.1	17.2	12.5	14.1	1.6
British civil servants	0.0	0.0	13.9	16.7	13.9	41.7	13.9	0.0
French MPs	26.2	23.1	20.0	15.4	4.6	10.8	0.0	0.0
French civil servants	16.4	21.3	31.1	19.7	6.6	4.9	0.0	0.0

See notes for Table 11.4.

concern. Table 11.4 begins this with an attempt to determine perceptions of the overall effect of MNCs on Britain and France. First, it is apparent that there are important national differences in perceptions. The French M.P.s and civil servants were clearly much more negative on the overall effect of MNCs than were their British counterparts. Indeed, in contrast to the French, an overwhelming majority of British respondents felt at least to some degree that the overall effect was good. Second, there appears to be an important difference between the perceptions of the M.P.s and the civil servants in each country, with the latter generally finding the overall effect somewhat more positive. This distinction would seem not to be difficult to understand, given the nature of the constraints and pressures on politicians as opposed to those on civil servants involved in the day to day work of improving the economy, and so on.

Rather similar findings are displayed in Table 11.5 in reference to a question on the net economic result of the operations of foreign-owned MNCs in the two countries. Again, the French respondents were considerably more negative, with the majority expressing the view that MNCs "take more than they give."

The two questions used to provide data for Tables 11.4 and 11.5 were taken from the 1970 survey conducted by John Fayerweather. Since the same survey procedures were used for both studies, this effort serves as a replication of the Fayerweather study and gives us some possibility of examining change over time. Table 11.6 presents a comparison of the two studies, with the findings expressed in terms of mean scores (the approach used in the Fayerweather study). Here we find some basic similarity in the findings, especially in terms of national differ-

TABLE 11.8. British and French Elite Perceptions of Beneficial and Detrimental Effects of MNCs (percentages)

(Question: Foreign-owned multinational companies have at the same time both important beneficial and detrimental effects on Britain [France].)

	Strongly Agree					Strongly Disagree		
	1	2	3	4	5	6	7	NA
British MPs	7.8	14.1	26.6	28.1	17.2	1.6	1.6	3.1
British civil servants	8.3	19.4	16.7	27.8	13.9	11.1	0.0	2.8
French MPs	13.8	16.9	18.5	32.3	12.3	4.6	1.5	0.0
French civil servants	21.3	13.1	24.6	27.9	6.6	4.9	0.0	1.6

See notes for Table 11.4.

TABLE 11.9. British and French Elite Perceptions of the Power to Control MNCs (percentages)

(Question: Do you consider that the British [French] Government has sufficient power to control the activities of foreign companies in Britain [France]?)

	The Government has enough power in all cases					The Government does *not* have enough power		
	1	2	3	4	5	6	7	NA
British MPs	21.9	18.8	15.6	4.7	7.8	14.1	15.6	1.6
British civil servants	22.2	47.2	16.7	0.0	8.3	0.0	0.0	5.6
French MPs	13.8	20.0	18.5	7.7	10.8	21.5	6.2	1.5
French civil servants	6.6	23.0	16.4	13.1	16.4	23.0	1.6	0.0

See notes for Table 11.4.

ences. However, the findings in the 1975 survey depict decidedly more negative perceptions, as one might expect if for no other reason than the wealth of largely negative opinion and analysis circulated in the press and academic writings of the early 1970s.

Table 11.7 refines the MNC threat issue by presenting data on whether the elites felt that the independence of business in Europe was being threatened by U.S. takeovers. Here it is also clear that the French respondents perceived the threat considerably more frequently and strongly than did the British.

TABLE 11.10. British and French Elite Policy Preferences for the Regulation of MNCs (percentages)

(Question: Given your views on the extent to which foreign-owned multinational companies are a detriment and/or benefit to Britain [France], what is the best policy or approach to deal with the situation?)

British MPs	British Civil Servants		French MPs	French Civil Servants
12.5	13.9	An international code of behavior for MNCs	12.3	4.9
32.8	13.9	International regulation through the EEC	21.5	16.4
4.7	2.8	International regulation through the OECD	3.1	0.0
3.1	0.0	International regulation through the UN	4.6	0.0
1.6	11.1	Stimulating industrial mergers in Europe	6.2	14.8
6.3	0.0	National efforts to discourage	1.5	0.0
1.6	5.6	National efforts to encourage with little regulation	0.0	0.0
9.4	16.7	National efforts to encourage with extensive regulation	13.8	32.8
1.6	5.6	No national or international encouragement or regulation	0.0	0.0
1.6	2.8	Other	0.0	0.0
23.4	27.8	Some combination	35.4	31.1
1.6	0.0	No answer	1.5	0.0

Note: N = 226.

TABLE 11.11. British and French Elite Policy Preferences for the Regulation of MNCs: National, International, or Mixed National and International Solutions
(percentages)

British MPs	British Civil Servants		French MPs	French Civil Servants
18.8	25.0	National solutions	15.4	32.8
17.3	19.4	Mixed national and international solutions	21.5	24.6
62.5	50.0	International solutions	61.5	42.6
1.6	0.0	No answer	1.5	0.0

Note: N = 226.

In an attempt to test the existence of a view, commonly referred to in academic literature and press accounts, that MNCs have at the same time both important beneficial and detrimental effects, the elites surveyed were asked whether they agree or disagree with the statement. As Table 11.8 indicates, while a large percentage of the respondents of each group took a middle view on the question (selecting alternative 4), nearly a majority (59 percent of the French civil servants) expressed some agreement with the statement.

Finally, the elites in the sample were asked if they felt their government had sufficient power to control the activities of foreign companies in their country. Table 11.9 indicates that a very large proportion of the respondents in each group felt that the government did have enough power. However, except for the British civil servants, some concern on this issue was expressed.

Turning to policy preferences for the regulation of MNCs expressed by the British and French governmental elites, national differences are not great. Indeed, Table 11.10 suggests that the apparent divisions of opinion are rather more prominent between M.P.s and civil servants than between the two countries. This is to be expected given the politicization of the issues involved and the amount of press attention devoted to them. However, the findings do suggest that there is no clear consensus on the optimal responses to MNCs and that a combination or series of responses may be appropriate. There also does seem to be some support for international responses or regulation. This last point can be seen more clearly in Table 11.11, which presents the findings in terms of preferences for national solutions, international solutions, or mixed national and international solutions.

Table 11.12 is a cross-tabulation that makes a direct attempt to test our main hypothesis by examining the relationship between perceptions of the

TABLE 11.12. Cross-Tabulation of Perceptions of the Overall Effect of MNCs by Policy Preference for the Regulation of MNCs: All British and French Elite Respondents (percentages)

Perceptions of the Overall Effect of MNCs	Policy Preferences for the Regulation of MNCs		
	National Solutions	Mixed National and International Solutions	International Solutions
Overall effect is good	11.3	7.7	29.4
	3.6	5.4	8.6
Overall effect is bad	8.1	7.7	18.1

Note: Chi square = 4.26 with 4 degrees of freedom (Sig. = .37); Kendall's tau B = −.05 (Sig. = .20); N = 220.

overall effect of MNCs and policy preferences for their regulation. Here we find that those who perceive the effect to be good are divided quite similarly to those who perceive the effect to be bad, on whether national, mixed, or international solutions are preferable. This finding remained consistent throughout the subgroups and when alternative recordings of the overall effect variable were utilized. Similar results were found when "overall effect" was replaced by the variable for perceptions of the net economic result of MNCs and by the variable for perceptions of the threat to business independence. These results are somewhat

TABLE 11.13. Cross-Tabulation of Perceptions of the Overall Effect of MNCs by Political Party Affiliation: British Civil Servants and M.P.s Affiliated with the Two Major Parties (percentages)

Political Party Affiliation	Perception of the Overall Effect of MNCs		
	Good Effect		Bad Effect
Labour party	10.3	25.0	14.7
Conservative party	30.9	19.1	0.0

Note: Chi square = 17.53 with 4 degrees of freedom (Sig. = 0.0002); Kendall's tau C = −.52 (Sig. = 0.0000); N = 68.

TABLE 11.14. Cross-Tabulation of Perceptions of the Overall Effect of MNCs by Political Party Affiliation: French Civil Servants and M.P.s Affiliated with the Two Major Parties (percentages)

Political Party Affiliation	Perception of the Overall Effect of MNCs		
	Good Effect		Bad Effect
Socialist party	1.4	4.2	26.4
R.D.S. (Reformers)	5.6	2.8	2.8
Union Centrists	4.2	1.4	5.6
Independent Republicans	5.6	5.6	2.8
U.D.R. (Gaullists)	9.7	9.7	12.5

Note: Chi square = 18.48 with 8 degrees of freedom (Sig. = 0.0179); Kendall's tau C = −.29 (Sig. = .0030); N = 72.

inconclusive because of the difficulty of categorizing possible regulation strategies into just three alternatives along a "scale" of increasing international cooperation; the loss of information here is great. However, they do suggest the need to explore possible sources of the attitudes in some detail. We can thus turn to a presentation of the relationship between background characteristics and these perceptions.

A considerable amount of background and attitudinal information was collected during the course of the survey. This information was used to provide a profile of the respondents and to check on the degree to which the sample was representative of the universe of British and French M.P.s and civil servants. However, it was also employed in an effort to determine the extent to which such factors account for variations in threat perception and policy preferences. By this analysis, we can began to explore the impact of the perception process (P) variables of our model.

The threat perception and policy preference variables were examined in terms of several different background variables, such as age, education, occupational specialization and training, political party affiliation, and years of service as an M.P. or civil servant. Age seemed to have some effect in some instances, and occupational specialization and training was apparently somewhat relevant, particularly for the British elites surveyed. However, the background variable that almost uniformly seemed to be a factor was political party affiliation.

Table 11.13 demonstrates this conclusively in the case of the relationship between British elite perceptions of the overall effect of MNCs and political party affiliation. The correlation is unusually high for survey data, and the

TABLE 11.15. Cross-Tabulation of Policy Preferences for the Regulation of MNCs by Political Party Affiliation: British Civil Servants and M.P.s Affiliated with the Two Major Parties (percentages)

Political Party Affiliation	Policy Preferences for the Regulation of MNCs		
	National Solutions	Mixed National and International Solutions	International Solutions
Labour party	12.1	12.1	27.3
Conservative party	7.6	1.5	39.4

Note: Chi square = 7.54 with 2 degrees of freedom (Sig. = 0.0231); Kendall's tau C = .25 (Sig. = 0.0168); N = 66.

direction of the relationship fits with expectations about the likely positions of the two parties. Table 11.14 provides roughly the same sort of analysis for French M.P.s and civil servants, with a similar but somewhat weaker relationship evident.

Finally, Tables 11.15 and 11.16 present an effort to examine the relationship between political party affiliations and policy preferences for the regulation of

TABLE 11.16. Cross-Tabulation of Policy Preferences for the Regulation of MNCs by Political Party Affiliation: French Civil Servants and M.P.s Affiliated with the Major Parties (percentages)

Political Party Affiliation	Policy Preferences for the Regulation of MNCs		
	National Solutions	Mixed National and International Solutions	International Solutions
Socialist party	4.2	5.6	21.1
R.D.S. (Reformers)	0.0	4.2	7.0
Union Centrists	2.8	1.4	7.0
Independent Republicans	2.8	1.4	9.9
U.D.R. (Gaullists)	8.5	8.5	15.5

Note: Chi square = 5.92 with 8 degrees of freedom (Sig. = 0.6558); Kendall's tau C = −.14 (Sig. = 0.0807); N = 71.

MNCs. As in the case of analyzing the latter variable in terms of threat perception variables, no clear relationship is discernible for either the British or French elites; both the political right and left seem to favor international solutions, though. To some this may begin to call into question the effectiveness of this variable for measuring policy preferences for the regulation of MNCs, but it may also belie the apparent lack of consensus, even at the political party level, on the appropriate policy response in this area.

The results of the survey analysis serve to provide us with a better picture of the nature of the initial threat perceptions and of their context in terms of other elite concerns and constraints. They also demonstrate that we must consider the impact that background factors seem to have on elite images and perhaps on the predispositions of elites toward certain types of perceptions. This is a complex area, which has already been treated extensively in the literature,[4] but it is also one that cannot be omitted from any model designed to investigate foreign policy behavior.

THE CASE STUDIES

It is now pertinent to move from the analysis of attitudes and perceptions of threat relating to MNCs to the question of policy response by national governments. However, directly addressing the question of the relationship between elite attitudes and governmental policies is a large task. In this section we shall begin to approach this task by briefly discussing French and British policy responses. In doing so, we shall broadly trace changes in policy and official attitudes for three political administrations in each country (the de Gaulle, Pompidou, and Giscard d'Estaing administrations of France; and the Wilson, Heath, and second Wilson administrations in the United Kingdom).

France

Prior to the de Gaulle administration, the French government encouraged foreign investment in France by its policy of remittance of earnings and repatriation of capital. By 1958, obtaining the authority to invest became more difficult, but the regulations were still not very restrictive. During the de Gaulle administration one can note significant variations in policy toward multinational corporations and foreign investment. Indeed, different phases can be delineated.

From 1958 to 1963, despite de Gaulle's apprehensions and his desire for national independence, the French actively sought to attract foreign investment. According to Gilles Y. Bertin, a consultant to the French Ministry of Finance, "During this period there was no single known instance in which the government permanently prevented a foreign investment undertaking."[5] France had signed the Treaty of Rome, articles 52, 58, and 67 of which had restraining implications on the restrictiveness of French policy, and in 1959 France concluded a bilateral treaty with the United States that guaranteed the right of establishment to each other's nationals. Indeed, on July 1, 1959, Prime Minister Michel Debré wrote to the French Economic and Social Council that it was preferable to have U.S. companies invest in France rather than in other EEC (European Economic Community) countries. In 1960, France signed the OECD (Organization for Economic Cooperation and Development) Code of Liberalization of Capital Movements.

However, this phase of relative openness came to a close as a result of the growth of negative public opinion in reaction to the behavior of U.S.-based MNCs in labor relations and takeovers in key French industries. In 1962, General Motors laid off 685 of 3,100 employees at its Frigidaire plant in Bennevillier, and Remington laid off 800 of 1,200 workers in Lyons. The French press pictured these actions as callous and out of touch with the traditions of French labor relations. French Minister of Industry Maurice Bokanowski and Minister of Finance Valéry Giscard d'Estaing added their own critical comments. While some doubt has been expressed as to whether the uproar was wholly justified, the impact of the episode was quite significant.[6]

Official concern was heightened when in January 1963 Chrysler acquired Simca stock, giving it 63.8 percent control. The threat of foreign domination of a key French industry thus became a point of concern. Finally, an article published in *Le Monde* (January 25, 1963, p. 14) leaked news of a proposal by the Libby, McNeil and Libby Corporation to build a cannery in southern France. Public opinion was again inflamed, particularly in view of the fact that a U.S. firm would be benefiting from a French government investment to rehabilitate the land in that region.

The impact of these events on French attitudes (and on reinforcing President de Gaulle's apprehensions) led to a period of restrictive regulation of foreign (especially U.S.) direct investment. In mid-January 1963, the French Ministry of Finance issued a public statement stressing the need for restrictions against investment from non-EEC countries and urging that the matter be examined at the meeting of EEC finance ministers scheduled to be held on February 1. After two postponements, the meeting was finally held on March 27, but France's EEC partners, already disturbed by recent French policies, showed little interest in the proposal.

For the next several years, the French government did indeed conduct a more restrictive national policy toward foreign investment. According to a statement from the French Finance Ministry,

all potential investments are scrutinized carefully to insure that they contribute substantially to French technology or business know-how, or provide aid to important but expensive lines of research. . . . We just object to anything that looks like speculation, a simple takover, or an investment which France can perfectly well handle itself.[7]

The implementation of this policy was initially centered around foreign exchange controls. From 1963 to 1965 new foreign applications for investment in France were generally discouraged, at least informally. However, in some ways this strategy was not sufficient for French goals. The European subsidiaries of U.S. companies could still invest in France unless the government was ready to be charged with violating the provisions of the Treaty of Rome, and in any case these subsidiaries would have tariff-free access to French markets. A common EEC policy was thus necessary.

Some French officials, most notably Prime Minister Georges Pompidou, were concerned that a negative posture would have adverse social and economic effects and would simply drive foreign investors to neighboring locations in EEC member countries. Indeed, this did happen on a number of occasions, including the loss of a Ford plant in 1966. Unfortunately for the government, a hesitant policy opened it to attack from the left, which charged that France was becoming colonized by foreign capital.

Irrespective of the general climate of opinion and the charges of the political left, U.S. foreign direct investment in France was relatively limited in comparison to that in other European countries, particularly West Germany and the United Kingdom. Table 11.17 indicates that investment in both France and the United Kingdom grew steadily during the period after 1958. However, the figures for France were consistently much lower, indeed usually less than one-third of the amount for the United Kingdom.

In any event, by 1965 it was certainly clear that French efforts for an EEC policy were unlikely to be successful. During that year, the Government carried out an extensive review of its policy toward foreign direct investment. This effort resulted in part in a report prepared by the Ministry of Industry, commonly referred to as the Bokanowski report. While the findings of the report were perhaps more positive toward foreign investment than might have been expected, it concluded that the true solution to the problem was located at the European level. For example, the Commission should make a more economic than strictly juridical application of articles 85 and 86, which deal with competition policy.[8]

By 1966 there were important changes on the national level. Much of the negative official commentary against the threat of foreign investment ceased for a time when Finance Minister Giscard d'Estaing was replaced by Michel Debré. Industry Minister Bokanowski was also replaced. The French government had reopened its office in New York (closed in the early 1960s), which was designed to interest foreign investors, and there was an apparent relaxation of national controls (a surprising development given the commitment to Gaullism held by the new finance minister). There was indeed some feeling within governmental circles that execution of the Fifth Plan would be difficult without foreign investment.

However, Debré also felt that a means of control was required. Accordingly, in December 1966 a law was passed that provided the government with direct approval power over all foreign investment moves except equity participations

TABLE 11.17. U.S. Direct Investment in France and the United Kingdom

Year	Total All Industries, Book Value at Year-End (millions of dollars)		Manufacturing, Book Value at Year-End (millions of dollars)	
	France	UK	France	UK
1958	546	2,147	—	—
1959	632	2,475	334	1,607
1960	741	3,194	402	2,164
1961	840	3,523	460	2,305
1962	1,006	3,805	582	2,512
1963	1,240	4,172	764	2,739
1964	1,446	4,547	909	3,010
1965	1,609	5,123	1,076	3,306
1966	1,758	5,657	1,201	3,716
1967	1,904	6,113	1,312	3,878
1968	1,910	6,703	1,345	4,257
1969	2,091	7,158	1,518	4,555
1970	2,588	8,015	1,867	4,988
1971	3,013	8,941	2,167	5,421
1972	3,432	9,509	2,482	5,851
1973	4,259	11,115	3,064	6,827
1974	4,886	12,461	3,411	7,201
1975	5,792	13,932	3,859	7,601
1976	5,954	15,696	3,968	7,776

Source: United States, Department of Commerce, *Survey of Current Business*, 1959–1977.

of less than 20 percent in listed companies.[9] According to a January 27, 1967, decree regulating the terms of the law, direct investments had to be reported to the Ministry for Economic Affairs and Finance; the ministry then decided (within two months) if the investment had to be postponed. Some argue that there was some arbitrariness in the law's application, especially discriminating against U.S. investments. The policy was certainly selective, and it is clear that the focus was to permit control of backdoor investment in France by U.S. companies through their European subsidiaries. In accomplishing this the measures were directed against other EEC members as well as against the United States.

The de Gaulle administration received much criticism from the other EEC members as a result of its new legislation, and the EEC Commission noted that French policy was in violation of the Treaty of Rome. The French response was that the new powers would only be used against non-EEC members. This explanation failed to satisfy either the Commission or the member states (most notably the Netherlands and West Germany), particularly given the ambiguity and dis-agreement over whether U.S. subsidiaries were in fact European firms. A pro-tracted argument between the Commission and the French government followed, eventually leading to a Commission decision to take the issue to the European Court of Justice in late 1969; the new Pompidou government eventually acqui-esced and modified the law.

The delay in French compliance to the provisions of the treaty and the directives of the Commission is understandable in light of the new wave of public concern about foreign investment that had developed in France. This concern was in part stimulated by the publication of *Le Défi Américain* by J.-J. Servan-Schreiber in 1967, which followed upon the government's desperate attempt to save its national computer industry from either financial insolvency or U.S. domination.[10] Noncompliance to EEC directives held lesser costs than relaxing the restrictiveness of national policy at this point.[11]

The de Gaulle administration supplemented its regulation policy with an effort to concentrate French industry and make it more competitive. The govern-ment adopted *Plan Calcul*, an ambitious effort to rebuild the national computer industry; more generally, it pursued a "national champions" policy, seeking to construct a limited number of large French corporations that could compete in international markets. However, cross-frontier European mergers were not favored. Indeed, de Gaulle even intervened to block Fiat's bid to take over Citroen.

The de Gaulle administration did not seek international cooperation in forums that included the United States (for example, the OECD) to deal with the threat of foreign direct investment and MNCs. Rather, French cooperative efforts seemed designed either to strengthen the French economic position within the EEC or to distract domestic opinion.

After the unrest of May 1968, with its attendant effects on the monetary position of France, foreign investment regulation became more relaxed. How-ever, a selective policy of investment rejection was still evident.

President de Gaulle resigned from office in April 1969, and the new admin-istration of President Pompidou modified French policy to a degree. Whereas investment regulation had not been a major electoral issue, the health of the French economy certainly had been. Pompidou had been a voice for moderation on foreign investment within the de Gaulle administration; given the needs of the economy, he soon began a gradual relaxation in the restrictiveness of French policy, at least to the degree permitted by public opinion.

However, the legal potential for a restrictive policy still remained. This can be seen first in the new administration's reaction to the EEC's directives and actions concerning the French investment regulation law of 1966. After numer-ous exchanges with the French government, the EEC Commission finally took the case to the European Court of Justice in November 1969. The government's initial response was to request a postponement of the case while it reconsidered the 1966 law. The law was then revised to meet the Commission's approval, and the case was closed. However, the government still retained the ability to block investments through foreign exchange controls established during the 1968 crisis and which required advance notice of investment proposals.

In general, foreign direct investment was encouraged during this period. In the words of Prime Minister Jacques Chaban-Delmas: "We do not wish to lose any opportunity to develop industrial plants in our country. We are not against, but for foreign investments."[12] But Pompidou saw attempts to dominate whole sectors of industry as a threat to French interests, and investment was encouraged in a controlled atmosphere, in line with regional development goals. The Territorial Planning and Regional Development Agency (DATAR), created in 1963, became actively involved in foreign investment questions to this end in mid-1969. Working closely with the National Planning Commission, DATAR encouraged new investment while seeking to channel it into zones other than the Paris region; five zones were delineated, with different incentives provided for investment in each zone. The new policy met with some success, especially since the government still had the potential ability to deny an undesirable investment proposal altogether.[13]

In February 1970 an interministerial council was held on the problem of foreign investment. Decisions taken here essentially reaffirmed the relaxation of French policy and the opening of the French economy to foreign investment. Investments that created new enterprises were to be preferred; the government was to aid French enterprises in order to facilitate their competitive strength and to encourage French foreign investment; and finally, the government would seek to harmonize its policies with those of other members of the EEC. President Pompidou announced elements of this policy the following month during the occasion of his visit to the United States.

As suggested in the above, the administration continued the "national champions" policy begun under de Gaulle. However, France also began to place emphasis on the need for developing an EEC industrial policy and for harmonizing company law to permit cross-frontier mergers of European firms. Indeed, as early as 1968, Olivier Guichard, minister of industry, discussed plans to introduce legislation in the French Parliament to this end.

The French proposals, indeed the Community industrial policy efforts as a whole, were not acted upon by the Community in any concrete sense during the Pompidou period. This stemmed in part from West German opposition, which resulted from a preference for a competitive market economy approach and a view that U.S. investment was beneficial and should not be discouraged. However, French officials continued to call for the development of European multinationals, and some discussions on the issue were held with German officials.[14]

The concept of a European industrial policy was revived briefly in 1972 at the Paris summit meeting of EEC heads of government, again with support from the French. The EEC Commission did open a Business Liaison Office in May

1973 in an effort to help and encourage joint ventures and transnational mergers of European firms. However, little else emerged from the EEC efforts, and the French returned to a view that national provisions were more practical.

In the early 1970s, the French continued to welcome investment from the United States. Indeed, DATAR's activities to attract investment to certain regions of the country were increased. By this time DATAR offices for this purpose had been established in Frankfurt, London, Madrid, New York, Stockholm, and Switzerland, and various publications were distributed in an effort to ease the installation of new investment. Press articles and reports pointing to the threat of U.S. foreign investment occurred less frequently. However, to some extent the gap seemed to be filled by accounts depicting the new threat of investment from the United Kingdom, following the decision to permit British entry into the EEC. Much of the concern here centered around what appeared to be a flood of investors in French real estate and in various sectors of the food industry.

Despite considerable discussion (especially in academic circles) about the need for the international regulation of MNCs, the Pompidou administration showed little interest (outside of the question of an EEC industrial policy) in the efforts of various national organizations to this end. By this time there had been important initiatives by other governments in the EEC, the OECD, and the United Nations.

French policy toward foreign investment continued to be favorable during the administration of president Valéry Giscard d'Estaing. During his service as Pompidou's finance minister, his expressed attitude toward foreign investment became much more favorable than it had been during the de Gaulle period. However, after being elected president, he maintained a low profile in his public statements on the subject; policy on foreign investment remained a point of contention with the French left.

However, the pursuit of a favorable (but guarded) policy toward foreign investment received support from both academic and governmental studies of the effects of such investment on the French economy.[15] Policy along the lines suggested by this counsel received further stimulus from the international economic environment of the time. The energy crisis dramatized by the events following the October 1973 war in the Middle East became a preoccupation in France, as it did in the rest of the industrial world. The "crise" on the minds of governmental decision makers was one of high-cost energy and world inflation, and not the impact of foreign investment. Indeed, the economic environment and the problems that dominated the debate during the 1974 French election campaign could only support the trend begun under Pompidou to encourage foreign investment in an effort to modernize industry and avoid unemployment. Stimulating industrial investment remained a concern of the government throughout the first few years of Giscard's term.

Policy statements issued by the new government reflected these concerns, and the efforts to encourage foreign investment begun under Pompidou were augmented. DATAR, under the direction of Jérôme Monod, became even more aggressive in seeking installations of foreign firms, in part by publicizing the opportunities and incentives available. With the support of Giscard, Monod also simplified the bureaucratic procedures that a foreign resident or firm must follow to locate in France.[16]

Indeed, industrial policy in general was the subject of controversy and disagreement within Giscard's administration as well as within the larger political arena. DATAR and elements within the Commissariat Général du Plan disagreed over the value of foreign investment to French industrial development at various points, and there was certainly disagreement on the issues between the administration and the political parties of the left opposition.[17] However, the most controversial element of the administration's industrial policy was the decision to seek an "Atlantic" solution to France's ailing computer industry, by permitting the U.S. MNC Honeywell to rescue Campagnie internationale pour l'informatique (CII) through a merger with Honeywell Bull. Given disappointment with the export performance of CII as a member of the European consortium (Unidata) that associated CII with Siemens, Philipps, and International Computers, the Honeywell merger was part of a new French policy to rebuild major high-technology industries for maximum export earnings at the lowest cost possible. According to French Minister of Industry Michel d'Ornano, CII-Honeywell Bull would have a French majority holding through a combined public and private sector participation. Despite this, the merger announcement was met by strong criticism from labor unions and both the political left and right. The decision profoundly divided the government, received a lively critical debate in the Senate, and was criticized by various quarters in the EEC. Similar lines of policy were pursued in the telecommunication industry. While not permitting foreign dominance, the government's decisions seem to have abandoned the Gaullist policy of expensive independence in favor of a strategy aimed at commercial success. The national champions policy of the previous two administrations had thus undergone important revision.

French industrial policy under Giscard also had an important impact on the small and medium-size industries and businesses in the country. Created under Pompidou in 1970 to facilitate the growth of medium-size enterprises through capital participation and merger aid, the Institut de Developpement Industriel (IDI) became increasingly active during the Giscard administration. In addition, the government began serious consideration of proposals for the "réforme de l'entreprise," stemming from a report submitted to the president in February 1975 by a committee under the leadership of Pierre Sudreau.[18]

The final element of the government's national investment and industrial policy was an effort to encourage direct investments abroad by French firms. Indeed, French investment in the United States grew dramatically between 1974 and 1977.

Proposals for an EEC industrial policy made little headway during the period after Pompidou, and the new French administration made no real effort to restimulate action. Indeed, one could argue (and the EEC Commission did) that Giscard's Atlantic solutions to the problems of French high-technology industry undermined the efforts of the Community.

There was some EEC effort during the Giscard period to follow up on the guidelines for MNCs submitted to the Council of Ministers in November 1973. For example, the Commission conducted an 18-month study that surveyed MNCs operating in member states.[19] However, the Council of Ministers took no real action on the proposals; after several postponements, the proposals ended up receiving only ten minutes of consideration. The European Parliament did discuss the original guidelines and raised the issue of regulating MNCs at various points, but the French were largely noncommittal on these efforts. Under Giscard, France was now cool to the drive for a European industrial policy, and was neither strongly in favor of nor strongly opposed to the Commission's efforts in other areas relevant to MNCs.

French policy toward the OECD discussions and negotiations on MNCs remained largely indifferent under the Giscard administration. France did sign the OECD declaration and voluntary guidelines for multinational enterprises on June 21, 1976 (along with the other 23 member states).[20] But the guidelines had been weakened considerably in the difficult negotiations (rarely attended by a representative from France) between October 1975, when the working party of government representatives agreed on a draft code of conduct, and the signing date for the final declaration and guidelines. The final guidelines were clearly closer to the proposals suggested by the representatives on the OECD's Business and Industry Advisory Committee than those proposed in the document of the Trade Union Advisory Committee.[21]

French policy toward the discussions and negotiations in the meetings of the United Nations Commission on Transnational Corporations and its working groups was initially as disinterested as was policy toward the OECD. France was represented at the first few meetings only by members of the permanent delegation to the UN in New York, while most other industrial countries sent special delegates from economic and industrial ministries in the capitals. As a result, French intervention in these meetings was neither concrete nor constructive. Indeed, the French representatives even left the role of response to criticism from the developing countries to other industrial countries. This enabled France to avoid offending the third world, while its formal participation in the efforts allowed the government to point to action in response to the MNC challenge, when that issue was raised by the political left at home. The UN was viewed as too political and diverse for effective action against MNCs, if indeed such action was indicated.

Some change in this posture became evident in late 1977, when the French representation at the meetings changed to special delegates sent from Paris. The new delegates became somewhat more active, and the government presented more concrete opinions on the issues. Moreover, in an official statement presented after some delay for inclusion in a document for the Working Group on the Code of Conduct, the government did articulate views on the code:

The Government of France views the elaboration of a code of conduct as an essential endeavour; a code to guide the activities of transnational corporations would be useful to encourage the positive role that they can play in the world economy. In this context the issue of a clear definition of a transnational corporation should receive priority attention. The criteria to be considered in establishing such a definition includes the size of the company, the diversity of its foreign activities, its importance in the sector in which it operates and its organizational pattern. State-owned corporations should be subject to the same regulations as private corporations.

A code of conduct should be voluntary, evolutionary and universal. An international treaty having binding force could not achieve broad acceptance; therefore the code should be an instrument in the form of recommendations, including principles of conduct addressed both to States and to transnational corporations.[22]

The statement went on to identify some principles regarding the behavior of transnational corporations and also to propose principles of governmental policies, the latter being a point of contention between the developed and developing countries. However, the government did not respond to a request from the secretary-general for all states to assist the Centre on Transnational Corporations in establishing a comprehensive information system.[23]

As one might expect, given French attitudes to the activities taking place in the UN itself, French policy toward the efforts of subsidiary and associated UN bodies reflected even less interest; this is particularly true of the UNCTAD efforts. However, the French position here was certainly not unique among the industrial countries, and French representatives voted for the adoption of the ILO voluntary principles and various UNCTAD resolutions on the subject.

In general, the foregoing leads to the conclusion that France under Giscard became increasingly satisfied with national approaches to the regulation of multinational corporations. The government even retreated somewhat from the efforts of previous administrations to employ the EEC in an international approach. French policy here has not been coherent and without ambiguity, but the EEC is still favored as the forum for any really useful international effort.

The stimulus for international action was not great because more investment was needed for the economy, and French industry perhaps now needed less protection from competition than in the past. Indeed, this can be seen in the aggressive posture of French corporations in increasing their own foreign investment activities, particularly in the United States.

Finally, it appears that domestic political discontent and concern about MNCs was largely diverted. The political parties of the left had sought to make an issue out of the threat of MNCs, calling for nationalization of some subsidiaries and the strict regulation of foreign banks, both in the common program of June 1972 and in later policy statements. However, consensus on a strict policy weakened, and the French Socialist party, as part of its quarrel with the Communist party, changed to a view that only very limited nationalization would be required. For a time, the nationalization issue, together with the predictions of a victory of the left in the 1978 legislative elections, did serve to discourage foreign MNCs from investing in France, but the surprisingly strong victory of the government coalition in those elections put the issue at rest, at least for the time being.

The United Kingdom

Foreign direct investment in the United Kingdom grew rather dramatically in the post-World War II period, particularly in the late 1950s. Indeed, the extent of foreign economic penetration, owing in part to a tradition of an open economy, was far greater than in France (see Table 11.17) or in any other European country for that matter. However, the issues surrounding foreign direct investment and the operation of MNCs, while important, were much less the subject of domestic political controversy there than in France. As a result, there was less real policy modification at the national level aimed directly at MNCs.

Despite the growth in foreign direct investment in the United Kingdom, a threat from this was not perceived at all well into the 1960s. MNCs and new foreign direct investment were regulated under authority provided in the Exchange Control Act of 1947, which limited investment financing, and the Companies Act of 1948, but the atmosphere was open and relaxed. Indeed, foreign investment was welcome. However, the government's concern over balance of payments problems and currency crises was reflected in its scrutiny of foreign direct investment through the Treasury's administration of exchange controls. Proposed investment was to be mostly self-financing and contributory to foreign exchange reserves. This constituted the only formal way in which foreign firms were treated differently from British firms, but foreign direct investment was generally seen as beneficial to the balance of payments situation; hence it was rarely discouraged or hindered by this means.

Impressed with the apparent success of planning initiated by Jean Monnet in France, Prime Minister Harold Macmillan did take a step in the direction of planning with the creation of the National Economic Development Council (NEDC), an organ that at various times sought to consider the impact of MNCs on the British economy.[24] Nevertheless, responsibility for oversight and policy toward MNCs was widely dispersed throughout the government until the early 1970s.

With the onset of the administration of Prime Minister Harold Wilson in October 1964 some relevant new governmental mechanisms and procedures were gradually instituted.[25] These measures reflected a more interventionist posture toward the economy in general rather than a response to a perceived threat or to specific instances of negative behavior by MNCs, at least initially. Unlike the experience of the de Gaulle administration in the same period there were no specific negative events or episodes that dictated or provided a justification for new governmental restrictions.

Shortly after the new administration took office, the key feature of British regulation of foreign direct investment was the government's ability and willingness to restrict the freedom of an MNC to choose the location for a proposed investment establishment or expansion. The government thus sought to make such investment conform to regional development and employment goals. Obviously this involved a bargaining process, and incentives including free depreciation allowances were provided for investment in certain regions. Aid for investment in development areas was greatly increased by the government with passage of the Industrial Development Act of 1966, which created a system of direct cash grants for certain types of capital investment. An incentive to increase employment by investment in underdeveloped regions was added with the establishment of a weekly Regional Employment Premium to firms for each employee involved in manufacturing in these underdeveloped regions. In administering investment grants, the Board of Trade did not distinguish between British and foreign companies.

Construction of all industrial installations was also subject to approval from local authorities. Significantly, those in excess of 5,000 square feet (3,000 square feet in the Midlands and the Southeast) also required approval from the Board of Trade in the form of an Industrial Development Certificate (IDC).

Interventionist machinery established by the Labour government included a new Ministry of Technology, headed by Anthony Wedgwood Benn, a prominent figure of the party's left wing. Under Benn's leadership, this ministry became quite active; among other things, he made initiatives with the Treasury to ensure that broader considerations than just the balance of payments were included when granting permission for new foreign direct investment. But the ministry's role in industrial policy only really began to be felt toward the end of the Wilson administration. A Department of Economic Affairs was also established in an effort to coordinate all elements of economic policy.

The Labour government embarked on an active legislative program with the aim of restructuring and rebuilding British industry, as well as strengthening the ailing economy in general. This effort included passage of the Monopolies and Mergers Act of 1965 designed in part to help strengthen business in the United Kingdom through mergers and to discourage foreign takeovers. Also in 1965, a National Board of Prices and Incomes (PIB) was established to replace the National Incomes Commission. But, perhaps the most significant action taken during the Wilson administration in this regard was the passage of a bill that established an Industrial Reorganisation Corporation (IRC) in December 1966. First presented in a white paper by George Brown, minister for economic affairs, the IRC was designed to improve the economic efficiency and competitiveness of selected industries.[26] It was independent from the government, and the mergers it fostered were not subject to scrutiny by the Monopolies Commission. The IRC began to have a significant impact on industrial concentration and rationalization by the end of the Wilson administration, but it was disbanded by the new Conservative government, which then created a somewhat weaker and less independent body for restructuring. Finally, in mid-1967, after considerable debate and controversy, a new Companies Act was passed, providing, among other things, for new degrees of disclosure of information by MNCs and some concessions for export-oriented companies.

As noted earlier, MNCs were for the most part not considered a real threat to the United Kingdom, except perhaps by certain trade unions, for the first two years of the Wilson administration. Indeed, they were looked upon quite favorably, especially by the financial and monetary sectors. Some positive impact on the balance of payments by MNCs was evident even if it was subject to executive decisions within various MNCs. For example, a survey report by the Board of Trade found that 22 percent of British exports in 1966 was accounted for by internal transactions within the branches and subsidiaries of MNCs.[27]

Even the takeover of the ailing Rootes Group motor manufacturer by Chrysler in late 1966 was largely viewed as a positive solution, though one not without some controversy and careful government scrutiny. Chrysler did have to make public promises on the future operation and balance of payments effects of Rootes in a letter to Technology Minister Benn, but it has been argued that this was to open communication channels and to provide a "political escape valve" for the government.[28]

However, by early 1967 official concern began to be expressed about the competitive dominance of U.S. MNCs and the existence of a technology gap between Europe and the United States. In separate speeches, Prime Minister Wilson and Chancellor of the Exchequer James Callaghan called for the creation of a European Technological Community. Public airing of this concern was then heightened with an extraordinary statement by Prime Minister Wilson during a speech to the Consultative Assembly of the Council of Europe on January 23, 1967. Warning that the United Kingdom was on the road to an industrial helotry, rather than partnership with the United States, Wilson said:

> there is no future for Europe, or for Britain, if we allow American business and American industry so to dominate the strategic growth industries of our individual countries, that they, and not we, are able to determine the pace and the direction of Europe's industrial advance, that we are left in industrial terms as the hewers of wood and drawers of water while they . . . enjoy a growing monopoly in the production of the technological instruments of industrial advance.[29]

This statement was widely taken to be aimed at making the United Kingdom seem more respectable in the eyes of de Gaulle, for the purpose of entry into the EEC. A copy of the speech was sent to the French president prior to a visit that Wilson and Foreign Secretary George Brown made the next day. However, the theme was stressed repeatedly by Wilson, even after the second French veto of a British application for admission to the EEC in late 1967, and in early 1968 British officials began to propose the creation of a European Institute of Technology. There was also some effort to establish other forms of European technological and industrial linkages outside of the EEC, which greatly annoyed the French.[30]

One outcome of this concern about the technology gap and the competitive dominance of U.S. MNCs was considerable British effort to stimulate mergers of firms. This began with the attempts of the IRC to concentrate and rationalize British industry to make it more competitive. Working as an outsider, the Labour government could, of course, have little impact on the activities beginning in the EEC on European company law and merger easing, but the government did make a spirited attempt to gain support for extending the IRC model to the European level. This extension never materialized, however, and the Conservative electoral victory in 1970 spelled an end to the British initiative.

Aside from official concern over the technology gap and the competitive dominance of U.S. MNCs, there were some instances of concern among members of British trade unions about the threat of foreign MNCs. Perhaps the most publicized episode in this was the labor dispute with the U.S.-owned Roberts-Arundel firm. Despite some government intervention, the plant was eventually closed, and the company expanded its activities in Belgium, Italy, and Spain. Ford in the United Kingdom also experienced considerable difficulty in labor relations, particularly in 1969, when more than 4.5 million man hours were lost in the first six months alone.[31]

In addition to disputes with individual foreign firms, several trade unions attempted to express their concern by action through the Trades Union Congress. Several unions submitted motions relating to MNCs to the annual congresses of the TUC during the mid to late 1960s.[32] As a result, some consultations with firms were conducted by the TUC and studies were made. In 1970, the TUC made proposals at a meeting of the National Economic Development Council, chaired by the prime minister, for a British initiative in studying problems relating to MNCs at the international level, possibly through the OECD.

The Labour government did begin to make initiatives to the OECD on this subject at about this time. Indeed, the United Kingdom served as the chairman of the early efforts of the OECD Industrial Committee, and by 1970 the government had become sufficiently mobilized by trade union and public concern to reevaluate its rather relaxed national policy. This mobilization was likely somewhat related to the increase in press coverage and scholarly works on MNCs. As one high official responsible for policy toward MNCs during that period and since put it, the beginning of official concern or threat perception in this area can be traced to the publication and circulation of Servan-Schreiber's *Le Défi Américain.*[33]

While the members of the Labour government did not all come to share the view of Technology Minister Anthony Wedgwood Benn that international companies would soon reduce national governments, including the British government, to "the status of a parish council,"[34] by 1970 there was some increasing interest in seeking international solutions. This included interest in referring the question to the OECD as well as in the efforts to ease cross-frontier industrial mergers in Europe, as described earlier. However, the government maintained the view that both national and international solutions had to be pursued with care. The British economy was still far from healthy, and new industrial investment (especially in export-oriented industries, much of which would have to come from MNCs) was seen as a crucial ingredient in the government's recovery program. The reality of this situation was to influence governmental policy in the administrations to follow, both Conservative and Labour.

With the Conservative electoral victory in mid-1970, Prime Minister Edward Heath found himself in a difficult situation with respect to MNCs. The British economy remained in difficulty and in need of both industrial investment and export earnings, yet the political environment had become considerably more hostile toward MNCs. Press coverage and analyses about MNCs increased, and soon concern was apparent in both academic and governmental circles, as well as in the trade unions and the Labour party.

In contrast to the period of the first Wilson administration, there were several episodes during the Heath administration when the behavior of specific U.S. MNCs received widespread negative publicity and elite concern. For example, the situation with Ford in the United Kingdom became greatly inflamed when corporation chairman Henry Ford II, in reaction to his corporation's continuing problems with British labor, threatened to prevent any future investment in Britain and to stop exporting components produced in Britain to other countries for final assembly in Ford plants. The point here was to avoid making production in other countries dependent on peace with British labor. Heath subsequently met with Ford, but the situation was not resolved; indeed, the chairman refused to meet with union leaders. Ford eventually carried out his threat to build a new plant (then in the planning stage) elsewhere in Western Europe; after considerable debate and country versus country bidding, the plant was built in Belgium.

A second example was the threat issued by the management of the Chrysler Corporation to end production in Britain because of continuing labor disputes at its plants in Coventry and Linwood. This caused considerable uproar, particularly when former Labour ministers Wilson and Benn charged that Chrysler was defaulting on the promises it had made at the time of its takeover of Rootes. As Michael Hodges has argued, the episode seemed to underscore the ineffectiveness of the government's measures for controlling or at least influencing the actions of MNCs after the point when a new investment was approved.[35]

These highly publicized events, among others, served to further sensitize public opinion on issues relating to the impact of MNCs. They also provided the Labour opposition with opportunities to criticize government policy and further politicize the issues. The Heath administration, caught in a dilemma of needing industrial investment and yet subject to political pressure for more control, wavered on the issue, but largely encouraged new investment, bowing to the imperatives of the economy.

A little more than a year after taking office, the government received a study on the impact of foreign direct investment in the United Kingdom, which had been commissioned by the Economic Services Division of the Board of Trade (subsequently a part of the new Department of Trade and Industry); a team of economists led by Professor M. D. Steuer of the London School of Economics had conducted the study.[36] While heavily qualified throughout, the study essentially found no compelling negative impact of foreign direct investment; indeed, important benefits were indicated. This of course provided the Conservative government with useful ammunition in its battle to justify its continued policy of favoring new foreign direct investment in the United Kingdom.

Given the impact of the Steuer Report, the Conservative government made little effort to upgrade national restrictions on foreign direct investment and the activities of MNCs. Indeed, it could be argued that, if anything, the government's ability to respond to MNCs was weakened. This stemmed largely from the government's decision to abolish the Industrial Reorganisation Corporation (IRC) in 1971. In March 1972, the Conservatives did introduce an Industry Bill White Paper to Parliament that eventually led to the establishment of an Industrial Development Executive (IDE).[37] The IDE was essentially a weakened form of the IRC without the latter's independence of action.

On the international level, the Heath administration did continue the campaign to encourage cross-frontier industrial mergers in Europe. As with the Wilson administration efforts, this campaign was closely tied to the government's attempt to gain admission to the EEC. Indeed, in an opening statement on June 30, 1970, at the EEC membership negotiations in Luxembourg, Anthony Barber said that an enlarged community could make more progress in industrial policy and technical cooperation; he added that the United Kingdom would welcome a common EEC industrial policy.[38]

However, as we have seen, little came from these proposals and expressions of support, even after the United Kingdom was admitted to the EEC. West German opposition remained strong, and the indifferent and vacillating positions of other governments discouraged further British follow-up. Except for its support of a common industrial policy and cross-frontier mergers, the United Kingdom in general did not favor EEC efforts to regulate MNCs. To the extent to which international regulation was favored at all by the Conservative government, the OECD was the preferred forum by far. The Conservative government did follow up on the OECD initiatives made by the Labour government, and, unlike the French government, it did actively participate in the negotiations for the creation of a voluntary code of conduct for MNCs and a data collection facility in the organization.

In part, this policy preference derived from a view that the United States should be involved in such efforts, but there were also important concerns about the legal implications of EEC action (the differing impact of restrictions here as opposed to OECD efforts). The potential legal and economic costs of an elaborate EEC policy were seen as problematic for the British, given both their relative economic weakness versus France and West Germany and their tradition of having an open economy.

Also in contrast to the French position, the British directed considerable attention to the efforts within the United Nations system during this period. A principal from the Department of Trade and Industry actively represented the Conservative government at an ILO meeting of experts on the Relationship between Multinational Corporations and Social Policy, and Professor John Dunning served on the UN's Group of Eminent Persons examining MNC questions. But the Conservative government attached a higher priority to the OECD efforts, in part as an effort to provide some structure, based on agreement among the industrial countries, for the more political UN negotiations to follow on such aspects as the code of conduct.

Prominent spokesmen within the Labour party criticized the Conservative government's relaxed policy, and pledged that a new Labour government would seek stricter controls and effective international response. Indeed, in January 1972, Anthony Wedgwood Benn, the chairman of the Labour party, argued that a framework of control for MNCs "will have to be constructed at various levels from the United Nations right down to the plant level."[39] In addition, the National Executive Committee of the Labour party published three "opposition green papers" relevant to MNCs, which among other things called for reforms in company law, including increased information disclosure provisions, and for the establishment of a National Enterprise Board (NEB). The NEB was to be designed in part to control British companies, which could then effectively challenge MNCs.[40] Similar proposals were included in the party's program, which stemmed from its annual conference in 1973.

The formation of a new Labour government under Harold Wilson on March 4, 1974, after the failure of Heath's election strategy, gave the Labour party an opportunity to deliver on its pledges to regulate MNCs more effectively. Initially, there at least appeared to be serious interest in examining the question thoroughly, and some important initiatives were taken. However, the realities of governing with a failing economy and the need to achieve consensus among quite disparate elements, both within and outside of the party, eventually led the government to encourage, indeed to actively campaign for, new foreign direct investment. In point of fact, the Labour government acted much in the same way (though not quite as aggressively) as did the French government during this period. Policy toward MNCs did not change precipitously as the United Kingdom shifted from a Conservative to a Labour government. Nonetheless, there were some modifications and institutional changes that should be noted.

First, the Department of Trade and Industry was separated into two distinct departments, and the new Department of Industry was put under the leadership of archinterventionist Anthony Wedgwood Benn, the minister of technology during the previous Labour administration. Furthermore, responsibility for all governmental policy toward MNCs, both national and international, was centralized within this new department; an Industrial and Commercial Policy Division served to coordinate the input and regulation efforts of all sectors of the government. This development was in great contrast to the diffusion of responsibility over MNCs and investment questions that had characterized the previous two administrations and which to a lesser degree still characterized the French government's situation.

Second, the Labour government actively pursued a new Industry Bill, which had potential for a significant impact on responding to MNCs. The bill proposed to set up a National Enterprise Board (NEB) with wide powers to promote industrial efficiency and competitiveness, along the lines called for when the party was out of office. The NEB, together with the other provisions of the Industry Bill, as set out in its original form at the end of January 1975 promised to go much further than even the IRC established during the previous Labour government.[41] However, the bill was the subject of extended controversy, both within Parliament and with the business community, which feared that the NEB would be used as a means for extensive nationalization of business and industry. In an effort to build support (particularly given its slim parliamentary majority), the government carried out extensive and sometimes acrimonious negotiations with the CBI and other leaders of industry. Some modifications in the bill were permitted, and there was an effort to specify clearly the circumstances under which state takeover could occur (not without a firm's expressed consent and extensive consultations) and to provide assurance that the new information disclosure requirements would be voluntary.

These modifications and interpretations, however, led to dissent from trade unions and a threatened revolt by the left wing of the Labour party, which charged that the bill was being watered down. The parliamentary consideration of the bill was lively, and the House of Lords attempted to revise it extensively, but the bill was eventually adopted with the NEB relatively intact.

The government was subjected to attack from the left wing of the party on MNC-related questions at other points as well, particularly when Benn was replaced by Eric Varley as secretary of state for industry. Benn was transferred to head the Department of Energy in the wake of the defeat of his anti-EEC efforts during the referendum (and in an effort to improve poor relations between the government and industry). In addition, the left wing Tribune Group of Labour M.P.s issued a statement in early 1975, calling for the government to adopt an entirely new economic strategy in face of the crisis. Among other things, the statement criticized government inaction in controlling MNCs and proposed a large increase in funding for the NEB to restructure British industry. The government, however, resisted significant change in this direction.

The government came to recognize that economic recovery, especially given the impact of higher oil prices and the attendant inflationary effects, would not be enhanced by discouraging new foreign direct investment. Indeed, a major report released by the National Economic Development Office in May 1975 pointed to a crisis in industrial investment in the United Kingdom. Criticizing the existing capital market, the NEDO report found that the annual growth rate of British manufacturing investment for the period 1960–72 (the years of maximum postwar economic expansion) was under half those of France, the United States, Japan, and the Netherlands.

Aware of the need for new investment, the government began a campaign to encourage more foreign direct investment by MNCs, along with some domestic reforms.[42] However, the most dramatic instance of the government's positive attitude toward MNCs and foreign direct investment was reflected in its effort to keep the economically failing Chrysler production facilities in the United Kingdom. Despite earlier pledges to Industry Minister Benn that it planned to stay in the United Kingdom and provide for worker participation in all levels of the company including the board of directors, continued labor strife and severe economic losses in the U.K. subsidiary led the parent corporation in Detroit to seriously consider essentially giving the subsidiary to the British government. However, Prime Minister Wilson weathered vocal attacks from labor union leaders, the Labour party's left wing, and the Conservative opposition to obtain parliamentary approval for a $355 million package of aid to rescue Chrysler's British factories.

This governmental action was extraordinary not only in terms of the amount of aid being given to a foreign-owned MNC but also because it seemed to represent a reversal of the government's "new industrial strategy," announced just a little more than a month earlier by the new industry minister, Eric Varley. In the new strategy, the government had announced that it would no longer use public funds to save jobs in failing companies, but rather would focus on promising companies and industries.

In the area of international responses to MNCs, British policy under the Labour government was rather clearly defined and consistent. The new administration remained in large measure hostile to EEC efforts to regulate MNCs, responding perhaps the most negatively among the member states to the Commision's November 1973 proposals.

The EEC was still not the favored forum for international responses to MNCs in the British view, and this view was accentuated with the Labour government's follow through on a campaign promise to hold a referendum on British membership in the EEC and to renegotiate the terms of entry. The final verdict of the referendum was "yes," but the British public remained among the most anti-EEC in its general opinion.

Of direct relevance to MNC policy and of considerable concern to the government in the renegotiation effort was its demand to retain national control over regional and industrial policy. One can understand the government's concern over this area, given the sensitivity and domestic implications involved, but these were areas of priority for the Commission and certain member states as well. As a result, accommodation to the British view was limited, and the government did come to the view that there were some benefits to common ground rules for aid to industries and uniform incentives for investment.[43]

As with earlier administrations, the forum preferred by the Labour government for international responses to MNCs was the OECD. However, British efforts here seemed to pick up a new impetus after the departure of the Heath government. In part, this was due to the fact that the government was consistently represented in OECD meetings by a high-level official from the Department of Industry, indeed the under secretary for the Industrial and Commercial Policy Division, the office that was now charged with responsibility for the coordination of the government's national and international policy toward MNCs. The OECD negotiations took place in the meetings of several different committees, and the Treasury sent a separate representative to the financial committee meetings. However, there was some coordination in London, and the OECD investment committee coordinated the relevant work of the other committees. The government did strongly support the predominant view that the OECD guidelines for MNCs should be voluntary, so that primary responsibility for control remained at the national level. Representatives of the government signed the declaration and guidelines on June 21, 1976.

The Labour government also directed considerable attention to the UN efforts, and, again in contrast to the French case, British participation here was rather constructive. However, much of this attention appears to be more a matter of form (perhaps in response to TUC pressure) than of substance, and the degree of politicization (especially during the early meetings of the Commission on Transnational Corporations and its working groups) often placed the British representative in a defensive, reactive position versus the developing countries.[44] In response to a request from the UN secretary-general, the British government submitted a statement of views and proposals on a UN Code of Conduct for MNCs on December 3, 1976. It is evident from the statement (and from subsequent negotiating behavior) that the United Kingdom was interested in maintaining the primacy of national efforts to control MNCs; investment flows (with their crucial beneficial effects on the economy) should not be disrupted or deterred by international action. Related to this was an interest in protecting the foreign investment activity of U.K. corporations, then second only to that of U.S. corporations.[45]

CONCLUSIONS AND IMPLICATIONS

The foregoing analysis does seem to provide support for the model of foreign policy behavior discussed earlier. The survey data analysis did not support the main hypothesis of the model about the impact of external threats on policy response; however, the case studies do provide some support, albeit limited and qualified, and the survey data demonstrate the importance of other elements of the model, namely the impact of individual variables on the threat perception/policy response processes.

Beginning with the French case, it is clear that the threat perception/cooperative response sequence came into play, at least to a limited degree, during the de Gaulle administration. Pompidou, who had been a voice for moderation during the de Gaulle administration, did modify policy somewhat. DATAR became increasingly active, and foreign investment was largely encouraged, with regional development goals in mind. The EEC Commission directives and Treaty of Rome provisions were finally complied with, and Pompidou was rather more interested in cross-frontier European industrial mergers than was de Gaulle.

With Giscard, policy continued to be directed toward encouraging foreign direct investment; indeed, efforts to attract it were stepped up, as higher energy costs and increased inflation had their impact on the domestic economy. However, Giscard, cautiously and with considerable opposition, pursued Atlantic solutions to the revitalization of high technology industries in an effort to maximize French export potential in this area. The EEC efforts to regulate MNCs were not supported, though the French still felt this forum was preferable to all other international organizations if there was to be international regulation, and there was no effort to restimulate the lagging efforts to develop a European industrial policy. Basically, the national control of regulation was to be maintained as much as possible. There was little difference between administrations on policy toward the work on MNCs taking place in the OECD and the UN.

Turning to the British case, the model again seems to have some validity. Both mass and elite perceptions of a threat from foreign-based MNCs were slower to develop in the United Kingdom than in France, and the issue was manipulated by elites for domestic and foreign political goals at various points. However, by the late 1960s there was a rather strong effort to react to the threat by stimulating European industrial and technological cooperation. At the behest of the trade unions, government initiatives were also made in the OECD. Changes in political leadership did lead to some modifications in policy toward the regulation of MNCs in the United Kingdom—indeed to a greater extent than in France.

In sum, we can discern that the French and British governments during the period of 1963–76 formulated MNC regulation policy under similar, important domestic political and economic constraints. Nonetheless, differences in governmental structure permitted the French administrations more freedom of action, as long as the levels of domestic concern were not too high nor the predilection of the political leadership too nationalistic. In weighing policy alternatives, the real priorities for the French government (indeed for both governments) were to maintain economic growth and employment and to stimulate regional development. As long as these were the goals, the president could adjust policy with a relatively free hand.

The British, especially the Labour administrations, were somewhat more constrained. The same goals predominated, but less domestic anxiety about MNCs could be accepted before some responsive or at least seemingly responsive actions were required. National differences in perceptions of threat from MNCs or in general concern about maintaining national independence were important but were not necessarily crucial in policy determination, nor were they necessarily related to the degree of economic penetration of MNCs in each country.

The foregoing analysis and conclusions do have important implications for the study of elite attitudes, perceptions, and policy response. First, it is clear that the processes involved are quite complex; suitable explanation requires treatment of the effects of many variables. Second, the measurement problems involved are immense, and it seems evident that effective analysis requires reliance on both quantitative and qualitative data sources. In the present effort we have sought to explain governmental attitudes toward MNCs and to determine the impact of such attitudes and perceptions on policy response. However, given the complexity of the undertaking, this can only be seen as a beginning effort.

NOTES

1. Norman A. Graham, "Threat Perception, Policy-Making and International Cooperation: A Comparative Study of the British and French Cases," unpublished Ph.D. dissertation, Columbia University, 1979. Extensive references to original sources may be found in the complete study.

2. Ernst B. Haas, *The Uniting of Europe: Political, Social, and Economic Forces, 1950-1957* (Stanford: Stanford University Press, 1968), p. xxxiii.

3. For a detailed specification of the model with several derivative hypotheses see Graham, "Threat Perception, Policy-Making and International Cooperation," Chapter 2.

4. See, for example: Robert Jervis, *Perception and Misperception in International Politics* (Princeton, N.J.: Princeton University Press, 1976), which provides an effective synthesis of much of the work done in this area. See also: Kenneth E. Boulding, "National Images and International Systems," *The Journal of Conflict Resolution*, III (1959), pp. 120-131; and Ole R. Holsti, "The Belief System and National Images: A Case Study," *The Journal of Conflict Resolution*, VI (1962), pp. 244-252.

5. Gilles Y. Bertin, "Foreign Investment in France," in *Foreign Investment: The Experience of Host Countries*, ed. by Isaiah A. Litvak and Christopher J. Maule (New York: Praeger, 1970), p. 119.

6. See: *Le Monde*, September 13, 1962, p. 12; *Time*, September 21, 1962, p. 88; and *Christian Science Monitor*, October 6, 1962, p. 5. For a detailed account and evaluation of these incidents and others see: Allan W. Johnstone, *United States Direct Investment in France: An Investigation of the French Charges* (Cambridge, Massachusetts: The M.I.T. Press, 1965), especially Chapter 2. See also: Robert W. Gillespie, "The Policies of England, France, and Germany as Recipients of Foreign Direct Investment," in *International Mobility and Movement of Capital*, ed. by Fritz Machlup, Walter S. Salant, and Lorie Tarshis (New York: Columbia University Press, 1972), pp. 397-443; Rainer Hellmann, *The Challenge to U.S. Dominance of the International Corporation* (New York: Dunellen, 1970), pp. 125-135; and Jonathan Wise Polier, *L'indépendance Nationale et L'investissement Etranger: La Politique Française a l'égard Des Investissements, 1945-1966*, Thèse pour le Doctorat de Recherche, Fondation Nationale Des Sciences Politiques, Paris, 1968.

7. *Wall Street Journal*, September 9, 1965, p. 10. See also: Peter G. Van der Spek, "The Outlook for Foreign Investment in the EEC," *Columbia Journal of World Business*, VI, 6 (November-December, 1971), p. 76.

8. France, Ministère de l'Industrie, *Rapport sur les Investissements Etrangers dans l'industrie Française*, 1965. See also: *Le Monde*, April 1, 1965, p. 7 and July 15, 1965.

9. Law 66-1008 (*Journal Officiel*, January 29, 1966, p. 11621).

10. See: *The New York Times*, February 5, 1964, p. 44 and July 24, 1964, p. 6; Denri Stern, *La Crise de la Compagnie des Machines Bull* (Paris: Bureau de Recherches et d'Action Economique, 1966); and Charles-Albert Michalet, "France," in *Big Business and*

the State: Changing Relations in Western Europe, ed. by Raymond Vernon (Cambridge: Harvard University Press, 1974), p. 112.

11. A persuasive discussion of this point is presented by Donald J. Puchala in "Domestic Politics and Regional Harmonization in the European Communities," *World Politics*, XXVII, 4 (July, 1975), pp. 502–503 and pp. 511–512.

12. Hellmann, *Challenge to U.S. Dominance*, p. 134; and *Frankfurter Allegemein Zeitung*, October 17, 1969. See also his statement reported in *Le Nouveau Journal*, April 18, 1970.

13. See: *Investissements Etrangers et Aménagement du Territoire: Livre Blanc* (Paris: DATAR, 1974); and Pierre Durand, *Industrie et Régions: l'aménagement industriel de la France* (Paris: La Documentation Française, 1972 and 1974).

14. *International Herald Tribune*, May 27, 1970. For descriptions of the subsequent attempts to revive EEC industrial policy, see: *The New York Times*, August 20, 1974; *International Herald Tribune*, September 19–20, 1970; and especially, Michael Hodges, "Industrial Policy: A Directorate-General in Search of a Role," in *Policy-Making in the European Communities*, ed. by Helen Wallace, William Wallace, and Carol Webb (London: John Wiley and Sons, 1977), pp. 111–135.

15. See: *Les conséquences économiques des investissements étrangers en France* (Paris: Service d'étude de l'Activité Economique, Fondation Nationale des Sciences Politiques, 1974), p. 97; and *Investissements Etrangers et Aménagement du Territoire: Livre Blanc* (Paris: DATAR, 1974), pp. 121–127. For a critical assessment of this report from the left, see *l'Humanité*, June 11, 1974.

16. For example, see the following publications issued by DATAR and distributed through its offices throughout the industrialized countries: *Investment and Export Financing* (Paris: March, 1975); *Research Centers in France* (Paris: March, 1975); *France: A New Investment Climate* (Paris: September, 1975); and *Investment Incentives in France* (Paris: September, 1976). See also: *Le Monde*, February 16–17, 1975, p. 18; and *DATAR: Newsletter from France*, 1975, No. 2, pp. 2 and 9.

17. See the assessment of the impact of MNCs contained in a study by G. Bertin for the Commissariat Général du Plan, entitled *L'Industrie Française Face aux Multinationales* (Paris: La Documentation Française, 1975). See also an article by Jacqueline Grapin entitled: "L'industrie frappeé par la Crise, Le second Défi Américain," *Le Monde*, December 13, 1975, p. 43. In early 1976 Socialist party leader François Mitterand presented a plan of industrial measures certainly more dramatic than the government was prepared to implement (see *Le Monde*, January 29, 1976, p. 29).

18. *Rapport du Comité d'Etude pour La Réforme de l'Entreprise* (Paris: La Documentation Française, 1975). For reports of the debate over the proposals, see: *Le Monde*, July 6, 1975, p. 30; July 19, 1975, p. 26; January 20, 1976, p. 15; and October 26, 1976, p. 22.

19. Commission of the European Communities, *Survey of Multinational Enterprises*, Volume I (Brussels, July, 1976).

20. OECD, *International Investment and Multinational Enterprises* (Paris, 1976).

21. Trade Union Advisory Committee to the Organisation for Economic Co-operation and Development, *TUAC Document on Multinational Corporations: Policy Proposals Adopted by the TUAC Plenary Session*, Paris, March 4, 1975. See also: *Financial Times*, March 4, 1975.

22. United Nations, Economic and Social Council, Commission on Transnational Corporations, *Transnational Corporations: Views and Proposals of States on a Code of Conduct*, E/C. 10/19/Add. 1 (March 22, 1977), p. 6.

23. United Nations, Centre on Transnational Corporations, *Establishment of a Comprehensive Information System on Transnational Corporations: Government Replies*, ST/CTC/1 (1977).

24. Trevor Smith, "The United Kingdom," in *Big Business and the State: Changing Relations in Western Europe*, ed. by Raymond Vernon (Cambridge: Harvard University Press, 1974), p. 89.

25. For an excellent detailed examination of these efforts, see Michael Hodges, *Multinational Corporations and National Government* (Westmead, Farnborough, Hants, England: Saxon House, D. C. Heath Ltd., 1974), pp. 61–122.

26. Cmnd. 2889, *The Industrial Reorganization Corporation* (January, 1966).

27. Christopher Tugendhat, "Transnational Enterprise: Tying Down Gulliver," *Atlantic Community Quarterly*, IX, 4 (Winter, 1971), p. 503.

28. Hodges, *Multinational Corporations and National Government*, pp. 81–83. See also an editorial supporting the government's decision in *The Times*, January 18, 1967.

29. *The Times*, January 24, 1967, p. 8.

30. See the statement by Technology Minister Benn, as reported in the *Survey of Current Affairs*, May 10, 1968, pp. 484–485; and the statement by French Deputy Foreign Minister Jean de Lipkowski, as reported in *Le Monde* and *Le Figaro*, October 22, 1968.

31. *Ford in Britain: The Company, the Unions, the Agreement* (London: IRIS Ltd., 1969), p. 15.

32. John Gennard, *Multinational Corporations and British Labour: A Review of Attitudes and Responses* (London: Alfred H. Cooper and Sons, 1972), pp. 50–51.

33. Interview, May 6, 1975.

34. *The Times*, November 28, 1968.

35. *The Times*, October 1, 1973.

36. The study was first presented to the government in September 1971. It was subsequently published in 1973 as a public document: Department of Trade and Industry, *The Impact of Foreign Direct Investment on the United Kingdom* (by M. D. Steuer, Peter Abell, John Gennard, Morris Perlman, Raymond Rees, Barry Scott, and Ken Wallis), London: HMSO, 1973. See also the statement on the report by John Davies, secretary for Trade and Industry, as reported in the *Financial Times*, October 12, 1971.

37. Cmnd. 4942, *Industrial and Regional Development* (March, 1972), pp. 5–7.

38. London Press Service, Verbatim Service, No. 174/70 (June 30, 1970).

39. Labour Party Information Department, News Release No. P55/72, p. 1.

40. *The National Enterprise Board, Labour's State Holding Company* (London: The Labour Party, 1973); *Capital and Equality* (London: The Labour Party, 1973); and *The Community and the Company: Reform of Company Law* (London: The Labour Party, 1974). See also: Wayland Kennet, Larry Whitty, and Stuart Holland, *Sovereignty and Multinational Companies* (London: Fabian Society Tract N. 409, 1971); The Labour Party, Scottish Council, *Scotland and the National Enterprises Board* (Glasgow: September, 1973); and Labour Research Department, *The Menace of the Multinationals* (London: LRD Publications Ltd., 1974).

41. See: Parliament, House of Commons, *Industry Bill: Explanatory and Financial Memorandum* (January 31, 1975).

42. For example, see: United Kingdom, Department of Industry, Central Office of Information, *Britain for Industrial Growth: The Facts* (London, March, 1974), and *Britain for Industrial Growth: The Opportunities* (London, August, 1975). In 1976, U.S. investment in the United Kingdom had declined by 15 percent from previous levels (see *The Economist*, May 13, 1978, p. 64).

43. Interview with British official, May 28, 1975. See the discussion of the government's reply to the Tribune Group's concern over EEC membership and its implications for industrial policy in *The Times*, March 21, 1975, p. 17.

44. Evidence for these points was obtained both through interviews with delegates to the various UN meetings and through personal observation of some of the proceedings. A striking example of defensive-reactive behavior versus the developing countries on MNC issues occurred during the debate in the Second Committee of the UN General Assembly (29th Session [1974], meetings 1638–40, 1642–44 and 1647–51) on Article 2 of the Charter of Economic Rights and Duties of States. Ultimately, the United Kingdom voted against the adoption of the charter along with five other developed countries; France abstained from voting.

45. Communication from the permanent representative of the United Kingdom to the United Nations to the secretary-general, December 3, 1976, pp. 1-2. A summary of this statement is contained in ECOSOC document E/C.10/19 (December 30, 1976), *Transnational Corporations: Views and Proposals of States on a Code of Conduct, Report of the Secretariat.*

12

ARE THERE LEARNING SIDE-EFFECTS ASSOCIATED WITH EMPLOYMENT IN A TRANSNATIONAL BUSINESS ENTERPRISE ?

Karl P. Sauvant
Bernard Mennis

Foreign direct investment—as carried out by transnational business enterprises (TNEs)—involves not only capital, technology, and similar resources. Intended or not, it is usually accompanied by sociocultural investments such as attitudes, values, and behavioral patterns, production patterns and processes, consumption patterns, and the like. TNEs, in fact, can be conceptualized as transmission belts through which sociocultural (or even broader: sociopolitical and economic) preferences of home countries are disseminated to other countries. Where this occurs, the sociocultural profile of host-country nationals tends to lose its national characteristics and tends to acquire those of the home countries in-volved. This is the essence of the processes associated with home-country-related sociocultural investments, that is, with the home-country effect. To illustrate: Coca-Cola replaces local soft drinks. In these processes, TNEs are merely trans-mission belts, even if they take an active part in the promotion of home-country-

Karl P. Sauvant is Transnational Corporations affairs officer, Centre on Transnational Corporations, United Nations, New York. Bernard Mennis is associate professor of political science, Temple University. The views expressed in this paper do not necessarily reflect those of the institutions with which the authors are currently affiliated.

This chapter is a revised excerpt from a longer monograph circulated through the *German Studies Notes*, published by the Institute of German Studies, Indiana University, Bloomington, Indiana. The generous support provided by the Institute of German Studies for the preparation of the research manuscript is gratefully acknowledged. Our thanks also go to John Fayerweather, Stephen A. Kobrin, Herbert I. Schiller, and John A. Smetanka, for their helpful comments on an earlier draft of this article.

related sociocultural investments. Any change in the sociocultural profile of host countries is entirely on account of the different sociocultural profile of home countries. As a result, the individuals involved would not become members of a "new tribe"[1] but rather would be coopted into the dominant one.[2]

Apart from this home-country effect, however, it is also conceivable that the special nature of the transmitting institution—its transnational character—has a socializing effect of its own on the individuals directly associated with any of its parts: the TNEs effect. If that were the case, a new tribe of transnationally oriented individuals with distinct characteristics of their own could, indeed, be emerging.

In this paper, we intend to investigate empirically whether, in fact, a TNE effect exists and, if it does, what magnitude it has.

CONCEPTUAL DISCUSSION

The essence of the processes associated with the TNE effect is that the sociocultural profiles of employees working in foreign affiliates (or, more generally, in any part of a TNE system) would over time become different from those of employees in indigenous enterprises. To give an example (which also illustrates the difference between the home-country effect on the one hand and the TNE effect on the other): in a French foreign affiliate in the Walloon part of Belgium one would not expect employees to exhibit attitudes, values, or patterns of behavior different from those of employees in a local company on account of home-country-related sociocultural investments (that is, the home-country effect) because of the high similarity of the sociocultural environments of the home and host countries. Nothing, in other words, could be transmitted. Differences may, however, occur on account of the fact that the foreign affiliate is part of a corporate system that transcends the host country and as such offers a special set of experiences. This example is particularly illustrative since distinctions in the sociocultural systems of host and home countries are a prerequisite for home-country-related sociocultural investments to operate. In our situation, therefore, any differences that would emerge between foreign-affiliate employees and local-company employees could only[3] be accounted for by a separate TNE effect.[4] (Conversely, the absence of any difference would suggest that no such separate effect exists.)

Corporate, not home-country variables, then would produce this effect. They would produce it through a subtle process of socialization. Its premise is captured concisely in the following quote from a paper by John A. Smetanka:

> The model rests on the basic assumption that the international attitudes of a host-country executive can be considered products of the experiences he encounters in his international business role, the parameters of which are determined by the organizational requisites of the multinational firms for which he works.[5]

The idea of such a socializing effect is advanced by a number of scholars. Robert C. Angell, Werner Feld, Joseph S. Nye, and Howard V. Perlmutter, for example, feel that transnational participation leads to a sociocultural profile different from that of individuals not involved in such participation.[6] In each case, the socialization process is assumed to take place in terms of a number of variables particularly germane to TNEs, such as the experience of being part of a large network that considers the world as its oyster, or because of increased chances for communication, travel, frequent face-to-face interactions with non-nationals, and the like.[7] Contact, in particular, plays a key role in these explanations, although it is generally overlooked that contact is independent from ownership, that is, is not necessarily exclusively associated with foreign affiliates but may also occur with similar frequency in export-oriented enterprises.

The specific conditions under which socialization takes place are not always systematically identified by the proponents of this approach. Obviously, however, the basic condition (and for some, this condition may be a sufficient one) is the knowledge of employees that they work in a foreign affiliate, in a part of a worldwide network with global interests. For those who emphasize the mediating role of contact (presumably primarily with other individuals in the network), the frequency of contact is important. These two variables could be considered as components of a more general variable, namely exposure to the transnational character of an enterprise. It would, however, not be correct to assume that, beyond the general knowledge of belonging to a TNE, all employees in a foreign affiliate are equally involved—or even involved at all—in the transnational aspects of the company. In fact, the trickle-down effect of such involvement may be relatively small.

It is argued by many that the impact of this socialization process—which, as already indicated, is not the result of any explicit message but rather a direct outflow of being associated with a TNE—is changes in the sociocultural profiles of TNE employees. However, there is no reason to assume that as a result of a transformation of attitudes, values, and patterns of behavior, host-country nationals would acquire the sociocultural characteristics of headquarters countries (as in the case of home-country-related sociocultural investments). Rather, one would have to assume that the transformation could proceed along another path[8] and toward, for instance, corporate or regional-global orientations or toward sociocultural profiles containing, for example, multiple loyalties, more complex images and stereotypes, improved abilities to communicate and understand non-nationals, or more status-quo oriented attitudes concerning, for instance, changes in the international economic system.

The general consensus is that changes toward more internationalistic and accommodative attitudes are the result—that, in fact, a new *peaceful* tribe is emerging. The title of Angell's book—*Peace on the March*—is indicative of this approach.[9] Thus, not only is a socializing effect being asserted, but the (positive) direction of this effect is asserted as well. This may well be the case if, for example, the TNE effect leads to a sociocultural profile characterized by more complex images and stereotypes. On the other hand, the TNE effect may also lead to more status-quo oriented attitudes concerning the international economic system; it would then combine with the consequences of the home-country effect and contribute to the maintenance of dependency structures in other spheres of home–host-country relations.

SOME PREVIOUS FINDINGS

Data supporting the existence of a socializing TNE effect are very scarce and, as a rule, do not pertain directly to the foreign affiliate situation and its TNE effect but rather to other forms of transnational participation.[10] Most importantly, as far as studies involving TNEs are concerned, they are not comparative in nature, that is, they only show that an impact exists (like Feld), but do not demonstrate that this impact is different from that in other types of business enterprises. A notable exception is Smetanka's study, reported in Chapter 10 of this volume.

In his analysis of the criteria for evaluating U.S. firms and their impact, Smetanka identified a number of variables that yielded significant results, but ownership (that is, whether or not executives worked for a Canadian or a U.S. firm) was not among them. In other words, foreign affiliates were not unique in producing certain effects. Other attributes that cut across domestic and foreign firms—like industry, degree of export orientation, degree of international work responsibility—proved to be of explanatory value. This would suggest that no specific TNE effect exists that was responsible for the differences observed by Smetanka.[11]

Similar findings were reported by us on the basis of a survey of managers in transnational as well as domestic-oriented independent enterprises headquartered in the Federal Republic of Germany. The degree of transnationality of an enterprise itself did not correlate with changes in attitudes regarding a number of important socioeconomic and political issues, while "external interest," a correlate of geographical work orientation (and after controlling for dependence sensitivity), did.[12] One could argue, however, that the situation in our previous study is not comparable since we did not compare managers working in domestic enterprises with those working in foreign affiliates, but rather managers in West German domestic-oriented enterprises with managers in West German TNEs. Still, the result should be quite relevant since what we were comparing were West German managers in one unit of a TNE (which happened to be the headquarters) with West German managers in a domestic enterprise in the same country. As discussed earlier, the TNE effect, if it exists, is a result of being associated with a transnational system per se and not (in contradiction of the sociocultural investment effect) the result of being associated with a particular part of the system, that is, the affiliate.

In fact, two arguments can be advanced which may suggest that this kind of comparison is superior to that of comparing foreign affiliates with domestic enterprises. The first one is that if an independent TNE effect exists, it would most likely materialize among headquarters managers since they are more exposed to the transnational character of their enterprise and are more involved in all its transnational functions than managers in any individual affiliate. The second argument concerns the question of isolating the TNE effect from sociocultural investment effects. If headquarters managers in a home country (or even in home-country affiliates) are compared with those in independent domestic-oriented enterprises in the same home country, the possibility of sociocultural investment is controlled for and hence cannot influence the findings. If foreign affiliates are compared with domestic enterprises, such a control does not occur (except by choosing variables that one would not expect to be susceptible to sociocultural investment or by selecting a home country with a similar culture). It may well be that the (uncontrolled) presence of sociocultural investments explains the differences found by Smetanka in his Canadian study. As a matter of fact, his variables (see the passage quoted earlier) appear to be highly susceptible to home-country related sociocultural investments, especially in a context where the sociocultural system of the United States is already of overshadowing importance.

In spite of these arguments, it remains a possibility that an effect materializes only in foreign affiliates. The reason is that the comparison made on the basis of our earlier study ignores the difference in one potentially important variable: ownership and control. In our earlier study, all enterprises involved were independent enterprises; foreign affiliates, however, are not. In fact, foreign-affiliate managers may be equally or even more exposed to the transnational character of their enterprise, exactly because they work in foreign affiliates and not in headquarters. An effect, therefore, might materialize. If this were indeed the case, one could no longer speak about a systemic TNE effect, since the absence of a TNE effect has already been demonstrated for headquarters managers. More properly, then, one would have to speak about a foreign affiliate effect.

Thus, we end this section with a question: Does working in a TNE—and especially within one of its foreign affiliates—as opposed to a domestic enterprise in fact make a difference for the sociopolitical preferences of employees?

ASSESSING THE TNE EFFECT

The Data Bank

In answering the question posed at the end of the preceding section, obviously care has to be taken to isolate the TNE effect from any home country sociocultural effect by choosing foreign affiliates of TNEs of different headquarter countries, by selecting enterprises in a host country whose sociocultural environment is relatively similar to that of the home countries involved, and by using items not likely to be susceptible to home-country sociocultural messages. If under these conditions a TNE effect can be demonstrated—if, in other words, the special transnational nature of enterprises gives rise to an effect of its own—we would have empirically established one of the component effects of the total sociocultural influence to which host societies and especially local employees of foreign affiliates are being exposed and we would be able to say something about the magnitude of this effect.

Our data base for investigating the TNE effect consists of responses from 3,300 members of the business elite (that is, managers) in 43 enterprises in the Federal Republic of Germany (FRG) to a highly structured survey questionnaire[13] (for the text of the questions that were used in this analysis, see Appendix 12.A). Managers are defined as those employees within an enterprise holding at least the rank of Meister or Gruppenleiter, positions generally acknowledged to represent the lowest level of management in enterprises in the Federal Republic of Germany.

For the purpose of our analysis, we divide these enterprises (and their mangers) into three groups[14]:

(1) foreign affiliates, that is, subsidiaries of enterprises headquartered outside the Federal Republic of Germany. Our foreign-affiliate sample comprises seven subsidiaries with 480 West German managers; the subsidiaries are distributed over five industries—chemical, construction, electrical, machinery, and steel/ metal—and their parent enterprises are headquartered in five other developed countries: France, the Netherlands, Sweden, the United Kingdom, and the United States.

(2) FRG-based TNEs, defined as those enterprises in our sample that are independent (that is, are not owned by another enterprise or combination of enterprises) and whose share of estimated sales to customers abroad (that is, exports plus sales by foreign affiliates) in total consolidated sales equals or exceeds 30 percent. This sample consists of 1,532 West German managers in 19 enterprises; the enterprises are distributed over the following five industries: chemical, electrical, machinery, steel/metal, and textiles.

(3) domestic-oriented FRG-based enterprises, defined as those independent enterprises with foreign sales of less than 30 percent. (Obviously we have divided our sample of FRG-based enterprises into two groups according to their degree of internationalization as indicated by foreign sales.) This sample contains 1,234 West German managers in 17 enterprises: the seven industries included are chemical, construction, electrical, machinery, steel/metal, textile, and utilities.

Our analysis focuses on these three groups of enterprises since they allow the clearest assessment of a TNE effect. Thus, the presence or absence of this effect is being ascertained through a comparison of managers employed in the headquarters of FRG-based TNEs versus those in domestic-oriented FRG-based enterprises; managers in foreign affiliates located in the Federal Republic of

Germany versus those in domestic-oriented FRG-based enterprises. As a matter of fact, we already know that no difference emerges in regard to the first comparison; as reported above, we have found that the degree of transnationality of an enterprise itself does not correlate with changes in attitudes regarding a number of important socioeconomic and political issues. (For this reason, we shall not report any statistical findings for this comparison in subsequent tables.) This finding is particularly important since in this comparison, as already noted, the possibility of a home-country effect and an ownership-control effect is controlled for.

On the basis of our preceding conceptual discussion, we also would not expect a difference to materialize for the second comparison: since managers in foreign affiliates as well as managers in headquarters are members of TNE systems, they would both experience the TNE effect, if it exists. Managers in TNE headquarters, in other words, cannot be used for control purposes to ascertain the presence or absence of a TNE effect. If, nevertheless, a difference should emerge, it could not be attributed to the systemic properties of a TNE network as a whole but rather either to differences in the ownership variable (that is, to the fact that headquarters managers are the controllers and affiliate managers the controlled) or to a limited independent foreign affiliate effect.

If the first two comparisons yield no intersample differences, logic would require that no difference emerges in the third comparison: managers in foreign affiliates versus those in independent domestic-oriented enterprises. Although this comparison directly tests (with the best control group available to us) for the TNE effect, the findings and considerations introduced earlier compel us to hypothesize that no significant difference between the two samples exists. Any differences that emerge are thus again either the result of the ownership variable or a limited TNE effect. It is not possible for us to ascertain whether a separate foreign-affiliate effect exists since this would require a comparison of domestic affiliates with foreign affiliates and we do not have data for the former. Obviously, however, the absence of any difference in this comparison would further confirm our earlier arguments and findings, and thereby suggest that a systemic TNE effect does not exist, or more accurately, that we are unable to establish empirically the existence of such an effect.

Moreover, it should be kept in mind throughout the data analysis that the parent enterprises of our foreign affiliates are headquartered in five other developed industrialized countries. Since the sociocultural systems of these countries and that of the FRG are relatively similar,[15] and considering that the strength of the indigenous (West Germany) sociocultural system is relatively high, we can be reasonably sure that the impact of home country-related sociocultural investments on West German managers in foreign affiliates in the FRG is not high. Therefore, any differences that become visible should not reflect the impact of home country-related sociocultural investments but rather should be the result of the TNE effect.

Furthermore, to assess the possible effects of TNEs, it is necessary to select variables that are relatively important and salient to our respondents, but in the main are not susceptible to home country-related sociocultural investments. In addition, they should be responsive to whatever TNE effect exists. These requirements quite obviously seriously restrict our options. After a perusal of the literature, we chose to concentrate upon a variety of dependent variables that can be grouped under the following three labels: national identification, regional integration, and patterns of information acquisition. Each of these three groups of variables will be introduced in greater detail below.

National Identification

Although it has been argued, as we have seen, that the experiences of employment in a foreign affiliate may influence national identifications, it remains unclear exactly what constitutes national identification and how it is to be measured. Put somewhat differently, no consensus presently exists in regard to the conceptualization or operationalization of national identification. Such a circumstance suggests caution and eclecticism. Hence, rather than restrict the analysis to a single selected indicator of national identification, it seems prudent at this juncture to work with several indicator-variables—all of which enjoy "face validity"—and to observe whether they in fact provide similar results.[16] Four indicators of national identification thus were selected for analysis.

The first is a so-called "patriotism scale" consisting of the following four six-point Likert-type items (strongly agree through strongly disagree, with no neutral midpoint): (1) "patriotism should be the primary aim of education"; (2) "it would be better to be a citizen of the world than of any particular country"; (3) "we should strive for loyalty to our country before we can afford to consider world brotherhood"; and (4) "our country is probably no better than many others."[17]

The second variable, "transnational solidarity," takes a somewhat different approach and is directed not at the absolute strength of patriotism as such, but at the relative strength of national versus class solidarity. Resting on the assumption that both the nation (nationalism) and class (cosmopolitanism) are reasonable and legitimate foci of identification, that one is not forced (or necessarily perceives onself to be forced) to choose between them, and that a condition of "multiple loyalties"[18] can exist, it attempts to describe the predominant orientation of the individual, if in fact there is one. Hence, respondents were asked how much they felt they had in common, first, "with Germans of other social classes" and, second, "with members of your social class in other EEC countries?" These two items were then merged and each respondent scored as to whether, and to what extent, he or she was class-oriented (that is, felt to have relatively more in common with members of his or her social class in other EEC countries than with West Germans of other social classes), nation-oriented, or, falling in between, identified with both with the same level of intensity. It should also be pointed out that as a result of the procedure used for computing individual scores for this indicator, discrepancies among individuals relating to the degree each of them identified (considered as a personal attribute) are canceled out here.

The third and fourth variables take yet another tack and assess whether, and to what degree, national identification intrudes when the individual manager is asked to think about the goals of European integration and the organization of production and business practices of the enterprise in which he or she is employed. In the former case, respondents were asked to indicate how worthy of support they considered six possible goals of integration. By design, three of them were "Eurocentric" in tone ("the increase of the standard of living in Europe," "the development of Europe as a third force," and "the collective development of the less developed regions in the EEC—southern Italy, Bayrischer Wald—with the aim of decreasing income differences within the EEC"), while three others were "ethnocentric" ("the increase of the standard of living in the FRG," "the opening of other European markets for German products," and the improvement of the position of the FRG in Europe"). An index of orientations regarding the goals of integration was constructed from these six items, summarizing the relative extent to which a respondent affirmed the three Eurocentric items and rejected the three ethnocentric ones.

A similar index regarding intrafirm organization was constructed by combining two corporate policy questions. They pertained to the geographical distribution of production within the enterprise (that is, to what extent should decisions on the location of production sites for technologically sophisticated products be influenced by noneconomic national considerations) and whether national (home-country) business customs should serve as guidelines in West German subsidiaries located abroad.

Thus four indicator-variables of national identification are distinguished. It should be noted that at least the first two do not appear to be sensitive to home-country related sociocultural investments, in the sense that there is nothing in, say, the sociocultural system of the United States that would emit any strong messages regarding any of the preferences distinguished for each of these indicators. In the case of goals of integration, however, one might expect a slight home-country effect in French affiliates ("la grande nation") while in the case of intrafirm organizations a slight home-country effect may intrude for United States affiliates (greater centralizing preferences).

Table 12.1 reports the results of the analysis for the patriotism and the transnational solidarity items and Table 12.2 for orientations regarding the goals of integration and intrafirm organization. Three analyses or modes of comparison are presented in the first table, as well as in all the subsequent ones. Initially, and at the most macro level of comparison, the total samples of managers employed in FRG-based enterprises and in foreign affiliates are directly compared. This provides an overall test of the similarity (or the contrary) between the two groups of managers regarding the variables under consideration—here, patriotism and transnational solidarity. A second mode of comparison includes only

TABLE 12.1. **The TNE Effect: Patriotism and Transnational Solidarity (FRG = FRG-based enterprises; FA = foreign affiliates in the FRG)**

Comparative Employment Situation of Managers	Patriotism[a]	Transnational Solidarity[b]
FRG vs. FA	.038	.061
FRG vs. only FA/EC	.043	.085
Partitioned by internationalization of FRG		
FRG/TNE vs. FA	.029	.016
FRG/domestic vs. FA	.071	.119

[a]Statistic: Pearson's product-moment correlation coefficient. The value range for the patriotism scale is 1 through 21, with value 1 representing minimum (lowest) patriotism. The overall mean = 8.66, and the standard deviation = 3.36. The following is the number of respondents found in each of the row categories: FRG-based enterprises, N = 2,776; foreign affiliates, N = 480; EC-based foreign affiliates, N = 384; FRG-based transnational enterprises, N = 1,532; FRG-based domestic enterprises, N = 1,234. A positive coefficient indicates that managers employed in foreign affiliates scored lower on the patriotism scale.

Please note that two statistical tests are used in this analysis according to the nature of the data being examined. Pearson's product-moment correlation coefficient is used where interval level data are present; the statistic gamma, a measure of association, is used where ordinal level data are present. For their computation formulas, see Nie et al., *Statistical Package for the Social Sciences*, second edition (New York: McGraw-Hill, 1975).

[b]Statistic: gamma. The value range for the index of transnational solidarity is 1 through 5 with value 1 representing maximum class identification and value 5 maximum national identification. A positive coefficient indicates that managers employed in foreign affiliates are relatively more likely to identify with class (versus nation).

managers employed in foreign affiliates whose headquarters are located in other countries of the European Community (EC). In other words, managers employed in Swedish or U.S. foreign affiliates in the FRG are not included, thereby restricting the analysis to a comparison of managers in FRG-based companies versus those in French, Dutch, and British affiliates. In this way, the specific character (and particularly its special susceptibility to a TNE effect) of the variables pertaining to integration, as well as the fact that (as far as formal economic-political distance is concerned) TNEs in other EC countries could almost be considered as domestic enterprises, would be taken into consideration. The third and final analysis is based on the partition of the FRG-based corporate sample into TNE and domestic oriented subgroups based on the extent of their corporate internationalization, as indicated by percent foreign sales.

Turning now to Table 12.1, we see that no impact on the part of foreign-affiliate employment is discernible with respect to both patriotism and transnational solidarity, and this is consistent across each of the modes of comparison. In other words, the two groups of managers that are compared each time manifest generally similar levels of patriotism and transnational solidarity. It is also the case that, where the FRG-based corporate sample is partitioned according to extent of internationalization, the coefficients that result are in every instance quite low, thereby suggesting that no difference probably exists between the two groups that are being compared. Needless to say, these findings are particularly important since a high susceptibility to a TNE effect appears reasonable where these two variables are involved. Essentially the same observations also apply to the analyses contained in Table 12.2.

Table 12.2 indicates that no differences exist between the samples with respect to both orientations regarding the goals of integration and intrafirm organization. This pattern is especially marked in regard to the latter, where the coefficients in fact are quite low.

In sum, then, the two tables and the analyses they contain indicate that no significant differences exist regarding national identification between West German managers employed in FRG-based enterprises (partitioned or not) and those employed in foreign affiliates, irrespective of the indicator that is applied. The coefficients that are obtained are generally marginal and are not substantial enough to establish the existence of a significant TNE effect.

TABLE 12.2. The TNE Effect: Goals of Integration and Intrafirm Organization

Comparative Employment Situation of Managers	Goals of Integration[a]	Intrafirm Organization[b]
FRG vs. FA	.135	−.039
FRG vs. only FA/EC	.139	−.068
Partitioned by internationalization of FRG		
FRG/TNE vs. FA	.106	.019
FRG/domestic vs. FA	.173	−.119

[a]Statistic: gamma. The value range for orientations regarding the goals of integration is 1 through 21, with 1 representing maximum Eurocentric and value 21 representing maximum nation-centric. A positive coefficient indicates that managers employed in foreign affiliates are more Eurocentric.

[b]Statistic: gamma. The value range for intrafirm organization is 1 through 3, with value 1 representing system-centric, 2 = mixed, and 3 = ethnocentric. A positive coefficient indicates that managers employed in foreign affiliates are relatively more system-centric.

Regional Integration

As with national identification, no consensus presently exists or even appears to be emerging, regarding the conceptualization or measurement of integration. This is not a trivial matter since different indicator-variables can, and in fact do, provide different results as to the status and progress of an integration effort.[19] Thus, we are once again driven to adopt a multiple-indicator approach. More specifically four indicators will be used to describe diverse aspects of (managerial) sentiments regarding regional integration in Western Europe. The first indicator is a general one and measures support for integration across nine analytically, operationally, and phenomenally distinguishable dimensions. These dimensions result from our previous work in which we demonstrated, through factor analytic techniques, that rather than being a unidimensional concept, support for integration could and should be disaggregated. Three of these dimensions fall under an aspect we have termed "formal governmental integration" (that is, where system-level decision-making institutions are created). The remaining six fall under "behavioral integration" (where actual transnational exchanges or interaction flows occur). The former aspect of formal governmental integration consists of three dimensions: "positive governmental integration regarding social and political functions" (that is, the establishment of system-level decision-making institutions for dealing with social and political matters), "positive governmental integration regarding economic functions," and "negative governmental integration regarding economic functions" (the abolition of administrative discontinuities with respect to transnational economic exchange). What we call behavioral integration includes two groups of three dimensions each. Three of the six behavioral dimensions are subsumed under economic-production integration (that is, the linking up and merging of industrial apparatus and the creation of a system-level economy), regarding corporate support functions (such as marketing, sourcing of capital), corporate control (for example, control of the parent company, personnel policy regarding opportunities covering promotion to top management positions, corporation-wide collective bargaining with a central union council), and production decisions (such as planning of product development, investment location). The final three dimensions are subsumed under social integration (that is, the linking and merging of sociocultural activities and the development of a system-sense of community), regarding political and economic interests, political and economic distance, and cultural distance.[20]

The second indicator is more case-specific and focuses on the quite controversial subject of the status of foreign workers in the FRG and, by implication, the acceptance of the principle of labor mobility within the European Community. The third and fourth indicators approach the matter of integration support from another angle and ask what the respondent is ready to do in order to promote integration in terms of commitment to a political party and an income contribution.

As indicated in the previous section, apparently a majority of researchers dealing with transnational participation appear to promulgate the general hypothesis that a difference in attitude regarding European integration will be evident between managers employed in FRG-based enterprises and those in foreign affiliates in the sense that the latter will tend to manifest more "prointegration" sentiments. To reiterate, this hypothesis rests on the proposition that the process of socialization of TNE employees encourages, or even forces, a more positive perspective on their part concerning the establishment of more comprehensive (economic, political, or social) communities. (For this reason, this set of variables appears to be particularly susceptible to a TNE effect while, on the other hand, none of them appear to be particularly sensitive to home country sociocultural investments). This proposition sounds disarmingly persuasive to many, but its assessment is far from being a simple task, even here where we are concerned with only one piece of the puzzle (that is, the relative increase in foreign-affiliate employment and its supposed sociopolitical effects).

Table 12.3 reports the differences, if any, in level of support for integration between managers employed in FRG-based enterprises and those in foreign affiliates. One immediately sees the advantage—and need— of not treating integration as a unidimensional concept. The overall coefficients of the two samples for each of the modes of comparison do not differ with respect to the six dimensions of governmental and social integration. In other words, contrary to the expectations of most analysts, foreign-affiliate employment appears to have little impact on support for these important dimensions of integration. The same result is obtained overall for the first economic-production dimension, but not for the other two.

It is with respect to economic-production integration regarding corporate control that for the first time one observes the manifestation of a strong difference in the two samples, as each pair is analyzed. And it is in the expected direction: foreign-affiliate managers are relatively more prointegration, in that, compared to managers employed in FRG-based enterprises, they are less anxious about the prospect of corporate control of FRG companies not remaining in West German hands.[21] Thus, familiarity (through actual experience) with foreign ownership and control appears to considerably diminish fears about such a circumstance. One possible reaction to this may be: "Why, of course." Perhaps, but is it indeed obvious and inevitable? Not really, since, if negative experiences in foreign affiliates were generally the case, the opposite could result and managers there would be relatively more, not less, concerned about non-national control of enterprises. Our finding suggests that anxiety over foreign control is greater among those managers who have not actually experienced it rather than among those who presently are actually working for foreigners. Yet we hasten to add that the impact of foreign-affiliate employment is almost reduced to this issue alone and, as the other findings indicate, is not being generally diffused. It only extends, although more weakly, to economic-production integration regarding

TABLE 12.3. The TNE Effect: Level of Support for Western European Integration

	Dimensions of Integration*								
	Governmental				Econ/Prod		Social		
Comparative Employment Situation of Managers	Soc/ poli	Pos econ	Neg econ	Supt funcs	Corp Cont	Prod	Poli/ econ inter	Poli econ dist	Cult dist
FRG vs. FA	-.010	.032	.010	.168	.210	.041	-.052	-.053	.015
FRG vs. only FA/EC	-.001	.059	.038	.163	.193	.060	-.070	-.073	.015
Partitioned by internationalization of FRG									
FRG/TNE vs. FA	-.009	.052	-.010	.185	.248	.017	-.051	-.055	.036
FRG/domestic vs. FA	-.016	.022	.039	.219	.255	.109	-.082	-.078	-.005

*Statistic: Pearson's product-moment correlation coefficient. The value range for these nine dimensions of integration support is 1 through 5, with value 1 representing maximum (positive) support for integration. The overall means reported consecutively from left to right are: 3.04, 2.99, 2.94, 2.95, 2.93, 2.99, 3.03, 3.02, 3.07, and the standard deviations consecutively reported are: .896, .836, .822, 1.03, 1.03, 1.03, 1.28, 1.19, 1.14. A positive coefficient indicates that managers employed in foreign affiliates are stronger in their support of integration.

support functions, where foreign-affiliate managers indicate that a more integrative perspective is desirable with respect to marketing, sourcing of capital, investment decisions, and so forth. But that is all. The general conclusion then is that it has not been demonstrated that employment in a foreign affiliate has an impact on the level of support for integration. What impact foreign affiliate employment has is narrowly confined to the two (but we emphasize, very important) economic-production dimensions of corporate control and support functions.

This conclusion is reinforced when the other indicators of integration are studied. As we have already mentioned, one of the central and very controversial issues in regard to integration has been the status of foreign (guest) workers. The issue involves such questions as: Are the various countries in the European Community (in particular, for our purposes, the FRG) prepared to accept the mobility of labor, as well as the mobility of goods, services, and capital? And, if they are, how should non-national workers be treated: for instance, as transients with temporary visas or as regular employees with rights and responsibilities similar to those enjoyed by national workers? An eight-point index on the status of foreign workers in the FRG was constructed, consisting of seven items relating to whether or not they should be allowed to work in the FRG, the nature of the visa that should be issued to them (temporary or permanent), whether they should be allowed to bring their families, whether they should be allowed to participate in the political life of the community in which they live (vote in community elections), and so forth.

The results of this analysis are reported in Table 12.4. Once again, no difference in sentiment appears to exist between managers employed in FRG-based enterprises (partitioned or not) and those in foreign affiliates, indicating that

TABLE 12.4. The TNE Effect: Status of Foreign Workers in the FRG

Comparative Employment Situation of Managers	Attitudes Regarding Foreign Workers*
FRG vs. FA	.046
FRG vs. only FA/EC	.058
Partitioned by internationalization of FRG	
FRG/TNE vs. FA	.020
FRG/domestic vs. FA	.078

*Statistic: gamma. The value range for attitudes regarding the status of foreign workers in the FRG is 1 through 8, with value 1 representing a position on status most supportive of integration and value 8 representing a position on status most adverse regarding integration. A positive coefficient indicates that managers employed in foreign affiliates express more integrative attitudes regarding the status of foreign workers in the FRG than those in foreign affiliates.

TABLE 12.5. The TNE Effect: Propensity to Defect Political Parties on Integration Issues

	Willingness to Defect among Party Identifiers Only*							
	Overall		CDU		SPD		FDP	
Comparative Employment Situation of Managers	Political Integration	Economic Integration	Political Integration	Economic Integration	Political Integration	Economic Integration	Political Integration	Economic Integration
FRG vs. FA	.016	.016	.000	−.038	−.067	−.017	−.038	−.022
FRG vs. only FA/EC	−.001	.065	.022	.097	−.064	.054	−.035	−.039
Partitioned by internationalization of FRG								
FRG/TNE vs. FA	−.081	−.045	−.029	.001	−.173	−.122	−.059	−.030
FRG/domestic vs. FA	.063	.091	.040	.085	.043	.090	.001	−.008

*Statistic: gamma. The value range for propensity to defect political party for adopting a contrary position regarding integration is 1 through 4, with value 1 representing a definite intention to vote for another political party. A positive coefficient indicates that managers employed in foreign affiliates are more willing to defect.

foreign-affiliate employment does not have a significant impact on attitudes regarding the status of foreign workers in the FRG.

A different tack is taken with the next indicator. Respondents were asked how probable it would be that they would vote for another political party if the one "you prefer took a position with respect to European economic and political integration that is quite contrary to your own ideas." Since the great majority of our managerial respondents were strongly prointegration[22] (as are an overwhelming percentage of the West German public, as indicated by the many public opinion polls on the subject), and since the three major political parties in the FRG were at the time of this survey (and still are) supportive of integration, we were actually asking essentially prointegration managers what they would do if the political party with which they presently identified switched and adopted a hostile position on European integration. More specifically, would foreign-affiliate managers, as compared to managers in FRG-based enterprises, be more likely to follow their party on this course or consider voting for another that remained sympathetic to the integration effort?

The results in Table 12.5 are divided into two parts. On the left, the overall findings are presented regarding both political and economic integration; on the right are the relevant figures broken down according to political party identification so that we are not misled by whatever party-specific tendencies may exist. First of all we see that overall no differences are manifest between managers in FRG-based enterprises (partitioned or not) and those in foreign affiliates in propensity to defect from their political parties on account of integration.

TABLE 12.6. Political Party Identification (mean differences)

Comparative Employment Situation of Managers	Political Party Identification			
	CDU	SPD	FDP	None
FRG vs. FA	−.03	−.07	−.05	.06
FRG vs. only FA/EC	−.01	−.10	.05	.06
Partitioned by internationalization of FRG				
FRG/TNE vs. FA	−.04	−.05	.02	.07
FRG/domestic vs. FA	−.01	−.11	.08	.04

Note: Excluded from this analysis are the few managers (N = 5) who indicated they identified with a political party other than the CDU, SPD, or FDP. Among managers employed in FRG-based enterprises, the percentage party identification was the following: CDU = 38 percent, SPD = 39 percent, FDP = 13 percent, no party identification = 10 percent. A positive coefficient indicates that managers employed in foreign affiliates have more representation in that particular party.

In virtually every case the figures approach zero. But will the same results be obtained when political party identification is explicitly taken into account? To answer this question, managers were separated according to whether they said they identified with the CDU (Christian Democratic Union), SPD (Social Democratic Party), FDP (Free Democratic Party), or do not identify with any party. As Table 12.6 shows, CDU and SPD representation is just about the same among managers (about 38 to 39 percent), FDP representation amounts to approximately 13 percent, and 10 percent say that they do not have a political-party preference. This table also reveals that the two samples have virtually the same political-party profiles. With this in mind, we can return to Table 12.5 and examine the relevant figures, this time disaggregated and analyzed by party. Not unexpectedly by now, the party-specific results do not deviate at all from the overall ones. Once again, the findings suggest that foreign-affiliate employment does not have a special impact; the two groups here as before express strong, similar rather than dissimilar views.

Essentially the same findings occur in Table 12.7 where the last integration indicator is presented. Here respondents were asked the following question: "How much of your monthly income would you be willing to contribute in the next three years" if it could be assumed that "it would be possible to achieve European economic and/or political integration through certain personal sacrifices by each individual, for example, financial sacrifices?" Although this question approaches the assessment of integration sentiment from a novel angle, the results obtained are very similar to the others. With respect to both political and economic integration, no significant difference appears to exist between foreign-

TABLE 12.7. The TNE Effect: Willingness to Contribute Financially to Further Integration

	Willingness to Contribute for*	
Comparative Employment Situation of Managers	Political Integration	Economic Integration
FRG vs. FA	−.047	−.017
FRG vs. only FA/EC	−.004	−.023
Partitioned by internationalization of FRG		
FRG/TNE vs. FA	−.044	−.017
FRG/domestic vs. FA	−.052	−.018

*Statistic: gamma. The value range for "willingness to contribute financially to political integration" and "to economic integration" is 1 through 4, with value 1 representing a willingness to contribute about five percent; 2, about three percent; 3 about one percent; and 4, not willing to contribute anything. A positive coefficient indicates that managers employed in foreign affiliates are more willing to contribute financially to further integration.

affiliate and FRG-based enterprise managers, irrespective again of the mode of comparison that is used.

Thus here, just as in nearly every other case, foreign-affiliate employment does not seem to have a socializing impact. Or, more cautiously, we have been unable to demonstrate that such an effect occurs with respect to sentiments regarding European integration. And this appears to be the case even for issues that would seem to be highly susceptible to the hypothesized TNE effect.

Patterns of Information Acquisition

The third and final category of dependent variables examined by us concerns the information acquisition patterns of West German managers employed in FRG-based enterprises and those in foreign affiliates. More specifically, two variables are initially distinguished: one describes the number of foreign professional journals that are regularly read; the second describes the number of foreign newspapers and magazines read. The former is intended to characterize professionally oriented patterns of information acquisition, whereas the latter variable denotes contact with more popular media. The objective is again to ascertain whether there exists an observable TNE effect that results in foreign-affiliate managers having a more transnational pattern of information acquisition. Note that since both our samples are composed of managers, and since moreover their rank profiles are similar, our analysis appears to take account of differences in the social class of respondents in the two samples, a factor that could have an important bearing on the frequency and transnational scope of reading habits.

The results of our analysis of patterns of information acquisition are presented in Table 12.8. We see that no differences exist between the two groups of managers in their reading habits of foreign professional journals as well as of newspapers and magazines. Recall that here we are inquiring whether foreign affiliate employment induces a general change, that is, a change in the direction of a more internationally oriented perspective regarding the acquisition of information. This does not seem to be the case, as the very modest coefficients signify.

And, as an aside, the responses of both groups of managers indicate that the amount of non-national reading they do is quite small (for example, only about 11 percent of the managers say they read a foreign professional journal and about 11 percent say they read a foreign newspaper or magazine), a finding that by itself throws some doubt on the TNE effect. Managers almost exclusively rely on national sources of information although most have prointegration sentiments and many even have international work responsibilities. They may be interested in developments occurring outside the FRG and believe these developments to have a strong impact on their personal well-being, as well as on the FRG itself, but they learn of them almost exclusively through national media. In this they apparently parallel the habit of U.S. business executives, even those who frequently travel abroad.[23]

TABLE 12.8. The TNE Effect: Information Acquisition

Comparative Employment Situation of Managers	Number of Foreign	
	Professional Journals Read[a]	Newspapers and Magazines Read[b]
FRG vs. FA	.067	.068
FRG vs. only FA/EC	.092	.067
Partitioned by internationalization of FRG		
FRG/TNE vs. FA	.023	.034
FRG/domestic vs. FA	.177	.157

[a]Statistic: Pearson's product-moment correlation coefficient. The value range for number of foreign professional journals read is 1 through 4, with value 1 representing three or more, and 4 = none. A positive coefficient indicates that managers in foreign affiliates read more foreign professional journals.

[b]Statistic: Pearson's product-moment correlation coefficient. The value range for number of foreign newspapers and magazines read is 1 through 4, with value 1 representing three or more, 2 = two, 3 = one, 4 = none. The overall mean = 3.001, and the standard deviation = .334. A positive coefficient indicates that managers in foreign affiliates read more foreign newspapers and magazines.

The findings in Table 12.8 relate, however, only to whether a respondent reads foreign media. No distinction is made as to the nationality of the particular foreign medium; such a control could be important here because the variables involved may be relatively receptive to sociocultural investments. The findings may fail to distinguish between a TNE effect and sociocultural investments. If this question were to be pursued, one would ask: "Are national managers in a foreign affiliate more likely to expose themselves to media of the country in which their foreign affiliate's parent company is headquartered?" Here one would be interested not in whether foreign-affiliate employment is associated with greater readership of foreign media in general, but in the more narrow, and perhaps more reasonable, query of whether the media effect is selective and extends only to the national newspapers and magazines of one's employer. In order to investigate the possibility of this more selective media impact, one first would have to isolate British, French, and U.S. managers employed in their respective foreign affiliates, and then describe the extent to which they read, respectively, British, French, and U.S. newspapers and magazines as compared to those managers in FRG-based enterprises. This analysis unfortunately could not be done because too few readers indicated they read U.S., and especially British and French, newspapers and magazines. More specifically, only 16 West German managers claim that they regularly read a French newspaper or magazine, and only 73 said they did so with respect to British media. A greater number of managers (137) indicate that they read U.S. newspapers and magazines, but the percentage is still very small (4 percent) considering the nature and combined size of our two samples (3,300). These numbers, of course, are considerably reduced when, by way of example, FRG-based enterprise managers are compared only to those in French foreign affiliates, or the latter are compared only with managers employed in FRG-based steel companies. In other words, the overwhelming national orientation of information acquisition patterns is again apparent; hence, the low number of readers of foreign media prevents us from further investigating statistically the existence of a TNE effect in this area.

Intervening Socialization Mechanisms

So far our analysis has assumed a uniformity of impact throughout each of the sampled firms. However, not all the employees in a foreign affiliate may be equally exposed to the circumstance of working in a transnational business system. One might speculate that only managers of relatively high rank or engaged in functional specializations that may be especially sensitive to non-national parent control are significantly receptive to the TNE effect. In addition, it could be argued that foreign affiliates may have proportionally fewer West German managers in high-level positions (for example, if foreign affiliates tend to staff these positions with home-country nationals) or that proportionally more managers are assigned to such relatively nontransnational functions as personnel and production, and that therefore the effects of foreign-affiliate employment on national identification, regional integration, and pattern of information acquisition are obscured. The argument is that if such attributes as rank or functional specialization were taken into account, the true impact of a foreign affiliate employment situation would be revealed.

Two related but analytically distinguishable "suppressor" variables are at issue here. The first is rank, and whether the hypothesized effects are more likely to appear among those holding higher level positions in the enterprise. The effect would be suppressed if there were substantially fewer such top level national managers in foreign affiliates and rank were significantly related to the dependent variables that we considered. The second is more subtle and features both rank and functional specialization. The point made here is that a combination of high rank and a functional specialization that is relatively transnational in scope may be necessary before the impact of foreign-affiliate employment is personally experienced. Thus, one may speak of "dependence sensitivity," a variable that isolates managers of relatively high rank whose work responsibilities also are primarily executive leadership or marketing and sales, from others of lower rank or alternative (more technical and insular) specializations. These two variables, rank and dependence sensitivity, allow us to make distinctions within the two samples and therefore to specify the particular subgroups where the impact of foreign-affiliate employment should be especially manifest.

However, several reinforcing bits of evidence tend to undermine seriously the contention that the TNE effect is in fact suppressed. First, the actual number of non-West German managers who were encountered in the total survey was minuscule; only 70 as against 3,300 West German nationals. Moreover, many turn out to be employed in FRG-based enterprises, and nearly one-third indicate they are of Austrian nationality, in spite of the fact that not a single one of the foreign affiliates in the study is Austria-based. Hence it is unlikely that the higher levels of rank within foreign affiliates located in the FRG are sufficiently dominated (if they are at all) by home-country nationals, at least to make a significant difference in this analysis—unless, of course, there are a considerable number of non-West German nationals who constitute the top management level of foreign affiliates, but who decided in quite disproportionate number not to participate in the study. But such systematic opting-out of non-West Germans is quite questionable.

Second, we also compared FRG-based enterprises and foreign affiliates in order to ascertain whether or not their rank and dependence sensitivity profiles were different. This turned out not to be the case; the profiles were, in fact, quite similar.

Third, and most compelling, a contingency analysis was performed where the same comparisons as above were made, but for subgroups of managers segregated on the basis of their rank and dependence sensitivity. The purpose was to see whether the hypothesized effects materialized among those of high rank and dependence sensitivity, and not among the others. The results, however, were not different from before, and once again failed to demonstrate the existence of a foreign-affiliate employment impact.

A second line of thought directs attention once more to what exactly is being investigated. We have been concerned with the relationship between foreign-affiliate employment and especially sentiments regarding the nation and integration. But why should such an association be direct? Or, put somewhat differently, maybe some mechanism (or intervening variable) is required through which the impact of the foreign-affiliate experience gets translated into sufficiently dissimilar sentiments so that this (otherwise indistinguishable) group of foreign-affiliate managers is set off from the majority of managers employed in FRG-based enterprises. The characteristics of one's job seem to be the logical choice as such an intervening mechanism. In other words, implicit in this hypothesis is the idea that work characteristics in foreign affiliates are different from those that exist in national companies, and it is this specific contrast that is associated with the hypothesized differences in sentiment between managers in foreign affiliates and those in FRG-based enterprises. Note that the above rests on two related but distinct propositions: first, that work characteristics in foreign affiliates differ from those in national companies; and, second, that because of the opportunities and experiences that work responsibilities afford, these differences are correlated with changing sentiments regarding national identification, regional integration attitudes, and patterns of information acquisition.

As is so often the situation, what is not especially clear in this formulation is the key issue of identifying those specific work-responsibility characteristics that can and should play a mediating role (that is, the operationalization of the intervening mechanism hypothesized to be associated with the attitude change that often is found under the rubric of "elite socialization"). One cannot be sure what these crucial work characteristics are since no theory is present to guide inquiry. Thus, left to our own means again, we have selected three attributes that appear to us at least to hold some promise. The first work-characteristic variable merely describes the geographical orientation of one's work, and specifically whether it is "primarily devoted to German issues in contrast to international issues." The second variable, which we have termed "work-related contact with non-nationals," indicates how often in their work respondents come into contact with foreigners. Finally, the third variable does not so much directly characterize work responsibilities as it depicts a particular change that may occur as the result of being employed in a foreign affiliate. This third variable, called "external interest,"[24] reflects the respondents' estimates of the direction and degree to which integration affects their personal well-being.

With the exception of the variable of "external interest," the results appear promising in regard to the possibility of establishing a TNE impact. First, in Table 12.9, we see that external interest fails to differentiate managers in FRG-

TABLE 12.9. The TNE Effect: Difference in External Interest, Geographical Work Orientation, and Contact with Non-Nationals

Comparative Employment Situation of Managers	External Interest[a]	Geographical Work Orientation[b]	Work Contact[c]
FRG vs. FA	.092	.433	.500
FRG vs. only FA/EC	.125	.514	.572
Partitioned by internationalization of FRG			
FRG/TNE vs. FA	.029	.253	.425
FRG/domestic vs. FA	.168	.648	.589

[a]Statistic: gamma. The value range for external interest is 1 through 7, with value 1 representing maximum positive external interest. A positive coefficient indicates that managers employed in foreign affiliates express a more positive external interest.

[b]Statistic: gamma. The value range for geographical orientation of work is 1 through 4, with value 1 representing primarily international issues and value 4 = only West German issues. A positive coefficient indicates that managers employed in foreign affiliates have a more international geographical work orientation.

[c]Statistic: gamma. The value range for work-related contact with non-nationals is 1 through 4, with value 1 representing contact once a week or more and value 4 = almost never. A positive coefficient indicates that managers employed in foreign affiliates have relatively more work-related contact with non-nationals.

based enterprises from those in foreign affiliates. Both samples feel dependent on regional developments to about the same extent. On the other hand, the variables of "work-related contact with non-nationals" and "geographical work orientation" provide more promising results. Fairly substantial variation between the two samples is evident; in other words, the relevant coefficients in every case are strongly positive.

Problems arise, however, regarding the consequence of the fact that managers in foreign affiliates have relatively higher work-related contact with non-nationals and more internationally oriented work responsibilities. They relate to the second part of the argument and involve the supposed association of these variables with differences regarding national identification and integration attitudes. Unfortunately for the argument, the association does not materialize.[25] Thus, whereas the first part of the follow-up (amended) hypothesis is affirmed, the second is not. And this situation casts serious doubt on the utility of work responsibilities and work-related contact with non-nationals as the intervening mechanisms translating the experience of foreign-affiliate employment into observably different sociopolitical and socioeconomic preferences.

In sum, our overall conclusion here is similar to, and therefore reinforces, the results of our earlier research in which it was demonstrated that the effects of transnational corporate activity on sociopolitical and socioeconomic preferences were tenuous, at best. In that work, a rather extensive list of dependent variables was introduced and analyzed, and no association was found in most of the cases. In only a few areas could an assocation be established, and it was neither a strong nor a direct one at that. This study extends that analysis to foreign affiliates for the question of the possible effects of the experience of "working for foreigners," that is, where parent-company ownership and control are in the hands of non-nationals. With only a few exceptions, it was found that no differences in national identification, attitudes regarding regional integration, and information-acquisition patterns exist between managers employed in FRG-based enterprises (partitioned according to extent of corporate internationalization or not) and those in foreign affiliates.

From the standpoint of sociopolitical and socioeconomic preferences, it seems to make no difference to managers that they are employed in a foreign affiliate of a transnational corporation—there is no TNE effect. "Robert T. Bloomberg is accustomed to working for companies whose home offices are far away. He used to work in Los Angeles for a company whose head office was in Michigan. Now he works in this industrial suburb of Chicago for a company based in Osaka, Japan. 'There isn't too much difference other than the distance,' he said. 'It's pretty much like working for an American company'!"[26]

CONCLUSIONS

The sociocultural profiles of host countries (both developed and developing) are the result of preferences that are derived from indigenous sources as well as preferences imported from abroad. We distinguished two types of such transnational transfers: home-country-related sociocultural investments (the home-country effect) and the specific effects of employment in a TNE (the TNE effect). In this chapter we discussed only the TNE effect.

More specifically, we examined the possible impact of work in foreign affiliates on sociopolitical and socioeconomic preferences of their employees. To accomplish this task, we used a number of indicator-variables relating to national identification, attitudes regarding Western European integration, and patterns of information acquisition. Alternative modes of comparison were identified and applied to the variables involved using data collected in a survey of managers in foreign affiliates and national business enterprises based in the FRG. In the case of national identification, the four variables were a patriotism scale, transnational solidarity, orientations regarding the goals of integration, and orientations regarding intrafirm organization. For regional integration, the pertinent variables were support for integration (disaggregated in terms of nine analytically, operationally, and phenomenally distinguishable dimensions), attitudes regarding the status of foreign (guest) workers in the FRG, propensity to defect from preferred political parties on account of integration, and willingness to contribute financially to promote integration. Finally, for patterns of information acquisition, we used reading habits concerning foreign professional journals and newspapers or magazines.

The general results of the analysis are quite easy to summarize since they are so consistent across the various indicators: with the notable exception of two of the nine dimensions of integration support (that is, economic-production integration regarding corporate control as well as corporate support functions), no significant differences were observed to exist between West German managers employed in FRG-based enterprises and those in foreign affiliates. In other words, our research has failed to demonstrate that foreign-affiliate employment has had an impact, at least with respect to the elite we surveyed and the areas with which this study is dealing. And, to reiterate, the only exception to this is that foreign-affiliate managers apparently are relatively more willing to accept a more integrative approach to non-national control of business enterprises and decisions relating to corporate support functions (such as marketing, sourcing of capital). In addition, dividing the FRG-based corporate sample according to extent of corporate internationalization does not alter this general finding. Although in some cases more strongly positive coefficients are evident when foreign-affiliate managers are compared with managers in FRG-based, domestic-oriented enterprises rather than with those in FRG-based TNEs, this certainly is not a consistent pattern; and, moreover, they are not different enough in degree to contradict the results of the other analysis.

Needless to say, these findings should be quite surprising to those analysts who believe in the socializing effect of transnational business enterprises and the experiences associated with them. The literature on the whole rather unambiguously leads one to anticipate that differences in sentiment would indeed be evident, and that the direction of these differences would be such that foreign-affiliate managers are, in particular, significantly less nation-oriented and more prointegration than those employed in FRG-based enterprises. On the basis of our analysis, these expectations have to be rejected.

Thus, we have to reject the thesis postulating the existence of a separate TNE effect, whether with respect to employees in headquarters (as already demonstrated elsewhere by us), or to employees in foreign affiliates. Working in a TNE itself apparently does not have a socialization impact on the sociopolitical and socioeconomic attitudes of employees.

NOTES

1. See James A. Field, Jr., "Transnationalism and the New Tribe," in *Transnational Relations and World Politics*, ed. by Robert O. Keohane and Joseph S. Nye, Jr. (Cambridge: Harvard University Press, 1977), pp. 3–22. Field, however, does not distinguish between home-country and TNE effects.

2. For a detailed discussion of the processes involved, see Karl P. Sauvant, "The Potential of Multinational Enterprises as Vehicles for the Transmission of Business Culture," in *Controlling Multinational Enterprises: Problems, Strategies, Counterstrategies*, ed. by Karl P. Sauvant and Farid G. Lavipour (Boulder: Westview Press, 1976).

3. Strictly speaking, this statement only applies to those sociocultural variables that are simultaneously susceptible to home-country-related sociocultural investments as well as TNE effects. Obviously, the existence of TNE effects can also be determined on the basis of differences with respect to variables that are only susceptible to TNE effects or, to put it more cautiously, that are not susceptible to home-country sociocultural investments.

4. Theoretically, a third effect could be present if TNEs themselves would originate messages, messages that originate, so to speak, in a distinct company culture and therefore could represent sociocultural messages in their own right. The potential for such a culture cannot be discounted since TNEs are, after all, powerful transnational socio-economic-political systems; but at the present time—especially under conditions of a complete domination of TNE systems by home-country nationals—it does not appear likely that such a company culture is appreciably distinct from the home-country culture, at least with respect to important variables.

5. John A. Smetanka, "Political Socialization in the Multinational Corporation: The Impact of Multinational Business on the International Orientation of Host-Country Executives" (Cambridge: Harvard University, 1977), mimeo, p. 3.

6. See Robert C. Angell, *Peace on the March: Transnational Participation* (New York: Van Nostrand Reinhold, 1969); Werner Feld, *Transnational Business Collaboration Among Common Market Countries* (New York: Praeger, 1970); Joseph S. Nye, *Peace in Parts: Integration and Conflict in Regional Organization* (Boston: Little, Brown and Co., 1971); and Howard V. Perlmutter, "L'entreprise internationale: Trois conceptions," *Revue économique et sociale* (Lausanne) 23 (May 1965), pp. 151–165 as well as his "View of the Future," in *The New Sovereigns: Multinational Corporations as World Powers*, ed. by Abdul A. Said and Luiz R. Simmon (Englewood Cliffs: Prentice-Hall, 1975).

7. For a review of a number of these variables and their hypothesized effect, see Bernard Mennis and Karl P. Sauvant, *Emerging Forms of Transnational Community: Transnational Business Enterprises and Regional Integration* (Lexington: D. C. Heath, 1976), especially chapter 4.

8. But not necessarily conflicting with the direction of changes in the case of home-country-related sociocultural investments, as suggested, for instance, by the development

of multiple loyalties; see Harold Guetzkow, *Multiple Loyalties* (Princeton: Princeton University Press, 1955).

9. These changes could potentially be disseminated into host and home societies through the mechanism of status-set linkages of TNE employees. But in the absence of any exposure to the TNE effect, receptivity to such secondary transmissions can be expected to be very low.

10. See some of the studies cited in note 6. See also Herbert C. Kelman, ed., *International Behavior: A Social-Psychological Analysis* (New York: Holt, Rinehart and Winston, 1965).

11. See also James Petras and Thomas Cook, "Dependency and the Industrial Bourgeoisie: Attitudes of Argentine Executives Toward Foreign Economic Investments and U.S. Policy," and "Politics in a Nondemocratic State: The Argentine Industrial Elite," in *Latin America: From Dependence to Revolution*, ed. by James Petras (New York: John Wiley and Sons, 1973); Brian Toyne, "Host Country Managers of Multinational Firms: An Evaluation of Variables Affecting Their Managerial Thinking Patterns," *Journal of International Business Studies* 7 (Spring 1976), pp. 39–55; and John D. Daniels, "The Education and Mobility of European Executives in U.S. Subsidiaries: A Comparative Study,"*Journal of International Business Studies* (Spring 1974), pp. 9–24.

12. Mennis and Sauvant, *Emerging Forms*. For similar results, see Linda J. Menard-Watt, "Transnational Business Elites and Their Attitudes towards Continental Integration: A Case Study of the Canadian Computer Industry," MBA thesis, University of Windsor, 1976.

13. Approximately 6,500 questionnaires were distributed throughout the ranks of these 43 enterprises; 3,370 were answered and returned, for a response rate of 52 percent. If there were less than 250 managers employed in a company, all the managers received questionnaires; otherwise participants were chosen by standard sampling methods.

14. Here we followed Wilhelm Grotkopp and Ernst Schmacke, *Die Grossen 500* (Düsseldorf: Droste Verlag, 1971). Financial service companies were excluded from consideration here. Because we cannot be certain that we have representative samples of foreign affiliates and FRG-based enterprises, the results of our subsequent data analyses can be generalized only with great caution. Our findings, therefore, ought to be considered as suggestive in nature.

15. This similarity is also perceived by our respondents: more than two-thirds of them thought that the culture of these five countries is "similar" to that of the Federal Republic of Germany, with one-third actually considering them as "very similar." (See Mennis and Sauvant, *Emerging Forms*, chapter 3).

16. Please note that we are not identifying national identification as a unidimensional variable comprising four items. This is not our intention here, or with regional integration and patterns of information acquisition. Except for the latter where the two variables are highly correlated (gamma = .390), the intercorrelations within each group are only moderate; that is, on balance in the range of gamma = .100 to .150. We group the variables in the way indicated because of their common content and convenience of presentation.

17. The "patriotism scale" is found in John P. Robinson et al., *Measures of Political Attitudes* (Ann Arbor: Survey Research Center, Institute for Social Research, University of Michigan, 1968). It was first used in a study by D. L. Sampson and H. P. Smith, "A Scale to Measure World-minded Attitudes," *Journal of Social Psychology* 45 (1957), pp. 99–106.

18. See Guetzkow, *Multiple Loyalties*.

19. For a demonstration of this situation, see Mennis and Sauvant, *Emerging Forms*, chapter 3.

20. See Mennis and Sauvant, *Emerging Forms*, chapters 2 and 3, for a full description of these nine dimensions of integration support.

21. Recall that this factor summarizes a variety of items.

22. Mennis and Sauvant, *Emerging Forms*, chapter 3.

23. See Ramond A. Bauer et al., *American Business and Public Policy* (Chicago: Aldine-Atherton, 1972).

24. For a discussion of this variable and its measurement, see Mennis and Sauvant, *Emerging Forms*, chapter 4.

25. The great majority of gamma coefficients for the relationship of work-related contact with non-nationals and geographical work orientation, on the one hand, and the many indicators of national identification and attitudes regarding regional integration on the other, are less than .100. With two exceptions—the relationship between geographical work orientation and transnational solidarity (= .212) and economic-production integration regarding production decisions (= .209)—all the remaining coefficients do not exceed .200. These findings are very consistent with those already reported in Mennis and Sauvant, *Emerging Forms*, chapter 4.

26. *The New York Times*, April 3, 1977, Section 3, p. 1.

APPENDIX 12.A

Text of Items Used from the Questionnaire

1. In your opinion, how similar is the political and economic system, and culture of the Federal Republic to that found in EACH of the countries listed below? Please use one of the following alternatives:

1. very similar	4. very dissimilar
2. somewhat similar	5. no opinion
3. somewhat dissimilar	

For EACH of the following countries and EACH of the columns, use ONE of the five alternatives provided above:

	POLITICAL SYSTEM	ECONOMIC SYSTEM	CULTURE
a. Sweden	. . .	. . .	. . .
b. Italy	. . .	. . .	. . .
c. Switzerland	. . .	. . .	. . .
d. France	. . .	. . .	. . .
e. USA	. . .	. . .	. . .
f. England	. . .	. . .	. . .

2. Please indicate whether the basic political and economic interests of West Germany and the countries below are:

1. very much in agreement	4. very different
2. fairly well in agreement	5. no opinion
3. rather different	

For EACH of the following countries and EACH of the columns, use ONE of the five alternatives:

	POLITICAL INTERESTS	ECONOMIC INTERESTS
a. Switzerland	. . .	. . .
b. France	. . .	. . .
c. USA	. . .	. . .
d. Italy	. . .	. . .
e. England	. . .	. . .
f. Sweden	. . .	. . .

3. Below is a list of objectives which frequently have been mentioned in connection with the integration of Europe. Please indicate the degree to which you believe that the objective is WORTHY OF SUPPORT. Use the following alternatives:

303

1. yes, certainly	4. no, certainly not
2. yes, probably	5. no opinion
3. no, probably not	

The objectives are:

WORTHY OF SUPPORT
_____

...   a. increase in standard of living in Europe

...   b. the development of Europe as a "third force"

...   c. the increase of the standard of living in West Germany

...   d. the opening of other European markets for German products

...   e. the collective development of the less developed regions of the EEC (e.g., southern Italy, Bayrischer Wald) with the aim of decreasing income differences within the EEC

...   f. the improvement of the position of West Germany in Europe

4. The following functions can be performed in the EEC in four different ways:

1. entirely by national governments according to the particular interests of the individual governments
2. by national governments but with prior consultation among (member) governments aiming at the harmonization of legislation and its administration
3. by an EEC government but with (member) governments having the right to veto in exceptional circumstances
4. entirely by an EEC government
5. no opinion

How should EACH of the functions be performed in the near future?
(USE THE ABOVE ALTERNATIVES)

...   a. Economic development and planning

...   b. International diplomatic representation

...   c. Fiscal policy

...   d. Military security

...   e. Education and training

...   f. Monetary and balance of payments policies

...   g. Social and welfare policies

...   h. Rules for political participation (e.g., voting regulations)

...   i. Judicial authority

...   j. Commercial relations with non-EEC countries

...   k. Public safety and order (e.g., control of crime)

5. Would increased political and economic integration within the EEC

      1. be very beneficial   4. be very harmful
      2. be moderately beneficial   5. have no effect
      3. be moderately harmful

with respect to: (USE THE ABOVE ALTERNATIVES)

	INCREASED POLITICAL INTEGRATION	INCREASED ECONOMIC INTEGRATION
your own well being	. . .	. . .

6. Let us assume that it would be possible to achieve European economic and/or political integration through certain personal sacrifices by each individual, for example, financial sacrifices. How much of your monthly income would you be willing to contribute in the next three years?

POLITICAL INTEGRATION (Check only one)	ECONOMIC INTEGRATION (Check only one)	
. . .	. . .	1. nothing
. . .	. . .	2. about 1% of my monthly income
. . .	. . .	3. about 3% of my monthly income
. . .	. . .	4. 5% or more of my monthly income

7. What degree of economic integration do you personally find desirable? For EACH of the following items, please indicate whether you are:

      1. strongly in favor   4. strongly opposed
      2. somewhat in favor   5. no opinion
      3. somewhat opposed

The items are: (USE THE ABOVE ALTERNATIVES)

	WITHIN THE EEC
a. the abolition of all tariffs and quotas	. . .
b. common external tariff in trade with non-members	. . .
c. free movement of labor	. . .
d. free movement of capital	. . .

8. This question concerns the treatment of foreign workers who want to come to West Germany for purposes of work. Please indicate your opinion about

EACH of the statements listed below by choosing between the following alternatives:

1. no
2. yes
3. no opinion

Foreign workers: (RESPOND TO EACH ALTERNATIVE)

. . . a. should be allowed to work in West Germany
. . . b. should, if they request, receive a TEMPORARY work visa
. . . c. should, if they request, receive a TEMPORARY work visa AND be allowed to bring their families
. . . d. should, if they request, receive a TEMPORARY work visa AND be allowed to participate in the political life of the community in which they live (e.g., vote in community elections; hold community political office)
. . . e. should, if they request, ALSO receive a PERMANENT visa
. . . f. should, if they request, ALSO receive a PERMANENT work visa AND be allowed to bring their families
. . . g. should, if they request, ALSO receive a PERMANENT work visa AND be allowed to participate in the political life of the community in which they live (e.g., vote in community elections, hold community political office)

9. The statements listed below concern future business strategies that can be pursued by your corporation in the EEC where the PRESENT LEVEL of economic integration in the EEC is maintained. Please indicate for EACH statement regarding corporate business strategies whether:

1. You strongly agree
2. You somewhat agree
3. You somewhat disagree
4. You strongly disagree
5. You have no opinion

PRESENT LEVEL OF INTEGRATION	POSSIBLE CORPORATE BUSINESS STRATEGIES (USE THE ABOVE ALTERNATIVES)
. . .	a. My corporation should employ in each of the countries of the EEC a completely differentiated marketing and sales strategy
. . .	b. Citizens from other EEC countries should have the same opportunity as German citizens to be promoted to the top positions of my company
. . .	c. Required capital, it possible, should be raised in the Federal Republic and only in other EEC countries if interest rates and other conditions there are favorable

   ...   d. My corporation should encourage the establishment of a central council, representing all employees from all EEC subsidiaries, that can then collec-
tively bargain with the corporation

   ...   e. Control of my (parent) company should always
remain in German hands

   ...   f. Product development within my corporation
should reflect the requirements of the EEC market
as a whole, even if this reduces the sales of some
products in the Federal Republic

   ...   g. Each subsidiary in the EEC should have its own
guidelines independent of the parent company, for
hiring and promotion

   ...   h. New investments by my corporation within the
EEC always should be made, other things being
equal, where wages are lowest even if this should
lead to a decrease of investment in the Federal
Republic

10. Below are three alternative ways in which the production of a company with
subsidiaries in other EEC countries can be organized. Which method should
be used by your company in the EEC in the future?

PRESENT LEVEL
OF INTEGRATION
(Check only one)

   ...   1. Subsidiaries should engage in an INTEGRATED
CROSSNATIONAL DIVISION OF LABOR with
the assembling of the product line at an optimal
(third) location (component specialization)

   ...   2. Each subsidiary should be the SOLE PRODUCER
in the parent system of a LIMITED NUMBER OF
COMPLETE PRODUCTION LINES (product
specialization)

   ...   3. Each subsidiary has its OWN COMPLETE PRO-
DUCTION PROGRAM of most of the products
produced by the parent company

   ...   4. No opinion

11. Let us assume that your company has producing subsidiaries in the other
countries of the EEC and the products of your company can be produced
approximately equally well in each of these countries. In your opinion,
what should be the geographical distribution of production under these
conditions? (CHECK ONLY ONE)

   ... 1. All products, regardless of their level of technical sophistication,
should be produced where costs are lowest in the EEC.

   ... 2. The most technically sophisticated goods should be produced in the

Federal Republic and less sophisticated goods produced wherever costs are lowest in the EEC.

... 3. A sufficient amount of each type of product should be produced in the Federal Republic in order to ensure national self-sufficiency. Production beyond this point should take place wherever costs are lowest in the EEC.

... 4. No opinion.

12. Should German business customs serve as guidelines in German subsidiaries abroad? (CHECK ONLY ONE)

    ... 1. Yes, certainly.
    ... 2. Probably yes.
    ... 3. Probably no.
    ... 4. No, definitely.
    ... 5. No opinion.

13. Which of the following groups includes the position you currently hold?

(NOTE—CORPORATE POSITIONS AND TITLES IN THE FRG ARE NOT ALWAYS EQUIVALENT TO THOSE FOUND ELSEWHERE. CONSEQUENTLY, THE ENGLISH TERMS USED HERE ONLY APPROXIMATE THE ORIGINAL TERMS.)

    ... Director, President, Vice-President (Unternehmensleiter, Vorstandsmitglied, Geschäftsführer)
    ... Subsidiary of division head (Betriebs-, Bereichs- und Hauptabteilungsleiter)
    ... Bureau, office or subdivision head (Abteilungsleiter)
    ... Supervisor (Meister, Gruppenleiter)

14. Please indicate those areas in which you have primarily worked since 1950 and also indicate the period you worked in them:

FROM — TO (Year) (Year)	PRIMARY WORK AREAS
. . . .	1. Production
. . . .	2. Marketing and sales
. . . .	3. Finance and accounting
. . . .	4. Personnel and training
. . . .	5. Research and development
. . . .	6. Organization and administration
. . . .	7. Executive leadership (Geschäftsleitung)

15. Since 1950, has your work been primarily devoted to German issues in contrast to international issues (e.g., foreign subsidiaries and/or import/export activities)? (CHECK ONLY ONE)

        ... 1. Only German issues
        ... 2. Primarily German issues
        ... 3. International and German issues received roughly the same working
              time
        ... 4. Primarily international issues

16. In your work, how often do you come into contact with foreigners?
    (CHECK ONLY ONE)

        ... 1. Once a week or more
        ... 2. Once a month
        ... 3. Several times a year
        ... 4. Almost never

17. Do you have a political party preference? 1. Yes ... 2. No ...
    IF YES:

    a. Which political party do you prefer?

        1. CDU/CSU ... 2. SPD ... 3. FDP ... 4. Other (Specify) ....
    b. Let us assume that you learn that the political party you prefer took a
       position with respect to European economic and political integration that
       is quite contrary to you own ideas—what would you do?

ECONOMIC (Check only one)	POLITICAL INTEGRATION (Check only one)	
...	...	1. definitely vote for another political party
...	...	2. probably vote for another political party
...	...	3. probably still vote for the same political party
...	...	4. definitely still vote for the same political party
...	...	5. no opinion

18. Which German and foreign newspapers, magazines and professional journals
    do you read fairly regularly?

19. How much in common do you have with respect to your "philosophical
    outlook" (Weltanschauung) with Germans of other social classes (CHECK
    ONLY ONE)

        ... 1. Very much in common
        ... 2. Something in common
        ... 3. Little in common
        ... 4. No opinion

20. How much in common do you have with respect to your "philosophical outlook" (Weltanschauung) with members of your social class in other EEC countries? (CHECK ONLY ONE)

... 1. Very much in common
... 2. Something in common
... 3. Little in common
... 4. No opinion

21. Below is a list of statements concerning a person's feelings about his country. Please indicate for EACH statement whether you:

1. strongly agree	4. mildly disagree	7. no opinion
2. agree	5. disagree	
3. mildly agree	6. strongly disagree	

The statements are: (USE THE ABOVE ALTERNATIVES)

... a. patriotism should be a primary aim of education
... b. it would be better to be a citizen of the world than of any particular country
... c. we should strive for loyalty to our country before we can afford to consider world brotherhood
... d. our country is probably no better than many others

22. Nationality: 1. German ...   2. Other (PLEASE SPECIFY) . . . .

13

A REVIEW OF THE
STATE OF THE ART

John Fayerweather

The purpose of this chapter is to pull together the content of the research studies reported in the rest of the book and the discussions in the workshop among the researchers. That endeavor is worthwhile because there are many common threads and opportunities for comparative analysis. However, it is also a hazardous process because of the inherent tendency in summarization to over-simplify and work toward conclusions. These tendencies are quite inconsistent with the characteristics of the research studies, which are notable for the variety of their methodologies and findings and for their inconclusiveness. With this caution in mind, the chapter will proceed, first looking at the nature of the attitudes toward MNCs found in the studies, then considering the varied influences shaping the attitudes, and finally contemplating the implications of the past work for future research.

COGNITIVE MAPS

The central purpose of attitude studies is to determine what is in the minds of people. It is therefore fundamental to the research that questions used in surveys relate meaningfully to what people actually think and feel, the set of stored information and associations resulting from the learning process that composes their cognitive maps.[1] Thus consideration of how the MNC fits into the cognitive maps of host nationals was a prime subject in our workshop and it recurs throughout the discussion of research studies in this chapter. As a prelude to that discussion of the specific manifestations of the subject, some general comments on its nature will be made in this introductory note.

The characteristics of multinational corporations and their impact on host nations are complex matters which are not fully understood even by experts in the field. Thus we start with the assumption that full knowledge and understanding of the subject is impossible even among the best informed people and, with a few exceptions, the great portion of the people covered by studies is substantially less informed than experts on the subject. Among the elite groups surveyed in several of the studies reported in this book, there is a fair comprehension of the basic aspects of MNC activities. Most government officials, businessmen, and other elites are reasonably well informed in business and economic matters and have a fundamental knowledge of foreign investment, operations of international firms, balance of payments, and the like. As one moves away from this relatively sophisticated core, however, the comprehension of MNC characteristics and effects becomes substantially less well informed. It is quite limited and highly unsophisticated among much of the less educated general public. However, there is some evidence that the general level of comprehension is rising. For example, Murray observed that the number of "no opinion" responses in his Canadian surveys had declined over the years. But the assumption still must be that the cognitive maps of large portions of host national populations contain very little pertaining to MNCs and even among relatively well informed people the information and views will be of a fairly modest and rather unsophisticated nature.

It is also quite evident that beliefs about MNCs will be a function of the nature of the host society and how the MNC fits into it. Thus, for example, in the developed countries of Europe and Canada the impact of the MNC on host control of national affairs is a widely recognized issue identified in several studies here. On the other hand, in Latin America the control issue as found in the Truitt-Blake study is incorporated into the more complex concept of dependencia, which embodies a blend of political and economic dependency-control relationships between the LDCs and the developed countries of which the MNC is a part. And yet another striking illustration is the set of subjects in Hilton's Nigerian study, which are quite distinct from those in the other countries, being representative of a much lower level of sophistication and of perceptions of MNCs in a notably less advanced country and one with a long colonial history.

In sum, these general characteristics of cognitive maps of host nationals identify three problems for research: first, that there are major limitations in the extent and sophistication of knowledge among respondents; second, that there is a wide diversity in the cognitive maps of respondents if a substantial range in population groups is covered; and, third, that there are distinct limitations in ability to do comparative studies between regions due to the difference in roles and perceptions of MNCs in varying host nation contexts.

These problems pertaining to cognitive maps have their major implications in two phases of research: first, the development of questions for surveys; and second, the interpretation of results. The determination of questions that relate meaningfully to the cognitive maps of respondents was recognized in our workshop discussions as a prime requirement for effective research. It appeared, however, that most people were satisfied that the methodologies being employed were reasonably effective in this respect insofar as they provided adequate gauges of respondent perceptions. Assorted problems existed with regard to those perceptions, but they are more in the province of interpretation, which will be discussed next in question formulation. This is not to say that the workshop participants were satisfied with the success in question formulation but that they did not regard it as one of the more serious complications of research in this field.

The consensus seemed to be that reasonable success could be achieved by employment of one or more of three methods of formulating questions that had been used variously in the studies reported in this book: analysis of newspaper content, presurvey interviews, and open-ended questions. The use of newspaper content as the basis of questions rests on the role of the press as a communicator of prevailing perceptions of MNC activities. The press content is largely based on the public output of the elites in government and business and therefore expresses their information and viewpoints. Likewise it provides a large part of the source of perceptions among broad segments of the population on a highly sophisticated subject of which relatively few people have direct information. On many aspects of an economic and political character, therefore, it is reasonable to assume that as far as terminology, types of issues, and the like are concerned, press material is quite relevant in identifying the content of cognitive maps of the people at least as far as the literate population is concerned. Thus for the elite surveys of Fayerweather and Truitt-Blake, this methodology seems to have been quite satisfactory for a large portion of the question formulation.

Presurvey interviews are a direct and in principle more exact procedure for identifying assumptions among respondents. However, they are more time-consuming and for this particular subject they may not be any more effective than the use of press content at least for surveys among the literate population. The experience of Marton, whose presurvey interviews resulted in substantially confirming the relevance of Fayerweather's press-determined questions as appropriate for the Canadian workers, would seem to bear out this assumption. On the other hand, Hilton found in Nigeria that the interviews added appreciably to the dimensions of his survey as he was reaching down into the less literate portion of the population. For example, his question about the "consideration" given by MNCs to workers, which was quite important to that stratum of the population, appeared in interviews subsequent to his initial preparation of the survey from press content. He also noted in the workshop that presurvey interviews were useful in identifying ostensibly unobjectionable terms found in press content that in fact carry a highly colored or potentially inflammatory import in certain contexts.

The open-ended question in which the respondent may phrase opinions independently is ideally the best solution to the problem. Presumably one gets exactly what is on the respondent's mind and not a response to the questioner's phrasing of what he assumes may be there. The major limitation, of course, is that the results of open-ended questions do not lend themselves readily to statistical analysis of the sophisticated kind that can be employed with the semantic differential types of questions typically used in the surveys reported here. Also a questionnaire with too many open-ended questions is time-consuming and often nonproductive in the load that it places on the respondent. But the limited use of open-ended questions can be quite productive in identifying perceptions that are prominent in respondents' views. Thus for example, both Murray and LeDuc in their Canadian studies and the Truitt-Blake study in Chile and Venezuela effectively used questions seeking the respondent's view of the primary advantages and disadvantages of MNCs.

While the questions employed in the surveys may have been reasonably accurate in determining what was in respondents' minds, interpreting the meaning of the content has proved to be extremely difficult. Where a question deals with quite straightforward factual information upon which the respondent has direct sources of information, answers may be taken more or less at face value. But with the types of questions asked in the surveys described here and the types of respondents involved, it is to varying degrees difficult to determine what responses are telling us about what is in people's minds and how it got there.

To illustrate this problem, we may consider, for example, responses to a question about balance of payments effects of MNC activities. Among a portion of the elite, knowledge of the nature of balance of payments accounts and of MNC financial transactions may be quite high, so a fairly knowledgeable response may be obtained from them. But even among these people the knowledge is likely to be limited to immediate balance of payments impact from capital, dividends, imports, and exports, which are the items commonly reported in the financial press. They are unlikely to have a highly sophisticated sense of such matters as import substitution or general effect on national import-export flows stemming from MNC operations.

Among less informed elites and the variety of people in the rest of the population, responses to a question on the balance of payments must be interpreted as arising from substantially less informed viewpoints. A considerable portion of the literate population doubtless understands that the balance of payments refers to the international economic relations of their nation. They also have some perception of how the MNC affects that relationship, probably based upon a handful of facts gleaned from the press, such as the magnitude of MNC dividend payments or licensing fees—whatever has been the subject of popular discussion in recent times. Or they may simply have a general sense of the MNC balance of payments impact in a perception, for example, that the outsiders get more benefit from their investment than the host nation, and a response will tap this vague feeling. There are doubtless other people who are so uninformed that they know only that the balance of payments refers to economic matters, and a response to a question on it therefore is based only on their general sense of the relation of MNCs to national economic affairs. Their response then may be based upon a variety of things ranging from personal experience in a limited number of employment or consumer contexts to some broad ideological perception of the role of large foreign firms in the world economy. And finally there are certainly some people who never heard of the balance of payments and yet will respond to a question simply on the basis of their general reaction to MNCs.

Existing research provides very little direct evidence related to this problem. The only findings reported in this book that explicitly relate to it are the responses given by Canadians in Murray and LeDuc's paper on the meaning of foreign investment. The range of responses on this apparently straightforward question are sufficient, however, to indicate how much more complex is the meaning of answers to questions on such matters as control of national affairs.

The problem of interpretation of responses pervaded the workshop discussions and appears throughout the reports in the preceding chapters, particularly in the efforts of researchers to identify relationships among responses and other information about respondents that may clarify the meaning of survey results. By such techniqes as cross-tabulation, correlation among responses, and factor analysis, they have attempted to determine patterns that may identify what it is that the respondents are thinking about MNCs, and how those thoughts relate to other perceptions and experiences. These efforts at interpretation have to varying degrees achieved some success, but they have also demonstrated by their limited accomplishments that we are far from understanding fully how MNCs fit into the cognitive maps of individuals.

Overall we may summarize the situation briefly as follows: on some points respondents have direct knowledge and reasonably clear and soundly formulated perceptions of MNC activities. On a large portion of questions, however, their information and thinking are quite limited and responses are based therefore on one or more of a limited range of perceptions of MNCs in their cognitive maps. These perceptions may range from highly specific experience, such as described in the Blake and Driscoll study of the paper firms in Brazil, to highly generalized ideological content, such as the nationalism and views of big business included in Marton's study of the Canadian workers.

Because of the importance and difficulty of this interpretation problem, researchers are thrown into the general area of the psychology of attitude formation. It is impractical to discuss such a general field here, but it is necessary to note such key points as appeared in the workshop discussions and in the research analyses because they point the way to an important area for future work in this field. Two interrelated directions of analysis appear to be required. The first is an understanding of how perceptions are formed. For example, in the workshop discussion Marton suggested that people commonly base their views about any particular point on consideration of a very limited number of factors, for example, three or four. Or to consider another tack, there is the question of the extent to which people are influenced by such diverse inputs as personal experience, opinion leaders, and general ideologies.

The other direction of exploration that is central to the analysis in survey research is understanding the mental process involved in the response to questions. The heavy employment of correlation and factor analysis is directed at determining patterns of related respondent perception on different questions. As the results of the studies reported here indicate, however, it is by no means clear what interpretation one should place on finding that responses on certain subjects are related to each other. At least three possibilities exist when a close relationship is identified by statistical analysis: (1) a direct cause and effect relationship; (2) an associational relationship with responses being similar because they derive from parallel patterns of thought; and (3) a "halo" effect in which responses on one question about which views are weakly held simply follow the responses on a second about which views are quite strong even though the two have no clear substantive relationship. In some cases the types of relationships seem clearly indicated. For example, in Marton's Canadian study the correlation between views of MNCs and big business seems logically to fall in the first category and there are strong indications that the halo effect accounts for the correlation between overall appraisal of MNCs and their effect on the Canadian way of life. However, in a great many cases it is quite difficult to determine which of these relationships may be at work. Thus, this aspect of the general problems of survey research is a critical one for work in studies of attitudes toward MNCs.

ATTITUDES TOWARD MNCs

The surveys reported in this book have covered a wide spectrum of attitudes toward multinational corporations. The totality and the range of questions in each study has had its separate meaning for the researcher. Therefore it is not easy to classify and compare results among the studies. But for our present analysis, such an approach is essential and it does appear possible to discern at least broad similarities in the structure of the surveys which will facilitate making generalized observations from their findings. In particular, subjects covered in the questions fall into three fairly distinct categories: overall appraisal of MNC effects on host nations; perception of impact in broad societal areas, notably economic, political, and cultural effects; and specific impacts chiefly of a business functional character. There are a number of questions that fall in the gray areas between these categories; so a precisely differentiated analysis of all aspects of the studies is not practical. However, pursuing this three-way breakdown is broadly productive because the characteristics of the responses under each heading are quite different.

Overall Appraisals

All of the studies included in this book contained at least one question that called for some form of overall appraisal of the impact of MNCs on the host nation. Clearly there is a common desire among researchers to have such a general appraisal, though one does not find explicit statements of the rationale for using such a general question. Presumably it stems in considerable part from a sense that host nations tend to have a general policy stance toward MNCs, and this has some relation to a generalized attitude toward them among various components of the population. And there is probably a natural inclination in research to include overall questions as a capstone to the broader range of questions on more explicitly defined subjects.

The results of the various questions show a generally favorable overall reaction to multinational firms, with negative responses notable only among labor groups. In Fayerweather's elite survey respondents were asked to rate the overall impact on the host nation on a one to seven scale of good to bad. The legislators, government officials, and businessmen were overwhelmingly favorable, with ratings on the good side ranging from 57 percent up to 78 percent among groups. Only with Canadian and French labor union leaders were there more bad than good ratings, 54 percent to 44 percent respectively. Using the same question on a sample of the first two groups five years later, Graham found strong favorable assessments among the British respondents, 62 percent of legislators and 94 percent of civil servants. However, the French data showed legislators 26 percent favorable versus 49 percent negative, and civil servants, 30 percent versus 41 percent, the balance taking a neutral position. The same question in Marton's survey of Canadian Ford workers gave a quite similar result with 56 percent appraising the effect as bad; in Smetanka's survey of Canadian executives it resulted in 83 percent favorable responses. In the Truitt-Blake survey of government, business, and academic elites, the respondents were asked to rate the economic and social impact of the firms as beneficial or harmful on a five-point scale. In Chile, 78 percent gave favorable responses, while in Venezuela 69 percent were positive in their reactions.

Hilton and Murray and LeDuc provide the only two examples of surveys of broad cross-sections of the population. Hilton's question in Nigeria asked whether or not the firms were contributory to the country on a five-point scale. U.S. firms in this question were rated as contributory by 65 percent of respondents. The Murray-LeDuc question asked whether U.S. investment was a good or bad thing for the economy, with the results of the latest year showing 48 percent favorable and 39 percent negative. The overall question in the Blake-Driscoll study in Brazil provides a somewhat different type of information because it asked respondents to rate the effects of two specific companies rather than of MNCs in general. It also dealt with different levels of impact. Respondents were asked to rate on a five-point scale whether the firms had a positive or negative effect. The responses were overwhelmingly favorable, with 99 percent rating both firms positively at the local level and over 90 percent giving favorable appraisals of the impact at the national level.

These findings are interesting in themselves as a counter to the publicly expressed adverse views, which often have high visibility in host nations. But they are particularly interesting in light of a number of other research findings reported here that are of a distinctly less favorable nature. In particular, it appeared that many people giving overall favorable responses had negative views of the impact of MNCs in quite important economic and political matters.

Such considerations led to a lively discussion in the workshop as to the meaning of the overall appraisals. The discussion brought a number of interesting ideas to the surface but led to no clear conclusions, suggesting that this is an area requiring considerable further research. A sampling of quotations from the workshop transcript is informative as to the directions in which exploration may proceed.

Hilton: "In each of our studies we have used some catholic question, but each of our questions is asking something very specifically different."

Murray: "I don't know if you can ask the 'good-bad' question. I think you have to ask a number of questions about jobs, balance of payments, etc. It's not like the buying intentions type of question. There you can look at ability to buy and other factors and come out with a high correlation of the overall intention but when you ask 'good-bad' there are so many dimensions that it may not have a meaning. I question whether there is a really general appriasal in the minds of most people."

Blake: "I think there is a general view, but I don't think the views on specific points about MNCs add up to it."

Hilton: "Even on a concept as amorphous as nationalism there is at least a consensus on what we are talking about among people in advanced societies. But a multinational corporation means different things to different people, especially in developing countries, so the aggregate of responses to the general question is not meaningful."

Sugges: "The interesting thing that came out of the factor analysis was that the general appraisal question did not load on any factor consistently. It tended to float around among the factors."

Fayerweather: "They reacted to different things: an economist one way, a worker another. They see things differently so they are reacting to different things. Even among groups they may see it differently."

Marton: "Psychological theory says that once you perceive something there is an immediate evaluation. You might be unstable in your evaluation, but you always have either a positive or a negative feeling."

Truitt: "We have asked them a series of questions which obviously show that they evaluate it different ways when you get specific. Does it create jobs? That's good. Does it take money out of the country? That's bad. So when you ask the overall question you already have a conflict."

Hilton: "The act of expressing an evaluation is behavior. The expression of attitudes may also be a surrogate for behavior. What we are measuring is not attitudes. We are measuring behavior which may or may not correspond to the attitudes we think we are measuring. There is also a predisposition of certain groups to state opinions in line with their environment. For example, there is a predisposition of government officials to state opinions consistent with government policy."

The analyses in the individual research studies confirm this varied and inconclusive pattern of explorations into the meaning of the overall appraisal of MNCs. Several of the studies have sought statistical relationships between the overall question and responses on other subjects. At least some statistically significant relationships are found in many cases, but for the most part the patterns are not conclusive. As noted in his quotation above, Sugges found that the overall question floated among the factors determined in his analysis of the Canadian, British, and French data. This would suggest that it was related to the elite views on key economic and political considerations but that the specific types and intensities of relationship varied substantially among groups and individuals. The correlation analysis by Fayerweather on the same data confirms this indication of varied influence of economic, control, and cultural factors. Smetanka's factor analysis determined that responses to the overall question fell into a large bundle of interrelated responses on economic and political matters, again suggesting that there is a relationship between the overall appraisal and views on these broad subjects.

Other correlation analyses suggest that the overall appraisal may stem from quite different sources. For example, Marton found a high correlation with the ideological factors of nationalism and views toward big business. Fayerweather determined a significant correlation with indicators of nationalism and satisfaction in relations with MNCs. The Blake-Driscoll study in Brazil may suggest an interesting element in the much more favorable appraisal of impact at the local level than on national affairs. It is possible that this differentiation may be explained by some rational appraisal of effects on the local community in contrast with appraisal of effects on the national economy or political processes. However, it is also likely that the explanation lies in the greater complexity of the impact on national processes and greater separation of respondents from them so that their views on MNC effects at the national level are more subject to generalized adverse influences. Supporting this line of exploration is the observation that in most of the surveys there is a tendency toward favorable reaction at the very broad general level and in specific matters particularly where there is close contact by the respondents with particulars of MNC operation. On the other hand, there is a tendency toward less favorable appraisal on questions focused on fairly broad economic, political, and control effects and where ideological considerations are notable.

Viewing this mixed and inconclusive picture, one is led to the tentative conclusion that a great many influences are probably at work in the overall appraisal. On the other hand, one is impressed with the possibility, which had considerable support in the workshop discussion, that the overall appraisal is something that exists more or less distinct from views on more specific effects of MNC operations.

Economic, Political, and Cultural Impact

We may turn now to the second level of breadth in impact of MNCs covered in the survey questions. By the nature of the results of the surveys, discussion of reactions to the broad societal impacts of MNCs may be usefully divided into two parts: economic and political, and cultural.

Economic and Political Impact

With great constancy, economic and political effects appear in survey results as prime aspects of host-national views of MNCs. In the open-ended questions seeking reasons for opinions about foreign firms, in both the studies of Murray in Canada and Truitt and Blake in Chile and Venezuela, economic and political factors were dominant. In Fayerweather's elite studies criteria in these categories stand out significantly as bases on which MNC performance should be judged.

Although the meaning of attitudes on economic and political impact are clearer than those on overall impact, there is still some uncertainty as to how these views fit into the cognitive maps of respondents. In the first place, as we noted in the previous section, there may well be connections between these attitudes and the overall appraisals. We do not know to what extent the influence runs from one to the other or vice versa, or indeed whether in the minds of some respondents the overall and the general economic and political considerations compose a largely undifferentiated blend. The fact that all of them combined together in one factor in Smetanka's analysis of the Canadian executives tends to support the latter possibility, though it is by no means convincing evidence of it.

The international business analyst has no difficulty in subdividing the economic from the political and differentiating components of each. The questions used in the surveys based variously on press content and interviews assume some degree of such differentiation in the cognitive maps of respondents. Thus, for example, Fayerweather's elite survey included one question that was essentially pointed at the balance of payments effect, referring to how much money companies took out of the country, while another question was intended to obtain an overall economic appraisal. The Truitt-Blake study elicited various responses to an open-ended question, which indicated an awareness among respondents of varied economic inputs, including technology, capital, and the like.

Differentiation on political aspects is less, because the subject is more amorphous and complex. One also observes a major difference in perceptions according to the nature of host nations noted previously. In the developed countries the questions geared to widely expressed concern in the press and political circles relate to control and decision making affecting the direction of national affairs. Questions with this terminology tap strongly held feelings about the extent to which MNCs control decisions on such matters as investment, the location of R&D facilities, employment, and the like in which host nationals have an inherent desire for full national control and a concern that MNC control will act contrary to their national interest. In Latin America, however, as observed in the Truitt-Blake study, the primary political issues revolve around the concept of dependencia, which goes beyond the concern for a loss of control of national affairs observed in the developed countries. It assumes not only that decisions are being made by external bodies including the MNCs but that in a broader and more enduring sense the whole pattern of the country's evolution is bound to that of the advanced industrial nations and directed to the advantage of the latter. The MNCs, rather than being perceived as separate entities disruptive of national control as in the developed countries, are in this instance seen as one of the major vehicles in the overall complex pattern of interdependence and consequent dependency in future development. Therefore this concept, while essentially political in nature, is heavily imbued with economic considerations as well.

Thus the economic and political factors may to a degree be segregated in the minds of respondents and to a degree may be expected to blend together. As far as they go, the research findings tend to confirm this mixture of blend and differentiation. Sugges' factors, for example, showed the economic and political questions running together in varied combinations. Smetanka, we have noted, found that responses to all of them were associated in one conglomerate factor. Yet the explicit differentiation of points previously mentioned in the open-ended questions of the Murray-LeDuc and Truitt-Blake studies indicates that many respondents do have in mind perceptions of certain discrete components of these subjects.

Another interesting indication of differentiation appears as a byproduct of the bias analysis of the elite data by Fayerweather and Marton. There was a correlation between the bias on each subject (economic, political, and cultural) and the questions relating to that subject. But there was not a close correlation among the bias indicators. The immediate conclusion from this pattern is that nationalistic biases tend to be oriented to particular subject areas rather than generalized. However, it seemed a logical corollary of this finding that viewpoints on each subject have a distinctive orientation differentiated from that of other subjects. Thus the political and economic effect appraisals were relatively well differentiated within people's minds, even though the work by Sugges on the same data would indicate that the appraisals in many cases did parallel each other, resulting in combination in the factor analysis.

These varied considerations were discussed in the workshop among the researchers with no clear conclusions. There was indeed some inclination to advance further hypotheses as to how the economic and political factors might sit in the cognitive maps of respondents. One possibility that seemed to gain particular support was that attitudes on political and economic impact might have substantially the character of ideology in people's minds. This view was supported by the assumption that most people would have very little factual basis for opinions in either major subject area, the political being extremely vague and the economic too complex and sophisticated for the most part even for most elites to understand thoroughly. Thus the proposition advanced was that many respondents would have in mind some very broad conceptual image of the economic and political impact of MNCs and that any questions identified by them as falling roughly in these areas would trigger responses keyed to the general concepts in mind without great differentiation as to the content of the question. This seems an interesting hypothesis to explore in an area in which future exploration should be fruitful.

The appraisals given by respondents on the political and economic impact of MNCs fall into a fairly consistent pattern among all of the studies. The political element stands out as the prime negative factor in most surveys. In the Truitt-Blake study in Chile and Venezuela respondents identified dependencia as the top disadvantage of MNCs. It is the only negative factor given by respondents in the Blake-Driscoll study in Brazil. In the Fayerweather elite studies, reactions to the effect of MNCs on control of national affairs elicited the strongest negative responses.

The viewpoints on the economic impact of firms come through in a distinctly mixed pattern, on the other hand. In the open-ended questions in both Murray and LeDuc's Canadian survey and the Truitt-Blake study economic factors rate high as both advantages and disadvantages listed by respondents. In the Brazilian study the appraisal of the economic impact of the two paper firms was overwhelmingly positive, even including the belief that they helped the country's balance of payments. This latter point is notable because other studies indicate a general tendency to view the balance of payments effects adversely. For example, in Fayerweather's elite study, in all three countries (Britain, Canada, and France) the views on external payments were more adverse than the opinions about the general economic impact of the MNCs. It should also be noted that there was greater consensus among all the elite groups on the balance of payments question than on others, suggesting that it is more a matter of national conviction approaching the ideological image proposition set forth above.

This same tendency towards generalized rather than discriminating response appears in an interesting way in the set of questions about joint venture effects posed in the Fayerweather elite survey. The data confirm the hypothesis that host nationals perceive the enhancement of local control by joint ventures as an all-purpose benefit to their interests rather than the reality of its being a mixed blessing serving their interests in some ways and not in others. Such indiscriminate response would tend to bear out the assumption that responses to such refined questions with political and economic implications are based in many cases, even among the elite, on some overall perception of the subject area, not on carefully thought-of refinements.

Cultural Impact

Attitudes on the cultural impact of MNCs compose quite a different picture from those concerning economic and political effects, both as to meaning and the character of responses.

To start with, surveys encounter a broad definitional problem because they have tended to seek a general appraisal of the cultural impact of MNCs. Questions about the general economic and political impact of MNCs present similar problems, but they are commonly met by supplementary questions that deal with more specific effects in these areas. Such amplification is much less common in covering the cultural effect, so surveys are afflicted in this respect with the same definitional problems that have bedeviled scholarly work on culture. In the classical work in the field, Kluckhohn and Kroeber identified some 164 definitions of culture.[2] They range from the broad concept that culture incorporates all man-created aspects of life to relatively confined subject areas. In studies of attitudes toward MNCs, researchers are generally concerned with tapping those feelings that lie behind such popular expressions as "the Americanization of Europe" and "Coca-Colization." Their definition would exclude attitudes toward economic and political effects, which are covered separately. Beyond that, what it would include is rather vague but would encompass particularly much of the sociology of life: attitudes, values, daily patterns of behavior, and the like.

This vagueness as to what effects are included forms an initial problem in phrasing questions for surveys. Those problems are then compounded by problems of popular semantics. The word *culture* to many people refers to painting, dance, music, and other art forms, so it is not practical to use in questions. Of various alternatives, the one that appears most often is "way of life," which was used in the Fayerweather and Murray-LeDuc studies. One finds this term quite commonly in popular literature, with essentially the meaning intended by researchers in this field.

Way of life, however, poses problems of interpretation just as great as those observed in the discussion of overall appraisals of MNC impact. It seems quite probable that it does represent a perception in the cognitive maps of a large portion of people. However, what it means to those people may vary greatly among them. For many it may mean quite specifically things that affect their daily life, such as their work activities, their entertainment, advertising influence on them, and the like. For others it may extend to a much broader range of things up to the broadest definition of culture noted above, namely all the man-made facets of society. For such people responses to a "way of life" question would encompass not only the more limited aspects of culture but also feelings on economic and political impact and therefore would approach the type of feelings tapped in the overall appraisal questions.

The findings of those surveys that do include the cultural impact of MNCs indicate that in general the attitudes about it among host nationals are favorable on balance and that it is a much lesser matter in their minds than other thoughts about MNCs. The fact that this element of attitudes does not appear in other surveys would tend also to confirm that this is a lesser component of the host-national concerns about MNCs. The lesser importance of views on cultural impact emerges explicitly from the set of questions on criteria for appraising MNCs in the Fayerweather and Smetanka surveys. Respondents ranked the effect on way of life as a distinctly lower criterion than economic and control considerations as well as a number of other factors. The same conclusion was drawn indirectly from the low frequency of mention of cultural impact in the open-ended questions of the Murray-LeDuc and Truitt-Blake studies. In the former, loss of identity and Americanization were noted by 4 percent of respondents as reasons for believing U.S. investment was a bad thing for the Canadian economy, while in the latter various responses grouped under the heading of "harms local culture" were noted as disadvantages by 2 percent in Chile and 5 percent in Venezuela.

The fact that mention of cultural impact appears as a negative factor in the open-ended questions might be construed to mean that there was a general negative reaction to MNCs on this issue. However, such an interpretation of the views of a very small portion of respondents does not seem justified. To the contrary, in the Fayerweather and Smetanka surveys the question seeking an overall appraisal of effect on national way of life produced consistently positive responses. Even the labor union leaders, who were negative on many considerations, were on balance favorable in this respect, with the exception of the French contingent, their mean score being slightly on the negative side. This inference of a generally favorable viewpoint on cultural impact may be drawn from responses to a number of questions that dealt with more specific matters that would be incorporated in the overall concept of cultural impact. For example, in Hilton's survey the Nigerians were clearly responsive to the value standards of MNCs embodied in the concepts of consideration and honesty. The Brazilian respondents in the Blake-Driscoll study expressed strongly favorable sentiments about a variety of social impact policies of the two paper firms. More broadly, other questions in the Fayerweather elite survey dealing with management and labor relations practices for the most part indicate a favorable reaction, the chief exceptions being negative perceptions among some, but definitely not all, labor groups.

Although the survey results are relatively clear in their indication of generally favorable response to the cultural impact of MNCs, but with low importance attached to it, the meaning of these reactions is uncertain in light of other findings and the definitional confusion noted at the outset. The uncertainties appear most conspicuously in the correlation analyses of the Fayerweather and Marton studies. In both instances high correlations were observed between the way of life question and the overall appraisal of the effects of the MNC on the host nation. As noted at the start of this chapter, the meaning of correlations in this sort of situation is difficult to determine. They may indicate anything from a strong cause-effect relationship to the presence of a weak element that tends to follow another factor to which it is vaguely associated in a halo effect. On the whole, it seems unlikely that the close correlation in this instance demonstrates that views of cultural impact are a strong determinant of the overall appraisal of MNCs, since that is logically inconsistent with the low rating accorded to the cultural factor. However, even this possibility cannot be ruled out, particularly if there is merit in the hypothesis advanced in the workshop that the overall appraisal is relatively independent of such other major factors as economic and political impact. Some further support for this line of reasoning might be found in the contrast between the generally favorable overall assessments and the generally negative economic and political appraisals. If the substantially favorable cultural impact reactions have considerable weight in the overall appraisal, that could at least partially explain the positive thrust found in them.

It seems somewhat more probable, however, that the halo effect interpretation is appropriate. This reasoning would incorporate the sense that culture and way of life appeared as very broad and diffused concepts in the cognitive maps of respondents. Thus in their minds the overall appraisal and effect on way of life would tap very similar viewpoints.

In the workshop discussion this definitional confusion in the minds of respondents was extended to another point on which evidence did not appear in any of the surveys but which seemed potentially important. That is the probability that reactions to the cultural impact of MNCs are combined in the minds of people with reactions to the general processes of modernization and industrialization in host nations. This phenomenon has been observed by a number of people. For example, a central theme of McCreary's *The Americanization of Europe* is that MNCs have been blamed by Europeans for many changes in the character of life that are a natural consequence of economic change.[3] Most people, being relatively undiscriminating in their thinking, have tended to associate those changes arising from major alterations in industrial and business processes with the major new factors in business life, notably the rapid growth and prominence of MNCs. In this context a favorable or unfavorable perception of the MNC may be more of a reflection of a favorable or unfavorable perception of the general modernization process than of the specific cultural impact of the MNC. This factor is doubtless a complicating element in the research findings observed here, but there is no way to discern its effect from the information at hand.

This discussion of attitudes toward cultural impact of MNCs presents a mixed picture as far as the research is concerned. On the one hand, the generally favorable reactions and low importance apparently attached to them suggest a low priority for further exploration of the subject. On the other hand, to the extent that it does have importance and possibly plays a significant part in the overall appraisals, the confusion as to people's views on cultural effects presents a challenging area for further exploration. It would seem that to clarify the subject a study devoted solely to it would be required. Such a study presumably would include a variety of questions on specific points like pace of work, advertising styles, and other elements of the way of life to determine what entered into the appraisals of cultural impact.

The Specific Effects of MNC Operations

The specific effects of multinational corporation operations covered in the surveys largely concern business functions such as employment, technology, exports, capital, and the like. These are less complex subjects than those previously discussed, and ones upon which factual information is potentially available, though in fact a large portion of respondents may have little actual or correct information at hand, as was indicated in the Truitt-Blake questions exploring the accuracy of respondent information. Presumably we do not have in this area the problems that have been noted in previous sections of high degree of uncertainty and variety in the character of the perceptions and the cognitive maps of respondents.

The survey findings indicate a general pattern of positive reactions among host nationals about the specific effects of MNC activities. In the Truitt-Blake study we find strong recognition of capital and technology inputs by MNCs among Chilean and Venzuelan elites. Blake and Driscoll found that respondents in Brazil rated the two paper companies highly in regard to a number of functional contributions. In Hilton's Nigerian study the employment created by MNCs was the source of strong favorable response. In Fayerweather's elite studies most groups gave generally positive ratings to the MNCs in their industrial relations practices, though some clear dissenting views among labor leaders are conspicuous. In the open-ended question used by Murray and LeDuc such specifics as creation of employment and inputs of capital rate high as reasons for believing U.S. investment is a good thing for the Canadian economy.

How significant the views on specific MNC impacts are in the total picture of attitudes toward MNCs is hard to determine and probably varies considerably from country to country. The prominence of these points in the open-ended questions of the Murray-LeDuc and Truitt-Blake studies suggests that they are the strongest source of positive feelings toward MNCs. The correlation analyses made in several studies are not particularly helpful on this point because they do not cover the key inputs of capital and technology specifically. Such specifics as are included in these analyses present a mixed picture in relation to the broader questions in the surveys. For example, Fayerweather's data show a low correlation between the overall appraisal question and responses on various aspects of industrial relations. Smetanka found that these industrial relations questions composed the only separate factor distinct from the all-encompassing factor, which included the economic, political, and overall appraisals. Marton's data on the Canadian workers showed that reactions to MNC wage levels had the second highest correlation with overall appraisal.

This latter finding suggests that the importance of specific impacts could be keyed to their relevance to the situation of particular respondents. That proposition is broadly confirmed by other findings in the surveys. For example, the value of the capital and technology inputs of the MNCs apparently was more strongly recognized in Chile than in Venezuela, the former being in greater need of economic development and support. Again in the Fayerweather data, which included LDC student and management program groups, certain distinctions among the criteria for appraising MNCs seem relevant. For example, the effect of MNCs on opportunities for investors was ranked distinctly higher in LDCs than in developed countries, presumably because this function is perceived in the LDCs as a general support for economic development whereas in developed countries it is perceived simply as helping particular investing businessmen, which has much less general relevance for the overall economy.

A rather puzzling finding in considering the overall importance of appraisal of specific impacts is the data in the Truitt-Blake study, which indicate that MNCs are perceived to make stronger efforts in R&D, exports, and training of management personnel than national firms, along with the view of the same respondents that on an overall basis national firms are more beneficial to the host country than MNCs. Of course, a number of other factors are at work in the overall appraisal. Nonetheless, it is interesting that the favorable ratings of the MNCs vis-à-vis national firms in areas that are of prime importance to national development should not apparently have weighed more in the overall ratings. Confirmation of their relatively limited significance is provided in the correlation analysis supplementing the Truitt-Blake study.

On another tack it would appear that the proximity factor developed in the Blake-Driscoll study is quite relevant to this subject of specific impacts. The indications of that study are that the specific impacts generate highly favorable responses; the degree of favorableness is a function of the closeness of people to the actual operations; and there is a distinctly less favorable overall appraisal of the firms' contributions at the national level than at the community level. This latter would suggest that the respondents do not perceive the specific contributions that are prominently visible at the local level to be as significant in the overall national picture. Taking the three points together, we would observe that the generally strong favorable reaction generated by specifics where they are readily perceived loses substantial force among the large portion of people who do not have direct contact with firms and among all people as they think of the firms in terms of their overall national role rather than in specific operating situations.

To summarize, it would appear that in this area of specific MNC impact, the determination of host-national attitudes is much easier than in the subject areas discussed previously and that the evidence of favorable response is quite general and strong. On the other hand, we have only an assorted and rather confused mixture of evidence providing leads but few firm conclusions as to how important these assessments are and the ways in which they may be related to other aspects of host-national attitudes on MNCs. Thus there would appear to be ample opportunity for further study to clarify this sort of relationship.

INFLUENCES AFFECTING ATTITUDES TOWARD MNCs

The preceding discussion has provided evidence that various aspects of MNC activities have substantial influence on attitudes toward them but also that the specific character of MNC performance is not sufficient to fully explain the prevailing opinions about them. The other possible influences that emerge from the research studies and our workshop discussion fall into three main categories: environmental conditions, ideologies, and personal experience. On each of these we have some useful if not conclusive evidence, which will be discussed below.

In considering these assorted influences, it is useful to set the MNC in perspective as part of the individual's total view of affairs. In the minds of most people MNCs are a matter of relatively minor concern. The Murray-LeDuc chapter provides a clear indication of this fact with U.S. investment identified as the most important issue facing Canada by only 4 percent of the population, far behind inflation, unemployment, pollution, and other major general national issues. Likewise among the four groups of government elites surveyed by Graham in Britain and France, foreign MNCs were ranked as the most serious economic threat by from 0 to 18 percent, with inflation and oil prices notably more significant. And in the total content of the individual's mind it must be recognized that even these major national issues are of minor regular concern compared to personal problems and needs: a person's job, family life, and so forth. Given this much greater significance of personal matters and more pressing national affairs, it is quite likely that views about the MNC will be affected by the individual's orientation to these more significant matters in his mind. This perspective provides overall confirmation of the probability of strong influence from the three types of factors to be discussed below. As far as environmental conditions are concerned, the individual may be expected to consider the MNC with respect to its relation to those general national issues that he sees as most significant; it is natural to expect that influences close to his personal life associated with MNCs will have a significant effect; and ideologies that he holds important may be expected to impinge with their values, objectives, and norms on views he will have on all subjects including the MNC.

Environmental Conditions

In the research studies and particularly in the workshop discussions a variety of environmental influences on attitudes toward multinational firms were suggested. They tend to cluster around three themes: general economic conditions, government policy, and visibility and the scapegoat concept.

Three of the research studies provide comparisons that bring out the effect of national economic conditions on views toward MNCs. The Truitt-Blake study emphasizes the notable contrast between conditions in Chile and Venezuela. The former was suffering at the time of the study from severe economic problems in trying to recover from the Allende period. On the other hand, Venezuela was booming with the prosperity of a strong oil-based economy. For Chile in these circumstances the contributions of MNCs were of major importance, particularly their capital along with technology and other resources. For Venezuela, on the other hand, capital was a minor consideration and in general MNCs were less essential to their progresss though their technology was certainly of significant value. The generally more favorable appraisals of the MNCs in Chile than in Venezuela appear to be substantially related to this difference in economic conditions.

The studies reported by Murray and LeDuc, extending over a number of years, bring out the same sort of influence as economic conditions have changed in Canada. During the 1960s, with the Canadian economy relatively prosperous, attitudes toward MNCs grew progressively less favorable under the influence of rising nationalism. As the 1970s progressed, however, economic conditions in Canada became more strained; in particular, the country was suffering from increasingly severe unemployment. In these conditions, attitudes toward MNCs began to turn more positive again. As their contributions to industrial expansion and employment became more important in the minds of the people, nationalistic goals received lower priority. Graham's historical analysis for Britain and France does not provide similar statistical evidence of changing attitudes except for the limited comparison with Fayerweather's results. However, the qualitative evidence from policy and press analysis suggests the same sort of sensitivity to national economic conditions, notably in the post-de Gaulle and Wilson administration shifts toward less adverse treatment of MNCs, in France and Britain respectively, as their value in bolstering sagging economies was given priority.

In addition to these indications of broad influence on overall attitudes toward MNCs, one finds among the research studies suggestions that the role of the MNC in the general economy affects views on a variety of specific points. For example, in Fayerweather's elite studies it appears that the larger role of foreign investment in Canada than in Britain and France is a factor in the pattern of attitudes. On certain points, for example, it is observed that the spread of attitudes among the four elite groups is less in Canada than in the two European countries. It seems a reasonable hypothesis that in the latter, where MNC influence is relatively modest, there is a greater fractionating of viewpoints among groups according to their particular perceptions of the interests or their individual viewpoints. In Canada, on the other hand, where foreign investment has a very broad national impact, there is greater likelihood that people will perceive more effects in an overall national perspective than in that of their particular group. Likewise, as noted in the discussion of the specific effects of MNCs, the

Fayerweather data show a comparison between the developed countries and LDCs, reflecting their relative priorities according to broad economic needs.

The influence of the overall national economic situation is closely related to that of government policy because the latter often stems from the former. However, the role of government policy forms a somewhat different type of influence, which was the subject of discussion among the workshop participants. The discussion was substantially concerned with who influences whom.

The data available present a mixture of evidence in this respect, particularly as they cover a range of people from top level elites who are closely associated with government decision making and leadership in national opinion formation to lesser government officials who are closely tied to official policy and others ranging out to the general public. Several of the studies gave attention to the association of government policy with attitudes toward MNCs but with varying degrees of intensity and depth of information, so the results tend to be suggestive rather than providing significant evidence.

The research most directly concerned with this subject is Graham's historical analysis of policy toward MNCs in Britain and France. In both cases it appears that attitudes of groups outside the government were significant factors moving toward official constraints on MNCs though the processes were different in each country. In France in the early 1960s, general public opinion, stirred by prominent events and popular literature projecting an adverse image of the MNCs, notably Servan-Schreiber's *The American Challenge*, encouraged nationalistic government policies, though by his nature de Gaulle easily moved in this direction. Somewhat later, the British government moved in a similar direction, substantially in response to organized labor union pressure. Graham perceives that the issue was manipulated by elites in Britain for political goals at various points. In both countries, the subsequent inclination of the governments to adopt more favorable policies toward MNCs was somewhat constrained by the adverse attitudes generated in the preceding years, though it is noted that in France the president is substantially more insulated from public pressures than is the prime minister in Britain. Overall the impression conveyed in Graham's work is that in these countries attitudes have tended to differ to a fair degree with government policy at various times and thus to be a source of pressure either for or against change in policy.

Murray and LeDuc reflect on the role of public opinion in the evolution of Canadian government policy in light of their study of the changes in viewpoint over time. It would appear that in Canada government policy has to some degree been independent of public opinion but to a substantial degree dependent upon and oriented toward what the public expects. In the workshop Murray added the observation that the government established a foreign investment screening system in the early 1970s, believing this to be desired by the public as evident from national polls. However, once the system was established and perceived to be potentially a source of discouragement for foreign investment, public support became notably less than appeared beforehand. Hilton advanced the hypothesis on this subject that the elite often act on the basis of what they perceive to be the public attitude and are often wrong. He noted that in Nigeria a law was enacted requiring that MNCs turn over a large portion of ownership to local investors and that subsequently it appeared that this went much further than the Nigerian public wished.

The Truitt-Blake studies deal only with one point in time, so one cannot assess the respective influences of policy and attitudes on each other as fully as in the analyses of Graham and Murray and LeDuc. They do show, however, that at the time of the surveys the attitudes of the Chilean and Venezuelan elites were closely in line with national government policy. The parallel appears not only in the broad viewpoint noted in the previous section but down to some refinements such as the attitude toward reinvestment of profits. The advocacy of a lower rate for MNCs than for national firms observed in Venezuela appears to be closely associated with the government policy of "fadeout" of foreign investment.

The third subject area, that of visibility and the scapegoat role of the MNC, was the focus of a stimulating discussion among workshop participants. It was initiated by Hilton on the basis of a major environmental difference between Nigeria and the countries covered in the other studies, namely the presence in Nigeria of a conspicuous foreign business group distinct from the MNCs, that is, the Lebanese* business community. The Lebanese were perceived quite adversely as compared to the MNCs, partly because their business practices were less enlightened, partly because they occupied a field of moderate size enterprises to which Nigerians aspired, and partly because of their closer operating proximity and visibility among the general Nigerian population. Hilton felt that these Lebanese businessmen functioned in effect as a buffer between the Nigerians and the MNCs, absorbing substantial adverse feelings, which in Latin America, for example, were directed toward the MNCs in the absence of other significant foreign-owned business activity.

From Hilton's initiative the workshop participants went on to develop the proposition that MNCs might be serving as a scapegoat in host societies. They were observed to have characteristics essentially appropriate to the scapegoat role, rather similar to those of the Jewish community in European countries in earlier eras. MNCs are essentially external to the main national body yet enough involved in it so that problems of national concern can be attributed to them. They also have a relatively limited ability to defend themselves, which seems to be characteristic of scapegoats. It was observed that the frustrations and problems of societies are so great that scapegoats, which can serve as emotional outlets, are perhaps essential. In these circumstances it is natural that the MNCs assume the role. Blake summed up this assessment with the following observation: "It is so much easier to get furious at a multinational corporation that

---

*"Lebanese" is used by Nigerians to include Syrians and Indians as well as Lebanese.

has assets and tangible things than to get livid at the nature of the international monetary system."

If the scapegoat role of the MNC has validity, its significance would vary depending upon the situation in each country. It was proposed that there were other areas in which buffer groups served the scapegoat role like the Lebanese in Nigeria, for example, the Indians in many parts of Africa, and the Chinese through much of Southeast Asia. Truitt noted that the relatively favorable view of MNCs in South Korea may for this reason be attributed to the direction of general national animosities and frustrations toward North Korea. It is also implicit in this line of thinking that the extent of adverse views toward MNCs originating in the scapegoat psychology would be a function of the general level of frustration and problems in the society.

The present research study provides no substantial evidence of the extent to which the scapegoat role and the relative visibility of the MNCs in the society influence attitudes. However, the general hypothesis appears to have merit and to be consistent with the information at hand. It therefore rests as an interesting area for future exploration.

Ideological Influences

Three elements that can be put in the classification of ideology seem to have a significant influence on attitudes toward multinational corporations: nationalism, internationalism, and feelings about big business.

Nationalism

An interrelation between nationalism and feelings about multinational firms is readily hypothesized because of the fundamental conflict between the MNC and the self-determination in control of national affairs and protection of the national wealth that are basic components of nationalism. The MNC, in the exercise of control over operations within a nation from its external headquarters and its extraction of profit from a nation, is inherently in conflict with those characteristics.

The general influence of nationalism can be sensed in all of the research studies, and it was explicitly demonstrated in several of them. In Marton's study of the Canadian workers, a high correlation was determined between Terhune's nationalism scale and both the overall appraisal of the effects of MNCs and a number of specific questions about their impact. The analysis by Marton and Fayerweather of the evidence of bias in the Canadian, British, and French elite data demonstrated the existence of substantial nationalistic bias and some correlations between it and attitudes of respondents. At a more refined level nationalistic feelings show up in a number of individual questions. For example, in the Fayerweather elite studies, nationalistic prejudices seem the only way to account for the much stronger worries of the French about German than about British control of firms within their country.

While the basic logics and research findings convincingly support the general proposition that nationalism affects attitudes toward multinational firms, exploration of this subject reveals a number of questions requiring further study. First, there is the determination of effective measures to identify nationalism. The fundamental problem here is not dissimilar to that noted in the discussion of culture. There are a number of definitions of nationalism, and some determination among them is inevitable in selection of research instruments. In the workshop, for example, Smetanka noted that there is a basic difference between offensive and defensive nationalistic viewpoints. The Terhune scale employed by Marton would fall essentially in the defensive category with its emphasis on national self-determination. This orientation seems particularly appropriate for studies of attitudes toward MNCs because of their primary impact on control of national affairs.

However, scales based on other orientations may have significant merit as well. One possibility is a patriotism scale. In the workshop Sauvant noted that in his work in Europe this did not seem particularly useful. However, it might be more relevant in those less developed countries where nationalism is relatively weak. A scale like Terhune's, which assumes the existence of a broad national consensus for self-determination, or particularly one oriented to aggressive nationalism may be too sophisticated for such a context. Finally, there are possibilities in the employment of questions designed to bring out nationalism in the specific context of the MNC attitudes, such as Fayerweather's mirror-image questions and those on the justness of treatment of foreign companies.

Second, the evidence is very mixed as to exactly what effects nationalism has on attitudes toward MNCs. The only solid finding is Marton's strong correlation of nationalism with overall appraisals of MNCs. The statistical strength of this finding is reinforced by the views expressed by some participants in the workshop that the overall appraisals may well be an ideological matter rather than being based on a combination of other attitudes about MNCs.

The evidence from more refined analyses is far less conclusive but quite intriguing. The Marton-Fayerweather analysis suggests that nationalistic bias may be selective as to subject matter. Their data show quite strong correlation between bias on economic and political effects and views about the impact of MNCs in those two areas respectively. However, there is poor correlation between the measures of nationalism on the two subjects and also with bias shown on the questions concerning the justness of treatment of companies by various countries.

The exploration for nationalism relationships in the Chile-Venezuela data was quite unproductive in an immediate sense, but the data suggest types of questions that might be productive for future research in this respect. Reasonable hypotheses may be advanced that nationalism has an influence, for example, in the comparison of effects of local and multinational firms and in the differentiation between them in such matters as proper profits and taxation. A significant problem in identification of the extent of influence of nationalism is the degree to which other factors are at work in responses to each question.

However, further exploration on these types of questions is particularly significant because they bear directly on host-national opinions in matters upon which specific governmental action of keen interest to multinational firms is taken.

A third problem area already suggested above is the effect of differences in nationalism among countries. Again the research findings present a number of suggestive leads on which further thought and research would be necessary before substantial conclusions could be reached. The intensity of nationalistic feelings appears to be a significant factor. For example, one might expect very strong concern in Canada about the control impact of U.S. subsidiaries in light of the relatively high portion of industry under foreign ownership. Yet the concern about control effects of U.S. firms found in Fayerweather's elite data was no greater in Canada than in Britain and France. This may be due to the character of Canadian nationalism, which is generally perceived as having a weak intensity compared, for example, with nationalism in Germany, Japan, and a number of other countries where intense national feelings are found.

Other intriguing evidence is found in Hilton's Nigerian study. He observes the endemic tendency among the Nigerians toward self-denigration and a perception of the United States and other developed countries as superior in a broad range of capabilities. Within this general pattern of negative self-perception, however, there is a distinct difference between the two major tribal groups—the Yoruba and the Ibos—with the former showing a substantially stronger sense of self-confidence. Hilton found that there was a correlation between this stronger self-assurance and adverse reactions toward foreign firms, from which he hypothesized that a greater degree of personal security fostered the ability to harbor less favorable sentiments toward foreign investors.

Internationalism

Internationalism concerns the extent to which people are committed to the expansion of economic exchanges among nations and collective approaches to economic and political problems. It is not in conflict with nationalism because it is quite possible for a person to be strongly committed to his own nation and to believe that in the present world its interests are best furthered through internationalist approaches. As a practical matter it is probably true that strong nationalists are generally less inclined to be strong internationalists, but the two concepts are distinct and therefore properly pursued as separate elements in research. It should be noted that internationalism is a lower order of generalized commitment in social psychological terms and some people might question placing it in the category of ideology. It has been put in this section as a matter of logical classification in the present discussion without an intention to argue its status on these grounds.

The MNC is readily perceived as consistent with the world scheme supported by the internationalists. It is a prime vehicle for accomplishing international economic exchange of resources with emphasis on rationalization and optimum economic performance. Thus one would expect those with an internationalist commitment to be favorable to multinational firms. The research findings available provide some support for this hypothesis, but the pattern is quite inconsistent.

In Fayerweather's elite study two questions with an internationalist thrust showed a high correlation with attitudes toward multinational firms. Graham's study of similar elites in Britain and France seems to convey a quite different picture, but this may be due to the nature of his questions. He sought the preferences of respondents among a variety of policy approaches to dealing with regulating MNCs, which were classified as national, international, or mixed national and international solutions. One might regard those favoring national solutions as less internationalist, but the views of many elites could be based on assessments of the practicality of international regulation rather than degrees of general internationalist orientation. Thus, the fact that Graham found no correlation between attitudes toward MNCs and international versus national solution preferences may not be significant to the present subject.

Internationalism appears in a less focused but much more pervasive form in Smetanka's research. A central thrust of his exploration is the identification of a sense of solidarity with people outside of Canada and a commitment to the international business process, both of which are facets of internationalism. He also found a strong correlation between these attitudes and views on MNCs.

The study of the transnational enterprise (TNE) effect by Mennis and Sauvant fits into the discussion at this point but with uncertain meaning. They have pursued the hypothesis that employment in a multinational firm would produce the TNE effect in the form of a greater commitment to internationalism in business matters. The findings of their study in West Germany seem to indicate the absence of a TNE effect in comparisons of managerial attitudes both between domestic German firms and headquarters of German MNCs and between domestic firms and affiliates of non-German MNCs in Germany. Furthermore, their work does not reinforce Smetanka's finding that structural influences affected key attitudes. The German data showed that managers in affiliates of foreign MNCs differed substantially from those in domestic German firms in both geographic orientation of their work and in work-related contact with non-nationals. However, the research could confirm no relation between these differences and national identification or integration attitudes. Despite these findings, the inherent logic of the TNE effect remains persuasive, and it may be that further research will demonstrate that it does have an effect on internationalism and other general attitudes and on perceptions of MNCs.

Attitudes toward Big Business

An association between attitudes toward MNCs and those toward big business has appeared conspicuously in the literature of this field in recent years. A number of prominent critics of the MNC have been critical of big business as well, with the two thrusts often blending indistinguishably together. Thus, for example, Kari Levitt's *Silent Surrender*, a major piece of the anti-MNC literature in Canada, can be read as much as a socialistic, anti-free-market-economy tract as a critique of foreign firms.[4]

Evidence to identify the extent of this sort of association is limited in the research findings available here. Some spotty preliminary indications were provided in Fayerweather's elite study, notably the particularly adverse reactions of the two most antibusiness groups included, namely the CGT, the communist union in France, and the NDP, the socialistically oriented political party in Canada. Following up on this lead, Marton included a scale for attitudes toward big business in her survey of workers in Canada. The high correlation with attitudes toward MNCs supports the presumed association, at least within that population sector.

One is inclined on the basis of this strong evidence both in the literature and the research findings to conclude that there is a clear and strong relationship. However, it would be desirable to have studies covering other population groups and countries before reaching a final conclusion.

Personal Influences

The final set of influences that may affect attitudes toward multinational corporations composes quite an assorted mixture. The common thread tying them together is their direct impingement on the individual with specific reference to the MNC as distinguished from the environmental and ideological factors, which have a broad character in which the individual-MNC relation is limited and somewhat indirect. These personal influences will be considered under three headings: press and the intelligentsia, information and contact, and personal feelings.

Press and the Intelligentsia

The role of the press and the intelligentsia in attitude formation concerning MNCs was mentioned earlier in the general discussion of cognitive maps. Because of lack of knowledge of MNCs, the complexity of many aspects of this subject, preoccupation with other matters, and further reasons, a large portion of people give little attention to MNCs. Such information as most of them have comes largely through public communications media. Thus the media are potentially a prime influence in attitude formation. Since the intelligentsia have much to do with the input and processing of media content, this potential then extends to them as well.

The research studies provide relatively little information on this type of influence. The Truitt-Blake report confirms the importance of media as a source of information. About two-thirds of the Chilean and Venezuelan respondents indicated that media were their primary source of information on MNCs. However, no correlations could be identified between the attitudes and sources of information.

We have no research that gets into the heart of determining the relation between what people receive from media sources and how it influences their views. Some items in the workshop discussion suggested leads for this type of investigation. Blake, for example, observed, "I'm not sure if the MNC had to be as major an issue as it is now or whether it was one thing that captured the imagination of a lot of people and it was articulated and formulated rather effectively so it became a leading issue." In like vein, some participants proposed that the idea of dependencia in Latin America was essentially articulated by the intelligentsia and disseminated by the media. In this case, however, the observation was that the middle class had never really accepted the concept as significant.

An intriguing item in the Truitt-Blake study is the finding that respondents considered MNCs superior to domestic firms in communicating information about their operations to the public. However, the research provides no basis for relating this finding to attitude formation among the respondents.

In general it appears that this is potentially an important aspect of the subject in which both research information and even hypotheses are relatively sparse at this stage. The lack of attention to it is probably attributable to a combination of two factors: first, that it is a difficult area in which to do effective studies; and, second, that research has tended to focus on elites because of their direct involvement with decision making. There is an assumption that media are a minor factor in attitude formation among elites and thus need not be given major attention. This assumption recognizes the major role of the media as a source of information for the elites but assumes that their capacity for discrimination and effective use of multiple sources of information limits the influence of the media per se. That is, the media are assumed to be an essentially passive conduit for information rather than an active influence in attitude formation. These considerations seem reasonably sound and as long as research resources are limited will probably act as a constraint on major efforts to explore the subject further. However, it would seem that the significance of the media would justify further limited explorations to determine the extent and nature of their influence on attitude formation.

Information

The central theme of the factors to be considered under this second heading is the nature of the information about MNCs that the individual has in his head. It involves consideration of the extent, prominence, and accuracy of the information and factors that bear on those characteristics. There is a general presumption that these characteristics must have an effect on attitudes, but the direction of effect is something upon which hypotheses vary.

The research findings in this area present a very mixed and inconclusive picture. The Blake-Driscoll study provides strong evidence that those who are most informed about specific MNCs have the most favorable attitude toward them. However, the significance of this evidence is uncertain because it may have as much to do with the personal satisfaction element to be considered in the next section as with the information component being considered here. Furthermore, this study deals with views toward individual companies, not attitudes toward MNCs in general. Thus the findings are suggestive but not clear.

Other research studies are of minor help on the relevance of direct contact. Fayerweather's elite surveys suggest a minor correlation between contact and attitudes. The Truitt-Blake study, on the other hand, indicated no relationship. During the workshop mention was made of a study by Wells of an extractive operation in Bougainville in which people close to the company were extremely negative. This finding taken in conjunction with the Blake-Driscoll study might suggest that contact would have more influence on the intensity than on the actual nature of attitudes, with the latter being a function of the realities observed through the contact.

A natural line of inquiry in this area is the accuracy of information held by people. One may theorize that accuracy will affect attitudes in three ways. First, and most directly, to the extent that perceptions of MNC performance or other specific effects influence attitudes, the quality of information contributing to those perceptions may be expected to be a factor. If, for example, the information a person has is substantially inaccurate, conveying an understanding that MNCs are less useful to the host country than is actually true, the inaccuracy element will presumably foster a less favorable attitude toward MNCs. Second, a person's perception of the degree of accuracy of his information may bear on his attitudes, or at least on the strength with which they are held. A well-informed person may have more clearly formed opinions. The theorizing is more tenuous here because the effects clearly depend greatly upon the type of person, the strong opinions held by many poorly informed people being a generally observed fact. Therefore, one may simply note that, other things being equal for any given individual, the more accurate he perceives his information to be, the stronger its influence on his attitudes may be. Third, there is the possibility that a propensity to accuracy or inaccuracy in an individual is associated with a propensity to a particular direction of attitudes. It may be true, for example, that some people are generally characterized by poor information and that the attitudes of such people typically lean in a particular direction, because they would be particularly prone to other influences, like nationalism. In pursuing these possibilities, we must note that it is likely to be hard to determine their validity, not only because of their inherent complexity but also because the direction of influence is difficult to hypothesize since inaccurate information may lead to perceiving MNCs either more or less favorably.

This line of inquiry was pursued in some of the research studies but with limited useful findings. The determination of the accuracy of perceptions about MNCs was a major component of the Truitt-Blake research. Their study demonstrates a very large degree of misinformation among the Chilean and Venezuelan elites. However, analysis of the data could not demonstrate a connection between the accuracy of perception and attitudes toward MNCs. Part of the problem in so doing may stem from the difficulty of establishing statistical measures of accuracy. However, it may also be significant that the accuracy questions were directed at aspects of MNC operations that were apparently either minor in respondent attitudes toward MNCs or ones upon which their views were relatively favorable. The study did not provide indicators of accuracy on MNC effects that are the source of major adverse perception, like the balance of payments and factors entering into the dependencia concept. A further interesting finding in this analysis is the indication that accuracy has a haphazard rather than consistent incidence. That is, individual respondents seemed typically to have misinformation on one or two topics and reasonably accurate information on others, rather than being either generally well informed or misinformed on all subjects. Again, the conclusiveness of this finding is limited by the statistical limitations of the study. However, it is an informative lead for further research.

Other studies provide some limited input on the accuracy of information. Hilton included some questions that indicated the accuracy with which the ownership of individual companies in Nigeria was perceived. He found a relatively high level of accuracy, which was a function of various demographic factors; however, he did not attempt to determine any relation between this accuracy and attitudes toward the firms. An earlier study by Moyer determined similar information in England.[5] It was notable particularly in confirming a widely held assumption that some major MNCs in developed countries are generally perceived as domestic firms, in this instance, for example, Hoover in England. The same is generally assumed to be true, for example, of firms like Lever Bros. in the United States. This element of identification of ownership undoubtedly has some bearing on the general question of attitudes toward MNCs, but present studies provide no indication as to the nature of that relevance.

Fayerweather's elite survey contained a question about the extent to which an individual's function required him to be informed on activities of foreign companies, which was designed to provide some measure of extent and accuracy of information. The findings did not indicate any relation to attitudes, but the question was probably too crude to be particularly informative in any case.

The impression conveyed by these varied research efforts is that the question of the effect of accuracy of information on attitude formation is quite uncertain and that it will be relatively difficult to explore it further by methods suitable for effective statistical analysis. The phrasing of questions even for the relatively straightforward matters covered in the Truitt-Blake study is clearly fraught with problems. For some other subjects of greater significance such as the balance of payments effects, it probably would be possible to phrase effective questions to determine the accuracy of information. However, on many important matters such as general economic impact, effect on control of national affairs, and so forth, assessment of the accuracy of information seems virtually impossible.

On the whole, this would appear an interesting area in which some improvement in research findings should be possible, and it would be desirable to have a better assessment of the significance of accuracy, if only because it is one area in which active efforts by MNCs might produce a change among host nationals. However, on the basis of present information, one cannot propose with any great confidence that accuracy in information will turn out to be a significant factor in attitude formation.

Personal Experience

The general proposition involved under this third heading is that attitudes toward MNCs may be a function of personal experiences that have had some psychological impact on the individual. Two main possibilities are considered: the first revolving around personal satisfaction and feelings, the second relating to the structural relationships of the individual and the attitudes that they stimulate.

The possibility that personal experiences in contact with MNCs will affect a person's attitudes toward them is an attractive hypothesis. But it is a subject that is quite complex and on which information is relatively limited. Only minor research has been devoted to exploring this hypothesis directly.

A question in Fayerweather's elite survey indicated that quite a high proportion of respondents had had satisfactory experience in contacts with MNCs, and there was a significant correlation between the extent of satisfaction and the attitudes toward MNCs. Marton's study contained a scale to determine job satisfaction among the Canadian workers; the results showed no correlation between satisfaction and attitudes toward MNCs. Probably the satisfaction element is one component of the influences at work in the Blake-Driscoll study of attitudes in Brazil. However, it is impossible to segregate its role from those of proximity, involvement, accuracy, and so forth.

The difference between the Fayerweather and the Marton findings would suggest that the influence of satisfaction in contacts with MNCs is a function of the contexts of the contact. Given the variety of contacts possible in customer, government, labor, business, and other roles, this is a significant complicating factor. It is also difficult to determine the extent of satisfaction. However, the logics for assuming its influence, reinforced by the findings of one of the two surveys, suggest that this is an area that should receive further research attention.

The proposition that structural relationships of an individual that somehow involve the MNC will affect attitudes toward foreign firms is also appealing. It is assumed that the ongoing influence of a structural position in which the impact of MNCs or concern with them in some other way is regularly present will affect a person's point of view substantially. Research to date has provided some confirmation of this proposition but leaves large dimensions of it lightly explored.

The fullest and most conclusive work is Smetanka's study of Canadian executives, in which structural relationships emerged as the primary determinant of attitudes. He found that favorable attitudes toward MNCs were fostered by structural relationships that developed an internationalist viewpoint. The variables included the kind of firm, those being actively interested in international markets having more favorable views; work responsibility, with executives regularly carrying international functions being more positive; and contacts, with those in frequent communication with overseas executives learning toward the positive side. Overall, the internationally oriented structural relationships have the effect of generating a greater sense that the executive has an interest in international business and a sense of solidarity with executives in other countries, all leading to an internationalist attitude on business affairs and support of MNCs.

Other evidence in the research is informative but rather scattered. One natural hypothesis is that employment in a multinational firm rather than a domestically owned one would enhance support of MNCs in general. Ownership did not, however, appear as a significant variable in Smetanka's survey. As we noted previously, it did not prove relevant to national identification attitudes in the Mennis-Sauvant study of the possible TNE effect in Germany. Likewise it showed no significance as a variable among the Canadian elites in Fayerweather's study.

Significant differences among major population groups have been demonstrated in the research. For example, the professional groups covered in the Truitt-Blake study varied in their perceptions of MNCs. Some differences were also observed among groups in Fayerweather's elite study. We have limited basis for refined analysis of the bases for these differences. However, they would appear to have more to do with the overall pattern of attitudes toward business in general than with any particular views relating to MNCs per se. For example, in the Fayerweather studies the substantially less favorable views of the labor leaders are a natural expectation in any views of business and do not appear to be particularly related to the foreignness of the companies. A single but apparently quite significant confirmation of this observation is the high rating on labor relations given to foreign firms by the communist CGT union leaders. This suggests that to the extent that their thinking discriminates between domestic and foreign business, the labor leaders are not particularly adverse to the MNCs. Thus the general disposition toward negative appraisals may reasonably be interpreted as essentially a negative appraisal of business firms in general.

Somewhat more significance may be attached to the difference between the perceptions of government and business groups. In Chile the government officials were found to be more favorable to MNCs than businessmen while the opposite was true in Venezuela. This difference is presumed to be related to the strong favorable thrust of government policy in Chile and the less favorable official viewpoints on MNCs in Venezuela. A reversal of relationships was also found by Fayerweather in Britain and France, with the government officials more favorable to MNCs in Britain and the businessmen more favorable in France. Here again the difference would appear to be related to the contrast in viewpoints of the two governments along with some difference in the business systems. The explanation in all of these cases, however, is based on very crude hypothecation and we have very little basis, as compared with Smetanka's type of study, on which to base conclusions.

Other explorations of structural relationships are even less conclusive. Among the variables considered in Fayerweather's elite studies, it appeared that some differences could be related to the hierarchical level of government officials and to whether or not they were in government units closely associated with international business. Graham found civil servants were somewhat more favorable toward MNCs than legislators. Smetanka observed a correlation with level of education. Murray and LeDuc note that those lower on the economic scale have been more favorable to MNCs in Canada, which they presume is related to concern about employment. These are intriguing possibilities, but none of them are substantially confirmed by the evidence at hand.

The strong reinforcement toward the general hypothesis in this area from Smetanka's work encourages the belief that further research would be fruitful. The variety of variables suggested by the leads drawn from other research studies, however, indicates the very broad range of possibilities that confront future research in this area. The inconclusiveness of the results of the limited exploration of the other studies and the intensity of the work required for the conclusive findings of Smetanka also indicate that any work in this field should be quite well focused. Smetanka's work suggests that the nature of significant structural influences may be relatively intricate and that therefore to isolate them it is necessary to control for a large number of other variables that may be at work, which is only practical in studies of relatively homogeneous groups.

SUMMARY

The great variety and inconclusiveness of the discussion in this chapter precludes neat summarization. It may be useful, however, to draw together a few reasonably clear patterns.

In certain broad dimensions, the varied research studies described in this book show considerable similarities of attitudes toward MNCs. On the whole the greater portion of the varied respondents surveyed expressed favorable appraisals of MNCs at the overall level and with respect to specific impacts on industrial operations. When it comes to broad economic, political, and cultural criteria, however, the pattern of reactions is mixed, with a leaning on the more important factors toward the adverse side. Specifically, the political impact is consistenly and quite strongly perceived in a negative light and overall economic impact is seen in both a positive and negative light with a tendency, if any, somewhat toward the negative side, though there are major differences among groups surveyed.

Among the potential influences on attitudes, it appears that environmental conditions, ideological views in the areas of nationalism and big business, and assorted factors bearing intimately on the individual's perception of the MNC are significant. Most prominent in the discussion, however, is the pervasive importance of variety. Central to it is the diversity in the cognitive maps of respondents noted at the outset. Seen with this orientation, a large portion of the chapter is essentially an elaboration of the diversity of patterns in which the MNC appears in cognitive maps of host nationals under the diverse influences of environmental conditions, ideology, information, personal experience, and other variables composing the totality of experience shaping viewpoints.

Summarizing the accomplishments of research to date is as difficult as summarizing the findings they have provided. Essentially one may safely say that the work has achieved a substantial reconnaissance level both as to substance and methodology. It is notable that each of the studies is quite distinct in important respects of content and groups surveyed. One might wish for a greater degree of commonality in some of their variables, which would permit a greater degree of comparative analysis among them. However, the diversity has resulted in a broader range of exploratory benefits than greater structural homogeneity would have permitted. Thus, for example, the two studies in Latin America provide distinct results and one would like to be able to compare and relate the findings. However, in fact they are quite diverse in methodological schemes and provide a very useful pioneer testing of distinctly different methodologies.

FUTURE RESEARCH

A number of comments have been made about the future direction of research in reference to individual aspects of attitude studies throughout this chapter. In conclusion a few broad observations seem in order, stemming from the view that in general work to date represents substantial accomplishment in a reconnaissance stage.

Essentially the question of future research is how one proceeds when this much reconnaissance has been accomplished. There seemed to be a consensus among our workshop participants that there has been enough exploratory fishing, that a continuation of the past pattern in which individuals thrust out in diverse directions in rather independently conceived projects is not in order. Accepting that view, we may consider at least three directions in which further research effort would be most useful: intensive studies of attitude formation processes, new exploratory efforts based upon careful theoretical formulation, and studies of the impact of attitudes on behavior.

The intensive study of attitude formation is encouraged by the great variety of variables that have been opened up in the reconnaissance process and by the productivity of the limited number of intensive studies in relatively homogeneous groups already undertaken, notably those by Marton and Smetanka. It would seem useful to undertake such case studies in carefully selected groups in other contexts where key variables can be explored further. Such studies would probably involve a greater amount of personal interviewing than work undertaken so far, followed by use of questionnaires permitting sound determination of the effect of significant variables influencing attitude formation.

While the doubts about further exploratory work expressed among the participants are justified, it is unsound at this stage to discourage exploration in a field that is still so poorly covered. The possibility of exploration opening up major new avenues, not so much in substance as in methodologies, should not be discouraged. What is needed, however, is clearly that exploration should be thoroughly grounded in past experience. If one criticism can be made of work to date, it is that too many of the studies have proceeded with very little application of findings from those of others that preceded them. A view was also voiced in the workshop that further work should be soundly based on theoretical concepts. The reconnaissance work accomplished to date would seem to provide an adequate basis for theoretical hypotheses. Thus for the future we should expect more intensive theoretical formulation incorporating the basic variables identified thus far and then the pursuit of hypotheses with such methodological innovations as appear promising in other areas of the world. This sort of exploration soundly based on past work may be quite productive.

The question of research on behavioral effects of attitudes takes a different direction from the work accomplished to date. The workshop participants expressed strong interest in exploring this territory. They were constrained in their efforts by the lack of any solid evidence upon which to proceed, but their interests suggest the value of research along this line.

Attitude researchers are somewhat in the same position as pure scientists. They generate extremely interesting findings but the value of their output is often not clear. Undoubtedly the findings of the research studies reported here are helpful in their present state to business and government policy makers. However, the value of attitude studies would be greatly enhanced if we knew which of the attitudes had what effect on which type of situation in what circumstances. Thus it is soundly proposed that the research extend to determination of the role that attitudes play. These studies may take assorted directions. For example, one may take a set of individuals and determine how the assortment of attitudes they hold affects their behavior in the range of activities in which they engage. Case studies may be undertaken of the evolution of specific government policies in which the attitudes of various participants are considered.

REFERENCES

1. E. C. Tolman, "Cognitive Maps in Rats and Men." *Psychological Review*, Vol. 55, 1948, pp. 189–208.

2. Clyde Kluckhohn and Alfred L. Kroeber, *Culture: A Critical Review of Concepts and Definitions.* (Cambridge, Mass.: The Museum, 1952).

3. Edward A. McCreary, *The Americanization of Europe.* (Garden City, N.Y.: Doubleday, 1964).

4. Kari Levitt, *Silent Surrender.* (New York: St. Martin's Press, 1970).

5. Reed Moyer, "British Attitudes toward U.S. Direct Investments." *MSU Business Topics,* Summer 1970, p. 63.

THE EDITOR

John Fayerweather is Professor of Management and International Business at the Graduate School of Business Administration of New York University. He has played a leading academic role in the expanding field of international business management over the past 30 years. He was the first president of the Association for Education in International Business (now the Academy of International Business) and has worked with several national and international organizations to advance education and research in the field. While a member of the faculties of Harvard, Columbia, and now NYU, he authored several textbooks including *Management of International Operations, International Business Management,* and *International Business Strategy and Administration.* His primary research interest has been the interaction of nationalism and multinational corporations. This work has resulted in three books, *The Mercantile Bank Affair, International Business-Government Affairs* (ed.), and *Foreign Investment in Canada,* and numerous articles.

THE CONTRIBUTORS

David H. Blake
Associate Dean
University of Pittsburgh

Robert E. Driscoll
Fund for Multinational
   Management Education

Norman A. Graham
Research Associate
Institute on Western Europe
Columbia University
   and
Senior Research Associate
The Futures Group

Andrew C. E. Hilton
International Bank for Reconstruction and Development

Lawrence LeDuc
Professor of Political Science
University of Windsor

Katherin Marton
Assistant Professor of Economics
Fordham University

Bernard Mennis
Associate Professor of Political Science
Temple University

J. Alex Murray
Professor of International Business
University of Windsor

Karl P. Sauvant
Transnational Corporations Affairs Officer
United Nations Centre
   On Transnational Corporations

John A. Smetanka
Assistant Professor of Sociology
State University of New York, Buffalo

Peter R. Sugges, Jr.
Assistant Professor of Management
Temple University

Nancy S. Truitt
Program Director
Fund for Multinational
   Management Education